The Hebrew Bible and Environmental Ethics

The environmental crisis has prompted religious leaders and laypeople to look to their traditions for resources to respond to environmental degradation. In this book, Mari Joerstad contributes to this effort by examining an ignored feature of the Hebrew Bible: its attribution of activity and affect to trees, fields, soil, and mountains. The Bible presents a social cosmos in which humans are one kind of person among many. Using a combination of the tools of biblical studies and anthropological writings on animism, Joerstad traces the activity of nonanimal nature through the canon. She shows how biblical writers go beyond sustainable development, asking us to be good neighbors to mountains and trees, to be generous to our fields and vineyards. They envision human communities that are sources of joy to plants and animals. The biblical writers' attention to inhabited spaces is particularly salient for contemporary environmental ethics in their insistence that our cities, suburbs, and villages contribute to flourishing landscapes.

Mari Joerstad is a research associate at the Kenan Institute for Ethics at Duke University, where she works on "Facing the Anthropocene," a project funded by the Henry Luce Foundation.

The Hebrew Bible and Environmental Ethics

Humans, Nonhumans, and the Living Landscape

MARI JOERSTAD
Duke University

CAMBRIDGE
UNIVERSITY PRESS

University Printing House, Cambridge CB2 8BS, United Kingdom

One Liberty Plaza, 20th Floor, New York, NY 10006, USA

477 Williamstown Road, Port Melbourne, VIC 3207, Australia

314-321, 3rd Floor, Plot 3, Splendor Forum, Jasola District Centre, New Delhi - 110025, India

103 Penang Road, #05-06/07, Visioncrest Commercial, Singapore 238467

Cambridge University Press is part of the University of Cambridge.

It furthers the University's mission by disseminating knowledge in the pursuit of education, learning and research at the highest international levels of excellence.

www.cambridge.org
Information on this title: www.cambridge.org/9781108700665
DOI: 10.1017/9781108568418

© Cambridge University Press 2019

This publication is in copyright. Subject to statutory exception and to the provisions of relevant collective licensing agreements, no reproduction of any part may take place without the written permission of Cambridge University Press.

First published 2019
First paperback edition 2021

A catalogue record for this publication is available from the British Library

Library of Congress Cataloging in Publication data
NAMES: Joerstad, Mari, 1984- author.
TITLE: The Hebrew Bible and environmental ethics : humans, nonhumans, and the living landscape / Mari Joerstad, Duke University, North Carolina.
DESCRIPTION: 1 [edition]. | New York : Cambridge University Press, 2019.
IDENTIFIERS: LCCN 2018047998| ISBN 9781108476447 (hardback) | ISBN 9781108700665 (pbk.)
SUBJECTS: LCSH: Bible. Old Testament–Criticism, interpretation, etc. | Environmental ethics–Biblical teaching. | Human ecology–Religious aspects–Christianity. | Ecotheology.
CLASSIFICATION: LCC BS680.E58 J64 2019 | DDC 221.8/1791–DC23
LC record available at https://lccn.loc.gov/2018047998

ISBN 978-1-108-47644-7 Hardback
ISBN 978-1-108-70066-5 Paperback

Cambridge University Press has no responsibility for the persistence or accuracy of URLs for external or third-party internet websites referred to in this publication, and does not guarantee that any content on such websites is, or will remain, accurate or appropriate.

Contents

Acknowledgments		*page* vii
1	Introduction	1
	Two Trees: Fryd and Glede	1
	Two Aims: Exegesis and Ecology	3
	Strangeness and Ethics	7
	Outline	12
2	Interacting with the World: "New Animism," Metaphor Theory, and Personalistic Nature Texts	14
	Introduction	14
	"New Animism"	19
	Metaphor and Relationality	37
	Personalistic Nature Texts and Patience	45
3	A Watchful World: Personalistic Nature Texts in the Torah	48
	Introduction	48
	Genesis	48
	Exodus	70
	Leviticus	72
	Numbers	80
	Deuteronomy	87
	A Note on Idioms and Metonymy	94
	Conclusion	95
4	A Sentient World: Personalistic Nature Texts in the Prophets	99
	Introduction	99
	War	101
	Theophany	110

	Address	122
	Grief	139
	Joy	145
	Conclusion	154
5	An Articulate World: Personalistic Nature Texts in the Writings	157
	Introduction	157
	Declaration in the Psalms	158
	Job's Negotiation with His Place	171
	Boundaries and Bliss	184
	Conclusion	193
6	Conclusion: Befriending the World	196
	Avenues for Further Study	197
	What Is the Good of a Concept?	201
	Living Together: Patricia Johanson and Jules Renard	210
	Religious Communities and Climate Change	216
	The Promise of Delight	219
Bibliography		221
General Index		239
Bible Index		242

Acknowledgments

This book has been a labor of love. Not only because I have loved working on it, but because the love of so many people have supported me in the writing of it.

First, thank you to my advisor Ellen Davis, who had confidence in me and my tree-hugger dissertation. This manuscript owes more than I can say to her careful attention and ongoing support.

Thank you also to my committee – Jennie Grillo, Anathea Portier-Young, Stephen Chapman, and Barbara Rossing – who offered thoughtful feedback and challenging questions.

Beatrice Rehl, Terence Fretheim, Stephanie Gehring Ladd, Blair Wilner, and Laura Lieber generously agreed to read and respond to this manuscript at a workshop sponsored by the Kenan Institute for Ethics at Duke University. Thank you for giving your time and thoughts to help me improve this book! Thank you also to Kenan and its director, Suzanne Shanahan, for providing the funds to bring the group together.

The group Writing and Academic Work at Duke's English Department has been invaluable as a space to explore academic writing and its potentials. Thank you especially to Toril Moi, Sarah Beckwith, and Cathy Shuman for all your work in organizing the group.

Norman Wirzba put me in touch with Cambridge University Press. Thank you for helping this manuscript along on its journey from my drawer into the real world.

Jedediah Purdy, Norman Wirzba, and the Henry Luce–funded project Facing the Anthropocene have given me time and space to revise and tinker, a valuable gift in a time of overtaxed schedules.

And finally, thank you to all the people who have provided me with companionship and friendship along the way. This book is an exploration of what it might mean to be friends with persons who are not human; it is because of you that I know the value of friendship in the first place. Thank you to my lovely Durham friends, who always make time for happy hour. To Ambereen, Zaid, and Amal: it is my delight to try (and mostly fail) to foil your constant insistence that every meal is on you. To Shannon, Yeon Joo, and Bradley – I cannot think of better people to eat and talk with. Most of my thoughts in some way depend on conversations with you. To my family, who know how to enjoy time and pay attention to the beauty of the world. And to Tyler, who daily shares with me Qoheleth's wonderful task:

Go, eat your bread with gladness, drink your wine with a happy heart, for God already approves of your work. Let your clothes always be white, and do not let oil be lacking from your head. Enjoy life with a [man] whom you love, all the days of your fleeing life that are given to you under the sun, all the days of your fleetingness. For this is your portion in life and in your toil, at which you toil under the sun. (Ecclesiastes 9:7–9)

I

Introduction

TWO TREES: FRYD AND GLEDE

I used to know two trees. I called them *Fryd* and *Glede*, Delight and Joy, but I do not know what they called themselves. They stood on a lawn, next to each other, their branches interwoven, a three-minute walk from my dorm; one a star magnolia, the other a northern magnolia. The star magnolia would blossom first, then the northern, but both bloomed before their leaves came in. They were, for me, messengers of spring. I would visit them. Once, with a friend, I licked moisture off their petals. The raindrops tasted faintly of flowers.

My roommates thought I was strange – beyond the occasional tree-hugger joke, they did not know what to make of my enthusiasm for the trees. Even I, when I think about it now, am unsure how to explain or conceptualize my interaction with the magnolias. The spring symbolism is clear enough, but that hardly exhausts my relationship with these trees. I went to them for comfort, for a kind of companionship. They contributed to my sense of home in ways I cannot put into words. But the difficulty of sorting out my side of things pales in comparison with the difficulty of sorting out their side of things. I do not know what the trees were to themselves, how they, as trees, experienced the world, or experienced my repeated presence. I know I thought they were sisters or friends, and that *Fryd*'s blooms would encourage *Glede* to get going. *Fryd*, to my mind, was extravagant, profligate. She dressed herself in floppy, crisp-white flowers, like a marshmallow wedding dress; lace, beading, silk, layers – why choose one when you can have all? *Glede* was more staid. Each bloom elegant: cream, with pink rising from the bottom. Her buds were precise and sculptural, like bone china, each poised and in its own space. Her flowers did not fall over themselves in giddiness; they sat on gray branches, profound and ecstatic, like queens and empresses.

But what were these trees in themselves? How did they experience each other? How did they feel the coming of spring, how did they know when to put out flowers? Did my passion for them register in any way? Did I encroach on their space, were they indifferent, or did they enjoy visits? I don't know and I don't know how to begin to know. I recognize that my thoughts about *Fryd* and *Glede* smack of anthropomorphism, of fruity sentimentality. But this shortcoming only begs the question of what real intimacy between humans and trees looks like. Is any such intimacy possible? I do not know, but I know that other people know. I have read about animists, people who interact with all kinds of persons – trees, rocks, foxes – and I have read the Bible: "The trees of the field will clap their hands..." (Isaiah 55:12); "I call today the heavens and the earth to witness against you..." (Deuteronomy 4:26)[1] – this from the mouths of Isaiah and Moses! The heavens and the earth, looking at us; so says Torah. What is all this about? What view of the world underlies these texts? What relationships did the biblical writers have with trees, soils, and skies?

What follows is an inquiry into these and related questions as they present themselves through the text of the Hebrew Bible. I use the classical tools of biblical studies, including close reading, historical comparison, and linguistic study, to think about intimacy and relationship between humans and nonhumans in the biblical text. The biblical writers return, again and again, to descriptions of the world that allude to a plenitude of persons: bellicose rivers, frisky mountains, fields draped in mourning. This book is an exercise in taking such language seriously; I don't mean literally – there is plenty of metaphor here – but seriously. What do these texts suggest about how ancient Israelites viewed and interacted with the world?

I will argue that texts across the Hebrew Bible demonstrate that its writers viewed nonanimal nature as active and alive, that is, as persons. By nonanimal nature I mean all elements of the cosmos excluding humans and animals, what in the modern West would be considered inanimate nature. I use the term "person" as a goad, a difficult term that is meant to make us uncomfortable. I hope that the tension between Western notions of personhood and of nonanimal nature will be a productive tension, one that might free our imagination to reconsider how we think of the

---

[1] All translations of biblical texts are my own, unless noted.

world and its relation to us. This is important if we are to understand the biblical text: a personalistic view of nonanimal nature influences how biblical writers narrate interaction among humans, nonhumans, and God. Rather than viewing nature and its elements as raw material or landscape, they describe the heavens and the earth, mountains, trees, and rivers as creatures that engage with other creatures and are able to hear and obey commands, protest human misconduct, lament and offer praise, and affect human history. Though a number of texts could be brought to bear on my thesis, I will mostly confine myself to texts in which nonanimal nature performs actions, displays affect, or is addressed in a manner similar to how one addresses a person; I collectively call them personalistic nature texts. These texts have not received sustained attention in previous scholarship and have never been studied together as a group.

TWO AIMS: EXEGESIS AND ECOLOGY

I have two aims. The first is exegetical: to arrive at a more accurate and detailed understanding of personalistic nature texts and their role in the Hebrew Bible. The second aim is ecological, namely to think about how we, in the contemporary world, interact with the world around us and to consider how engaging with the Bible's active understanding of nonhuman nature might influence our ethics and the scope and nature of contemporary environmental action. As such, my aims echo Jane Bennett's, in her book *Vibrant Matter: A Political Ecology of Things*, in which she explores "the capacity of things – edibles, commodities, storms, metals – not only to impede or block the will and design of humans but also to act as quasi agents or forces with trajectories, propensities, and tendencies of their own."[2] Bennett writes about these "capacities" with two goals in mind, one philosophical and one political. The philosophical project of her book is "to think slowly an idea that runs fast through modern heads: the idea of matter as passive stuff, as raw, brute, or inert."[3] This aim is much like my exegetical aim; I will "think slowly" through texts in which nonanimal nature behaves like persons. I will treat with suspicion the common-sense "fast" idea that nonanimal nature is inert, and the concomitant assumption that ascribing activity to it is, therefore, always only

---

[2] Jane Bennett, *Vibrant Matter: A Political Ecology of Things* (Durham: Duke University, 2010), viii.
[3] Ibid., vii.

symbolic or ornamental. Bennett's political goal is "to encourage more intelligent and sustainable engagements with vibrant matter and living things," and she uses as a guide the question, "How would political responses to public problems change were we to take seriously the vitality of (nonhuman) bodies?"[4] I ask the same question, but use the biblical text as the source material for ecological reflection. Bennett hopes to contribute to "more ecological and more materially sustainable modes of production and consumption."[5] "My hunch," she writes, "is that the image of dead or thoroughly instrumentalized matter feeds human hubris and our earth-destroying fantasies of conquest and consumption. It does so by preventing us from detecting (seeing, hearing, smelling, tasting, feeling) a fuller range of the nonhuman powers circulating around and within human bodies."[6] Like Bennett, my hope is that attending to personalistic nature texts will prove useful for contemporary ecological engagement.

In particular, I hope to contribute to discussions in Christian and Jewish communities, for whom the Hebrew Bible is scripture. Richard Bauckham, in his book *Living with Other Creatures: Green Exegesis and Theology*, uses language similar to Bennett's, though with a religious bent, to describe what is at stake in taking seriously nature's praise of YHWH.[7] He writes: "The more we praise God with the other creatures, the more we shall want to resist the relentless trend towards a total humanizing of the world in which the rest of creation will have become no more than the material from which we have fashioned a world of our own creation."[8] Attention to how nonhumans praise YHWH is, he says, "the strongest antidote to anthropocentrism in the biblical and Christian tradition."[9] Terence Fretheim, in his book *God and World in the Old Testament: A Relational Theology of Creation*, also considers texts in the Hebrew Bible in which nonhumans praise YHWH. He asks: "[W]hat kind of thinking about God and what kind of thinking about nature would have occasioned this kind of language?"[10] The language he refers

---

[4] Ibid., viii.   [5] Ibid., ix.   [6] Ibid.
[7] YHWH is the English rendition of the four Hebrew letters יהוה, which make up the divine name. Orthodox Jews do not say or write with vowels the divine name. In consideration of Orthodox readers, I have rendered the divine name as YHWH throughout, including in quotations.
[8] Richard Bauckham, *Living with Other Creatures: Green Exegesis and Theology* (Waco, TX: Baylor University, 2011), 154.
[9] Ibid., 150.
[10] Terence E. Fretheim, *God and World in the Old Testament: A Relational Theology of Creation* (Nashville, TN: Abingdon, 2005), 250.

to includes Isaiah's call to the mountains, the forest, and its trees to "break forth into shouts of joy" (Isaiah 44:23), and the incorporation, in Psalm 148, of the sun, the moon, the heavens, the waters above the heavens, the deeps, fire and hail, snow and frost, strong wind, the mountains and all hills, fruit trees, and cedars in YHWH's chorus of praise. Bauckham and Fretheim query one particular kind of personalistic nature text, namely those in which nonanimal nature receives summons to praise, but texts that attribute activity to nonanimal nature are much more diverse than this. Jeremiah says to the heavens, "Be desolate ... at this, be horrified, be very dry" (Jeremiah 2:12), Joshua commands the sun and the moon to stand still in the sky (Joshua 10:12), and Moses recruits the heavens and the earth to witness against Israel (Deuteronomy 4:26; 30:19; 32:1). This project resists anthropocentrism not only by exploring nature's praise, but also by attending to its mourning, its responsibilities in creation, its attentiveness to humans and YHWH, its articulateness, and its joy.

This kind of attention requires putting aside commonsense notions about where life begins and ends, what a person is, and who and what can be in a relationship. Bennett writes that studying the vibrancy of matter "requires that one is caught up in it."[11] "One needs," she says, "to suspend suspicion and adopt a more open-ended comportment. If we think we already know what is out there, we will almost surely miss it."[12] Bauckham points to the eighteenth-century poet Christopher Smart as an example of someone who embodies this kind of "open-ended comportment." Nature's praise is a key theme in Smart's poetry, as exemplified by his poem about his cat:

For I will consider my Cat Jeoffry.
For he is the servant of the Living God, duly and daily serving him.
For at the first glance of the glory of God in the East he worships in his way.
For this is done by wreathing his body seven times round with elegant quickness.
For then he leaps up to catch the musk, which is the blessing of God upon his
   prayer.[13]

The poem is both a detailed observation of the behaviors and habits of Smart's cat and a celebration of these behaviors as Jeoffry's forms of worship.

---

[11] Bennett, *Vibrant Matter*, xv.   [12] Ibid.
[13] Jubliate Agno, Fragment B. The section of the poem that concerns Jeoffry can be read at www.poets.org/poetsorg/poem/jubilate-agno-fragment-b-i-will-consider-my-cat-jeoffry. The poem in its entirety is over 1,200 lines.

In Bauckham's words, the poem is "playful as well as serious."[14] It is a charming, funny portrait of a cat, and a serious theological reflection on the relationship between God and a nonhuman creature. Reading personalistic nature texts require something of Smart's spirit, or of the spirit he attributes to his cat, "a mixture of gravity and waggery."

Another person who embodies this spirit is Martin Buber. In *I and Thou*, he writes about two ways of looking at a tree:

> I consider a tree. I can look at it as a picture: stiff column in a shock of light, or splash of green shot with the delicate blue and silver of the background ... I can subdue its actual presence and form so sternly that I recognize it only as an expression of law ... In all this the tree remains my object, occupies space and time, and has its nature and conditions.[15]

This is the tree as *It*, as object, but Buber insists there is another way to look at a tree: "It can ... also come about, if I have both will and grace, that in considering the tree I become bound up in relation to it. The tree is no longer It."[16] Buber emphasizes that becoming "bound up in relation" to a tree is not an instance of humans projecting meaning onto the world. For the relation to be real, it must be mutual. "The tree is no impression, no play of my imagination, no value depending on my mood; but it is bodied over against me and has to do with me, as I with it." To deny the mutuality of the relationship would be "to sap the strength from the meaning of the relation." Buber is unsure of what this means for how we think about trees (does the tree have consciousness?), but he is unambiguous about the reality of the meeting, that the *Thou* he meets is the tree: "I encounter no soul or dryad of the tree, but the tree itself."[17]

For Buber, the *I–Thou* relationship between humans and trees is one that is beyond words. When we address nonhuman creatures as *Thou*, "our words cling to the threshold of speech," he says.[18] To meet the world and be met by it is something that must be lived; "Believe in the simple magic of life, in service in the universe, and the meaning of that waiting, that alertness, that 'craning of the neck' in creatures will dawn upon you," he offers in encouragement. "Every word would falsify; but look! bound about you beings live their life, and to whatever point you turn you come upon being."[19] This book is an attempt to heed Buber's encouragement to look, while engaging with texts that do not seem to think that "every word

---

[14] Bauckham, *Living with Other Creatures*, 154.
[15] Martin Buber, *I and Thou*, trans. Ronald Gregor Smith (Edinburgh: T. & T. Clark, 1950), 7.
[16] Ibid.   [17] Ibid., 8.   [18] Ibid., 6.   [19] Ibid., 15.

would falsify." I share Buber's sense that my words are inadequate, but not his claim that they are, therefore, necessarily false (the fact that Buber writes at length about meeting a tree suggests that he, too, has more confidence in words than he lets on). Instead, I hope, with Maggie Nelson and Ludwig Wittgenstein, that "the inexpressible is contained – inexpressibly! – in the expressed,"[20] that, despite my inability to definitively describe the point of view of *Fryd* and *Glede*, I can yet say something that might help me and us be receptive to the "mutual giving" between humans and the world so tantalizingly promised by Buber.[21]

Observed at a distance, through the lens of Western concepts, personalistic nature texts appear naive and primitive, or at least the interpreter who takes them seriously appears so. From up close, with an openness to their sense of engagement, entanglement, and wonder, they reveal the rich thought of Israel's poets on the life of other-than-human creatures and their relationship with YHWH. Taken seriously, they can provide stimulus for more careful ecological thought, a prod to make us reconsider how we treat creatures that the modern West does not consider persons: mountains, forests, soils, and bodies of water. Mountaintop removal, clear cutting, aggressive use of fertilizers and pesticides, and careless oil drilling looks very different when these acts are not only extractive resource management, but also dysfunctional relationships with persons created and valued by God.

STRANGENESS AND ETHICS

One of the challenges of using personalistic nature texts for ethical reflection is their enduring strangeness. Knowing *about* animist understandings of nonanimal nature, that is, the idea that "the world is full of persons, only some of whom are human, and that life is always lived in relationship with others," does not easily translate into experience or familiarity.[22] To most Westerners, myself included, study does not erase the strangeness of interacting with trees or rocks as subjects capable of response. The enduring alienness of personalistic nature texts does not, however, mean that these texts cannot inform ethics. On the contrary,

---

[20] Maggie Nelson, *The Argonauts* (Minneapolis, MI: Graywolf, 2015), 3.
[21] Buber, *I and Thou*, 33.
[22] Graham Harvey, *Animism: Respecting the Living World* (London: Hurst & Co., 2005), xi. See Chapter 2, "Interacting with the World," for a more in-depth definition of animism.

their strangeness is itself informative. It opens up space for new questions, approaches, and methods.

One thing that personalistic nature texts and animist traditions provide is a new language. One may infer from personalistic nature texts that interactions with mountains, trees, and, especially, farmland are social. That means that the language of social interactions is suitable for thinking about ecology. Words like etiquette, respect, generosity, and gratitude, borrowed from animist traditions and implied by biblical discourse, convey new ways of relating with nonanimal nature. For example, the Bible repeatedly insists that the ground "gives" its produce and that trees "give" their fruit (see, for example, Leviticus 25:19; 26:4; Deuteronomy 11:17); this terminology implies that the ground and trees act with generosity towards humans when they provide food for human consumption. Leviticus emphasizes that the land needs sabbath (see Leviticus 25:2; 26:34–35), and requires humans to respect this needs and to adapt their actions to it. Humans must return the generosity of the land by granting it rest. The prophetic theme of the mourning of the land (see Isaiah 24:4; 33:9; Jeremiah 4:28; 12:4, 11; 23:10; Hosea 4:3; Joel 1:10; Amos 1:2) solicits repentance and compassion from the audience. To say that a land is in mourning exceeds accusations of mismanagement. It names the land as an aggrieved person, a person entitled to restitution and consolation. Using social language to describe the relationship between humans and nonanimal nature alters the meaning of sustainability and responsible use; instead of focusing primarily on what is sustainable for human populations, the language requires that attention also be paid to the land's needs and desires.

The difference between animistic understandings of the world and modernistic ones can seem absolute – the difference unbridgeable – yet there are people who, though they do not necessarily identify as animists, model respectful engagement with nonanimal nature. These people can serve as "tutors" in the endeavor to change how we interact with that which is not human. Contemporary farmers, scholars, and writers model how language might mold interactions with nonanimal nature. Chickasaw poet and writer Linda Hogan speaks about misuse of land in terms of broken treaties: "It is clear that we have strayed from the treaties we once had with the land and with animals. It is also clear, and heartening, that in our time there are many – Indian and non-Indian alike – who want to restore and honor these broken agreements."[23] Logan, like Leviticus

---

[23] Linda Hogan, *Dwellings: A Spiritual History of the Living World* (New York: W.W. Norton, 1995), 11.

(see, for example, 26:42), frames the relationship between people, land, and animals in covenantal terms. Extractive resource management, water pollution, and global warming are deplorable not only because they adversely affect human life, but also because they fail to honor proper relationships between humans and all that is nonhuman. Such practices are forgetful of the fact that "all things are connected."[24] The title of an edited volume by Wes Jackson, Wendell Berry, and Bruce Colman, *Meeting the Expectations of the Land: Essays in Sustainable Agriculture and Stewardship*, points to a similar logic.[25] Sound treatment of nature extends beyond making sure humans will have access to food, water, and clean air in the future; it includes respect for the land's own "expectations." Attention to the expectations of the land changes the sort of questions we might ask when faced with a decision that will affect humans, soils, forests, and rivers. We must ask both "How will our choices affect us, our children, our neighbors, people in faraway countries?" and "How will they affect pines, beeches, soil, rivers, creeks, and groundwater?" Will our action permit only a minimal living space for these creatures? How might we instead act with generosity? What might it mean to extend hospitality towards a valley, or respect towards a stand of trees?

Such questions are not new questions, though they are new to me. The anthropologist Hugo Reinert relates how the Sami reindeer herder and philosopher Nils Oskal describes proper interaction with *sieidi*, stones to whom Sámi people have traditionally sacrificed. Oskal does not describe such sacrifices as worship, but as politeness: "Common courtesy indicates that you should greet it and wish it well in your thoughts when passing it by. It is unheard of to argue with a *sieidi* or to enter into conflict with it."[26] Oskal compares politeness towards *sieidi* to Christian charity; both, he claims, express "an obligation to 'extend politeness to all beings that cross your path.'"[27] Extending politeness to stones, tundra, trees, and fungi will not feel natural to most people raised in the modern West, but it can nonetheless shape our thinking and action. Politeness, respect, and gratitude as measures of the value of an action set a higher standard than costs and profits, questions about human benefits and losses, even

[24] Ibid., 41.
[25] Wes Jackson, Wendell Berry, and Bruce Colman, *Meeting the Expectations of the Land: Essays in Sustainable Agriculture and Stewardship* (San Francisco: North Point, 1984).
[26] Hugo Reinert, "About a Stone: Some Notes on Geologic Conviviality," *Environmental Humanities* 8, no. 1 (2016): 99.
[27] Ibid.

questions about environmental impact. Reinert himself thinks of it as a matter of recasting questions about harm: "Can a stone be harmed?" he asks, before suggesting that one way to include stone in politics is to view it as "a vulnerable subject."[28]

Reinert describes two immersive, relational "experiments" in which he attempts to act as if the world is alive and sentient. The first involves a *sieidi* stone. Reinert is visiting Kvalsund in northern Norway, when the people there learn of his interest in stones. They tell him about a near-by *sieidi* stone, named Stallogargo. Reinert writes that "on [his] second day [he] went to see the stone and introduce [himself]."[29] He brings the stone gifts: a few coins and tobacco. His sacrifice does not make him feel either familiarity or comfort, nor does it cause a sudden change in him. He speculates, however, that it affects a second "experiment," this time involving a property on the coast of Denmark with which he is entrusted. Everything about the property requires work: "There are floors to take up, foundations to excavate and reinforce, literal mountains of earth and stone to move and remove and fill in."[30] His bodily engagement with the property changes what he sees when he looks at it:

> As time and the work press, the land reveals itself to me in new ways ... I feed the birds and hedgehogs, water the trees, pay attention to root systems and earthworms and to the time it takes for things to grow, to seasonal shifts and patterns of rain, to water flows as they articulate with the topography of dips and trenches and heights.[31]

The new owner of the next-door property models a different way of seeing and treating the land; in the space of an afternoon, he "razes the lot to the ground."[32] Reinert is grief-stricken: "I watched a hundred years of trees, plants, hedgehog habitats, and bird nests destroyed."[33] His own engagement with his plot of land has changed how he understands interactions between humans and the spaces in which they live. The leveling of the next-door plot no longer appears to him as a reasonable building and landscaping strategy, but as a "horror," a violation of "the mutual enmeshment of soil and self and beings."[34]

Of the two experiments, the second, I suspect, is the easier for most people to understand. But Reinert draws a close connection between his gift to the *sieidi* stone and his engagement with the plot of land on the coast of Denmark. He writes: "Could it be, by some logic of hidden

---

[28] Ibid., 104. [29] Ibid., 107. [30] Ibid., 108. [31] Ibid. [32] Ibid. [33] Ibid.
[34] Ibid., 108–9.

agency, that I invited all this – that in the gesture of offering I opened myself to the stone as an influence?"³⁵ Perhaps it is because Reinert introduced himself to Stallogargo and treated it with generosity that he can now see the deep connections between himself, his land, and its animals and plants. Perhaps the land is returning his respect and generosity.

Reinert cautions against quick recourse to the question "But is it real?"³⁶ Can stones really return generosity? Instead he suggests other questions: "What happens if I do this? If I follow this lead?"³⁷ Or, as Martin Buber says about the world addressed as *Thou*: "It comes, and comes to bring *you* out; if it does not reach you, meet you, then it vanishes; but it comes back in another form."³⁸ Similar to Reinert, Anishinaabe writer Louise Erdrich suggests moving away from questions of belief and instead focusing on behaving relationally: "There was a time when I wondered – do I really believe all of this? I'm half German. Rational! Does this make any sense? After a while such questions stopped mattering. Believing or not believing, it was all the same. I found myself compelled to behave toward the world as if it contained sentient spiritual beings."³⁹ Personalistic nature texts can engender in us a kind of openness; when the world comes to "bring us out," when the world compels us, when a tree reaches out to us in greeting, perhaps we might, if we have paid attention to the Bible's stories of the joys and sorrows of creation, be ready to greet it in turn.

Another word for this openness is attention. The writers of the Hebrew Bible display close attention to nonanimal nature. Theophanies include both close observation of the effects of earthquakes and storms on the land, and a multifaceted connection between such physical phenomena and the experience of awe and fear at YHWH's coming. Attention need not be particularly mystical. Reinert's interaction with his property is physical and practical, but it also involves love and commitment. Wendell Berry describes how feeding livestock requires minute perception: "One must pay attention – not just throw the feed in, but stay and watch; see if it is eaten with relish and cleaned up; see if all the animals are eating, if all are healthy, if the feed is doing the good it is supposed to do."⁴⁰

---

³⁵ Ibid., 109. ³⁶ Ibid., 110. ³⁷ Ibid.
³⁸ Buber, *I and Thou*. Emphasis in original.
³⁹ Louise Erdrich, *Books and Islands in Ojibwe Country* (Washington, DC: National Geographic, 2003), 16.
⁴⁰ Wendell Berry, "Whose Head Is the Farmer Using? Whose Head Is Using the Farmer?," in *Meeting the Expectations of the Land: Essays in Sustainable Agriculture and Stewardship* (San Francisco: North Point, 1984), 27.

This is not a passive attentiveness, an outsider observing the world without affecting it. This is an interactive attention, a participatory awareness. As Thom van Dooren, Eben Kirksey, and Ursula Münster insist, attention involves both observation and action:

> [A]ttentiveness is a two-part proposition: both a practice of getting to know another in their intimate particularity – steadily applying one's observant faculties and energies, as the *Oxford English Dictionary* puts it – and, at the same time, a practice of learning how one might better respond to another, might work to cultivate worlds of mutual flourishing, that is ... how one might be "assiduous in ministering to the comfort and pleasures of others, giving watchful heed to their wishes."[41]

In the chapters to come, I will "steadily apply [my] observant faculties and energies" to personalistic nature texts in the Bible, in order that we might become "assiduous in ministering to the comfort and pleasures" of all creatures, human, animal, and other-than-animal. It is my hope that, through this process, personalistic nature texts may help us reframe approaches to ecology. They can help us think beyond the human, beyond human needs, and help us "[give] watchful heed" to the wishes of all God's creatures, including those with whom most of us rarely think to relate in personal terms, such as soil, forests, rivers, oceans, and clouds.

OUTLINE

This study consists of two parts: the first (Chapter 2) lays the theoretical groundwork, while the second (Chapters 3–5) turns to exegetical studies of personalistic nature texts in the Hebrew Bible.

Chapter 2, "Interacting with the World: 'New Animism,' Metaphor Theory, and Personalistic Nature Texts" begins with a discussion of Cora Diamond's article "Losing Your Concepts,"[42] in order to situate the distance between the concepts of personhood, relationality, and nature in the modern West and in animistic traditions. The rest of the chapter outlines current research on how animists think about personhood and relationships between persons (both human and other-than-human), and the unsuitability of applying the nature–society dualism to such societies. Throughout the chapter, I draw parallels to texts and traditions in the

---

[41] Thom Van Dooren, Eben Kirksey, and Ursula Münster, "Multispecies Studies: Cultivating Arts of Attentiveness," *Environmental Humanities* 8, no. 1 (May 2016): 17. The quote within the quote is from the *Oxford English Dictionary*.
[42] Cora Diamond, "Losing Your Concepts," *Ethics* 98, no. 2 (1988): 255–77.

Hebrew Bible. I also discuss the social and pedagogical functions of metaphors, as well as the importance of approaching personalistic nature texts with patience and humility.

Chapters 3–5 form the bulk of the study, each chapter focusing on personalistic nature texts in one of the three sections of the Hebrew Bible. The activity of nonanimal nature in Torah is the topic of Chapter 3, "A Watchful World: Personalistic Nature Texts in the Torah." The land is a central character in this section; it observes cultic regulations, guards against pollution caused by human faithlessness, and punishes transgressors. In Chapter 4, "A Sentient World: Personalistic Nature Texts in the Prophets," nonanimal persons are more diverse. Trees and stars join battles, fields mourn, mountains witness, and seas tremble. This chapter is divided into five thematic sections, each of which discusses a particular form of activity or context of activity: war, theophany, address, grief, and joy. Chapter 5, "An Articulate World: Personalistic Nature Texts in the Writings," covers the Psalms, Job, and Song of Songs. The first part of the chapter concerns nature's speech in the Psalms, the second looks at Job's negotiation of his innocence vis-à-vis his land, and the third looks at the blurred boundary between humans and vegetation in Song of Songs.

In the conclusion (Chapter 6) I look at further avenues for research, including implications for studies of theological anthropology, architecture and artifacts in the Hebrew Bible, and iconographic interpretation. I also consider the difficulty of establishing whether one set of concepts is superior to another (I return to Diamond's work), ethical implications of personalistic nature texts, and possible rewards of reading personalistic nature texts with attention. I briefly look to artists and poets as examples of people who might help us cultivate attentiveness and perception.

2

Interacting with the World

"New Animism," Metaphor Theory, and Personalistic Nature Texts

INTRODUCTION

This project began with a fascination with Genesis 4. In a dispute between two brothers, a dispute God steps in to moderate, the ground is a central character. After Cain kills Abel, the ground swallows Abel's blood and lends it voice to call out to God, notifying God of the murder. Though it would be too much to say, I think, that the ground impedes Cain's violence – Abel dies, after all – it certainly participates in God's judgment on that violence.

So, I formed an hypothesis: in the Hebrew Bible, other-than-human characters moderate and respond to human violence. When humans turn especially bellicose and aggressive, the world protests. I started at the beginning, combing through the canon start to finish, looking for other texts in which nonanimal nature actively intervenes in the story. I quickly realized that my hypothesis was wrong. Or, rather, not wrong so much as inadequate. I was looking for nature to do one thing, to fill a defined slot in the history of Israel's life with God and each other, but what I encountered was much more diffuse. Nature did all kinds of things, played many different roles, not just the one that I had noticed. Even trying to organize the texts I found into well-defined categories, either in terms of kinds of actions or kinds of actors, proved impractical; the texts were too diverse.

This is when I first started to feel the poverty of my own language. I did not have the words to describe what I was seeing.

I poked around the library, read articles on related topics, picked the brains of colleagues, talked it over with my partner, and scribbled notes and questions in the margins of books. Eventually, this research led me to anthropology, specifically to the field "new animism."

Animism has been a darling concept of anthropology since the birth of the field. It was first developed by Edward Burnett Tylor, in his book *Primitive Culture* of 1871. Defined as the "doctrine of universal vitality,"[1] Tylor believed animism was the first stage in the evolution of culture or civilization (the other stages are civilized religion and absolute science).[2] Racist assumptions tinted early views of animism – Tylor, for example, wrote that one of the roles of ethnography was "to expose the remains of crude old culture which have passed into harmful superstition, and to mark these out for destruction"[3] – the most important of which was that animism was an initial stage of human evolution, one that ought to be replaced by higher, more enlightened versions of religion.[4] For early anthropologists, animism was a kind of epistemological mistake. It was a step towards true religion or true science (depending on whom you asked), but no more than a step on the way. It was certainly not a worldview equal to Christianity or Western empiricism.

Despite this dubious beginning, late twentieth century scholars have refurbished the concept of animism.[5] The person responsible for this renaissance was A. Irving Hallowell, whose insight that animist conceptions of personhood extend beyond the human sparked a flood of research.[6] Hallowell's writing, and that of subsequent anthropologists, provide

---

[1] Edward B. Tylor, *Primitive Culture: Researches into the Development of Mythology, Philosophy, Religion, Language, Art, and Custom*, vol. II (New York: Holt, 1889), 285.
[2] Tylor's stages resemble those proposed by Hegel (the religion of nature, the religion of spiritual individuality, and absolute religion; see Georg Wilhelm Friedrich Hegel, *Lectures on the Philosophy of Religion*, trans. Peter Crafts Hodgson and J. M. Stewart, vol. I [Berkeley: University of California Press, 1984], ix–xi); and George Frazer (magic, religion, science; see James George Frazer, *The Golden Bough: A Study in Magic and Religion*, vol. 11 [London: MacMillan and Co., 1925], 304).
[3] Edward B. Tylor, *Religion in Primitive Culture*, vol. II (Gloucester, MA: Peter Smith, 1970), 539.
[4] See, for example, William Robertson Smith, *Religion of the Semites* (New Brunswick, NJ: Transaction, 2002); James George Frazer, *The Golden Bough: A Study in Magic and Religion*, Vol. 11 (London: MacMillan and Co., 1925); John Lubbock, *The Origin of Civilization and the Primitive Condition of Man: Mental and Social Condition of Savages* (New York: D. Appleton and Company, 1874).
[5] For a historical overview of the study of animism, starting with Edward Burnett Tylor, see Nurit Bird-David, "'Animism' Revisited: Personhood, Environment, and Relational Epistemology," *Current Anthropology* 40, no. S1 (1999): S69–72; and Graham Harvey, *Animism: Respecting the Living World* (London: Hurst & Co., 2005), 3–29.
[6] A. Irving Hallowell, "Ojibwa Ontology, Behavior, and World View," in *Readings in Indigenous Religions*, ed. Graham Harvey (London: Continuum, 2002), 18–49.

fruitful comparisons for personalistic nature texts. Their rethinking of the concepts of personhood, nature, and relationality, and their ethnographic investigations into various animist traditions provide fresh lenses with which to study biblical texts in which nonanimal nature acts or is spoken to. Also important for understanding personalistic nature texts is metaphor theory. Most of the texts we will look at involve metaphor in some way or another; understanding the role of metaphor, in particular how it can provide access to relationships, is key for understanding how biblical writers describe trees, mountains, and clouds. The figurative language of personalistic nature texts does not indicate poetic fancy or artificiality, but instead serves to guide human interactions with persons whose bodies and ways of being in the world differ from human ones.

The main reason modern scholars struggle to interpret personalistic nature texts is that the concepts that guide our interaction with the other-than-human world are not the same as those that guided ancient Israelites. Furthermore, the modern English vocabulary of action, agency, and life is both unsatisfying and inadequate for describing how the writers of the Bible narrate interactions between God, humans, and nonanimal nature. So are the words we use to describe literary devices, words like personification, anthropomorphism, and animation. Each of these words assumes that writers attribute personal traits to that which is not personal, as if a writer first sees an inert mountain and *then* decides to attribute humanlike features to it. Such words bend the concepts of the text to fit our own, and so distort them. New animism and metaphor theory can provide a better vocabulary, a way of speaking that introduces us anew to biblical texts.

That said, some of the vocabulary I use will be deeply uncomfortable for many Western readers. Most uncomfortable, probably, will be my use of the term "person." As I have said, I use this term as a goad. It is intended to provoke thought, to make visible prior assumptions about what is and is not a person, and to open up space to rethink the roles of other-than-human nature in the Hebrew Bible. I offer it as a means to creativity, not as dogma. The term (in this use of it) arose from attempts of anthropologists to translate animists ways of life into language legible within Western academic discourse. Animists themselves have many ways of speaking of those with whom they are in relation; there is nothing original or indisputable about the term "person." I offer it as an invitation into the biblical text. Personalistic nature texts are a rich record of one people's interaction with their world. To read them is to listen in on a passionate and vital conversation between humans and the other-than-human persons with whom they share life. If we insist that this conversation is in fact a monologue, we will miss much of what is said.

"Losing Your Concepts": *Cora Diamond, Personalistic Nature Texts, and Articulating Conceptual Distance*

The difficulty of listening well to the biblical text is that the world of the biblical writers is so different than our own; intellectual openness to their ideas does not necessarily make us less confused. Their concepts of what it is to be a human being, the place of humans in the world, the life of other-than-human beings – these all differ substantially from our own patterns and ideas of life. Even nailing down what exactly the differences consist of is complicated, because we are so habituated to our own world, our own thoughts. How then do we learn about concepts that differ from our own, and how do we evaluate the relative goodness of those concepts? In her article, "Losing Your Concepts," philosopher Cora Diamond surveys discussions of conceptual loss in the field of moral philosophy. She does so in order to ask "what sort of good a concept is, and what kind of loss it is to lose concepts."[7] Is it possible, she asks, that some conceptual changes leave us better off (for example, make us less sexist)? Or might conceptual loss disrupt the relationship between our experiences and our thoughts in ways that leave us worse off than we were before the conceptual loss? These may seem like abstract questions, with little connection to the role of nonanimal nature in the Hebrew Bible, but Diamond's exploration can help clarify why it matters how we think and speak about all that is not human. Her writing also provides pointers for how we might set about changing or recovering our concepts, even as she makes clear that this is no easy task.

A key aspect of Diamond's argument is that concepts are not simply intellectual ideas, but instead ways of life: "[G]rasping a concept (even one like that of a human being, which is a descriptive concept if any are) is not a matter just of knowing how to group things under that concept; it is being able to participate in life with the concept."[8] The problem facing modern scholars writing about personalistic nature texts is that we do not live the way people who believe that mountains and the sun are living

---

[7] Cora Diamond, "Losing Your Concepts," *Ethics* 98, no. 2 (1988): 256.
[8] Ibid., 266, 276.

beings do. To understand fully what it means that God gives the sun and the moon responsibility to rule the day and the night (Genesis 1:16) we must live the way the writers of this ancient text lived, in their world, with their language and their concepts. We must participate in their life with the concepts. In other words, understanding biblical texts is not simply an intellectual exercise, but an exercise in how to live. We are ill equipped to interpret the texts of the Bible, because our daily life is so removed from the people who produced them. To span the gap between our concepts and theirs, to find language that is both accurate and satisfying, requires more than regular effort and a suspension of commonsense ideas and categories.

Diamond distinguishes between disagreement between people who share a conceptual world and the sort of responses we have when "someone's words show, or seem to show, some departure from the shared conceptual world."[9] When faced with a departure from familiar concepts, we respond not with "I disagree," but with "How can he have adduced *that* here? How can he so much as think that relevant?" and "What is this?" "What is going on?" "Huh?"[10] In the face of foreign concepts, our ability to make meaning and our language fall short; we are reduced to "a kind of inarticulateness."[11]

This does not mean that all mentions of nonanimal nature in the Bible must prompt confusion and disorientation in modern Western readers. Texts like "And Noah ... planted a vineyard" (Genesis 9:20) seem straightforward. The text is meaningful and clear to a reader, who assumes that the words "planted" and "vineyard" mean more or less what they mean now. The difference between ancient Israelite concepts and modern concepts is here either nonexistent or invisible.[12] Personalistic nature texts produce a different response. When we read, in 2 Samuel 18:8, that "the forest devoured more people than the sword in that day," we must engage with metaphor, but it is difficult to know *how* exactly. It is easy enough to construe a metaphorical meaning for "devour" in

---

[9] Ibid., 273.   [10] Ibid., 273–74.

[11] Diamond quotes Iris Murdoch to illustrate the connection between loss of concepts and loss of language: "We have suffered a general loss of concepts, the loss of a moral and political vocabulary" (Ibid., 261, 262). Quoting Iris Murdoch, "Against Dryness: A Polemical Sketch," in *Revisions, Changing Perspectives in Moral Philosophy*, ed. Stanley Hauerwas and Alasdair C. MacIntyre (Notre Dame: University of Notre Dame Press, 1983).

[12] Diamond discusses invisibility in the context of certain philosophies of language and the mind which *makes invisible* conceptual loss. See Ibid., 266–72.

relation to "the sword," but what does it mean for a forest to devour? To say that this is "just metaphor" gets us nowhere; it amounts to saying that the text here is meaningless. To invent a rationalistic explanation (the soldiers were lost in the forest and died of starvation?) is also unsatisfying; why talk as if the forest performs an action if it really comes down to poor orienteering skills?

Diamond insists that the experience of encountering concepts foreign to our own "does not need to remain at the level of 'Huh?'"[13] "Reading," she writes, "involves in various ways a sensitivity to the conceptual world in which the work lies," a responsiveness that is simply a part of "an ordinary human responsiveness to words."[14] This responsiveness can move towards articulateness; it is possible to explore and talk about the distance between our own concepts and strange concepts encountered in texts and conversations. It is not now possible to share in the life of ancient Israel, but it is possible to listen attentively to the stories and poems they created. In particular, we can pay attention to texts in which conceptual distance is clear and visible, and we can try, to the best of our abilities, to use "concepts internal to [their] thought."[15] One way to approach this task is to seek help from present day peoples whose concepts more closely resemble those of ancient Israel. Contemporary animists consider beings beyond humans as persons; their conceptual world potentially provides parallels to the biblical text. Western anthropologists and ethnographers have written extensively about their attempts to make articulate the fissure between modern Western cosmologies and those of contemporary animists, and their work provides a more adequate and precise vocabulary than what has previously been applied to personalistic nature texts in biblical studies.

"NEW ANIMISM"[16]

The challenge faced by Western students of animism is not unlike the challenge posed by personalistic nature texts. Though animism has been studied since the birth of modern anthropology, Graham Harvey writes that, for the most part, animist "modes of discourse and enquiry have been opaque and invisible" to Western scholars.[17] It is not simply that

---

[13] Ibid., 274. [14] Ibid., 273. [15] Ibid., 276.
[16] The adjective "new" in "new animism" refers to a new direction in scholarship, not to a new phenomenon in the world. For a discussion of the term, see Harvey, *Animism*, xi–xiv.
[17] Ibid., 203.

animism is confusing to modern scholars, but that scholars have been unable to see their own lack of insight and the distance between their own concepts and the concepts of the peoples they study. Philippe Descola argues that early studies into animism were motivated by "a logical scandal": the peoples with which anthropologists came into contact blurred or simply ignored the demarcation between "human beings and 'natural objects.'"[18] In Diamond's words, when faced with animist societies, scholars thought: "'What is this?' 'What is going on?' 'Huh?'"[19] Until recently, efforts to reduce this dissonance focused on assimilating animist concepts and ontologies to Western ones. Contemporary scholars, like Irving Hallowell, Nurit Bird-David, Graham Harvey, Tim Ingold, Philippe Descola, Eduardo Viveiros de Castro, and Marilyn Strathern, try to change this and seek to understand animism using concepts and vocabulary internal to animist thought. A. Irving Hallowell formulates the importance of setting aside Western categories:

[I]n the social sciences and psychology, "persons" and human beings are categorically identified ... The same identification is implicit in the conceptualization and investigation of social organization by anthropologists. Yet this obviously involves a radical abstraction if, from the standpoint of the people being studied, the concept of "person" is not, in fact, synonymous with human being but transcends it ... [A] thoroughgoing "objective" approach to the study of culture cannot be achieved solely by projecting upon those cultures categorical abstractions derived from Western thought.[20]

While biblical scholars cannot go back in time and interview the communities that produced and used the texts of the Hebrew Bible, anthropologists studying animism can talk and live with the people whom they study. They can use ethnography to address and explore how animist ways of life differ from modern Western patterns of living. Keith Basso offers an illustrative anecdote. He is sitting with five Apache friends, but he is unable to follow their conversation. The people around him speak and respond to each other with a series of place names, and Basso cannot stitch them together into a meaningful whole. He sees no sequence or sense in their words, and describes himself as "superfluous, slightly stupefied, and roundly perplexed."[21] He cannot position himself in the

---

[18] Philippe Descola, *Beyond Nature and Culture*, trans. Janet Lloyd (Chicago, IL: University of Chicago Press, 2013), xix.
[19] Diamond, "Losing Your Concepts," 273–74.
[20] Hallowell, "Ojibwa Ontology, Behavior, and World View," 20–21.
[21] Keith H. Basso, *Wisdom Sits in Places: Landscape and Language among the Western Apache* (Albuquerque: University of New Mexico Press, 1996), 82.

conversation or take part, not because he fails to understand individual words, but because he has no idea what they have to do with each other:

> What is puzzling about this snippet of Western Apache talk is that we are unable to account for the ways in which its constituent utterances are related to each other. Put more exactly, we lack the knowledge required to establish sequential relations among the utterances, the unstated premises and assumptions that order the utterances, just as they occur, into a piece of meaningful discourse.[22]

This problem cannot, Basso writes, be solved simply by studying Apache language. A clearer understanding of vocabulary, grammar, and syntax is insufficient. In order to understand the conversation he has heard, he must share in life with his Apache interlocutors. He quotes a statement by Samuel Johnson that recalls Cora Diamond's words: "To inhabit a language ... is to inhabit a living universe, and vice versa,"[23] and describes his own ethnographic work as an attempt to understand what it is like to live inside culturally constructed worlds that differ from his own.[24] Ethnographers studying animism can do what no biblical scholar can do: they can live and speak with the people whom they study. They can, at least to a certain extent, participate in the life with the concept.

The fact that biblical scholars studying personalistic nature texts and ethnographers studying animism both experience conceptual confusion is not in itself enough to justify using new animism as a point of comparison. It is not just that ethnographers and biblical scholars must both wrestle with a conceptual gap, but that their conceptual gaps share many characteristics. Most importantly, biblical texts and animist discourses do not draw a sharp line between human persons and other beings and landscape features. They share a social understanding of the cosmos. Graham Harvey defines animism as follows:

> Animists are people who recognize that the world is full of persons, only some of whom are human, and that life is always lived in relationship with others. Animism is lived out in various ways that are all about learning to act respectfully (carefully and constructively) towards and among other persons.[25]

Other definitions of animism, though not identical, highlight similar themes. Philippe Descola writes that the characteristic common to animist societies

---

[22] Ibid., 80.   [23] Ibid., 69.
[24] Ibid. See also Graham Harvey's discussion of changes in the methodology of ethnography, as well as his gratitude for conversations with hosts in his acknowledgements: Harvey, *Animism*, xv–xvii, xxii.
[25] Harvey, *Animism*, xi.

is that they "treat certain elements in the environment as persons endowed with cognitive, moral, and social qualities analogous to those of humans."[26] The Sisseton-Wahpeton Oyate scholar Kim TallBear writes that, to indigenous peoples, "nonhumans are agential beings engaged in social relations," and "'forces' such as stones, thunder, [and] stars are known within our ontologies to be sentient and knowing persons."[27] In the Hebrew Bible, the land has moral and cultic responsibilities (Leviticus 25:4–5; 26:34–35), people and YHWH talk to mountains and the skies (Isaiah 1:2; Micah 6:1–2), stars participate in warfare (Judges 5:20), and trees and billows offer praise to God (Psalm 98:7–9; 148:3–10). Sociality, emotion, and moral responsibility are not confined to humans and human society, but extend into the whole world. The ontologies of animists and the writers of the Hebrew Bible share a family resemblance. Personhood is not a human characteristic, but a concept that "is anterior and logically superior to the concept of the human."[28] The concept of personhood encompasses humans, but is not limited to us. In addition to human persons, there are also mountain persons, river persons, wind persons, etc.

If this similarity is at the level of a yet to be proven thesis, other points of comparison are easy to demonstrate. First, both animists and the Hebrew Bible place great emphasis on specific plots of land. In the Hebrew Bible, land is not a commodity for sale or exchange. This is true both of the national territory as a whole and of specific family holdings.[29] Animists also do not view land as a commodity or a natural resource.

---

[26] Descola, *Beyond Nature and Culture*, 31.
[27] Kim TallBear, "An Indigenous Reflection on Working Beyond the Human/Not Human," in "Theorizing Queer Inhumanisms," *GLQ: A Journal of Lesbian and Gay Studies* 21, no. 2–3 (2015), 209–48. See also Eduardo Viveiros de Castro's definition of animism as "an ontology which postulates the social character of relations between humans and nonhumans: the space between nature and society is itself social" ("The Transformation of Objects into Subjects in Amerindian Ontologies" [The 98th Annual Meeting of the American Anthropology Association, Chicago, November 17, 1999], quoted in Anne-Christine Hornborg, *Mi'kmaq Landscapes: From Animism to Sacred Ecology* [Aldershot, UK: Ashgate, 2008], 37); and Vine Deloria's description of Indian metaphysics as "the realization that the world, and all its possible experiences, [constitute] a social reality, a fabric of life in which everything has the possibility of intimate relationships because, ultimately, everything [is] related" (Vine Deloria Jr. and Daniel Wildcat, *Power and Place: Indian Education in America* [Golden, CO: Fulcrum, 2001], 2).
[28] Eduardo Viveiros de Castro, *Cannibal Metaphysics: For a Post-Structural Anthropology*, trans. Peter Skafish (Minneapolis, MN: Univocal, 2014), 58.
[29] See, for example, the story of Naboth's vineyard in 1 Kings 21, and the emphasis in Leviticus on YHWH's ownership of the land (Leviticus 25:23).

Harvey writes that, for animists, "particular places and lands are vitally important."[30] Places are "persons in their own right," and they contribute to the formation of human persons.[31] Standing Rock Sioux author and theologian Vine Deloria writes that "[t]ribal religions are ... complexes of attitudes, beliefs, and practices finetuned to harmonize with the lands on which the people live."[32] The importance of the land, of the relationship between humans, the land, and YHWH will be a prominent theme in Chapter 3, which explores personalistic nature texts in Torah.

Two other parallels between animism and the Hebrew Bible are striking, though they will not receive attention in this study. Animists tend to have detailed dietary laws and extensive methods for constructing the body.[33] These are also central concerns of the biblical law codes. For the biblical writers, what you eat and how you treat your body are not questions of taste, preference, or esthetics, but are governed by divine law. For animists, eating requires proper etiquette, because to eat an animal or a plant is to interact with another person.[34] Hunting, husbandry, agriculture, and eating are social acts. Klaus Koch uses similar language when talking about ancient Israelite interactions with "mountains, wells, trees, and ... animals." Because these "had a sacred dignity of their own, [Israelites] had to live circumspectly in company with them."[35]

In terms of the body, animists hold that the body must constantly be constructed to maintain its humanness.[36] As in the Hebrew Bible, what you wear, how you shave (or not shave), the use of tattoos or scaring, the

---

[30] Harvey, *Animism*, 109.
[31] Ibid., 109, 66. See also Basso, *Wisdom Sits in Places*, 7, 34, 62–63, 101–2; and Marilyn Strathern, "Partners and Consumers: Making Relations Visible," in *Readings in Indigenous Religions*, ed. Graham Harvey (London: Continuum, 2002), 61.
[32] Vine Deloria, Jr. *God is Red: A Native View of Religion* (Golden, CO: Fulcrum, 1994), 70.
[33] See Harvey, *Animism*, 211; Richard K. Nelson, "The Watchful World," in *Readings in Indigenous Religions*, ed. Graham Harvey (London: Continuum, 2002), 356; Viveiros de Castro, *Cannibal Metaphysics*, 52–53; Istvan Praet, *Animism and the Question of Life* (New York: Routledge, 2014), 19–20.
[34] Since relationships between humans and nonhumans are personal and social, Graham Harvey uses the term "etiquette" to describe the relationship between, in this case, the Maori and their land (Harvey, *Animism*, 63).
[35] Klaus Koch, "The Old Testament View of Nature," *Anticipation* 25 (January 1979): 49.
[36] If the body is a given in Western cosmologies, while the soul or the mind must be constructed, the opposite is true in animist cosmologies. The soul (not to be confused with the Christian soul) is a given, a common feature of all beings, while bodies must be made and maintained. In the West, each agent is responsible for its soul; for animists, persons are instead responsible for their bodies. See Viveiros de Castro, *Cannibal Metaphysics*, 53; Philippe Descola, *The Ecology of Others*, trans. Geneviève Godbout

creation and collection of ornaments, and so on, are not optional bodily practices, but part of what it means to be a person. The body is not a given, nor a neutral reality, but a project that must be maintained in order to continue to be a human person.[37] Similarly, Koch writes that, in Genesis, when God creates humans, "he does not create a perfect *physis* in the Greek sense. He creates [them] as a kind of project who must find [their] way to completion (in Hebrew *tamam därak*) by *sedaqā*-deeds."[38] Humans become fully human over time, by living in a particular way, and by performing certain deeds and avoiding others. This suggests further fascinating parallels between the Hebrew Bible and animism, indicating multiple connections between present day animism and the cosmology of the Hebrew Bible.

There is no denying that the Hebrew Bible is far removed in time from present day animism. Is it reasonable to compare the two, given this temporal distance? The problem resembles that which faces anthropologists in new animism. Contemporary animism is diverse and multifaceted; for example, some animists believe in a creator god or gods, while others do not.[39] In his book *Beyond Nature and Culture,* Philippe Descola demonstrates that present day animism is geographically widespread, existing in North and South America, Siberia, South Asia, and Australia,

---

and Benjamin P. Luley, Paradigm 42 (Chicago: Prickly Paradigm, 2013), 32; and Descola, *Beyond Nature and Culture*, 62.

[37] Many animist traditions do not automatically identify humans from outside their own communities as properly human, precisely because they do not participate in the same rituals and practices to maintain humanness. The identification of humanness in animist traditions is one of the primary topics of Istvan Praet's *Animism and the Question of Life*.

[38] Koch, "The Old Testament View of Nature," 50. Koch's transliteration is idiosyncratic. The final transliterated word is clear enough (צְדָקָה, "righteousness"), but the first phrase is less so. It most closely resembles the expression תָּם־דָּרֶךְ, "way of integrity" (Proverbs 13:6). See also Job 4:6; 22:3; Proverbs 10:29; 28:6.

[39] Harvey, *Animism*, 128. For a discussion of supreme beings in animist traditions, see Rane Willerslev, "'The One-All': The Animist High God," in *The Handbook of Contemporary Animism*, ed. Graham Harvey (Durham, UK: Acumen, 2013), 275–83. Viveiros de Castro's book *From the Enemy's Point of View* includes a list of spirits named in Amazonian traditions, including creator spirits like Aranāmī, who "raises up the sky" (Eduardo Viveiros de Castro, *From the Enemy's Point of View: Humanity and Divinity in an Amazonian Society* [Chicago, IL: University of Chicago Press, 1992], 77). Even within specific traditions, it can be difficult to determine whether a creator god is present. For example, Kristina Lindell argues that the Kammu people of Laos for the most part attribute the creation of the world to cultural heroes, but that one of the legends she collects credits the celestial spirit *róoy lwàaŋ* with the feat (Kristina Lindell, "Himmelens Andar," in *Kammu – Om Ett Folk i Laos*, ed. Håkan Lundström and Jan-Olof Svantesson [Lund: Lunds universitetshistoriska sällskap, 2006], 41–42).

and that it does not originate from a common cultural source.⁴⁰ What makes these traditions similar is not genetic relatedness, but instead a similarity in "the siting of ontological boundaries, and thus the structure of cosmologies."⁴¹ Present day animist traditions are no more related to each other than to the traditions of the Hebrew Bible. Scholars have classed traditions as animist and studied them together, because to do so has been illuminative and instructive. The proof of the appropriateness of new animism as a point of comparison for personalistic nature texts will be whether it provides an incisive perspective on the biblical text.

The Hebrew Bible is not, of course, similar in every way to present day animism. But the expertise of anthropologists can increase sensitivity to the texts of the Hebrew Bible, moving us beyond inarticulateness. Or, as Graham Harvey says in defense of the term "animism," the purpose of grouping geographically and temporally disparate phenomena under one label is to "aid recognition, establish communication, permit familiarity, and enable mutual understanding."⁴² Comparing personalistic nature texts to animistic beliefs opens up new venues for conversation, and lends

---

⁴⁰ See Descola, *Beyond Nature and Culture*, 3–31. Animism has been a less salient category for scholars studying African peoples. It is unclear whether this is due to scholarly trends (that is, anthropologists of Africa preferring other theoretical frameworks), or whether animism is simply less prevalent on the African continent. A few examples of scholars using animism to elucidate African practices and traditions exist, including Harry Garuba, "Explorations in Animist Materialism: Notes on Reading/Writing African Literature, Culture, and Society," *Public Culture* 15, no. 2 (2003): 261–85; and Caroline Rooney, *African Literature, Animism and Politics* (London: Routledge, 2000).

⁴¹ Descola, *The Ecology of Others*, 87. Descola argues that human communities organize social relations using "formulas of which there is probably a limited number" (Ibid.). Ontological boundaries can be drawn in different ways, but there are only so many options. His argument is similar to Westermann's argument about creation stories. Westermann writes that creation stories from all over the world show similarities, not because they are dependent on each other, but because the options available for speaking of creation are limited. See Claus Westermann, *Genesis 1–11: A Commentary* (Minneapolis: Augsburg, 1984), 22, 26. Descola argues for four basic ways of drawing ontological boundaries: 1) animism, 2) totemism, 3) naturalism, and 4) analogism. In animism, all beings have similar interiorities, though their bodies are different. In totemism, both interiority and physicality resemble each other across beings. In naturalism, beings have significantly different interiorities, though they are made up of more or less the same stuff. In analogism, all beings are radically different, both inside and out (Descola, *Beyond Nature and Culture*, 122). For this project, the two important categories are animism and naturalism; naturalism describes the cosmology of the modern West: all things are made up of the same stuff – atoms, molecules, the elements of the periodic table – but differ in terms of interior life. Animists instead emphasize shared cultural categories – all things have dwellings, eat food, and perform rituals, etc. – but do so in markedly different bodies.

⁴² Harvey, *Animism*, xiii.

that conversation a rich vocabulary.⁴³ It provides resources that the field of biblical studies lacks: a precise and extensive discussion of ontologies that differ radically from modernist ones, and sustained engagements with the peoples who structure their lives by such ontologies.

The Western concepts personhood, relationality, and nature are rendered strange and foreign by animism, and they mark the sites at which animism most clearly differs from modernist cosmologies. Roy Wagner, in his article "The Fractal Person," labels terms like these and the concepts they represent "hegemonic ideas," drawing on the work of the Italian Marxist Antonio Gramsci. "Hegemonic ideas," Wagner writes, are "concepts that have come to be taken so much for granted that they seem to be the voice of reason itself."⁴⁴ Hegemonic ideas are not concepts we think *about*, but concepts we think *with*. They structure our thinking. A key contribution of students of new animism is that they have been able to think critically about hegemonic ideas central to Western cosmology. The prime example is Irvin Hallowell's realization that personhood extends beyond humans in the Ojibwa⁴⁵ worldview.⁴⁶ While personhood in modern Western thought is coterminous with humanness, in Ojibwa ontology, as well as in other animistic worldviews, personhood is a "more comprehensive categorization" that encompasses both human and "other-than-human persons."⁴⁷ Hallowell writes:

---

⁴³ Anthropologists have made a concerted effort to produce vocabulary suitable to the societies they study. That said, finding fitting language remains a challenge. Several scholars emphasize that a major difficulty in studying animism is that the vocabulary of Western languages is inadequate to the task. See Basso, *Wisdom Sits in Places*, 39; Hallowell, "Ojibwa Ontology, Behavior, and World View," 28; Harvey, *Animism*, 190; and Hornborg, *Mi'kmaq Landscapes*, 154.
⁴⁴ Roy Wagner, "The Fractal Person," in *Big Men and Great Men: Personifications of Power in Melanesia*, ed. Maurice Godelier and Marilyn Strathern (Cambridge: Cambridge University, 1991), 159.
⁴⁵ The names Ojibwe/Ojibwa, and Chippewa are all names attributed to Anishinaabeg peoples. Ojibwe/Ojibwa was invented by Henry Rowe Schoolcraft, and this name was then misheard as Chippewa and recorded in nineteenth century treaties. See Gerald Vizenor, *Everlasting Sky: Voices of the Anishinabe People* (St. Paul, MN: Minnesota Historical Society, 2000), 8–10; Lauret Savoy, *Trace: Memory, History, Race, and the American Landscape* (Berkeley, CA: Counterpoint, 2015), 51–52. I have chosen to use whatever name the author of an article uses, in order to avoid confusion, but want to note the long history of misnaming indigenous peoples.
⁴⁶ The concept of "person" has always been central to anthropology. Alfred Gell writes that "the entire historical tendency of anthropology has been towards a radical defamiliarization and relativization of the notion of 'persons'" (Alfred Gell, *Art and Agency: An Anthropological Theory* [Oxford: Clarendon, 1998], 9).
⁴⁷ Hallowell, "Ojibwa Ontology, Behavior, and World View," 22, 29.

[I]n the universe of the Ojibwa the conception of "persons" as a living, functioning social being is not only one which transcends the notion of person in the naturalistic sense; it likewise transcends a human appearance as a constant attribute of this category of being.[48]

Other-than-human persons include the sun, rocks, and the wind, all of which participate in social relations with other persons.[49] Such social relations are especially "charged" in Ojibwa interactions with the world, because persons, human or otherwise, are "*loci* of causality in the dynamics of their universe."[50] Personhood, in other words, is not defined by reference to the human, but by the ability to cause changes in the surrounding world.[51] As Hallowell states, the Ojibwa attribute events not to "impersonal 'natural' forces," but instead always ask "*Who* did it, *who* is responsible."[52] This "personalistic theory of causation" means that the Ojibwa maintain "reciprocal relations" not only with other humans, but also with other-than-human persons.[53] The idea of other-than-human persons is one of the central building blocks of new animism; it has been productive for scholars writing on people groups in North and South America, Siberia, South Asia, and Australia.[54]

When I say that elements of nonanimal nature are persons in biblical writing, that is not to suggest a categorization system like the division of mammals into Boreotheria, Supraprimates, and Laurasiatheria,

---

[48] Ibid., 33. In Western worldviews, angels are a clear example of nonhumans who are considered persons due to humanoid bodies.
[49] Nurit Bird-David paraphrases Hallowell's point as follows: "The Ojibwa conceives of 'person' as an overarching category within which 'human person,' 'animal person,' 'wind person,' etc, are subcategories" (Bird-David, "'Animism' Revisited," 71).
[50] Hallowell, "Ojibwa Ontology, Behavior, and World View," 42. Emphasis in the original.
[51] I avoid the term "agency" as a shorthand for the ability to effect change, because agency assumes the presence of a mind. I discuss agency below.
[52] Hallowell, "Ojibwa Ontology, Behavior, and World View," 43. Emphasis in the original. See also Kenneth Morrison's claim that "indigenous life is organized around the existence of persons, human and otherwise, rather than around materiality, functionality and abstraction" (Kenneth M. Morrison, "Animism and a Proposal for a Post-Cartesian Anthropology," in *The Handbook of Contemporary Animism*, ed. Graham Harvey [Durham, UK: Acumen, 2013], 39).
[53] Hallowell, "Ojibwa Ontology, Behavior, and World View," 45.
[54] See, for example, Bird-David, "'Animism' Revisited." (she changes the term to "superpersons"); Hornborg, *Mi'kmaq Landscapes*; Eduardo Viveiros de Castro, "1. Cosmologies: Perspectivism," *HAU: Masterclass Series* 1 (July 8, 2012), www.haujournal.org/index.php/masterclass/article/view/106; Rane Willerslev, *Soul Hunters: Hunting, Animism, and Personhood among the Siberian Yukaghirs* (Berkeley, CA: University of California Press, 2007); and Harvey, *Animism*.

depending on their DNA.⁵⁵ An animal can, according to the rational of classification, only be classified in one way (you can disagree about the right way, and about which categories to use, but the idea of classification assumes that there *is* a right way), and not sometimes one way and sometimes another. Nor does this classification say anything about our everyday interactions with mammals. I do not know which category my dog belongs to (or my husband, for that matter), but we get along fine anyway. To say that biblical writers use personal vocabulary for skies is to say that they relate to the skies as persons; the word "person" captures a form of life, not a category. As Diamond writes, using as example the concept "human being," "[t]o be able to use the concept 'human being' is to be able to think about human life and what happens in it; it is not to be able to pick human beings out from other things or recommend that certain things be done to them or by them."⁵⁶ That is why it makes little sense to ask if every tree in the Hebrew Bible is a person; the answer can only be "yes and no." The biblical writers are not dividing the world into categories, but describing relationships. All trees have the potential to participate in relationships; recognizing when and how these relationships take place is important, not whether or not to affix the label "person" to any given cypress. This is why, when Hallowell asks an Ojibwa man, "Are *all* stones we see about us here alive?" he responds, "No! But *some* are."⁵⁷ The man is not saying that all rocks in the world can be piled into two piles: alive rocks in one, dead rocks in the other. Instead he is saying that he, or someone in his community, or an ancestor reports having interacted with some stones and not with others. As Hallowell writes, "The Ojibwa recognize, *a priori*, potentialities for animation in certain classes of objects under certain circumstances ... The crucial test is experience. Is there any personal testimony available?"⁵⁸ Some stones have proven themselves alive; the rest are potentially alive, but there's no way to know. Or, as Alfred Gell explains, "we recognize agency, *ex post facto* ... we cannot tell that someone is an agent before they *act as an agent*, before they disturb the casual milieu in such a way as can only be

---

⁵⁵ See Jan Ole Kriegs et al., "Retroposed Elements as Archives for the Evolutionary History of Placental Mammals," *PLOS Biology* 4, no. 4 (March 14, 2006).
⁵⁶ Diamond, "Losing Your Concepts," 266.
⁵⁷ Hallowell, "Ojibwa Ontology, Behavior, and World View," 24.
⁵⁸ Ibid. Bird-David makes a similar argument about understandings of relationality among the Nayaka. Nonanimal nature is considered relational when it acts in relational ways. Anything has the potential to interact, but not all things do (Bird-David, "'Animism' Revisited," 73).

attributed to their agency."⁵⁹ The term "alive" is not a category, but a concept, and it names ways of life rather than provides a label.

Another difference between animism and modernism is how each tradition understands relationality. Marilyn Strathern, in her article "Partners and Consumers: Making Relations Visible," argues that animists understand relationality and sociability in ways that do not map onto Western Euro-American understandings of relationships. "[R]elationships do not," she writes, "link individuals."⁶⁰ Instead, persons are constituted by relationships.⁶¹ Drawing on Roy Wagner's formulation "the fractal person," she writes that individuals cannot be "expressed in whole numbers."⁶² That is not to say that persons are less than whole, as if each person is a half or a third of something. Wagner uses the term "fractal person" as a way to circumvent the false alternative between "individual and group," in order to describe persons who are "neither singular nor plural."⁶³ A person is not a single unit (an individual), which, if added to other single units, becomes a collective of related members (a group). Relationships do not flow between unitary, freestanding persons, who would exist in the absence of such relationships. Persons are constituted by their relationships, relationships with kin, with land, with specific bodies; take those relationships away, and the person "fades away."⁶⁴ In Bird-David's terms, personhood is not a given, but is "[made] ... by producing and reproducing sharing relationships."⁶⁵ This is

---

⁵⁹ Gell, *Art and Agency*, 20. Emphasis in the original.
⁶⁰ Strathern, "Partners and Consumers," 59.
⁶¹ See also Bird-David's article "'Animism' Revisited," which draws on Strathern's work, and Descola's discussion of the Chewong term *kamo* ('personage') (Bird-David, "'Animism' Revisited," and Descola, *Beyond Nature and Culture*, 25).
⁶² Strathern, "Partners and Consumers," 59. See Wagner, "The Fractal Person," 162. Wagner writes that "[a] fractal person is never a unit standing in relation to an aggregate, or an aggregate standing in relation to a unit, but always an entity with relationships integrally implied" (Ibid., 163).
⁶³ Wagner, "The Fractal Person," 162. Wagner uses the example of genealogy and reproduction: "People exist reproductively by being 'carried' as part of another, and 'carry' or engender others making themselves genealogical or reproductive 'factors' of these others. A genealogy is thus an enchainment of people, as indeed persons would be seen to 'bud' out of one another in a speeded-up cinematic depiction of human life" (Ibid., 163).
⁶⁴ Descola, *Beyond Nature and Culture*, 25. Martin Buber's "primary words" communicate a similar conviction. In Buber's understanding of people, there are no "I," "you," or "it" in isolation. The primary words are always "combined words," always "I–Thou" or "I–It," and through the primary words persons come into being (Buber, *I and Thou*, 3, 11).
⁶⁵ Bird-David, "'Animism' Revisited," 73. See also Tim Ingold, who writes that "[t]hings *are* their relations" (Tim Ingold, *Being Alive: Essays on Movement, Knowledge and Description* (London: Routledge, 2011), 70).

something more than interdependence or mutual need. People are not organized into individuals and groups, into the particular and the general. Wagner compares Western attempts to split the fractal person into whole units, into discrete individuals, to trying to split meaning into parts: "Though we may well persuade ourselves, through grammars, sign-systems ... and the like, that the means by which we elicit meaning can be eminently partible, the meanings so elicited do not and cannot have parts."[66] Sociality and relationships are not things a person can engage or not engage in; relationships are not *between* persons. A person is someone who relates, and relationships make persons.[67]

Animist understandings of personhood and relationality challenge the Western dualism of nature and society. Philippe Descola writes insightfully about why the nature/culture dualism should not be applied to animist societies.[68] Descola argues that the modern West organizes the world into two distinct spheres of phenomena.[69] On the one hand is nature, which is given and unitary. Nature is always and everywhere the same, it has "stable frontiers," and includes everything that is not the product of human ingenuity: the environment, the human body, the climate, and the laws of physics.[70] It provides "the condition of the life of humans," that which is given before humans begin to interpret, build, and organize. On the other hand is culture, the many means by which humans make sense of the world around them. In contrast to nature, culture is arbitrary, multiple, and heterogeneous.[71] Humans all over the world interpret their environment differently, but their environments are all part

---

[66] Wagner, "The Fractal Person," 166.

[67] A consequence of the fact that relationships make persons is that humans become persons over time, through practice. For example, Bird-David describes *devaru* ceremonies among the Nayaka as a form of education: "Participants learn from conversing and sharing with devaru characters to discriminate mutually responsive changes in themselves and things they relate with; they become increasingly aware of the webs of relatedness between themselves and what is around them" (Bird-David, "'Animism' Revisited," 77). By participating in rituals and in daily sharing relationships, the Nayaka "*make* their personhood" (Ibid., 73).

[68] The nature/culture dualism is the subject of Descola's book *Beyond Nature and Culture*. His smaller work, *The Ecology of Others*, explores the same topic, but from the point of view of controversies within the field of anthropology. The nature/culture dualism goes by different names (nature/culture, nature/society, and nature/history), all of which refer to more or less the same thing: the contrast between the physical world as a given and history as the product of human ingenuity and intentionality.

[69] See, for example, Descola, *Beyond Nature and Culture*, xv, 7; and Descola, *The Ecology of Others*, 1, 4, 36–37.

[70] Descola, *The Ecology of Others*, 36, 46.

[71] Ibid., 61; Descola, *Beyond Nature and Culture*, xv.

of one set of clearly defined phenomena. But this parcelling out of existence is not, according to Descola, universal. It is not even particularly common.[72] Animist ontologies, for example, operate differently. Culture here is the given. All beings have culture, of which human culture is only one example. Culture is diversified by bodies and by points of view: all beings see the world in distinct ways, as determined by their bodies, but do so by means of a shared set of cultural categories.[73] This is not a case of flipping the Western dualism on its head. Because culture is shared by humans and nonhumans, understandings of what is related, what belongs together in ontological categories, are different. Descola points to the example of the Chewong, a people group in the Pahang Province of Malaysia. The Chewong are dualists of a sort, but their dualism is based on what is near and what is far off:

> Despite their different appearances, all the entities within this forest cosmos mingle together in an intimate and egalitarian community that, as a whole, stands in opposition to the threatening and incomprehensible world outside, which is inhabited by "different people" (*bi masign*): Malaysians, Chinese, Westerners, and other aboriginal peoples.[74]

The important community, the circle of similarity, is determined and constituted by those with whom the Chewong relate, the plants, animals, and people with whom they interact on a daily basis. Rather than understanding all humans as related due to a common biological makeup, the Chewong prioritizes the sameness of those who live close together, despite differing bodies. Their dualism is not the inverse of the Western nature/culture one. It produces a way of life that prioritizes different relationships, produces different categories, and makes possible different comparisons.

Rather than seeing personalistic nature texts simply as examples of literary devices like anthropomorphism and personification, research on animism provides concrete examples of alternative understandings of personhood, and illustrates how such understandings are integrated into a coherent way of life. Notably, animistic views on personhood sidestep the problem of agency. In Western thought, agency requires the ability to make plans, which in turn requires a mind. Brian Walsh, Marianne Karsh, and Nik Ansell call agency "the central stumbling block" to

---

[72] Descola, *Beyond Nature and Culture*; see also Marshall Sahlins, *The Western Illusion of Human Nature: With Reflections on the Long History of Hierarchy, Equality and the Sublimation of Anarchy in the West, and Comparative Notes on Other Conceptions of the Human Condition* (Chicago, IL: Prickly Paradigm, 2008), 88.
[73] Descola, *Beyond Nature and Culture*, 11.   [74] Ibid., 22.

understanding biblical texts that say that trees "praise, sing, clap, and rejoice."⁷⁵ They go so far as to say that to use or understand such language is "almost impossible for our modern Western minds."⁷⁶ The problem lies in the Cartesian split between mind and body, the mind being assigned the task of thinking and envisaging plans, and the body the task of carrying out the purposes of the mind.⁷⁷ The idea that any action must first be planned in the mind and, secondarily, executed by the body precludes the possibility that anything that does not have a brain can act. This assumption makes nonsense of statements like Isaiah's declaration that "the trees of the field clap their hands" (Isaiah 55:12). It is not just that trees do not have hands, but, more importantly, trees do not have minds. They cannot conceptualize applause, and, therefore, such actions cannot seriously be attributed to them.

The anthropologist Tim Ingold calls agency a problem "of our own making."⁷⁸ He writes:

How is it, we wonder, that humans can act? If we were mere lumps of matter, we could do nothing. So we think that some extra ingredient needs to be added to liven up our lumpen bodies. And if, as sometimes seems to us, objects can 'act back', then this ingredient must be attributed to them as well. We give the name 'agency' to this ingredient.⁷⁹

Nowhere in the Hebrew Bible is nonanimal nature described as having a mind or some other "extra ingredient" that makes it possible for it to listen, act, and communicate. Its activity is stated matter-of-factly and appears in texts without warning or preamble. Text such as Habakkuk 3:10, "The mountains saw you and writhed" and Zechariah 11:2, "Wail, O cypress, for the cedar has fallen," do not posit a spirit acting in the mountains, or dryads animating trees, but mountains and trees taking part in the story as their own, material selves.⁸⁰ Ingold's skepticism of modern ideas of agency spring from his observation of animist peoples. Referencing his ethnographic work, Ingold states that "people do not

---

⁷⁵ Brian J. Walsh, Marianne B. Karsh, and Nik Ansell, "Trees, Forestry, and the Responsiveness of Creation," *Cross Currents* 44, no. 2 (June 1994): 159–60.
⁷⁶ Ibid., 152.
⁷⁷ Tim Ingold summarizes this understanding of body and mind as "the thinking mind and the executive body" (Ingold, *Being Alive*, 77).
⁷⁸ Ibid., 16. ⁷⁹ Ibid.
⁸⁰ Ingold described the conventional view of animism as "a system of beliefs that imputes life or spirit to things that are truly inert" (Ibid., 67). It is this view, among others, that scholars of new animism seek to refute. While there are certainly people who believe that some trees or mountains are inhabited by spirits, such beliefs are not marks of animism.

universally discriminate between categories of living and nonliving things."[81] Though animism is often misunderstood as "a system of belief that imputes life or spirit to things that are truly inert," Ingold describes it instead as the recognition of "the dynamic, transformative potential of the entire field of relations within which beings of all kinds, more or less person-like or thing-like, continually and reciprocally bring one another into existence."[82] All matter relates, though to different degrees, and all matter contributes to and influences the life of other matter. Ingold's work is important because he illustrates the conceptual value of animism as a means to throw light on commonsense Western concepts. The study of personalistic nature texts need not be mired in concerns about how things without brains and nervous systems can act. Animist traditions provide a coherent understanding of causation and action without recourse to the Cartesian split. These traditions demonstrate that, to dismiss personalistic nature texts because they suggest conceptualizations of liveliness that fall outside the range of what modernism allows, is to impose a modern understanding of agency on ancient texts.

Numerous scholars have pointed to the interrelatedness of all creation in the Hebrew Bible.[83] This is another area in which animism can contribute to biblical studies. Scholars of new animism have thought more deeply about what interpersonal relationships mean, challenging the Western idea of exchange between individuals. While the relationship between humans and nonanimal nature is not the primary relationship into which the Israelite cult and tradition introduce and train its adherents – the primary relationship being the one between Israel and YHWH – for Israel to relate to YHWH requires that Israel also maintain a wide set of relationships with other creatures. Israel's relationships to their animals,

---

[81] Ibid.
[82] Ibid., 67, 68. Ingold contrasts his own definition of animism with that of Peter Pels, who writes that animism "is a way of saying that things are alive because they are animated by something foreign to them, a 'soul' or ... spirit made to reside *in* matter" (P. J. Pels, "The Spirit of Matter: On Fetish, Rarity, Fact and Fancy," in *Border Fetishisms: Material Objects in Unstable Spaces*, ed. P. Spyer [London: Routledge, 1998], 94. Quoted in Ingold, *Being Alive*, 28).
[83] See, for example, Fretheim, *God and World in the Old Testament*, 264; William P. Brown, *The Ethos of the Cosmos: The Genesis of Moral Imagination in the Bible* (Grand Rapids, MI: William B. Eerdmans, 1999), 48; Norman C. Habel, *The Book of Job: A Commentary* (Philadelphia: Westminster, 1985), 57; Michael Welker, *Creation and Reality* (Minneapolis: Fortress, 1999), 42; Hilary Marlow, *Biblical Prophets and Contemporary Environmental Ethics: Re-Reading Amos, Hosea, and First Isaiah* (Oxford: Oxford University Press, 2009), 120.

their land, and, more broadly, to the cosmos, are nested within their relationship to YHWH. Without these other relationships, Israel does not have a relationship with YHWH. The first words from YHWH to Israel in Leviticus are "When any one of you offers a livestock offering to YHWH ..." (Leviticus 1:2), and Deuteronomy describes its laws specifically as laws for "when you enter the land that YHWH your God is giving to you ..." (Deuteronomy 18:9; see also 26:1). Israelite identity is enacted through a host of agricultural, dietary, and cultic regulations, most of which require the presence and participation of more than a human person or human community. Israel is not Israel in isolation; to be Israelite means to engage in specific relationships with your field, your trees and vines, your animals, and your human kin and neighbors.

The centrality of relationship and sociability in animism casts light on the amount of time spent in the biblical law codes on issues that seem less than spiritual. Sacrifice and the system of land tenure are prominent examples of practices that moderate and determine how humans interact with nature, both animal and nonanimal.[84] For example, Mary Douglas argues that the Levitical distinction between clean and unclean animals is not a matter of hygiene, or of evaluative judgments (the clean animals are not "better" than the unclean animals), but instead a way of protecting animal life: "[YHWH's] love for his animal creation lies behind his laws against eating and touching their corpses."[85] Israel is only permitted to eat certain domestic animals, and, in order to eat even these, Israel must observe rituals that recognize the participation of such animals, specifically domesticated animals, in Israel's covenant with YHWH.[86] All other

---

[84] For the role of sacrifice in regulating the relationship between humans and animals, see Mary Douglas, *Leviticus as Literature* (Oxford: Oxford University Press, 1999), 134–37; and Jonathan Morgan, "Sacrifice in Leviticus: Eco-Friendly Ritual or Unholy Waste," in *Ecological Hermeneutics: Biblical, Historical, and Theological Perspectives*, ed. David Horrell et al. (London: T & T Clark, 2010), 32–45. For the role of land tenure in regulating the relationships between humans and land, see Christopher J. H. Wright, *God's People in God's Land: Family, Land, and Property in the Old Testament* (Grand Rapids, MI: William B. Eerdmans, 1990).

[85] Douglas, *Leviticus as Literature*, 1–2.

[86] Douglas bases her argument of covenantal participation by sacrificial animals on analogies between the sacrificer's body, the body of the sacrificed animal, the temple, and the holy mountain: "In sacrifice the body of the sacrificial animal becomes [a] microcosm in its own right, corresponding to the tabernacle and the holy mountain ... the body of the worshipper is [also] made analogous to the sanctuary and the altar" (Ibid., 134). Both Israelite bodies and the bodies of their sacrificial animals must maintain purity in a way not required of non-Israelites or nonsacrificial animals. The one counter example is the fact that Leviticus allows the eating of wild game, which falls outside

animals are protected from human use by their status as unclean. Douglas further argues that the prohibitions on touching animal carcasses in Leviticus 5:2 and 11:8 serve to "[protect] [an animal] in its lifetime."[87] The prohibition not only rules out humans *eating* the animal, but also raising it for other uses: "Since its carcass cannot be skinned or dismembered, most of the ways in which it could be exploited are ruled out, so it is not worth breeding, hunting, or trapping. These unclean animals are safe from the secular as also from the sacred kitchen."[88] In other words, the sacrificial system sets out broad guidelines for how humans are to relate to animals.[89] With most animals, humans are permitted only a distant sociability, that of sharing the same land. In terms of animals with whom Israelites interact on a daily basis, their domestic animals, Leviticus provides a more detailed etiquette, an exacting set of rules for when and how an animal may be used for food. Speaking of the biblical ban on eating blood (see Genesis 9:4), Klaus Koch argues that blood symbolizes the value God places on nonhuman living creatures.[90] He questions the Christian church's abandonment of this and other cultic regulations, arguing that it has led to nature "[becoming] mere raw matter for human culture and humanity's self-realization."[91] Inattention to the Bible's dietary laws and other ceremonial laws, according to Koch, is not innocent or ethically neutral, but instead "looks like 'Christian ignorance toward nature.'"[92]

Douglas's schema of covenantal participation. She does not offer a satisfying explanation for the permission to eat game that "divide the hoof and chew cud" (Leviticus 11:3). For a critique of this lacuna in Douglas's argument, see Walter J Houston, "Towards an Integrated Reading of the Dietary Laws of Leviticus," in *The Book of Leviticus: Composition and Reception* (Leiden: Brill, 2003), 154–55.

[87] Douglas, *Leviticus as Literature*, 141.

[88] Ibid. Douglas's argument builds on Milgrom's claim that the purpose of restricting the kinds of animals Israel may eat is to teach respect for life. See Jacob Milgrom, *Leviticus: A New Translation with Introduction and Commentary* (New York: Doubleday, 1991), 735.

[89] See also Blenkinsopp's statement in "Creation, the Body, and Care for a Damaged World" that "Ritualization ... provides a symbolic context for our interaction with other living forms. It delimits and channels options" (Joseph Blenkinsopp, "Creation, the Body, and Care for a Damaged World," in *Treasures Old and New: Essays in the Theology of the Pentateuch* [Grand Rapids, MI: William B. Eerdmans, 2004], 44); and Morgan's claim that "the sacrificial system serves as a key example of a wider priestly concern to establish, uphold, and habitualize boundaries as a temper to anthropogenic violence" (Jonathan Morgan, "Land, Rest & Sacrifice: Ecological Reflections on the Book of Leviticus" 2010, 94, ore.exeter.ac.uk/repository/handle/10036/119945).

[90] Koch, "The Old Testament View of Nature," 50.   [91] Ibid.   [92] Ibid.

Christopher Wright argues that biblical laws of land tenure reflect the conviction that the land ultimately belongs to YHWH: "The land is not to be sold in perpetuity, the land is mine" (Leviticus 25:23).[93] YHWH's care for the land, like YHWH's care for animals, regulates how Israelites are to interact with their land holdings. "[T]he relationship between God and Israel," Wright states, "was thoroughly 'earthed' in the socioeconomic facts of life – shaping and being shaped by them."[94] The corollary of this is that Israel's relationship with its land was thoroughly religious, regulated by YHWH's instructions to Israel and by YHWH's relationship with the land. Israelite families could farm their land and pass it on to their children, but they could not sell it. Wright primarily describes this form of land tenure as a protection against the abuse of smallholding families, but it can equally well be read as a protection of land itself.[95] As we will see in Chapter 3, the land of Israel is responsible to observe various cultic regulations, the most prominent of which is sabbath rest.[96] The possession of the land of Israel by Israelite families ensures (or should ensure) that the land is able to uphold its duties before YHWH. Just as eating meat is not simply a matter of nutrition, but a complex relationship that involves both YHWH and animals, so land tenure is not only an economic equation, but a participation in the relationship that YHWH maintains with the soil of Israel. Dietary laws and the rules of land tenure are not abstract regulations without moral or religious value, but modes to ensure that humans, animals, and nonhumans interact in ways that honor God's ordering of the world.

By participating in the cult and in the system of ancestral land tenure, Israelite families and communities are trained to interact with the world in specific ways. This makes little sense if the focus of religious life is a clearly bounded individual. But if all persons are made up of their relationships, including their relationships with food and land, the Levitical attention to what you eat, when and where you eat it, what you wear,

---

[93] Wright, *God's People in God's Land*, 58. [94] Ibid., 23.

[95] Wright describes the land tenure system as one example of how "Israel [stands] under the protection of Yahweh" (Ibid., 64), though on the next page he writes that "the most explicit assertion of divine land ownership in the Old Testament is made for the sake of protecting the *family* and its *land*" (Ibid., 65, Emphasis in the original).

[96] Levitical instructions also suggest that the land has different responsibilities for which human participation is necessary. Farmers are not to reap the corners of their fields or strip the vineyard bare (Leviticus 19:9–10; 23:22); fruit trees are not to be harvested in their first three years of bearing (Leviticus 19:23); and fields should not be planted with two kinds of seeds (Leviticus 19:19).

how you cut your beard and your field, when you pick your fruit, and what years you sow your grain, coheres with more pious sounding commandments. If personhood in the Hebrew Bible extends beyond humans, then Israelite life demands maintaining a wide set of relationships in a way that respects YHWH's presence in their midst. For this kind of life, agricultural practices, land ownership, and dietary rules are as important as prayers and internal intentions. Though it is difficult to state in the vocabulary of modern English, Israelite relationship to nature is not simply a gauge of their faithfulness, a litmus test of devotion. Nature does not stand outside Israel and YHWH's relationship as an external and arbitrary measure of adherence to YHWH's statutes. There *is* no nature distinct and apart from humans. Humans participate in a great mesh of creatures, "a domain of entanglements,"[97] and the Hebrew Bible sets forth human responsibilities within this meshwork.

METAPHOR AND RELATIONALITY

Early anthropologists thought animism was a spontaneous belief system, a holdover from stages of childhood in which children cannot distinguish between what is alive and what is not.[98] This assumption stems from a distortion of Edward Tylor's comparison of animistic societies to early childhood, and it gained popularity within and outside anthropology.[99] Ethnography has shown, however, that animism is a learned perspective. Graham Harvey writes that animism "is found more easily among elders who have thought about it than among children who still need to be

---

[97] Ingold, *Being Alive*, 71.
[98] A more recent example of this line of thinking is Stewart Guthrie's book *Faces in the Clouds: A New Theory of Religion* (New York: Oxford University Press, 1993). Guthrie transforms the idea into an evolutionary theory. The confusion of animate and inanimate objects is, according to Guthrie, beneficial for survival. Better to mistake a rock for a lion, than a lion for a rock. Guthrie's theory still assumes that animism is a kind of mistake, just a useful one.
[99] For a discussion of Tylor's comparison of animism and childhood, see Bird-David, "'Animism' Revisited," 69. Tylor himself did not argue that animism was instinctual (in the words of Harvey, he claimed that animism was "the first significant theory that humans thought and taught to their descendants" [Harvey, *Animism*, 6]), but others built on his association between animism and childhood to make this claim. For a discussion of the afterlife of Tylor's scholarship in anthropology, see Ibid., 5–9. Martin Buber's work is an example of Tylor's influence beyond anthropology. Buber compares "the primitive man" to "the child" (Buber, *I and Thou*, 26).

taught how to do it."[100] Nurit Bird-David argues that the pandalu ritual of the Nayaka, a South Indian people group, is a means of learning how to engage well with other-than-human persons. A pandalu ritual is a two-day celebration, in which entranced performers bring to life other-than-human persons, called devaru. Other participants then engage with the devaru, by striking up conversations, sharing food, and making requests. By means of pandalu events, persons "are educated to perceive that animals, stones, rocks, etc., are things one can relate with – that they have relational affordances, that is, what happens to them (or how they change) can affect and be affected by what happens to people (or how they change)."[101]

I have already mentioned land tenure, dietary laws, and rules for managing the body as examples of practices that educated ancient Israelites in how to relate to YHWH and the world. Personalistic nature texts are another aspect of such training; they train by means of metaphor, poetry, and story. If the other practices are primarily bodily and material, the use of metaphor in personalistic nature texts trains through language. Metaphor gives the audience particular language to talk about that which is not human, language that posits certain kinds of relationality and excludes others. They are, in a sense, literary pandula events; they educate the audience to perceive the "relational affordances" of the world with which they interact. And, unlike terms like personification, metaphor need not suggest fictiveness. A metaphor can accurately describe using figurative language; it is a way of speaking that covers situations in which literal words are inadequate or imprecise.

Metaphor theorists disagree about almost everything: how to define metaphor, what elements make up a metaphor (and what to call them), how such elements relate to each other and to the meaning of a metaphor, the nature of the difference between metaphorical and literal speech, the extent to which metaphors are descriptive, etc. That said, we all use metaphors in daily speech without difficulty. What follows assumes that sort of familiarity – I do not aim to arrive at a more precise terminology for its workings. Technical language only enters in when it helps illuminate the pedagogical role of metaphor in personalistic nature texts; other than that, I will leave it to the side.

Compare the use of metaphor in the following two biblical texts:

Look! Assyria, the cedar of Lebanon: beautiful branches and shaded forest and great height, and its top is among the clouds. (Ezekiel 31:3)

---

[100] Harvey, *Animism*, 18. [101] Bird-David, "'Animism' Revisited," 77.

For you will go out with rejoicing and in peace you will be brought in. The mountains and the hills will burst into jubilation before you, and all the trees of the field will clap their hands. (Isaiah 55:12)

The metaphors of Ezekiel 31:3 and Isaiah 55:12 both involve trees. But the role played by trees is not the same. In the verse from Ezekiel, the writer evokes a tall cedar in order to describe the imperial might of Assyria. To use the terminology of I. A. Richards, Assyria is the tenor of the metaphor (that which is described), the cedar is the vehicle (the means by which Assyria is described).[102] Together they form the metaphor, whose topic is the power of empire.[103] In Isaiah 55:12, the trees themselves are the tenor, the act of applause the vehicle, and the resulting metaphor speaks about the joy of the hill country at the return of exiled Israel. Ezekiel uses plants to better describe humans; Isaiah does the reverse.

The tendency in biblical studies has been to read both metaphors as descriptions of humans or human emotions, approaching the Isaiah text and others like it as oblique renditions of human (or in some cases divine) reactions and experiences, mirrored in the landscape.[104] The trees are joyful because humans project joy onto them, not because they themselves respond to the exiles or feel affect. The alternative to this approach is not to read the texts literally, but to take seriously their metaphors. Speaking of Isaiah again, trees do not have hands and they do not clap. But that is to be expected; to read Isaiah 55:12 in such a way would be to misunderstand how metaphor works. When someone describes themselves as being "in seventh heaven," we understand that they are talking about their mood, not their geographical location (or their idiosyncratic cosmology): they are very, very happy. Isaiah's metaphor is no more difficult to understand (the trees are celebrating); the difficulty is not in the metaphor

---

[102] I. A. Richards, *The Philosophy of Rhetoric* (New York: Oxford University Press, 1936), 96.

[103] Ibid., 100.

[104] For example, Ronald Simkins argues that nature is capable of reflecting back human actions because such actions "[produce] ramifications in nature that affects humans" (Ronald Simkins, *Creator & Creation: Nature in the Worldview of Ancient Israel* [Peabody, MA: Hendrickson, 1994]). A similar line of interpretation is Bernard Anderson's view of the snake in Genesis 3. Anderson reads the snake as an externalized part of the human psyche, not as an actual snake. He quotes Ricoeur's statement that the snake "would be a part of ourselves which we do not recognize; he would be the seduction of ourselves by ourselves" (Bernhard W. Anderson, *Creation versus Chaos: The Reinterpretation of Mythical Symbolism in the Bible* [New York: Association Press, 1967], 156. Quoting Paul Ricœur, *The Symbolism of Evil* [Boston: Beacon, 1969], 132).

itself, but in its claim about trees. Isaiah attributes mood to trees, mood, and historical awareness. I might describe a tree as happy or unhappy, say, if it is flourishing and bearing fruit, or looking wilted and blighted. But it would not occur to me to talk about trees rejoicing at the end of World War II or at the return of refugees to the Balkan peninsula. Biblical writers do so – though the historical events are not the same, of course – and frequently. This is what I want to understand! How do they view trees, how do they interact with them, to make such language sensible and important?

Janet Soskice writes that a primary purpose of metaphor is to guide access to a referent. She uses "the fine edge" between negative and positive theology as an example.[105] Apophatic theology, the insight "that we say nothing of God," does not mean that theology has nothing to offer except silence. The realization that we are unable to define God "is the basis for the tentative and avowedly inadequate stammerings by which we attempt to speak of God and [God's] acts."[106] Such stammerings point towards God and give access to a relationship with God, but they do not exhaustively describe God: "[T]his separation of referring and defining is at the very heart of metaphorical speaking and is what makes it not only possible but necessary that in our stammering after a transcendent God we must speak, for the most part, metaphorically or not at all."[107] Metaphors are necessary when speaking of referents that are imperfectly known; the metaphors permit relationships to exist in the absence of exhaustive knowledge.

Soskice's description of metaphor bears a resemblance to Rowan Williams' description of the role of icons in the Eastern Orthodox church:

There is in the theological tradition and in modern Orthodox discussion a distinction between saying that the ultimate truth of God is incapable of being captured definitely by any picture or idea and saying that the truth of God is radically different from what is represented. It is not that the image is somehow untruthful ... They neither deliver a complete grasp of the underlying reality nor act only as a trigger to wordless contemplation; they create a relationship in which discovery occurs, and continues to occur as the contemplation of images goes on. The negativity is less a matter of an absolute "this is not it" – ... than of "this is not, and can never be, all."[108]

---

[105] Janet Martin Soskice, *Metaphor and Religious Language* (Oxford: Clarendon, 1985), 140.
[106] Ibid.   [107] Ibid.
[108] Rowan Williams, *Dostoevsky: Language, Faith and Fiction* (Waco, TX: Baylor University Press, 2008), 221–22.

Metaphors are a bit like literary "icons," in the sense that they "create a relationship in which discovery occurs." Their purpose is not definitional; they do not state how, exactly, mountains are personal, or put into precise philosophical terminology what enables fields to mourn. Instead, they open up the possibility of ongoing interaction. They enable Buber's "mutual giving." Literary descriptions of nonanimal nature are particularly suited to perform this function, because personalistic clouds and rivers look exactly like clouds and rivers; it is not that ancient Israelites went about in the world seeing Disney-like anthropomorphic creatures everywhere (think of the grandmother tree in *Pocahontas*). Metaphor allows biblical authors to explore the multiform relationships between humans, nonhumans, and God, and to invite readers into these relationships, thereby enabling discovery in the absence of definitional knowledge. Metaphors open up a space for interaction, a space that privileges not exhaustive knowledge, but intimacy.

None of this is to suggest that reading metaphors is easy. Soskice writes that metaphors do not simply describe things as they are; to read them in this way would be "naïve realism."[109] It would mean assuming "there [is] no difficulty in describing God by the same terms we use of observables; that God simply and truly gets 'angry', 'hardens his heart,' or is the king of heaven.'"[110] Metaphors posit both an "is" and an "is not"; when the Bible describes God as angry, that does not mean that divine anger is indistinguishable from human anger; equally important, it also does not mean that human and divine anger have nothing in common.[111] To understand a metaphor requires navigating between its "is" and "is not." To read personalistic nature texts with a naïve realism would be to assume that, when the prophets describe the land as mourning (see Isaiah 24:4; 33:9; Jeremiah 4:28; 12:4, 11; 23:10; Hosea 4:3; Joel 1:10; Amos 1:2), or the psalms call on nonanimal nature to break out in praise (see Psalm 69:35[34],[112] 89:6 [5]; 96:11–12; 148:3–10), the mourning and praise in question are identical to human mourning and human praise.

---

[109] Soskice, *Metaphor and Religious Language*, 119. See also Kirsten Nielsen's claim that metaphors "speak about reality," but do not "[illustrate] reality" (Kirsten Nielsen, *There Is Hope for a Tree: The Tree as Metaphor in Isaiah* [Sheffield, UK: JSOT, 1989], 42–43).
[110] Soskice, *Metaphor and Religious Language*, 119.
[111] The language of "is" and "is not" is borrowed from Ricoeur (Paul Ricœur, *The Rule of Metaphor: Multi-Disciplinary Studies of the Creation of Meaning in Language*, Toronto: University of Toronto Press, 1981, 7, 248–49.
[112] When the versification of the Hebrew and English Bibles differ, the first number refers to the Hebrew versification and the number in brackets refers to the English versification.

The opposite reading, also inappropriate, would be to dismiss out of hand the possibility that the biblical writers attribute forms of mourning and rejoicing to nonanimal nature. What both these readings fail to see is how metaphors are "social."[113] Human mourning, human praise, and human anger act as suggestions or guidelines in complicated relationships – with God, with trees, with the soil; they enable humans to respond to nonhuman grief and nonhuman happiness. They use the known (what it is like to be human) to help people relate to that which is less known (God, nonhuman persons). But they require a careful balancing act: In what ways is the mourning of fields like the mourning of humans? In what ways is it not? These are not simple questions; they are the complicated field of inquiry that opens up once you start paying attention to personalistic nature texts.

What is necessary for a word to be appropriate to different contexts? Why is "to mourn" such a flexible verb for biblical writers? In "Projecting a Word," a section of his "Excursus on Wittgenstein's Vision of Language" in *The Claim of Reason: Wittgenstein, Skepticism, Morality, and Tragedy,* Stanley Cavell writes about what constitutes "appropriate projections [of a word] into further contexts."[114] Why, instead of coining new words for every thing, action, and situation, do we instead make do with old words? "Why," asks Cavell, "haven't we arranged to *limit* words to *certain* contexts, and then coin new ones for new eventualities?"[115] He uses as his example the verb "feed": "'feed the kitty,' 'feed the lion,' 'feed the swans' ... 'feed the meter' ... 'feed the film' ... 'feed the machine' ... 'feed his pride' ... 'feed wire.'" The different uses cause us no trouble; the projection of "feed" into different contexts is perfectly intelligible. To imagine a group of people whose language has a different word for each instance requires imagining a people who sees "no connection between giving food to eels, to lions, and to swans, that these [are] just different actions, as different as feeding an eel, hunting it, killing it, eating it."[116] Furthermore, we would have to assume "not only that they [see] [these activities] as different, but that these activities [are] markedly different; and not different in the way it is different for *us* to feed swans and lions ... but different in some regularized way," for example

---

[113] Soskice, *Metaphor and Religious Language*, 132.
[114] Stanley Cavell, *The Claim of Reason: Wittgenstein, Skepticism, Morality, and Tragedy* (New York: Oxford University Press, 1999), 180. Note that Cavell and Diamond are both associated with the "New Wittgenstein" school.
[115] Ibid. Emphasis in the original.   [116] Ibid., 182.

requiring different dress, different songs, and different rituals.[117] The life of these imagined people would have to be very different from our own.

But, Cavell argues, the tolerance of a language for projection does not mean that all projections are acceptable: "what will count as legitimate projection is deeply controlled."[118] Returning to the example of "feed," he writes that "You can 'feed peanuts to a monkey,' and 'feed pennies to a meter,' but you cannot feed a monkey by stuffing pennies in its mouth."[119] Language is both stable and tolerant; an infinite number of projections are possible, but that is not to say that all projections are valid (though it is important to note that what makes a projection invalid is not that it is "wrong" or "counterfactual," but that it is unintelligible).

The particular projections possible in a language are not predetermined, but depend on "forms of life"; "You cannot use a word to do what we do with them until you are initiate of the forms of life which give those words the point and shape they have in our life."[120] Here Cavell's argument is similar to Diamond's point about "life with the concept"; understanding a concept is not a matter of grasping certain categories and then being able to slot the world into them, but of sharing in the forms of life that give shape to those concepts. To understand why you'd need different words for feeding a lion and an eel, or a lion and a meter, requires participating in forms of life in which those really are different actions, and, therefore, require different words.

Biblical language is not obviously like the language of the imaginary people who have a different word for ever instance in which we use "feed."[121] Such a degree of specificity in verb usage suggests a gulf between us and the imaginary people that would make it hard for us to carry on conversation. Biblical language, in contrast, is very familiar – it is part and parcel of our linguistic inheritance. But this familiarity disguises the ways in which the valid projections in the language of ancient Israel differ from valid projections in modern European languages. The biblical writers use the verb אבל, "to mourn," with any number of subjects: people mourn (Gen. 37:34; Amos 8:8), gates and walls mourn (Isa. 3:26; Lam. 2:8), soil mourns (Joel 1:10), wine and vines mourn (Isaiah 24:7).

---

[117] Ibid. Emphasis in the original. [118] Ibid., 183. [119] Ibid. [120] Ibid., 184.
[121] Cavell extends the metaphor to imagine a language completely intolerant of projection; no language, including biblical language, is like that. Such a language is not possible, as Cavell's rhetorical question, "Can everything be just different?" implies (Ibid., 182).

Comfort is also extended to nonhumans:[122] "For YHWH has comforted Zion, he has comforted all her dry places and made her wilderness like Eden, and her dry places like the garden of YHWH" (Isaiah 51:3). These projections differ from modern projections of grief and consolation, but how? To simply say that the one usage is literal and the other metaphorical gets us nowhere: "Being willing to call ideas (or objects) 'the same sort' and being willing to use 'the same word' for them is one and the same thing" – the biblical uses of "mourn" are no more metaphorical than the use of "feed" in "feed his pride."[123] If there is no similarity between two things or ideas, projecting a word from one context to the other will produce nonsense.

At the end of "Excursus on Wittgenstein's Vision of Language," Cavell turns to Wittgenstein's discussion of "'figurative' or 'secondary' senses of a word."[124] Such uses, Cavell writes, "such shades of sense, intimations of meaning ... allow certain kinds of subtlety or delicacy of communication; the connection is intimate, but fragile."[125] Then he writes: "Persons who cannot use words, or gestures, in these ways with you may yet be in your world, but perhaps not of your flesh."[126] He is of course not referring to the Bible, but the sentence is suggestive of our relationship to the biblical writers. We live, in a sense, in their world. Their words shape our life, our literature, our culture. But we are not of their flesh; we cannot easily trade words and gestures. But their words may yet teach us new ways to live. Living well as a human, according to the Hebrew Bible, requires being able to relate appropriately to the land, to the environment, to rivers and waterways. Metaphors guide and give access to these relationships, without systematizing or defining them. Just as divine metaphors aid access to YHWH, so nature metaphors aid access to nonanimal nature.

In other words, metaphors give us a way to respond to Buber's invitation to "look!"; they give us language to say something, but not too much, of the beings that "round about [us] ... live their life."[127] And it is important that we say something. Humans are not isolated individuals, but communities. Buber claims that, when speaking to the world as *Thou*, "you cannot make yourself understood with others concerning it, you are alone with it," and perhaps if that were true, we could do without

---

[122] Cavell writes that "What will be, or count as 'being fed' is related to what will count as 'refusing to eat'" (Ibid., 183). To the biblical writers, what counts as mourning is related to what counts as comfort.
[123] Ibid., 188.   [124] Ibid., 189.   [125] Ibid.   [126] Ibid.   [127] Buber, *I and Thou*, 15.

metaphors, or do with personal, private metaphors only.[128] But this is not the world presented to us by the biblical writers. Living well with other-than-human creatures is to them a communal responsibility; it is part and parcel of everyday life together. And for this we need shared language. Metaphors allow biblical writers to acknowledge and narrate relationships that "cling to the threshold of speech,"[129] they make it possible to train others in these relationships, and they make visible lives that might otherwise go unnoticed. Metaphors are tools for relationality; they are a way in which human language is brought into service of human relationships with that which is not human.

PERSONALISTIC NATURE TEXTS AND PATIENCE

Though new animism provides wonderful tools for studying personalistic nature texts, it also generates frustration. Despite my best intentions, I cannot share the experience of living in a world full of persons, only some of whom are human. I have not been trained in animist ways of relating to animals, trees, and rocks, and reading academic monographs on the topic is not sufficient education. In fact, the writings of "new animists" suggest that even in-depth ethnographic work cannot wholly overcome this experiential barrier. A distinct tone of longing surfaces. Graham Harvey writes that, through his scholarship, he is "fumbling towards a richer experience of the world," and muses that "perhaps ... animists ... have ways of speaking that more adequately represent [a] rediscovered sense of human belonging in a deeply conscious and relational world."[130] Tim Ingold describes animism as a liberating alternative to modernist ideas about matter and form.[131] Even Descola, who insists that "for anthropology, no ontology is better or more truthful in itself than another," speaks of the study of animism with urgency. "One does not have to be a great seer," he writes, "to predict that the relationship between humans and nature will, in all probability, be the most important question of the present century."[132] For Descola, animism provides one part of "a framework" by means of which the West can "reflect upon the effects of the disintegration of our notion of the natural world."[133]

---

[128] Ibid., 33. [129] Ibid., 6. [130] Harvey, *Animism*, 69, 190.
[131] Tim Ingold, "Being Alive to a World Without Objects," in *The Handbook of Contemporary Animism*, ed. Graham Harvey (Durham, UK: Acumen, 2013), 225.
[132] Descola, *The Ecology of Others*, 66, 81. [133] Ibid., 82.

To engage with animism, and with personalistic nature texts, is an engagement with a particular modern ignorance. It is to come face to face with our loss of concepts. Attention, responsiveness, and careful listening do not produce overnight, or even perhaps in a lifetime, the ability to enter into the experience of those who speak with mountains, and relate to trees as kin. In her essay "Teaching a Stone to Talk," Annie Dillard dwells on her efforts to listen to the world: "The sea pronounces something, over and over, in a hoarse whisper; I cannot make it out. But God knows I have tried."[134] She announces her stance of readiness, her pose of attention: "At a certain point you say to the woods, to the sea, to the mountains, the world, Now I am ready. Now I will stop and be wholly attentive."[135] What she hears, however, is not a great chatter of woods, sea, and mountains, but silence:

After a while you hear it: there is nothing there. There is nothing there but those things only, those created objects, discrete, growing or holding, or swaying, being rained on or raining, held, flooding or ebbing, standing or spread ... This is it: this hum is the silence.[136]

Her words share continuities with animist traditions, who also relate to "those things only." But, in contrast to animists, for whom this hum is meaningful, to Dillard it is silence. The world for humans is mute, and humans are mute "in relation to all that is not human."[137] Dillard's approach contrasts with recent attempts in biblical studies to listen to nonanimal nature, like the Earth Bible Project's principle that its participants should "see things from the perspective of Earth."[138] This principle assumes that we know *how* to see things from the perspective of earth; Dillard does not. She responds to the silence of the world with an image of patience, namely that of a man trying to teach a stone to talk:

Reports differ on precisely what he expects or wants the stone to say. I do not think he expects the stone to speak as we do, and describe for us its long life and many, or few, sensations. I think instead he is trying to teach it to say a single

---

[134] Annie Dillard, "Teaching a Stone to Talk," in *Teaching a Stone to Talk: Expeditions and Encounters* (New York: Harper & Row, 1982), 71.
[135] Ibid., 71–72.   [136] Ibid., 72.   [137] Ibid., 74.
[138] Norman C. Habel, ed., *Readings from the Perspective of Earth* (Sheffield: Sheffield Academic, 2000), 33–34. One conclusion that can be drawn from new animism is that "seeing things from the perspective of Earth" is a difficult task. Viveiros de Castro writes about the philosophical questions raised by worldviews that attribute personal perspectives to other-than-human persons: "What these persons see ... – and therefore what they are as persons – constitutes precisely the philosophical problem posed by and for indigenous thought" (Viveiros de Castro, *Cannibal Metaphysics*, 2014, 56).

word, such as "cup," or "uncle." For this purpose he has not, as some have seriously suggested, carved the stone a little mouth, or furnished it in any way with a pocket of air which it might then expel. Rather – and I think he is wise in this – he plans to initiate his son, who is now an infant living with Larry's estranged wife, into the work, so that it may continue and bear fruit after his death.[139]

Larry leaves the stone as it is. Instead of speeding up the project by changing the stone, Larry plans to pass it on to other people, who in turn might pass it on to others. In Dillard's narration, it is not the stone that must change; the humans around it, who wish to communicate with it, must wait. Either the stone will speak, or it will not. Or, as Buber says, the world encountered as *Thou* "is unreliable ... you cannot hold it to its word ... [I]t comes even when it is not summoned, and vanishes even when tightly held."[140] Animists maintain mutual relationships with other-than-human persons. Such relationships cannot be forced, cannot be made to appear by means of study and determination, but must be waited for. They require patience.

The West has made a practice of assuming that our own concepts, our science, objectivity, and rationality, are better and more enlightened than those of other peoples. It is humbling, at times even humiliating, to be made to feel the limitations of our ways of parcelling out the world and our experiences. I would like to know what it is like to talk to a tree or what a stone might say to me. Furthermore, as an academic, it is somewhat embarrassing to write about personalistic nature texts. There is always the nagging sense that maybe it would be more professional to dismiss them all as rhetoric, as ornamentation or anthropomorphizing. Jane Bennett writes that her own investigation into the vibrancy of matter requires "a certain willingness to appear naive and foolish."[141] This project is an exercise in waiting, in listening to others who have listened to the world. Along the way it will be important to suspend the knee-jerk reaction that mountains cannot be afraid, soil cannot mourn, and skies cannot speak, and to risk a bit of foolishness. And if we are very lucky, perhaps the biblical texts might reveal in the world a similar patience, a similar waiting, a "craning of the neck" towards our attention and our desire, a readiness out there to know and be known.

---

[139] Dillard, "Teaching a Stone to Talk," 68. [140] Buber, *I and Thou*, 32.
[141] Bennett, *Vibrant Matter*, xiii.

3

A Watchful World

Personalistic Nature Texts in the Torah

INTRODUCTION

The books of Torah tell the story of Israel's beginnings: creation, the patriarchs, the exodus from Egypt, the journey towards the land of Canaan. It is a story of how YHWH and Israel get to know each other, how they prepare for life together. But it is not a story of humans and God only; in these books, the earth (אֶרֶץ) and the ground (אֲדָמָה) are key characters. The earth participates in the creation of vegetation and draws God's attention to Cain's murder of Abel in Genesis. In Exodus, it swallows the Egyptians pursuing the Israelites through the Reed Sea. Leviticus attributes cultic responsibilities to the ground, and warns that it will resist human inhabitants who obstruct its ability to fulfill these. Numbers describes the earth as a devouring being, which swallows Korah and his company. In Deuteronomy, the earth, together with the heavens, stands as witness against Israel, should they fail to maintain their covenant with YHWH. The activity of the ground and the earth reflects its context; a key theme of Genesis through Deuteronomy is the relationship between the Israelites and the land into which they are about to enter. The character of the land, its obligations to YHWH, its relation to humans – these themes come to the fore in personalistic nature texts in the Torah.

GENESIS

Genesis 1: The Earth Brought Forth ...

In Genesis 1, nonanimal nature plays two roles: it participates in God's creation of the world and receives responsibilities for the world's ongoing maintenance. The first of the two belongs to the earth. When God commands the earth to sprout vegetation, the earth "[brings] forth vegetation – plants seeding seed according to its kind and trees making fruit with its seed in it according to its kind" (Genesis 1:12). The earth *itself* brings forth vegetation in obedience to God's command; God initiates the work, but leaves its execution to the earth.[1]

Claus Westermann associates the earth's activity in Genesis 1:12 with a particular kind of mythic genre: origin stories. Westermann distinguishes between creation stories, in which gods create the world or parts of the world, and origin stories, in which they spontaneously appear.[2] He notes that, in stories from Israel's neighbors, origin stories occur with some frequency, and, though he argues that Genesis 1:11–12 demonstrates a continuity or relationship with them, he maintains that "creation completely dominates origin in the Old Testament."[3] The trace of an origin story is, for Westermann, evidence of a bridge between the story of Genesis 1 and those of Israel's neighbors, but nothing else. He treats the words "the earth brought forth" as not genuinely Israelite; in his argument they are vestigial and ought not to be taken as evidence that Israelites thought that the earth is able of its own accord to put forth new creatures.[4]

---

[1] Similar commands occur in verses 1:20 ("God said: Let the waters teem ...") and 1:24 (God said: Let the earth bring forth ..."), but in each case the following verse specifies that God creates the new beings (1:21: "God created the great sea monsters ..."; 1:25: "God made the wild animals of the earth ..."). Fretheim cautions against making too much of this difference in stated subjects: "Genesis 1:12 differs from 1:20, 24 in that it specifically states that "the earth brought forth." That such a statement is not present in 1:20, 24, however, should not be interpreted to mean that the earth and waters were not actual participants in these cases; rather, God's creative act is mediated in and through these creatures, and God as sole stated subject is a variation of 1:11–13, where the earth is stated as the only subject." See Fretheim, *God and World in the Old Testament*, 38.

[2] See Westermann, *Genesis 1–11*, 26.

[3] Ibid., 25–26. Though Westermann bemoans the tendency to use comparative material as a means to devalue the stories of Israel's neighbors, his argument that Israel's writers reject mythology has a decided evaluative flavor. He describes the reworking of mythic material in the Bible as an intentional rejection of myth (see, for example, his discussion of the rejection of hero narratives in Ibid., 12), and describes the result as "a process of liberation" (Ibid., 65).

[4] In general, Westermann tends to distribute agency in Genesis between humans and God only. For example, Westermann applies the logic of demythologizing to his interpretation of God's commands in Genesis 1 and to human achievement stories throughout Genesis. In his treatment of God's commands in Genesis 1, Westermann states: "The only difference between God's acting in history and his action in creation is that in the one case his command is directed to a person (Abraham) or a mediator (Moses), while in the

An alternative to Westermann's contrast between origin stories and creation stories is to consider the making of the world as a joint effort of God and creatures. God initiates creation – God makes light and dark, dry land and wet, and so on – but once these creatures exist, they add their labor to God's. This is how Michael Welker understands Genesis 1. In this text, the earth is "an active, empowering agent that brings forth life."[5] In other words, the earth shares some of God's ability to make living beings. God does not hoard this skill, but bestows it on the world. Welker emphasizes that the anxiety to differentiate cleanly between God's actions and the actions of creatures is one that readers impose on the text – we do not have to choose between assigning actions to God or to creatures; the two overlap and intertwine and merge.[6] In the words of Terence Fretheim, "God makes a decision to create in community rather than alone; at the divine initiative, the creation plays an active role in God's creative work."[7] Framed this way, creation carries responsibility, alongside God, for its own existence, and it is vulnerable to its own actions. What creatures do matters, and can influence the world is enduring ways; this will be a running thread throughout this book. So will be Welker's insistence that the Bible draws no more than a fuzzy line between divine and creaturely activity. God does not present creatures with a ready-made world, à la the watchmaker analogy. Instead, the activity of creatures, both human and other-than-human, is "a constitutive element in the process of creation."[8]

---

other it is a command *without an addressee*, and hence a creation command." (Westermann, *Genesis 1–11*, 85. Emphasis added). In other words, the earth, the heavenly bodies, the waters – none of these are addressees. The text itself does not necessitate this reading. It is based on the assumption that nonanimal nature cannot be spoken to. In terms of human achievement stories, Westermann writes that, in other Ancient Near Eastern myths, creation includes not only the creation of the natural world, but also elements of civilization, like the pickaxe, the plough, irrigation, and weaving (Ibid., 57–58). In biblical stories, however, especially in the list of achievements in Genesis 4:17–26, all progress in civilization is due to human ingenuity: "Faced with the mythology of the Ancient Near East, the Bible takes the same stand as does the modern secular historian: all progress in civilization is a human achievement" (Ibid., 61). This shift from divine creation of civilization to human discovery is labeled by Westermann as a move away from myth. Myth distributes acts between a number of gods and phenomenon, while, Westermann argues, the Bible restricts all such agency to either God or humans.

[5] Welker, *Creation and Reality*, 42.   [6] Ibid., 11–12.
[7] Terence E. Fretheim, *Creation Untamed: The Bible, God, and Natural Disasters* (Grand Rapids, MI.: Baker Academic, 2010), 11.
[8] Welker, *Creation and Reality*, 13.

The second role of nonanimal nature in Genesis 1, that of maintaining the world's order, falls to the sun and the moon: to make a distinction (הַבְדִּיל) between light and dark, to be signs for seasons, to give light to the earth, and to rule (מָשַׁל) the day and the night (Genesis 1:14–18). The task that sounds most incongruous to modern ears is the task of ruling, and, even in biblical Hebrew, the root מׁשל ("to rule") usually refers to humans or God exercising authority over other humans.[9] Westermann calls ruling "a personal function," and, therefore, takes the verb to be "an echo ... of the divinity of the sun and the moon."[10] The divinity of the luminaries is precisely what Herbert Brichto claims the text denies; he writes that the sun and the moon have been "demoted ... to mere artifacts, lamps rising and setting on the command of the One Creator."[11] Brichto's interpretation is based on the assumption that nonhuman nature must either be inert or divine; either they are gods or stage dressing. But, in this text, the sun and the moon are simply creatures like other creatures, alive but not gods. There's certainly an echo of traditions in which they *are* divine, but the text counters this echo not by presenting them as inanimate lamps, but as responsible persons, created by and subordinate to God.

Irvin Hallowell's description of Ojibwa understandings of the sun is a helpful parallel. Hallowell writes that "to the Ojibwa ... the sun is a 'person' of the other-than-human class."[12] The Ojibwa attribute the sun's daily rising and setting to its personal habits, not to natural law.[13] Harold Fisch makes a similar argument, though using different terms, in his description of the daily and seasonal rhythms established by the luminaries in Genesis 1: "To the Hebrew mind, the Law of Nature has an imperative character; like *torah* in the human sphere, it involves *command* and *responses*."[14] The fact that nonanimal nature performs "personal functions" need not mean that they are divinized, but instead that the circle of creatures capable of performing "personal functions" is bigger in the Hebrew Bible than it is in modern Western thought.

---

[9] The noun מֶמְשָׁלֶת ("rule, dominion") usually refers to human or divine rule, except in Genesis 1:16 and in Psalm 136:8; both of these verses describe the rule of the sun and the moon. The verb מָשַׁל ("to rule") always refers to human or divine ruling, except in Genesis 1:18. (Note: all concordance work is my own, unless I refer to dictionaries or word books.)

[10] Westermann, *Genesis 1–11*, 127.

[11] Herbert Chanan Brichto, *The Names of God: Poetic Readings in Biblical Beginnings* (New York: Oxford University Press, 1998), 69.

[12] Hallowell, "Ojibwa Ontology, Behavior, and World View," 28.   [13] Ibid.

[14] Harold Fisch, "Analogy of Nature: A Note on the Structure of Old Testament Imagery," *The Journal of Theological Studies* 6, no. 2 (October 1955): 170. Emphasis in the original.

The responsibility to distinguish (הַבְדִּיל) between light and dark should also be considered a "personal function." The word הַבְדִּיל ("to distinguish") has strong cultic overtones, and in Leviticus it designates Israel's responsibility to distinguish between the holy and the common.[15] With respect to the luminaries, both מָשַׁל ("to rule") and הַבְדִּיל ("to distinguish") refer to their role in upholding and maintaining the order of the cosmos, which parallels the purpose of Israel's cultic system.[16] Jeffrey Cooley, for example, writes that "the great lamps are created as agents whose responsibility is to rule day and night and thereby create a significant cultic chronological order of the cosmos."[17] The activity of the sun and the moon, therefore, differs from that of the earth in Genesis 1:12. While the earth takes part in the creation of the world, the sun and the moon participate in its ongoing governance, and make possible human worship. Both cases have in common that nonanimal nature cooperates with the divine effort to organize creation and ensure its fertility and growth.

Although the sun and the moon are not divinized in Genesis 1, the text is, among other things, a polemic against the gods worshipped by Israel's neighbors.[18] The sun is not god, the moon is not god, the sea serpent and the sea in which it swims are not gods. These are creatures in a world made by the one whom Israel worships, living furnishings in this one God's cosmic temple.[19] The text is studded with borrowed material, with more or less obvious references to other religious traditions and divinities; it is a

---

[15] See Leviticus 10:10; 11:47; 20:24–25.

[16] Kirsten Nielsen writes that "[t]he ultimate purpose of the Israelite cult, broadly construed, is the preservation of the cosmos" (Kirsten Nielsen, *Yahweh as Prosecutor and Judge: An Investigation of the Prophetic Lawsuit (Rîb-Pattern)* [Sheffield: Dept. of Biblical Studies, University of Sheffield, 1978], 45). God's acts of creation begin with a series of distinctions (Genesis 1:4, 7); the task of making a distinction (הַבְדִּיל), given to the luminaries, also associates their work with that of God. See also John Barton, "Reading the Prophets From An Environmental Perspective," in *Ecological Hermeneutics: Biblical, Historical and Theological Perspectives*, ed. David G. Horrell et al. (London: T & T Clark, 2010), 53.

[17] Jeffrey L. Cooley, *Poetic Astronomy in the Ancient Near East: The Reflexes of Celestial Science in Ancient Mesopotamian, Ugaritic, and Israelite Narrative*, History, Archaeology, and Culture of the Levant 5 (Winona Lake, IN: Eisenbrauns, 2013), 317. See also Mark S. Smith, *The Priestly Vision of Genesis 1* (Minneapolis, MN: Augsburg Fortress, 2009), 98.

[18] The most obvious point of comparison is with the Babylonian creation narrative *Enuma Elish*, in which the god Marduk slays the sea serpent Tiamat and then creates the world from her body.

[19] For example, the sun and the moon are called מְאֹרֹת, "lamps," a word used elsewhere in the Torah only for the lamps of the tabernacle. See Exodus 25:6; 27:20; 35:8, 14, 28; 39:37; Leviticus 24:2; Numbers 4:9, 16. In Ezekiel 32:8 and Psalm 74:16, מָאוֹר refers to

palimpsest of Israel's interactions with other religions and of its own past religious practices.²⁰ It is tempting to read this polemic as definite proof that the personal functions of the luminaries do not indicate any personalistic understanding of the luminaries themselves. After all, they are called "lamps" (מְאֹרֹת), which suggest passive tools, not personal beings. But humans too are furnishings, in a sense. They are "images" (צֶלֶם), statues, and Eve, like a house, is "built" (בָּנָה) from materials taken from Adam (Genesis 2:22).²¹ Being furnishings in God's world is a grave and wonderful responsibility, not a sad demotion. Since monolatery or monotheism are the norms throughout the biblical writings, at least in terms of their final form, scholars tend to assume that any activity on the part of nonanimal nature must be a trace of foreign or past worship practices, left in place to prove its opposite.²² For example, as cited above, Brichto writes that, while most Ancient Near Eastern traditions personified the sun, moon, and stars, these are reduced "in Genesis to mere artifacts."²³ Brichto's general point is correct – Genesis 1 polemicizes against the worship of celestial bodies – but his corollary point – the sun, moon, and stars are mere artifacts in Genesis 1 – is not. The sun and the moon are "demoted" from gods to powerful creatures, whose responsibilities include ruling over day and night and making possible seasonal and cultic calendars. Inertness and divinity

---

luminaries. In Psalm 90:8, it refers to the "light of [YHWH's] face," and in Proverbs 15:30, to the "light of the eyes."

[20] For a discussion of solar worship in Israel, see Glen Taylor, *Yahweh and the Sun: Biblical and Archaeological Evidence for Sun Worship in Ancient Israel* (Sheffield, UK: JSOT, 1993).

[21] Elsewhere in the Bible, the noun צֶלֶם ("image") most often refers to various sculpted or cast images, often of gods, but not always. See, for example, Numbers 33:52; 1 Samuel 6:5, 11; 2 Kings 11:18; Ezekiel 16:17, 23:14; Amos 5:26; and 2 Chronicles 23:17. For a discussion of "the image of God," especially as it relates to the ruling function of humans in Genesis 1, see J. Richard Middleton, *The Liberating Image: The Imago Dei in Genesis 1* (Grand Rapids, MI: Brazos, 2005). Thank you to Laura Lieber for pointing out that Eve is built.

[22] On the development of monotheism in biblical traditions, see Mark S. Smith, *The Early History of God: Yahweh and the Other Deities in Ancient Israel* (Grand Rapids, MI: William B. Eerdmans, 2002); and Thomas Römer, *The Invention of God* (Cambridge, MA: Harvard University Press, 2015).

[23] Brichto, *The Names of God*, 69. Bill Arnold cites Brichto's statement with approval in his Genesis commentary (Bill Arnold, *Genesis*, Cambridge: Cambridge University Press, 43). Matthew Michael makes a similar assertion concerning the role of the celestial bodies in Deuteronomy 33:13–14. He writes that the sun and the moon have been turned into "mere agents of Israel's deity," in a polemical move against the solar worship of Israel's neighbors (Matthew Michael, "Twilight of the Gods: Hidden Polemics in Joshua 10:12–14," *Hebrew Studies* 55 [2014]: 65).

are not the only options. Living humans are not divine, but neither are they dead. The same is true for celestial bodies.

Does this mean that Genesis 1 is somewhat pantheistic, or at least not properly monotheistic? Richard Bauckham writes that, in the Bible, "Nature is certainly de-divinized but it is not de-sacralized."[24] He argues that much discussion of the active role of nonanimal nature in the Hebrew Bible assumes a false alternative between pantheistic, animistic visions of nature (nature as an object of worship), and modern, secular ones (nature as an object of use).[25] His particular terms are not especially helpful, but the general point is instructive. There are more ways to relate to nature than as god or as resource. Where I would disagree with him is his assumption that animistic visions of nature are necessarily pantheistic. Animism is not a dogmatic system, but a way of relating to other persons, human and otherwise. To understand the earth and the luminaries in personalistic terms does not require divinizing them, any more than relating to your grandma in personalistic terms means assuming that she's a goddess. Animist societies are diverse in terms of religious beliefs: some are theistic, some are not; some have creator gods and some do without, and so on. Furthermore, it is clear from ancient sources that elements of the world could be recognized as persons without being understood as gods. For example, in a discussion of the phrase "I call to witness the heavens and the earth" in Deuteronomy 4:26, 30:19, and 32:1, Delcor contrasts different witness lists in Ancient Near Eastern treaty texts. In some, gods are listed first, then the heavens, the earth, and other natural elements, suggesting that the natural elements are not considered divine.[26] In others, the heavens and the earth are listed among the divinities, suggesting that they were worshipped as gods.[27] In the first case, the

---

[24] Richard Bauckham, *Bible and Ecology: Rediscovering the Community of Creation* (London: Darton, Longman & Todd, 2010), 86.

[25] Ibid.

[26] M. Delcor, "Les Attaches Litteraires, l'origine et La Signification de l'expression Biblique 'Prendre a Temoin Le Ciel et La Terre,'" *Vetus Testamentum* 16, no. 1 (January 1, 1966): 11–12.

[27] Ibid. Delcor points to the Treaty of Mursil II (1334–1306 BCE) and Duppi-Tessub king of Amurru as an example of a treaty in which the heavens and the earth do not appear to be divine. See James B. Pritchard, *Ancient Near Eastern Texts Relating to the Old Testament* (Princeton, NJ: Princeton University Press, 1950), 203–5. Note that Delcor himself does not make much use of his own argument. He goes on to say that biblical writers demythologized the role of the heavens and the earth in treaties, though he does not explain what he means by demythologizing. See Delcor, "Les Attaches Litteraires, l'origine et La Signification de l'expression Biblique 'Prendre a Temoin Le Ciel et La Terre,'" 15.

natural elements are simply powerful creatures, whose permanence makes them particularly suited to the role of witnessing.[28]

The personal function of the earth and the celestial bodies sheds light on the refrain of Genesis 1: "it was good" (Genesis 1:4, 10, 12, 18, 21, 25, 31). Though the earth, the sun and the moon, and the sea and the sea serpent are not gods, they are afforded dignity and power *as creatures*. They are given responsibilities, and, in the case of the great lights (and humans,) are tasked with ruling the world. This is extraordinary, given that this text serves in part as polemic. Consider how it could have been different. Instead of its refrain "it was good," it could have described the world as a host of vanquished enemies. In fact, that is how the sea and Leviathan are depicted in some biblical texts (see, for example, Habakkuk 3:8–15; Isaiah 27:1; 50:2; Nahum 1:4; Psalm 74:14). But that is not how it goes in Genesis 1; God repeatedly declares that the world is good, very good. The refrain of Genesis 1 may serve, among other things, as a counter to potential hostile responses to creation. The sun is not to be despised because the god *Shamash* ought not to be worshipped, nor is the sea an enemy because Israel does not worship *Yam*. It is often noted that, in contrast to the Babylonian creation story *Enuma Elish*, in which humans are created as slaves to the gods, Genesis 1 presents humans in a much more favorable light: they are made in God's image. What is less often noted is the generosity that Genesis 1 extends to other beings: they too are valued creatures in God's world.

If neither the polemical nature of Genesis 1 nor its monotheistic stance requires an impersonal understanding of nonanimal nature, what about the structure of the chapter, which many argue depends on a clear separation between nonliving and living things? Scholars observe a parallel or two-panel structure in Genesis 1. The days of creation correspond to each other, so that day one corresponds to day four, day two to day five, and day three to day six, with the seventh day, the day of God's rest, as the capstone.[29] The first panel, it is argued, represents the creation of habitants or domains,

---

[28] Delcor, "Les Attaches Litteraires, l'origine et La Signification de l'expression Biblique 'Prendre a Temoin Le Ciel et La Terre,'" 12.

[29] See Arnold, *Genesis*, 30; Bauckham, *Bible and Ecology*, 13; Brown, *The Ethos of the Cosmos*, 37; Terence E. Fretheim, *Creation, Fall, and Flood: Studies in Genesis 1–11* (Minneapolis, MN: Augsburg, 1969), 47; Middleton, *The Liberating Image*, 75, 278. Middleton claims that the identification of this parallel structure dates from at least the eighteenth century. He cites Henri Blocher, who in turn names Johann Gottfried von Herder (1744–1803) as the originator of the observation (Ibid., 74, citing Henri Blocher, *In the Beginning: The Opening Chapters of Genesis* [Leicester, UK: Inter-Varsity, 1984], 51).

while the second panel represents the populating of these habitats. For example, Richard Bauckham names the first panel "Environments and Names" and the second "Inhabitants and Tasks,"[30] and Richard Middleton labels the two panels "forming static regions" and "filling with mobile occupants."[31] The language of these labels, especially the words environments, regions, inhabitants, and occupants, is misleading. It brings to mind modern assumptions about animation, liveliness, and personhood. For example, Fretheim summarizes the overall movement of Genesis 1 as "from the inanimate to the animate,"[32] and William Brown calls day four the day when "life begins."[33] Perhaps most misleading is Middleton's use of "static regions" to describe that which is created on the first three days, since "static" suggesting not only lifelessness, but unchangeability.

The text itself resists any clear distinction between animate and inanimate. First, the habitats created in days one to three participate in the creation of their inhabitants, as we've seen with respect to the earth in Genesis 1:11–12. Not what one would expect from a static region! Second, the sequence of creative acts complicates the picture. Vegetation is created on day three, that is, on a 'domain' day. The luminaries, however, are created on day 4, a "populating" day. Middleton calls vegetation and the luminaries "borderline creatures,"[34] and concludes that, while "Genesis 1 is clearly concerned with ordered categories, this order is not rigid," and its categories have "fuzzy boundaries."[35] This reasoning is backwards. It is not that Genesis 1 has unclear categories, but that the categories of modern interpreters do not quite fit the picture. An interesting example of mismatched categories is Bonhoeffer's theological commentary on Genesis 1–3. Bonhoeffer is forced to treat the creation acts out of order, because he distinguishes between the creation of "that which is firmly fixed" and "that which lives."[36] He places Genesis 1:6–10 and 14–19 in the first category (the creation of the firmament, the dry land, and the great

---

[30] Bauckham, *Bible and Ecology*, 13.
[31] Middleton, *The Liberating Image*, 279. See also Brown, *The Ethos of the Cosmos*, 37.
[32] Fretheim, *Creation, Fall, and Flood: Studies in Genesis 1–11*, 47.
[33] Brown, *The Ethos of the Cosmos*, 37. Note that Brown, in his later book *The Seven Pillars of Creation: The Bible, Science, and the Ecology of Wonder*, highlights the active participation of the earth and the sea in the creation of its respective creatures. See William Brown, *The Seven Pillars of Creation: The Bible, Science, and the Ecology of Wonder* (Oxford: Oxford University Press, 2010), 44–45, 61, 73.
[34] Middleton, *The Liberating Image*, 280.   [35] Ibid.
[36] Dietrich Bonhoeffer, *Creation and Fall: A Theological Exposition of Genesis 1–3*, ed. Martin Rüter et al., trans. Douglas S. Bax, Vol. 3, *Dietrich Bonhoeffer Works* (Minneapolis, MN: Fortress, 1997), 50–55, 56–59.

lights) and Genesis 1:11–13 and 20–25 in the second (vegetation, and land and sea creatures). The difficulty disappears if we abandon the idea that days one through three describe the creation of lifeless environments, while days four through six describe the creation of living beings. All things created in Genesis 1 are active and able to interact with other beings. The creatures are organized and differentiated, but not into the categories "animate" and "inanimate."

Attending to Genesis 1 itself, the writer differentiates creatures based on how God makes each being, on their various material conditions, and on their functions and roles. Westermann points out that, on the first three days, God "separate[s]" and "name[s]."[37] Days four through six lack a clear verbal repetition, but several interlocking repetitions give coherence to the panel. First, God gives a task to each creature. The luminaries are to make distinctions, rule, give light, and be signs (Genesis 1:14–18). The birds, fish, and humans are tasked with being fruitful, multiplying, and filling (Genesis 1:22, 28).[38] Humans are given the additional responsibility of subduing and having dominion (Genesis 1:28). Second, on days five and six, God blesses the sea, air, and land creatures with fertility.[39] A third oft-noted feature of days four to six is that all creatures belonging to these days move: luminaries move across the sky, fish swim in the sea, birds fly in the air, and land animals and humans walk and crawl. What emerges from the details of the text is an organized and diverse world. The distinctions between creatures are based on how God creates each creature, what tasks God gives to them, the particulars of their bodies, how they reproduce, what they eat and their use value as food, and where they live. Such distinctions between creature organize the days. It is the description of a closely observed and lived-in world, albeit

---

[37] Westermann, *Genesis 1–11*, 87. The verb "to make a distinction" (הַבְדִּיל) does not appear in the third day. Instead the distinction between dry land and the sea takes place through the gathering (קָוָה) of the sea.

[38] The land animals are given no explicit task.

[39] Westermann ties blessing to animation: "P distinguishes between animate and inanimate creatures. The animate creatures are blessed by God. To bless means 'to bestow with a dynamism to increase.' ... and this is primarily the power of fertility given to humans and to beasts" (Westermann, *Genesis 1–11*, 88, quoting Ludwig Köhler, *Vom Hebräischen Lexikon* [Leiden: E. J. Brill, 1950]). Westermann's argument mingles abstract categories with more concrete considerations. What ties fish, birds, animals, and humans together is that they have young. The salient feature is not that they are animate, but that they reproduce in a certain way.

an idealized one.⁴⁰ The various creatures all participate in the life of the world, in ways proper to their bodies and their location. Humans and animals reproduce and eat (and in the case of humans, subdue and have dominion), the earth puts forth vegetation, the sun and the moon distinguish between night and day and rule over them. All creatures are active – there are no static domains here – but active in different ways and to different ends. Together they carry out the creaturely side of the formation and continuation of the world.

Genesis 4: The Soil ... Opened Its Mouth

Genesis 4 introduces a prominent way in which nonanimal nature interacts with humans: it intervenes when people commit particularly egregious transgressions. In this case, the ground makes known and responds to human violence:

> YHWH said: What have you done?! The voice of your brother's blood cries out to me from the ground. And now, cursed are you from the ground that opened its mouth to take your brother's blood from your hand. For you will serve the soil, but it will not again give its strength to you; a vagrant and a wanderer you will be in the earth. (Genesis 4:10–12)

A number of features of Genesis 4:10–12 indicate that the ground intervenes after Cain murders Abel. First, the ground (אֲדָמָה) is the subject of several active verbs. The ground "opens its mouth," "takes" blood from Cain's hand, and refuses to "give its strength." The verbs that apply to Cain are either passive (אָרוּר – "you are cursed") or describe the futility of Cain's future actions ("you will serve ... but it will not give"). This stands in stark contrast to Cain's busyness at the beginning of the story: he tills (4:2), brings sacrifices (4:3), dialogues with God (4:6, 9–15), speaks to his brother (4:8), and rises up and kills (4:8). Then, in verses 4:10–12, it shifts. The ground is now in control of Cain's life. In Kristin Swenson's words, "The land, which defines the object of Cain's vocation ... becomes a source of testimony and indictment against him."⁴¹ Previously, Cain would till the ground, and the ground would

---

⁴⁰ See, for example, Ellen Davis' argument that "Genesis 1 represents in specific terms the plant world as it was known to those who occupied the highlands of the Levant" (Ellen F. Davis, *Scripture, Culture, and Agriculture: An Agrarian Reading of the Bible* [Cambridge: Cambridge University Press, 2009], 49).

⁴¹ Kristin M. Swenson, "Care and Keeping East of Eden: Gen 4:1–16 in Light of Gen 2–3," *Interpretation* 60, no. 4 (October 1, 2006): 381.

supply fruit (4:2–3). Now, no matter what Cain does, the ground will not share its produce. Cain is no longer the protagonist of his story. Instead the ground shapes his life; it refuses to yield to Cain, and forces him to take up a life of homelessness and wandering.

The vocabulary of Genesis 4:10–12 also draws attention to the activity of the ground. Verse 4:11 uses the verb לָקַח, "to take," to designate the exchange of blood between Cain and the soil. The verb can describe anything from passive receiving to active taking, though, in most cases, it is used to describe someone willingly taking hold of something.[42] Significantly, Genesis uses the phrase "take from the hand" another eight times. Four times it refers to characters transporting objects,[43] twice to characters persuading someone to accept a gift,[44] once to recovering property,[45] and once to seizing spoils in war.[46] In every case, the subject of לָקַח is active and willing. In the case of Genesis 4:11, English translations tend to choose a more passive sounding translation of לָקַח, like "receive."[47] This translation is not technically wrong, but it disguises the participation of the ground in this story. The ground does not passively soak up blood; it actively takes the blood from Cain's hand.

Also interesting is the nearly unique use of the noun כֹּחַ, "strength," to refer to the abilities of the ground, abilities that include the production of produce. It highlights how vegetation is not first and foremost a product of human labor, but instead the result of the ground's labor.[48] It is a gift that it can offer or withhold, depending on how humans live. The giving and withholding of produce on the part of the ground is commonly evoked in texts related to curses and blessings. Leviticus 26:4 is representative: "I will give your rains in their time, and the earth will give its produce (יְבוּל) and the trees of the field its fruit (פְּרִי)."[49] Both Genesis 4:12 and Leviticus 26:4 use the same verb (נָתַן) to describe how the earth and the ground will produce fruit, but they use different nouns to describe the fruit itself. Leviticus uses common and straightforward nouns for

---

[42] For an example of an instance in which לָקַח ("to take") describes a situation of passive or unwilling receiving, see Isaiah 40:2.

[43] Genesis 22:6; 32:14[13]; 43:12, 15.   [44] Genesis 21:30; 33:10.   [45] Genesis 38:20.

[46] Genesis 48:22.   [47] See NSRV, ESV, KJV, NIV, NAB.

[48] Genesis 4:12 is one of two places in which כֹּחַ ("strength") appears with the word אֲדָמָה ("ground"). The other is Job. 31:39. Note that the logic of Job 31:39 is similar to that of Genesis 4:11–12: the consequence of inappropriate use of the ground is frustrated agriculture and poor yield. It is possible that Hosea 7:9 also uses כֹּחַ ("strength") to refer to produce ("Strangers eat his strength (כֹּחוֹ), but he does not know it"), but this example is less clear.

[49] See also Leviticus 25:19; 26:20; Deuteronomy 11:17; Zechariah 8:12; Psalm 85:13.

produce: יְבוּל ("produce") and פְּרִי ("fruit"). The writers of Genesis 4 instead choose the word כֹּחַ ("strength"). This noun denotes the ability to perform actions, in particular actions that require effort, and it is associated with God, youth, and military personnel.[50] While the common expression "the earth will give its produce" is ambiguous about the extent to which the ground actively engages in the production of vegetation, due to the wide lexical range of נָתַן ("to give"), the use of כֹּחַ ("strength") focuses attention on the central importance of the ground's participation in farming and food production.

Genesis 4:12 is one of two places in which כֹּחַ ("strength") appears with the word אֲדָמָה ("ground"), the other being Job 31:38–40. After a long discussion with his friends, Job turns to his farmland for confirmation of his innocence:

If my farmland (אֲדָמָה) has cried out against me, and its furrows have wept together, if I have eaten its strength (כֹּחַ) without payment, if I have made the throat of its lord breathe [its last]: instead of wheat, may thorns come forth, and instead of barley, weeds. (Job 31:38–40)

For Job, the kind of vegetation his soil produces is his final proof of his innocence. For Cain, the ground's refusal is a consequence of his guilt. In both cases, the ground assesses human conduct and responds accordingly. The ground is not a passive tool that God manipulates to judge or reward; it is a creature that participates in God's interactions with humans.

The story of Cain and Abel is so familiar, it is difficult to imagine what it would be like to read it without knowing its end. But if you do, you might discover a sense of plot development, of suspense. As discussed, the verb לקח, "to take," usually designates an act of willingly taking or receiving something. If you did not know that the ground comes to Abel's aid, this verb makes it look as if the ground works in concert with Cain when it swallows Abel's blood, as if the ground is Cain's accomplice. Consider, for example, Job 16:18 – "O Earth, do not cover my blood; may there not be a resting place for my cry" – which suggests that swallowed blood is hidden blood, is blood that does not cry out. This raises important questions at the beginning of the canon. To what extent does the ground mirror or aid human action, regardless of the nature of that action? Is other-than-human nature always obedient to God's commands? Can nonanimal nature be disobedient? I will return to these

---

[50] Christo H. J. van der Merwe, "Lexical Meaning in Biblical Hebrew and Cognitive Semantics: A Case Study," *Biblica* 87, no. 1 (2006): 91.

questions when I look at the sea in the Prophets, and at Ezekiel's oracles to hills and valleys. For now, it is enough to flag it. After all, in this particular story, the ground does not side with Cain; it swallows blood in order to reveal it, not to conceal it.

Many modern interpreters of the Cain and Abel story downplay the role of the ground in Genesis 4 because the ground's intervention has been classified as a trace of Canaanite magical beliefs and myths. An example is Westermann's treatment of the passage. Westermann writes that, in this passage, "we are ... in the realm of magic."[51] He argues that the magical element, including the active participation of the ground, is no longer operative in the text; it has been "neutralized" by its inclusion in God's speech to Cain.[52] According to Westermann, the fact that God speaks the words of judgment means that God, not the ground, punishes Cain. An earlier version of the text still shines through, one in which "[t]he earth's jaws gaped open to swallow the blood of the one murdered by his brother and denied the farmer its produce," but this version is different from the final version of the text.[53] Scholars can reconstruct the earlier version, but, in his view, what they reconstruct is a story that the writer or redactor of Genesis 4 has gone to pains to negate. This is a puzzling line of argument, since the redactor could easily have omitted all references to an active ground. If they have attempted to "neutralize" the participation of the ground, they have done a poor job. If anything, including the role of the ground in the divine speech lends authority and legitimacy to the ground's response to Cain.

Although the participation of the ground is not "neutralized" in Genesis 4, evidence from other Ancient Near Eastern texts supports Westermann's claim that Genesis 4:10–12 echoes magical practices and beliefs. One example is the parallels between Hittite and biblical blood rites, which Yitzhaq Feder explores in his book *Blood Expiation in Hittite*

---

[51] Westermann, *Genesis 1–11*, 306. See also Umberto Cassuto's argument that Genesis 4:11–12 reflects the Canaanite tradition that those who die are swallowed by Môt, the god of death, and descend into his gullet. (Umberto Cassuto, A Commentary on the Book of Genesis [Jerusalem: Magnes; Hebrew University, 1961], 220.) Note that magic is a highly contested term. For a helpful overview of the history of magic in Western scholarship and a reevaluation of the term, see Ariel Glucklich, *The End of Magic* (Oxford: Oxford University Press, 1997). Glucklich writes that "[m]agic is based on a unique type of consciousness: the awareness of the interrelatedness of all things in the world by means of simple but refined sense perception." The purpose of magic is to "[restore] the experience of relatedness in cases where that experience has been broken by disease, drought, war, or any of a number of other events" (Ibid., 12).

[52] Westermann, *Genesis 1–11*, 306.   [53] Ibid.

and Biblical Ritual: Origins, Context, and Meaning. Most pertinent to this study is Feder's discussion of the role of chthonic deities in Hittite purification rites, in particular his close reading of the text "Ritual for Purifying a House."[54] The purpose of this ritual is to remove evil from a house, be it "blood, impurity, threat, (or) perjury."[55] The priest addresses the ritual to the underworld deities, and attempts to attract the deities to the house using a blood libation. The priest hopes that, when the deities come to take the libation into the underworld, they will also take with them the impurity of house. The language of the rite shares features with the language of Genesis 4:10–12, especially in its evocations of "the Dark Earth."[56] The priest first mentions "the Dark Earth" in his plea to the chthonic deities: "Decide the case of this house! The evil blood that is inside, you take it and give it to the Deity of Blood. Let him carry it to the Dark Earth. Let him nail it down there."[57] Later in the ritual, he addresses "the Dark Earth" directly: "O Dark Earth, restrain their inclination. May it swallow down the blood, sin, impurity, perjury, evil foot, and common gossip of the house and the city."[58] In this rite, much like in

---

[54] Yitzhaq Feder, *Blood Expiation in Hittite and Biblical Ritual: Origins, Context, and Meaning*, Writings from the Ancient World Supplements 2 (Atlanta, GA: Society of Biblical Literature, 2011), 211–15. For a full text of the ritual, see Billie Jean Collins, "Purifying a House: A Ritual for the Infernal Deities (1.68)," in *The Context of Scripture: Vol. 1: Canonical Compositions from the Biblical World*, ed. William W. Hallo and K. Lawson Younger (Leiden: Brill, 2003), 168–71; or Emmanuel Laroche, *Catalogue Des Textes Hittites* (Paris: Klincksieck, 1971), 446. For a more indepth study of Hittite rituals involving 'The Dark Earth," see Billie Jean Collins, "Necromancy, Fertility and the Dark Earth: The Use of Ritual Pits in Hittite Cult," in *Magic and Ritual in the Ancient World*, ed. Paul Mirecki and Marvin Meyer (Leiden: E. J. Brill, 2002), 224–41. Collins' article is especially interesting in that it connects "the Dark Earth" with fertility rites, both human and agricultural (see Ibid., 231–32, 235). Despite her translation of *dankuiš daganzipaš* as "underworld," Collins points to the ambiguity of the term "earth" "as both cultivated/fertile soil and underworld" to explain the involvement of chthonic deities in fertility rites (Ibid., 238).

[55] Feder, *Blood Expiation in Hittite and Biblical Ritual*, 211, quoting the introduction to the ritual in the Hittite text.

[56] *dankuiš daganzipaš*. Billie Jean Collins argues that "The Dark Earth" "refers to the realm of the chronic deities" and may, therefore, be translated as simple "Underworld" (Collins, "Necromancy, Fertility and the Dark Earth," 224). As such, the term differs from the term אֲדָמָה in Genesis 4. While אֶרֶץ sometimes serves as a term for the underworld, it is less clear that אֲדָמָה carries this lexical range. Cassuto argues that אֶרֶץ and אֲדָמָה ought to be considered synonyms in the case of Genesis 4 (see Cassuto, *A Commentary on the Book of Genesis*, 219).

[57] Feder, *Blood Expiation in Hittite and Biblical Ritual*, 213.

[58] Feder, *Blood Expiation in Hittite and Biblical Ritual*, 214. Feder does not explain what "evil foot" is. A missed opportunity.

Genesis 4:10–12, the earth has a mouth and an appetite for blood. Though the genres of Genesis 4:10–12 and "Ritual for Purifying a House" are different – the first is a narrative, the second a ritual text – both depend on a nexus of ideas that associate spilled blood with the active participation of the ground in human affairs.

If Genesis 4:10–12 were the only biblical text that presented the ground along these lines, Westermann might be justified in considering it a trace that has been neutralized by the writer. It is not. Several texts describe the ground or the earth swallowing people. The earth swallows Pharaoh's army in Exodus 15:12, and, in Numbers 16:30–34, Korah, Dathan, and Aviram are swallowed together with their households.[59] The expression "a land that devours its inhabitants" appears several times,[60] and many texts attribute a mouth or throat to Sheol.[61] In contrast to the Hittite text, these instances of swallowing do not mention bloodthirsty subterranean deities, nor are they attempts to appease or barter with such gods. Instead, the earth swallows on God's command, or at least in service to God's ends.[62] The activity of the ground in Genesis 4:10–12 is not unique, but instead reflects a common biblical idea that the ground reacts to human transgression. The element of the text that has been "neutralized," as Westermann writes, is not the contribution of the ground to Cain's punishment – that is still very much present – but the idea that the earth houses a host of divine beings.

---

[59] The incident of the earth swallowing the rebels is also mentioned in Numbers 26:9–10, Deuteronomy 11:6, and Psalm 106:17.

[60] See Numbers 13:32: "a land that devours its inhabitants" (אֶרֶץ אֹכֶלֶת יוֹשְׁבֶיהָ). Similar expressions are also found in Leviticus 26:38 and Ezekiel 36:13–14.

[61] See, for example, Isaiah 5:14; Habakkuk 2:5; Psalm 141:7; and Proverbs 1:12. Sheol and the earth are related, though not identical. They are sometimes conflated, as in Numbers 16:30–33. In this text, though it is the earth which opens up and swallows Korah, Dathan, and Aviram, they are said to go down "alive to Sheol."

[62] Pseudo-Philo reads Genesis 4 and Numbers 16 together, and notes that the ground acts without command in Genesis 4. He interprets this to mean that the ground is an accomplice in the murder of Abel. He then asks why the ground has been inactive between Genesis 4 and Numbers 16, and concludes that it must be because of the curse, with which God has sealed its mouth. See Bruce N. Fisk, "Gaps in the Story, Cracks in the Earth: The Exile of Cain and the Destruction of Korah in Pseudo-Philo (Liber Antiquitatum Biblicarum)," in *Of Scribes and Sages Volume 2, Later Versions and Traditions*, ed. Craig A. Evans (London: T&T Clark International, 2004), 26–28. For a similar reading by a modern interpreter, see Cassuto, *A Commentary on the Book of Genesis*, 220–21. In contrast to Pseudo-Philo's reading, Habel calls the ground in Genesis 4:12 "the agent of Yhwh's action" (Norman C. Habel, *The Birth, the Curse and the Greening of Earth: An Ecological Reading of Genesis 1–11* [Sheffield: Sheffield Phoenix, 2011], 72).

The germane question in regard to the role of the ground in Genesis 4 is not *whether* it echoes magic, but *how* the writers has made use of such echoes. What aspects of the traditions on which the writers draw have been suppressed, and what aspects have been brought to the fore? The short answer is that the writers of Genesis 4 emphasize the ground's sensitivity to human violence and responsiveness to God and God's intentions, and they avoid references to any deities aside from YHWH. There are no chthonic gods in Genesis 4. There is just the ground. Though the text uses language similar to that of Hittite blood rituals, the writers use it to set up a situation much like that of the covenant curses found in Leviticus, Deuteronomy, and the Prophets.[63] In these texts, communal failure to uphold covenant obligations leads to a set of negative consequences, including agricultural infertility. But, whereas the covenant blessing and curses are always communal – they affect all of Israel – Genesis 4 presents the same situation as a microcosm. Rather than the people of Israel, the text focuses on one person, Cain. The disciplining agents are also reduced in number. Rather than the earth, the sky, disease, foreign armies, and so on, we have the ground only.[64] By placing this story at the beginning of the canon, the writers tie covenant blessings and curses back to the beginning of the world, anchoring them in the fabric of creation. The role of the ground in Genesis 4 is not idiosyncratic or in conflict with major strands of tradition in the Hebrew Bible; instead it articulates, by means of narrative, the common idea that the world responds to and resists human transgression.

Although Genesis 1 and 4 belong to different textual sources, it is possible to see resonances between the roles of nonanimal nature in the two texts.[65]

---

[63] See, for example, Leviticus 26:14–33; Deuteronomy 28:15–68; Jeremiah 3:3; Micah 6:13–15; Haggai 1:5–6, 10–11.

[64] For an example of a plentitude of agents, see Deuteronomy 28:21–29.

[65] Genesis 1 is usually attributed to the Priestly source (P), while Genesis 4 is attributed to the Yahwist source (J). See Westermann, *Genesis 1–11*; von Rad, *Genesis*. Traditionally the J source has been considered the older of the two (see Julius Wellhausen, *Prolegomena to the History of Israel* [Atlanta, GA: Scholars, 1994]). The J source and its dating has come under scrutiny due to a collapse of the consensus surrounding the documentary hypothesis, and some scholars now avoid using J as a source designation. For example, Martin Arneth calls the two sources P and non-P (nP) (Martin Arneth, *Durch Adams Fall Ist Ganz Verderbt...: Studien Zur Entstehung Der Alttestamentlichen Urgeschichte* [Göttingen: Vandenhoeck & Ruprecht, 2007]). See also Andreas Schüle, *Die Urgeschichte (Gen 1–11)* (Zürich: Theologischer Verlag, 2009). Arneth argues that nP was never an independent source, but that it was written to supplement the Priestly primeval history (Arneth, *Durch Adams Fall Ist Ganz Verderbt...*, 21). In other words, he both challenges the idea of J as such and reverses the chronological ordering of Genesis 1 and 4.

First, in both texts the ground takes an active role in the production of vegetation. In Genesis 1, the earth (אֶרֶץ) is assigned responsibility to make plants. In Genesis 4, the ground (אֲדָמָה) withholds plants in order to punish Cain. The noun is not the same in each case, but in both texts the earth and its soil have the ability to give or withhold vegetation. The ground uses this ability to support God's ordering of the world, as is also the case in Genesis 3, in which Adam and Eve's transgression causes the ground to produce thorns and thistles (Genesis 3:18). In Genesis 1, God tasks the earth with producing food for humans, birds, and land animals. This task is impeded in Genesis 3 and 4, when the ground aids God in disciplining human transgression. The compliance comes at a cost; in Genesis 3:17, God calls the ground cursed (אֲרוּרָה), and, in both chapters, the ground's fertility is checked. The ground participates in God's justice, even when it means sacrificing aspects of its own wellbeing.

Second, both stories deal in some fashion with boundary maintenance. The sun and the moon set the boundary between day and night in Genesis 1, and, by so doing, they maintain the order of creation. Genesis 4 includes no explicit mentions of boundaries or divisions, but there is no question that fratricide is a serious boundary violation. Cain appropriates the divine prerogative over the boundary between life and death.[66] The ground steps in to witness against and discipline an intolerable transgression of God's ordering of the world. Nonanimal nature repeatedly plays this role throughout the Pentateuch and elsewhere, as will become clear when we progress through the parts of the canon. It does not step in to adjudicate every instance of human offense, but rather becomes active in moments of heightened importance, be it unusual violence (like here), cultic rebellion, or covenantal failure. If Genesis 1 shows us the role of nonanimal nature in a harmonious world, Genesis 4 begins to flesh out its activity when that harmony breaks down.

Genesis 31:48, 52: The Witness Stone

Genesis 31 is the first text in the Hebrew Bible in which a human character summons an other-than-human character to witness an agreement.

---

[66] Genesis 4 contains no formulated rule against murder, though God warns Cain in 4:6–7 against the dangers of giving in to anger. Reading in canonical order, we first see an explicit rule against murder in Genesis 9:4–6, where it is tied to God's claim on all blood. For prohibitions on murder, see Exodus 20:13 and Deuteronomy 5:17. For prohibitions on eating blood, see Leviticus 17:10–16 and Deuteronomy 12:23–25.

The chapter forms part of the story of Jacob's stay with Laban in Aram. Jacob has just left Laban, who is now pursuing him. Once Laban catches up with Jacob, and after an incident involving household gods, camels, and "the way of women," Laban and Jacob make a covenant. Laban formalizes the covenant by naming witnesses:

> Laban said: This heap is a witness between me and between you today. Therefore its name is *Gal-Ed* [witness heap] ... A witness is this heap and a witness the pillar, that I do not cross to you beyond this pillar and that you will not cross to me beyond this heap and this pillar for evil. (Genesis 31:48, 52)

The witnesses to their agreement are a stone heap and a pillar, and, as such, the text resembles passages in Deuteronomy and Joshua. In Deuteronomy, Moses calls on the heavens and the earth to witness the covenant between Israel and YHWH (Deuteronomy 4:26; 30:19; 31:28), and in the Book of Joshua, a stone pillar serves the same purposes, witnessing to the people's commitment to "the God of Israel" (Joshua 24:23–27). The Deuteronomic texts have received more scholarly attention than the passages from Genesis and Joshua, the latter sometimes being understood as precursors to the former.[67] Regardless of the relative age of each text, the passages evince a conviction that nonanimal nature, be it stones or the heavens and the earth, can observe human oaths and respond when such oaths are broken. Joshua, for example, specifies that the stone pillar is a fitting witness because "it has heard all the words that YHWH has spoken to us" (Joshua 24:27). I will deal with this motif in more detail in the section on Deuteronomy. Here I will only point out that the notion that elements of nonanimal nature can observe covenants and agreements resonate with and expand on the role of the ground in Genesis 4. Nonanimal nature not only reacts to disruptions of the order of creation established in Genesis 1, but can also witness the terms of more specific agreements, be they between human parties or between Israel and YHWH.

Genesis 47:13–26: Should We Die ... Us and Our Land?

The writers of the Hebrew Bible sometimes speak about human and other-than-human characters using the same words, a practice that serves to indicate their mutual dependence. One example is found at the end of Genesis, in the story of how Joseph comes to buy the people and land of

---

[67] See Richard M. Davidson, "The Divine Covenant Lawsuit Motif in Canonical Perspective," *Journal of the Adventist Theological Society* 21, no. 1–2 (January 1, 2010): 55–56.

Egypt for Pharaoh (Genesis 47:13–26). During a famine, the Egyptians make increasingly desperate exchanges with Joseph: first they exchange their silver for seed, then their livestock, and finally themselves and their farmland. In this narrative, humans and farmland suffer together, and their suffering is described using identical language:

> Why should we die before your eyes, both us and our land? Buy us and our land in exchange for bread and we will be, us and our land, slaves for Pharaoh. But give seed, that we may live and not die, and our land not become desolate.
> (Genesis 47:19)

The Egyptians use the same verbs to refer to themselves (אֲנַחְנוּ) and their farmland (אֲדָמָה). They even specify that the plural verbs and verbal phrases they use, such as "die" (נָמוּת) and "be slaves" (נִהְיֶה עֲבָדִים), refer not only to people, but to "us and our land" (אֲנַחְנוּ וְאַדְמָתֵנוּ). Only in the last line do they make a demarcation: they describe their own plight as death, and that of their land as desolation. The Egyptians do not differentiate between themselves as persons and the land as a commodity. Both are described in personal terms; they understand the fate of the one as analogous to and interdependent with that of the other.

Few commentators speak about the wording of Genesis 47:19. An exception is Victor P. Hamilton, whose textual notes on the passage include a brief remark on Genesis 47:19:

> The expression 'why should we die ... we and our land' is strange. This expression is called a zeugma, i.e. the use of a verb ("die") to govern two words, with only one of which ("we") it makes sense.[68]

Hamilton's conclusion that the verb "to die" only makes sense in relation to "we," and not "our land," depends on his understanding of land. To die one must be alive. The assumption underlying Hamilton's comment is that the land does not live, and therefore cannot die. And yet it cannot be taken for granted that ancient Israelites would have shared this assumption about land, nor that they would have attributed such an assumption to Egyptians. In fact, the Egyptians go out of their way to specify that the verbs do not refer to humans only.

It is important to stress that the context for this passage is not primarily Egyptian understandings of land, but Israelite ones. Jürgen Ebach argues that attempts to match the story with a period in Egypt's history are

---

[68] Victor P. Hamilton, *The Book of Genesis: Chapters 18–50* (Grand Rapids, MI: William B. Eerdmans, 1995), 615, n. 18.

misguided. Instead, he says, the purpose of the passage is to act as a mirror for Israel. It explores and reflects ambivalence about the monarchy, especially royal appropriations of land and labor.[69] He compares Genesis 47:13–26 to Samuel's description of royal prerogatives in 1 Samuel 8:11–18:

> [H]e will take your sons ... your daughters ... your best fields, vineyards, and olive groves ... a tenth of your seed and your vineyards ... your slaves, male and female ... your donkeys ... [and] a tenth of your flocks, and you will be his slaves.

The words of the Egyptians connect this passage with a major concern in the Hebrew Bible: how are people and land related, and how should that relationship govern land distribution? We have had several hints leading up to Genesis 47:19 that land is not simply a tradable commodity. When Joseph proposes to Pharaoh that he ought to collect grain as insurance against the famine, his stated purpose is that "the land (הָאָרֶץ) not be cut off by famine" (Genesis 41:36). Later, when Joseph's brothers arrive in Egypt, he accuses them of having come to see "the nakedness of the land (עֶרְוַת הָאָרֶץ)" (Genesis 42:9).[70] The noun used for "land" in these verses is different than the noun in 47:19, and in both cases it is possible that it is used as a metonym. Perhaps Joseph is simply describing the people of Egypt using אֶרֶץ, "the land," as a collective term. This is unsatisfying. The land (אֶרֶץ) is here a collective term that refers *both* to the Egyptian people *and* to their land. Famine threatens both in more or less the same way. Human suffering and the suffering of nonanimal nature are not incommensurable, but instead resemble each other and intertwine.

The use of identical verbs to describe humans and land is not, as Hamilton says, a kind of mistake, a malapropic use of the noun אֲדָמָה ("ground"). It is a signal that Joseph and the Egyptians are now bartering

---

[69] Jürgen Ebach, *Genesis 37–50* (Freiburg: Herder, 2007), 496–97, 501–4. Janzen, like Ebach, compares Genesis 47:13–26 with Israelite land practices, but instead of following Ebach by focusing on 1 Samuel 8 and Leviticus, Janzen cites the story of Naboth's vineyard in 1 Kings 21 (J. Gerald Janzen, *Abraham and All the Families of the Earth: A Commentary on the Book of Genesis 12–50* (Grand Rapids, MI: William B. Eerdmans; Handsel, 1993), 180–81).

[70] The expressions "be cut off (תִּכָּרֵת) by famine" and "the nakedness of the land (עֶרְוַת הָאָרֶץ)" are borrowed from vocabulary usually associated with human bodies. For the former expression, see, for example, Genesis 17:14; Leviticus 18:29; and Ezekiel 14:13, 21. The two Ezekiel passages include references to famine. For the latter, see Genesis 9:22; and Exodus 28:42.

for that which ought not to be commodified, namely "life and land."[71] Whereas land is private property *par excellence* in modern Western society, the Hebrew Bible places similar restrictions on the sale of land as on the sale of people. Leviticus 25 imagines situations in which extreme financial hardship entail the need to sell one's land and oneself, using the same language for each: "If your relative falls into poverty, and sells his holding ... if your relative who is with you grows poor and sells himself to you ..." (Leviticus 25:25, 39).[72] The sale of land is almost unheard of in the Hebrew Bible, and no Israelite would voluntarily sell ancestral holdings.[73] Neither land nor people can be owned in perpetuity, but must be returned in the year of Jubilee. The explanation for this rule is the same in each case: the land and the people belong to God. In Leviticus 25:23, God states that "the land is mine," and in 25:42, God calls the people "my slaves." The surprise in Genesis 47:19 is not that the same verbs can apply to both people and land, but that all the people and all the land sell themselves as slaves to Pharaoh.

Genesis 47:19 speaks about the affinity between humans and land and their common suffering. Without the land, the people will starve, and without the people, the land will go unsown. The situation recalls Genesis 2:5, in which God's motivation for creating humans is that "there was no human to work the ground." The people equate their own death with the death of their land, and their enslavement is also the enslavement of their land. In this passage, nonanimal nature does not intervene in human affairs, but instead

---

[71] "[D]as Leben und das Land," Ebach, *Genesis 37–50*, 500. Since I am using "life" as a category that covers human, animal, and nonanimal nature, I would have phrased this differently. That said, Ebach's basic insight, that the sale of persons and land are both inherently problematic, and at some level unacceptable, still holds.

[72] It should be noted that Leviticus 25 does not speak about land in general or people in general, but of the land of Israel and people of Israel. Land outside of Israel is not mentioned at all, whereas the text specifies that non-Israelites can be "held as property" and passed as inheritance to children (Leviticus 25:45–46). 'Property' translates the noun is אֲחֻזָּה, the same word used elsewhere in Leviticus 25 to denote inalienable family land (see Leviticus 25:13, 24, 25).

[73] Leviticus 27:20 speaks somewhat cryptically of selling land in the context of consecrating lands to YHWH, but otherwise the verbs מָכַר (to sell) and קָנָה (to buy) are not used to describe financial transactions involving farmland (whether the noun is אֶרֶץ, "earth," or אֲדָמָה, "land"), except to forbid it (see Leviticus 25:23, 34). Fields (שָׂדֶה) are sometimes sold, though these transactions take place within the kinsman redeemer system (see Ruth 4:3 and Jeremiah 32:7–9, 15, 25, 43–44). Two exceptions are Abraham's purchase of the field near Mamre and Jacob's purchase of a plot of land by the city of Shechem, but, since these are not purchased from Israelites, they are also anomalous (See Genesis 23:1–20; 25:10; 33:19; 49:30; 50:13; Jacob's plot is also mentioned in Joshua 24:32).

suffers alongside humans. Genesis 47:13–26 is not only about the survival of people through famine, but about the survival of people *and their land*.

EXODUS

Exodus 15:12: Earth Swallowed ...

The Book of Exodus focuses on God's activity in delivering Israel from Egypt, to the exclusion of other actors (Moses helps, of course). Though the plagues certainly involve both animal and nonanimal nature, they do not initiate or shape their activities; they are tools in the hands of YHWH.[74] In every case, YHWH instructs Moses and Aaron, they perform the actions, and some disaster comes to pass. In these texts aspects of nature appear as God's weapons, rather than as God's collaborators. The disasters are not described as the activity of nonanimal nature itself.

The one exception to this pattern is in the Song of the Sea: "You stretched out your right hand, Earth (אֶרֶץ) swallowed them" (Exodus 15:12). That the text highlights the activity of earth at this particular point is unexpected; the Song, more so than the rest of Exodus, "celebrates God's direct, unmediated, personal incursion into the world of humankind."[75] As Nahum Sarna points out, the Song has no interest in the intermediaries between God and Israel: Moses is not mentioned, neither are angels, the cloud, or the darkness.[76] Aside from this one line, the emphasis falls entirely on God as Israel's deliverer.[77] So how have scholars explained the activity of the earth in this verse?

The first explanation should be familiar: Exodus 15 reflects mythological elements borrowed from Israel's neighbors, in this case the Baal cycle.[78] The first person to make this argument was Frank Moore Cross, who argues that the Song of the Sea reflects a period in Israel's history when their religion "stood in clear line of continuity with

---

[74] For a discussion of the role of nonanimal nature in the plagues, see Terence E. Fretheim, "The Plagues as Ecological Signs of Historical Disaster," *Journal of Biblical Literature* 110, no. 3 (1991): 385–96.

[75] Nahum M. Sarna, *Exodus = [Shemot]: The Traditional Hebrew Text with the New JPS Translation* (Philadelphia, PA: Jewish Publication Society, 1991), 75.

[76] Ibid.

[77] See also Brevard S. Childs, *The Book of Exodus; a Critical, Theological Commentary* (Philadelphia, PA: Westminster, 1974), 249.

[78] For an overview of the similarities between the Song of the Sea and the Baal cycle, see Brian D. Russell, *The Song of the Sea: The Date of Composition and Influence of Exodus 15:1–21* (New York: Peter Lang, 2007), 39.

the mythopoeic patterns of West Semitic, especially Canaanite myth."[79] He contrasts this with later texts that memorialize historical events and focus on Israel as "a historical community."[80] Cross does not take this to mean that the text describes ideas outmoded when the text was written, only that such ideas later held a less central place in Israelite religion and religious institutions. He also emphasizes a significant difference between the Baal cycle and the Song of the Sea. In the Baal cycle, Baal battles against Yamm, the god representing the watery chaos; in Exodus 15, "the sea is not personified or hostile ... There is no question here of a mythological combat between two gods."[81] While Yamm is Baal's opponent, the sea is God's ally.

Cross does not discuss the role of the earth in 15:12, but his argument suggests a possible explanation for the verse. Perhaps the writer chooses to describe the earth as active in Exodus 15:12, in order to contrast it with the recalcitrant sea in the Baal cycle. It serves as a reminder that the earth is not an enemy for God to defeat, but instead a creature obedient to YHWH's command.[82] The role of enemy is reserved for the Pharaoh and his army. Cross's argument does not, in other words, rule out reading the earth as an active being in Exodus 15.

The second common explanation is that this is simply a figure of speech. Earth, ארץ, it is argued, is a synonym for "the underworld," and the verse ought to be read as a flowery way of saying "they met their death."[83] This explanation fails to take into account the fact that the earth swallows people several times in the Hebrew Bible. The motif appears not only in short sayings such as we have here, but also in longer narratives in which the ground's ability to swallow people is

---

[79] Frank Moore Cross, "Song of the Sea and Canaanite Myth," in *Canaanite Myth and Hebrew Epic: Essays in the History of the Religion of Israel* (Cambridge, MA: Harvard University Press, 1973), 143. The Song of the Sea is usually considered to be one of the oldest pieces of writing in the Hebrew Bible. See, for example, Mark S. Smith, "Warfare Song as Warrior Ritual," in *Warfare, Ritual, and Symbol in Biblical and Modern Contexts* (Atlanta, GA: Society of Biblical Literature, 2014), 165–66.
[80] Cross, "Song of the Sea and Canaanite Myth," 143.   [81] Ibid., 131–32.
[82] Cross describes Yamm and Môt as together representing the chaotic elements of the cosmos: "If Yamm represented the unruly powers of the universe who threatened chaos, until restricted and tamed by Baʻal, then Môt, ʼĒl's dead son, represents the dark chthonic powers which bring sterility, disease, and death" (Ibid., 116). Though Cross does not mention it, Exodus 15:12 might relate to Baal's battle against Môt, the god of the underworld (see Ibid., 116–18, for a description of the battle).
[83] Sarna, *Exodus* = *[Shemot]*, 80. See also Childs, *The Book of Exodus: a Critical, Theological Commentary*, 243; and Helmut Utzschneider and Wolfgang Oswald, *Exodus*, trans. Philip Sumpter (Stuttgart: Verlag W. Kohlhammer, 2015), 324.

central to the narrative.⁸⁴ The fact that the "figure of speech" explanation cannot account for longer narratives weakens the explanation's commonsense appeal; if the logic of other narratives depends on an active earth, there is no reason to dismiss out of hand that the same is true in Exodus 15:12.

Though I am persuaded that the Song of the Sea borrows from a similar cultural background as the Baal cycle, for my purposes it makes more sense to read the Song of the Sea against the background of the ground's activity in Genesis 4. There the ground disciplines an individual for a specific transgression. Here the earth swallows the people who seek to hinder God's deliverance of Israel. Commentators note that the Song of the Sea moves from speaking about God's deliverance of Israel at the Sea of Reeds to describing Israel's entry into the promised land. Exodus 15:12 sits at the center of this structure; as Nahum Sarna notes, "the use of *eretz* in verse 12 smooths the transition" between the two parts of the poem.⁸⁵ But the word אֶרֶץ, "Earth," does more than contribute to the poem's stylistic structure; at the tipping point of the poem, the moment at which Israel transforms from a group escaping Egypt into a community journeying towards their new home, the writer points to the sympathetic involvement of the nonanimal world. God is the main actor in the poem, but, in contrast to Baal, God's actions take place within an obedient and compliant world. Much like the ground participates in God's judgment of Cain, so here the earth aids in God's defeat of Pharaoh's army.

LEVITICUS

Scholarship on Leviticus stands out among writing on the books of Torah as the one instance in which the life of nonanimal nature has been written about in some detail. In his article "Transgressing, Puking, Covenanting: The Character of Land in Leviticus," Jonathan Morgan argues that "these later chapters of Leviticus [18–27] reflect a genuine, strange and yet profound recognition that the land is not an inanimate object, but rather is ... 'a semi-autonomous moral agent.'"⁸⁶ Morgan identifies ten instances of "the land performing various actions" – Leviticus 18:25, 28;

---

⁸⁴ The most prominent example is Numbers 16. See also Genesis 4.
⁸⁵ Sarna, *Exodus = [Shemot]*, 80.
⁸⁶ Jonathan Morgan, "Transgressing, Puking, Covenanting: The Character of Land in Leviticus," *Theology* 112, no. 867 (May 1, 2009): 177. Morgan is quoting Davis, *Scripture, Culture, and Agriculture*, 100. See also Morgan, "Land, Rest & Sacrifice," 78.

19:29; 20:22; 25:2, 4, 5; and 26:34, 38, 43 – and differentiates his own approach to these texts from the more common one:

[F]or many commentators [the land] stands primarily as the stage on which the drama of the people's covenant relationship with YHWH is played out ... According to this approach, the land is the location of the experiment of constructing a community which, in every aspect of its life, pays tribute to the holiness of God who dwells in its midst, and, thereby, which stands itself as holy and distinct – a community bearing testimony to the creative work of YHWH.[87]

The emphasis in this approach is squarely on people and YHWH. The land matters as far as it is the context for the relationship, but it is background rather than participant in Israel's covenant with YHWH. Significantly, aside from the occasional scholar like Jonathan Morgan, the trend is to resist implications in the text that the land is a responsive creature, one that is able to maintain relationships with people and with YHWH. An example is Jacob Milgrom's excellent Anchor Bible Commentary on Leviticus. Milgrom recognizes that, on its surface, Leviticus 18:25 says that the land will spew out its inhabitants. Yet he qualifies this interpretation in a number of ways. When speaking of the land as a punishing agent, he repeatedly uses the word "automatic," suggesting that the land does not choose to vomit out its inhabitants, but that instead this response is built into the land's makeup in a mechanistic way.[88] Supporting the claim that Milgrom reads the land's involvement as automatic are his comparisons of the land with a barometer and the painting in Dorian Gray.[89] He also contrasts what he calls "realistic" portrayals of the land with "anthropomorphic" portrayals.[90] "Realistic" portrayals, such as those found in Leviticus 26 and Numbers 33, attribute the exile to "human agency."[91] Milgrom speculates that the "unabashed anthropomorphic imagery" of Leviticus 18 and 20 suggests that these texts are particularly old.[92] Instead of allowing for the possibility that the text describes the land as an active being, Milgrom instead attributes its actions

---

[87] Morgan, "Transgressing, Puking, Covenanting," 177, 175–76.
[88] See Milgrom, *Leviticus*, 1572, 1577. To be fair, Milgrom once uses the word "automatic" to refer to God's action, but then softens it by saying that "it is as though [God] had no choice" (Ibid., 1580).
[89] Milgrom, *Leviticus*, 1777, 1580. See also Jeanne Kay, "Human Dominion over Nature in the Hebrew Bible," *Annals of the Association of American Geographers* 79, no. 2 (June 1989): 217. Christopher Wright describes the land as a "covenantal thermometer" (Christopher J. H. Wright, *Old Testament Ethics for the People of God* [Leicester, UK: Inter-Varsity, 2004], 77, 96).
[90] Milgrom, *Leviticus*, 1577.   [91] Ibid.   [92] Ibid.

to either God or humans. It is not *really* the land that vomits out its inhabitants; the text "picturesquely describes the result of YHWH's decision, not that of the land."[93] He explains that the emphasis on the land's obligation to keep the sabbatical year serves to ensure that the sabbath laws will apply to everyone, Israelite and resident alien alike, and also that it is a way to manage human anxiety about the duration of the exile.[94] In other words, verses like Leviticus 26:43a, "and the land will be forsaken by them, that it may enjoy its sabbaths ..." do not speak about a need of the land, but instead provide an explanation to anxious exiles who do not understand why God has failed to return them to their land.

The reason for the divergence between the readings of Milgrom and Morgan cannot be attributed to a lack of care on Milgrom's part in observing the details of the text. Most of the exegetical observations that undergird Morgan's argument are found in Milgrom's commentary, and several of Morgan's arguments build on lines of interpretation found in Milgrom's work.[95] Milgrom simply does not consider the possibility that the land is "a separate character," with "a distinct relationship with God."[96] Milgrom's discussion of the fact that the land is never explicitly called holy in Leviticus may provide an explanation for his reluctance. He writes that the author of the Holiness Code avoids calling the land holy, because it would imply that "holiness inheres in the land – indeed, in nature."[97] This, according to Milgrom, cuts too close to the beliefs of Israel's neighbors: "It would not be a far remove from the theology of the pagan world, which hypostatized nature as representing, even embodying, various deities, who were members of the divine assembly, or independent and even malevolent forces."[98]

I would argue that Milgrom here merges two distinct "apprehensions": the ancient Israelite reluctance to speak of divinities aside from YHWH and the concern of modern biblical scholars to distinguish between ancient Israelite religion and so-called nature religions.[99] But the fact that the

---

[93] Ibid., 2321.   [94] Ibid., 2152, 2336.
[95] For example, Morgan's argument that YHWH's relationship with the land predates YHWH's relationship with the people depends on Milgrom's observation that the land belongs to God long before the Israelites enter it (Morgan, "Land, Rest & Sacrifice," 73).
[96] Ibid., 31.   [97] Milgrom, *Leviticus*, 2185.   [98] Ibid.
[99] The idea of "nature religions" is based on Hegelian philosophy and early anthropology. Hegel suggested that religion develops in three stages: the religion of nature, the religion of spiritual individuality, and absolute religion (Hegel, *Lectures on the Philosophy of Religion*, 237). The father of modern anthropology, Edward Burnett Tylor, proposes similar stages, but replaces absolute religion with positive science (Tylor, *Religion in Primitive Culture*, 441–44). The idea of "nature religions" was then picked up by biblical

land is not a separate divinity in Leviticus cannot be taken as evidence for its inertness. Personalistic nature texts suggest that ancient Israelites were as likely as their neighbors to think about nonanimal nature as alive and active. The writers of the Bible do not appear to have felt any pressing need to distinguish between their religious thought and that of their neighbors along these lines. Though modern biblical scholars often assume such a distinction, arguments to support it tend to be circular – because the writers of the Hebrew Bible must have wanted to differentiate their own religion from Canaanite traditions, texts in which the land relates directly with God or intervenes in human affairs cannot be taken at face value. This is to prioritize a modern assumption about what ancient Israelite religion *must* have been like, rather than to attend to evidence in the text.[100]

Leviticus 18:24–28: The Earth Vomited ...

The activity of the land in Leviticus follows a rough temporal schema.[101] The writer first looks to the past, when other people inhabited the land. He or she then turns to the soon-to-be present, to Israel's life in the land. Third, the writer considers the far away future, that is, Israel's exile. Finally, set within considerations of exile lies the hope of a return to the land.

Leviticus 18 describes the expulsion of the Canaanites as an act of the land, and frames it as a warning to Israel:

Do not make yourself unclean by means of all these things, for by these the peoples became unclean, whom I am sending out before you. The earth was unclean and I visited its iniquity upon it and the earth vomited out its inhabitants. But you are to keep my ordinances and my judgments and not do any of these abominations ... so that the land does not vomit you out when you make it unclean just as it vomited out the people who were before you.
(Leviticus 18:24–28)

---

scholars, who contrast the Bible's focus on history with the attention to nature in other Near Eastern religions. Numerous examples exist, but representative are G. Ernest Wright, *The Old Testament Against Its Environment* (London: SCM, 1950), 22; and Gerhard von Rad, *Old Testament Theology*, vol. 2 (New York: Harper, 1962), 104.

[100] James Barr writes: "The picture of the ancient religions, against which the Hebrew contribution has been set, seems to depend excessively on purely theological and philosophical analysis of what it *must* have been like, too little on expert historical analysis of what is *was* like" (James Barr, "Man and Nature: The Ecological Controversy and the Old Testament," in *Ecology and Religion in History* [New York: Harper and Row, 1974], 71).

[101] Jonathan Morgan points to the importance of the land's past, as it is seen in Leviticus 18:24–28, for establishing what he calls 'a temporal dimension' for the life of the land. See Morgan, "Land, Rest & Sacrifice," 78.

In these verses, the land's responsibility to avoid becoming unclean predates Israelite presence in the land. The land is judged for the iniquities of its inhabitants, which the text describes simply as "its [the land's] iniquities," and it responds by vomiting them out. The description of God's chastisement of the earth is unique. It is unusual for אֶרֶץ, "earth," to be the object (direct or indirect) of the verb פָּקַד, "to visit"; the only other example is Psalm 65:10 [9]: "You visit the earth and water it." Whereas Psalm 65 describes God as a benevolent farmer, whose visitation produces agricultural bounty, Leviticus outlines what happens to the land if it becomes a place unfit for God's presence. God's visitation, in this case, serves to restore its cultic purity. That the land was required to maintain cleanness prior to the entrance of Israel shows that YHWH's relationship with the land predates the exodus from Egypt and the conquest of Canaan. This land always belonged to YHWH, and the land and its inhabitants were always responsible to live in a way compatible with YHWH's presence.[102]

Second, this passage demonstrates that the status of the land depends on the behavior of its inhabitants. The land needs its residents to act in certain ways in order to remain clean. If the people act in ways contrary to purity, God will account their actions *both* to the people and to the land, and *both* will be disciplined. As Morgan writes, in this text and others like it, "we encounter ... the notion that one of the implications of [the] polluting effect of sin is that it infringes upon and disrupts the relationship between YHWH and the land."[103] The people who live in the land, be they Israelite or not, have a responsibility to live in such a way that the land can maintain its relationship with God. If they do not, the land will vomit them out.

Leviticus 19:29: That the Land Not Prostitute Itself ...

Once Leviticus moves to the future, to Israel's future occupancy in the land, its texts instruct Israel in how to aid and not hinder the land's relationship with YHWH. The rationale given for the injunction against prostituting one's daughter is that to do so would also prostitute the land: "Do not defile your daughter by prostituting her so that the land (הָאָרֶץ) does not prostitute itself and the land (הָאָרֶץ) become full of

---

[102] See Milgrom, *Leviticus*, 2186.   [103] Morgan, "Land, Rest & Sacrifice," 81.

adultery" (Leviticus 19:29). Milgrom states that the land (הָאָרֶץ) here is a metonym for "the people of the land," but the only evidence he offers is that the land (הָאָרֶץ) is elsewhere used as a metonym.[104] Undermining his own argument, he points out that, perhaps, the verse might reflect the theology that "the promised land is polluted by Israel's sin." He references Jeremiah 3:2 ("You have polluted the land with your prostitution"), in which, he argues, the land refers to the physical landscape itself, not the people living in the land. He further writes that the "explanation that land is a metaphor for people" is an "admittedly weak explanation."[105] For all this he does not consider the possibility that the prostitution of Israelite daughters might force the land into a similar kind of prostitution. Ellen Davis writes that Leviticus 19 is "a highly condensed exemplar of analogical thinking."[106] The author does not explain commandments by giving rationales, but instead by giving more commandments, "a string of concrete examples ... showing what holiness looks like on the ground."[107] Leviticus 19:29 is preceded by an injunction against certain religious practices ("You are not to make cuts in your flesh on behalf of a person..." [Leviticus 19:28a]), and followed by a command to observe others ("You are to keep my sabbaths..." [Leviticus 19:30a]). Based on this string of religious legislation, it is likely that the prostitution of the land relates to the land's cultic responsibilities. The fact that prostitution is associated with idolatry throughout the Bible supports this conclusion.[108] A prostituted land is a land that is no longer fit for YHWH's presence. The idea that human behavior affects the standing of the land before YHWH is a common theme in Leviticus, and this text is simply a variation on the warnings given in Leviticus 18:24–28 and 20:22: "You are to keep all my ordinances and all my judgments and do them, in order that the land, into which I am bringing you that you may dwell in it, not vomit you out" (Leviticus 20:22). The rationale behind the prohibition on prostitution and the admonition to keep YHWH's laws is the same: the laws and ordinances given to Israel not only mediate and safeguard their own relationship with YHWH, but also that of the land.

---

[104] Milgrom, *Leviticus*, 1967–68.   [105] Ibid., 1967, 1968.
[106] Davis, *Scripture, Culture, and Agriculture*, 85.   [107] Ibid.
[108] See, for example, Exodus 34:15–16; Leviticus 17:7; 20:5–6; Numbers 15:39; Deuteronomy 31:16; Judges 2:17; and Jeremiah 3:6, 8.

Leviticus 25 and 26: The Land is to Rest ...

At the heart of YHWH's relationship with the land is the sabbath. In Leviticus 25 and 26, Israel is repeatedly informed that the reason they must keep the sabbath year and the year of Jubilee is so that the land may observe *its* sabbath:[109] "When you enter the land which I am giving you, the land is to rest – a sabbath to YHWH" (Leviticus 25:2). The instructions that follow focus on human actions ("you are not to sow"; "you are not to prune"; "you are not to harvest"; "you are not to gather" [Leviticus 25:4–5]), but the purpose for these actions is entirely focused on the land: "in the seventh year, there will be a complete sabbath for the land ... a complete sabbath it will be for the land" (Leviticus 25:4, 5). Though other sabbath laws focus on humans and animals resting, here the rationale for the cessation of labor is that the people must not disrupt the land's ability to observe sabbath.[110]

This attention to the land's sabbath is what occasions the turn to the far future, to Israel's eventual exile. If the people refuse the land its sabbaths, the people will go into the exile so that the land can rest in their absence:

Then the land will enjoy its sabbaths, all the days it lies desolate and you are in the land of your enemies. Then the land will pay off its sabbaths. All the days it lies desolate it will rest, [the rest] it did not rest during your sabbaths when you rested[111] upon it. (Leviticus 26:34–35)[112]

In this text, the exile is not first and foremost a judgment on the people, though it is that too (see Leviticus 26:16–20), but a purging necessitated by the land's obligation to keep sabbath. Exploiting the similarity

---

[109] See Morgan, "Land, Rest & Sacrifice," 76.
[110] For an example of a sabbath law focused on humans and animals, see Exodus 20:10. Emphasis in the original.
[111] I have translated יְשָׁב here as "rested" (usual glosses include "to sit," or "to dwell"), in order to reproduce in English the wordplay between the root שבת ("to rest") and בְּשָׁבְתְּכֶם ("when you dwelt"), the infinitive construct of יָשַׁב.
[112] Milgrom reads Leviticus 26:33b–35 as an interpolation, the purpose of which is to indicate a new theme (Milgrom, *Leviticus*, 2322). His reasoning is that, having turned to the exile of Israel, "there is no reason to mention again the condition of its land" (Ibid.). This reasoning only holds if we assume that the people are the primary focus of the passage. If the land is an equally important focus, the vacillation between the experience of the land and the experience of the people makes sense. Milgrom also speculates that verses 43–44 may be "a parenthetical remark ... written in exile, together with 33b–35, as a consolation for the delay of redemption" (Ibid., 2336). It is hard to escape the sense that Milgrom feels uncomfortable with the text's emphasis on the *land's* rest, as opposed to anything having to do directly with the people.

between the root שׁבת ("to rest") and the word שֶׁבֶת ("to sit, dwell,"), the infinitive construct of the verb יָשׁב, the writer contrasts the land's inability to rest while the people "rested" on the land with the future rest the land will have when the people are in exile. The exile is not a means to prompt the people to repentance, but is instead the condition necessary to restore the land to covenant observance. The final consequence for the people, after they have experienced famine, war, and illness, is that they will live in a different sort of land; no longer will they live in a land that observes YHWH's injunctions, but instead they will be banished to the land of their enemies, which "will devour [them]" (Leviticus 26:38).

Leviticus 26:42–43a: I Will Remember the Land ...

A glimmer of hope interrupts the grim predictions of Leviticus 26. Once the land has observed its sabbaths, YHWH will again remember the covenant with the people and with the land:

> And I will remember my covenant with Jacob, and also my covenant with Isaac, and also my covenant with Abraham, I will remember. And the land I will remember. And the land will be forsaken by them that it may enjoy its sabbaths when it is desolate without them ... (Leviticus 26:42–43a)

This verse, like the description of the land's past in Leviticus 18, highlights the temporal priority of God's relationship with the land. Ellen Davis writes:

> The inverted order in which the ancestors are listed – Jacob, Isaac, and Abraham – points to the preeminence of the land, which takes its rightful place in covenantal history, even at the head of the line of ancestors. Before Abraham was, the land is.[113]

The people's hope is here intertwined with hope for the land. Because God remembers the land, God will also remember the people. This verse is, in a sense, the inverse of the Egyptian farmers' insistence in Genesis

---

[113] Ellen Davis, "The Pain of Seeing Clearly: Prophetic Views of the Created Order," in *Biblical Prophecy: Perspectives for Contemporary Ministry*, Interpretation: Resources for the Use of Scripture in the Church (Louisville, KY: Westminster John Knox, 2014), 85. Davis's reading contrasts with that of Milgrom, who argues that the phrase "I will remember the land" simply means that God will remember the covenant with the patriarchs, the "essence" of which "is the promised land" (Milgrom, *Leviticus*, 2335). Morgan points to Leviticus 25:23 ("The land is mine") as evidence that "the relationship between the land and YHWH exists independently of, and ... prior to, the one between YHWH and the people" (Morgan, "Transgressing, Puking, Covenanting," 178).

47:19 that their death is also the death of their land: the hope of the land is the hope of the people. And yet this hope lies at the other end of exile; only after the land has "been forsaken" and "[enjoyed] its sabbaths" will YHWH turn and remember. The requirement that the land observe its sabbaths in full cannot be circumvented or rushed.

The description of the life of nonanimal nature in Leviticus resonates with two themes we have seen in other Torah texts. First, the writers of Leviticus attribute activities to the land that have, in the words of Morgan, "strong cultic overtones."[114] Recall that, in Genesis 1, the sun and the moon receive the task of distinguishing (הַבְדִּיל) between the day and the night, the same verb which in Leviticus refers to the responsibility of Israel to distinguish between the clean and the unclean, the common and the holy.[115] The cultic behavior of the land in Leviticus is not described as an act of distinction, but instead focuses on the land's obligation to keep sabbath and remain clean. These obligations, also reminiscent of Israel's cultic responsibilities, are more important than any other responsibilities of the land, including its support of the continuation of Israel's life on the land.

These texts from Leviticus also resonate with stories in which the land swallows people.[116] If the vomiting texts in Leviticus are read together with these earlier texts, they suggest that Israel must maintain a fine balance if they are to live on the land. Transgressions may lead either to being consumed by the land or being expelled by it. Maintaining their relationship with the land is an important feature of the way of life enjoined on Israel throughout the books of the Pentateuch. The land is by no means a mechanistic measure of the people's faithfulness, but instead a creature sensitive to its own obligations to YHWH and to the behavior of the people who dwell upon it.

NUMBERS

Numbers 13:32: A Land That Devours Its Inhabitants

The first reference to the life of nonanimal nature in Numbers is a brief one. The verse in question is Numbers 13:32, part of the report of the scouts who have surveyed the land of Canaan:

---

[114] Morgan, "Land, Rest & Sacrifice," 79.   [115] See Leviticus 10:10; 11:47; 20:25.
[116] See Genesis 4:10–12 and Exodus 15:12. In the Genesis text, of course, the land only swallows Abel's blood, not his whole body.

They brought a report of the land which they had surveyed to the children of Israel, saying: The land which we crossed into in order to survey it – it is a land that devours its inhabitants, and all the people we saw in it were men of great size!

(Numbers 13:32)

"A land that devours its inhabitants (אֶרֶץ אֹכֶלֶת יוֹשְׁבֶיהָ) . . ." Commentators fall into two camps when they attempt to explain this expression. On the one hand, some call it at idiom, and seek to determine its precise meaning. For example, Jacob Milgrom rejects arguments that the expression refers to agricultural infertility or disease, and instead concludes that "this idiom can only mean that the nature of the land is such that it will perpetually keep its inhabitants at war."[117] In other words, Milgrom's strategy is to rationalize the metaphor. George W. Coats follows the same course and interprets the phrase to mean that the inhabitants of the land are "geared for war."[118] On the other hand, some scholars, like Dennis Olson and William Brown, argue that the Israelite scouts "mythologize the land," and that they do so illicitly.[119] They mistake a "land flowing with milk and honey" for a devouring beast.[120]

These lines of interpretations include important insights, but also blindspots. Milgrom helpfully focuses on material concerns: what practical considerations lie behind the spies' report? While I do not think the text offers any evidence that can help scholars determine whether the problem is infertility, disease, or war, I do think Milgrom is right to locate the anxiety of the scouts in real life dangers.[121] Where his interpretation

---

[117] Jacob Milgrom, *Numbers = [Ba-Midbar]: The Traditional Hebrew Text with the New JPS Translation* (Philadelphia, PA: Jewish Publication Society, 1990), 106–7. Martin Noth makes a similar suggestion. He writes that "the statement ... probably means that it is full of warlike dissensions" (Martin Noth, *Numbers: A Commentary*, Old Testament Library [Philadelphia, PA: Westminster, 1968], 107). See also Norbert Lohfink, "The Strata of the Pentateuch and the Question of War," in *Theology of the Pentateuch: Themes of the Priestly Narrative and Deuteronomy*, trans. Linda M. Maloney (Minneapolis, MN: Fortress, 1994), 203.

[118] George W. Coats, *Rebellion in the Wilderness: the Murmuring Motif in the Wilderness, Traditions of the Old Testament* (Nashville, TN: Abingdon, 1968), 141; and Rolf P. Knierim and George W. Coats, *Numbers*, The Forms of the Old Testament Literature 4 (Grand Rapids, MI: William B. Eerdmans, 2005), 186.

[119] Dennis T. Olson, *Numbers*, Interpretation: A Bible Commentary for Teaching and Preaching (Louisville, KT: John Knox, 1996), 79; and Brown, *The Ethos of the Cosmos*, 92.

[120] Olson, *Numbers*, 79. See also Brown, *The Ethos of the Cosmos*, 92.

[121] Baruch Levine contrasts the report in Numbers 13:38, which he says is "realistically concerned about force and fortification," with the report in 13:32, which he says "malign the Promised Land itself" (Baruch A. Levine, *Numbers 1–20: A New Translation with Introduction and Commentary* [New York: Doubleday, 1993]). The question of whether

falls short is that he does not consider the possibility that the scouts think the land may have a hand in bringing these sorts of problems on its inhabitants. The expression is not simply a fanciful idiom, but rather part of a general way of talking about land, which includes expressions like "the land will give its produce (וְנָתְנָה הָאָרֶץ יְבוּלָהּ)" and "the land is not able to support them (לֹא נָשָׂא אֹתָם הָאָרֶץ)."[122] Such sayings exist on a spectrum – for example, the verb "to give" (נָתַן) has such a diverse usage that it is difficult to determine the level of activity attributed to the land in "the land will give its produce" – but each saying in some way communicates the idea that land contributes to the wellbeing or lack thereof of its inhabitants. The scouts worry about material conditions that make a land unlivable, and they attribute these conditions to the land itself.

The strength of Olson and Brown's interpretation is that they focus on misidentification.[123] Rather than seeing the land as it is, a generous land, the scouts see the land as greedy and dangerous. The problem with their interpretation is that they call this misidentification "mythologizing." This term suggests that the scouts' misidentification centers not on the character of the land, but on the extent to which the land is alive. Brown, in fact, argues that Numbers 13 "serves the Priestly polemic against *Chaoskampf*," disclosing that "all fears, socially based and mythologically construed, [are] wholly unfounded."[124] We have seen in other texts in the Torah that the idea that the land is alive does not preclude the possibility that the land is good. The spies' fears are unfounded, not because they mistake that which is not alive for a "voracious monster," but because they mistake a land obedient to YHWH for a hostile and unpredictable power. Their crime, as Norbert Lohfink writes, is "calumny of the land" (דִּבַּת הָאָרֶץ [Numbers 13:32]) "a negative judgement on the good and saving gift offered by YHWH."[125] In human terms, their crime is the crime of slander.

---

it is "realistic" or "unrealistic" to claim that the land devours its inhabitants depends entirely on where one draws the line between mechanistic forces and personal forces.

[122] See, for example, Genesis 13:5–6; 36:7; Leviticus 25:19; 26:4. Note that, in Genesis 13:6, אֶרֶץ ("earth") takes a masculine verb, instead of the expected feminine.

[123] Brown writes that "the conflicting reports hinge completely on how the land is perceived" (Brown, *The Ethos of the Cosmos*, 92). See also Adriane Leveen, *Memory and Tradition in the Book of Numbers* (New York: Cambridge University Press, 2008), 108–9.

[124] Brown, *The Ethos of the Cosmos*, 92, n. 148.

[125] Lohfink, "The Strata of the Pentateuch and the Question of War," 197.

Numbers 16:30–34 and 26:10 (with Deuteronomy 11:6 and Psalm 106:17): The Earth Opened Its Mouth

In Numbers 16, the scouts' fears come to pass, but it is not the land of Israel that does the honors. Instead, a patch of earth in the wilderness swallows up rebels within Israel's camp. And it is not the deed of a capricious land, acting outside the influence and control of humans and YHWH, but a response to Moses's bidding and YHWH's creating. When Dathan, Aviram, Korah, and the Levites challenge the leadership of Moses and Aaron, Moses devises a test:

> By this you will know that YHWH has sent me to do all these works; [they] are not from my own heart. If these die the death of all humankind, and if the fate of all humankind is visited on them, YHWH has not sent me. But if YHWH creates a creation and the soil opens its mouth and swallows them and all that is theirs and they go down alive to Sheol, you will know that these men spurned YHWH.
> (Numbers 16:28–30)

Immediately, just as Moses finishes speaking, the earth "[splits] apart" under the rebels:

> And the earth opened its mouth and swallowed them and their households and every person who belonged to Korah and all the possessions. And they went down – they and all who belonged to them – alive to Sheol, and the earth covered over them and they disappeared from the middle of the camp. And all of Israel that was around them fled from their voice, for they said: lest the earth swallow us.
> (Numbers 16:32–34)

Numbers 16 (with its echoes in Numbers 26:10, Deuteronomy 11:6, and Psalm 106:7) is a story about intracommunal challenges to YHWH's deliverance of Israel. If the Egyptians at the Reed Sea represent the external enemy that tries to intervene in YHWH's deliverance of Israel, Korah and the other rebels represent an internal challenge. Their challenge is not a military one, but instead they undermine Moses' interpretation of the exodus from Egypt, the wilderness wandering, and the newly established cult. Egypt is to them "a land oozing milk and honey," the wilderness a place of death, Moses holds power illegitimately, and Aaron has no special claim to serve at the tabernacle (Numbers 16:3, 13).

As in Exodus 15, the earth swallows up those who stand in the way of YHWH's deliverance of Israel. Scholars have linked both texts to the Baal cycle, in the case of Numbers 16, focusing on texts concerning Môt, the god of death and the underworld.[126] Aside from the language of

---

[126] See, for example, Milgrom, *Numbers = [Ba-Midbar]*, 138.

swallowing, the close association between the underworld (שְׁאֹל) and the earth and ground (אֶרֶץ and אֲדָמָה, respectively) suggests that the writers are working against the background of cultural ideas similar to those found in stories about Môt. The earth's mouth provides a passage which allows Korah and his household to go down "alive to Sheol" (Numbers 16:33), resembling Baal's descent into the netherworld through Môt's throat: "Ba'al entered [Môt's] mouth, descended into his maw."[127] This story, however, much like those in Genesis 4 and Exodus 15, does not speak of the ground or the underworld as YHWH's opponent. They are allies who offer their assistance in order to squelch those who oppose YHWH's chosen leaders. Speaking of a possible connection between the myth of Môt and Numbers 13:32, Lohfink suggests that the priestly writer is "playing with this mythological background,"[128] and that seems to me an accurate description of the relationship between the myth and the biblical text. The writer has not reproduced the myth, but has instead creatively borrowed aspects of the myth in order to show that the world, be it the underworld, the sea, or the earth itself, does not battle against YHWH, but instead aids YHWH's purposes.

Numbers 16 differs from Genesis 4:10–12 and Exodus 15:12 in that the earth's ability to swallow is here marked as unusual. Moses describes it using the term "creation": "If YHWH creates (יִבְרָא) a creation (בְּרִיאָה), and the earth opens its mouth and swallows them ... then you will know that these men have despised YHWH" (Numbers 16:30). Martin Noth argues that the root ברא, "to create," is "reserved for the productive, generative action of God."[129] Milgrom proposes that this language is occasioned by "the pagan background of the imagery," which the writer "tries to counter by emphasizing that it is solely the creative act of the Lord that is responsible for the activity of the earth."[130] Milgrom's argument is similar to my own, in the sense that he too argues for an intentional reworking of the mythological material. Where we differ is over his use of the word "solely." If the writer wanted to describe this act as being "solely" the work of YHWH, then surely he or she could have avoided using such active language to describe the involvement of the earth. If we consider this story together with Numbers 13:32, it clarifies

---

[127] Quoted in Frank Moore Cross, *Canaanite Myth and Hebrew Epic: Essays in the History of the Religion of Israel* (Cambridge, MA: Harvard University Press, 1973), 117.
[128] Lohfink, "The Strata of the Pentateuch and the Question of War," 203. Lohfink goes on to argue that the story of Dathan and Aviram reflects the same mythological background as Numbers 13:32.
[129] Noth, *Numbers*, 128.   [130] Milgrom, *Numbers = [Ba-Midbar]*, 138.

the issues with which the writers contend. The negative report of the scouts has suggested that YHWH is not in control of the land into which they are about to enter. YHWH has said it is a land flowing with milk and honey, but the scouts suspect that it is instead a voracious land, a land that will kill them. The noun בְּרִיאָה, "creation," and the verb בָּרָא, "to create," in Numbers 16:30 recall YHWH's creation of the world in Genesis 1, and so establish God's control, a control that extends over the land of Canaan, the wilderness, and all lands. The earth is not an unreliable monster that at any moment may gobble up the Israelites; it is a creature under the control of Israel's God.

The relationship between God's action and the action of the ground in Numbers 16 is just one example of the general problem of agency in the Hebrew Bible. It is just as pressing in stories with human actors as in stories with nonhuman ones. A prominent example is God's use of foreign armies to judge Israel.[131] When God sends armies against Israel and Judah, are the foreign armies responsible for their actions? Are they really choosing to do what they do or do the actions belong to YHWH? The words of prophets are another example. When prophets preface their words with "Thus says YHWH," do the words that follow belong to the prophet or to God? Because humans with no agency is as uncomfortable and unacceptable a thought as mountains that skip about and serve as witnesses, commentators have tended to say that the actions of foreign armies and the words of the prophets are *both* the actions of YHWH *and* of the respective human subjects. The main reason scholars conclude differently about personalistic nature texts is that thinking of nonanimal nature as inert accords better with modern ideas about mountains, trees, and luminaries. Yet the biblical text does not warrant such divergent conclusions. Just as the prophets are not talking puppets, so the earth in Numbers 16 is not a stage set with levers that God manipulates. The actions of nonanimal nature and of YHWH overlap and intertwine; this intermingling does not require that all action be ascribed to YHWH. The earth is responsible for its part in the story of Israel, just as the

---

[131] See, for example, Deuteronomy 28:49–52; Isaiah 5:26–30, 10:5–6; Jeremiah 4:6; 5:15–17; 34:21–22; Amos 6:14; and 2 Chronicles 36:17. Isaiah 10:7 explicitly raises the problem of how to interpret the relationship between YHWH's actions and those of Assyria. After God has described Assyria as "the rod of my anger," the text reports on Assyria's attitude: "But he, this is not what he intends, and his heart does not think [it]. For in his heart is to destroy, and to cut off nations, not few." Assyria's confidence in its own strength is then used to justify God's future judgment on the empire (Isaiah 10:12).

prophets are responsible for their words and the foreign armies for their bloodshed.

Numbers 21:17–18: The Song of the Well

Numbers 21 summarizes several of Israel's stages of traveling through the wilderness. When they reach Be'er, YHWH declares that he will provide the people with water. In response, Israel sings a song:

> Go up, O well! Sing to it!
> A well; officials dug it,
> The nobles of the people quarried it,
> With a sceptre, with their staffs.
> (Numbers 21:17–18)

Scholars have next to nothing to say about the first line of this song. It begins with a singular imperative (עֲלִי, "go up"), before switching to a plural imperative (עֱנוּ, "sing"). The change in person confirms that the two verbs are addressed to different audiences, the first to the well, the second, presumably, to the people gathered around it. Though the prose account makes clear that the well is a gift from YHWH, the song suggests a similar intertwining of actions and responsibilities as we saw in Numbers 16. The water is a gift from YHWH. It also requires the cooperation of the well itself, whose "going up" is an obedient response to YHWH's promise to Moses. In this it resembles the officials' choice to dig; they too are contributing to the creation of the well.

Daniel Hillel describes two kinds of wells dug in ancient Israel. The first is a shallow well, "dug into the source of groundwater," which is fed over time by "seepage from the surrounding strata."[132] The second is a deep well, dug to the depth of 30–160 feet, which "tap[s] into a deep, perennial aquifer."[133] The difference between the two in terms of use is that shallow wells tended to dry out during periods of drought, whereas deep wells "provided a reliable, longterm supply of water."[134] Both are distinct from cisterns, which "collect surface runoff during rainstorms."[135] This last difference is especially important. While cisterns are dug, then filled with water, the successful quarrying of a well means *finding* water. It comes bubbling up from the ground. It meets the diggers.

---

[132] Daniel Hillel, *The Natural History of the Bible: An Environmental Exploration of the Hebrew Scriptures* (New York: Columbia University Press, 2006), 299.
[133] Ibid.   [134] Ibid.   [135] Ibid.

This story probably describes the completion of either a shallow or deep well, a shallow one making more sense in the present context, since Be'er is only a stop of the way, not a permanent village. The poet does not describe the well as the solitary action of YHWH, but as the result of cooperation between three parties. YHWH names the place and promises water, the well "goes up," and the diggers dig down. YHWH's care for Israel is not unilateral, but involves obedient participation from other persons, both human and other-than-human.

DEUTERONOMY

Deuteronomy 4:26, 30:19, 31:28, and 32:1: I Call to Witness the Heavens and the Earth

In Deuteronomy, the heavens and the earth serve as witnesses to the covenant between Israel and YHWH. Three times Moses calls on them to witness against Israel: "I call to witness against you today the heavens and the earth ..." (Deuteronomy 4:26, see also 30:19; 31:28). The opening of Moses's song in Deuteronomy 32:1 also draws on the idea of the heavens and earth as witnesses, or at least as audience: "Give ear, O heavens, and I will speak; let the earth hear the words of my mouth." In each of the four cases, the context is the covenant between Israel and YHWH, especially as it relates to the possession of the promised land. In Deuteronomy 4:26, the heavens and the earth witness God warning the people; if they "act ruinously" (הִשְׁחַתֶּם), they will "disappear quickly from upon the land." In 30:19, they are called on to vouch for the fact that God presents the people with a choice: "Life and death I have set before you, blessings and curse; choose life, that you might live, you and your offspring." The context in 31:28 is Moses' concern that the people will turn away from God after his death; in his absence, he calls on the heavens and the earth to examine the people. The song itself serves as a witness against the people (Deuteronomy 31:19), by chronicling God's care for Israel despite their repeated turns to other gods.

Traditionally, these texts, alongside a number of texts in the prophets, have been studied as examples of the genre "prophetic lawsuit."[136] First identified by Hermann Gunkel, it became a hotly debated topic a

---

[136] The texts commonly grouped together as "prophetic lawsuit" texts are Deuteronomy 4:25–26; 30:15–19; 31:28–29; 32:1; Isaiah 1:2; Jeremiah 2:12; Micah 6:1–2; and Psalm 50:4–7.

generation or two after him.¹³⁷ Two issues were especially contested. First, do these texts reflect any particular Ancient Near Eastern literary form? A common suggestion was that the texts borrow the language of Ancient Near Eastern suzerainty treaties, especially Hittite ones.¹³⁸ Though some scholars argued that the heavens and the earth stand for the deities listed in Hittite treaties, a more common claim was to tie the heavens and the earth to the natural phenomena that often follow deities in the list of witnesses in such documents.¹³⁹ An example is the treaty between Mursil II and Duppi-Tessub, king of Amurru. After naming many deities, the list of witnesses concludes with "the mountains, the rivers, the springs, the great Sea, heaven and earth, the winds (and) the clouds – let these be witnesses to this treaty and to the oath."¹⁴⁰ According to this line of argumentation, the authors of the Deuteronomic passages borrowed the language of suzerainty treaties to describe the formation of the covenant between YHWH and Israel.

Second, scholars disagreed about whether the Deuteronomic passages belonged to the same genre as the prophetic passages. Should these texts be read together at all? How scholars answered this question depended in large part on whether scholars recognized the prophetic lawsuit genre as a legitimate genre designation. Those who defended the prophetic lawsuit form argued that the prophetic passages call on the heavens and the earth because they witness the covenant in Deuteronomy. The Deuteronomic and prophetic passages, according to this argument, share a common background in suzerainty treaties. Scholars who denied the validity of the prophetic lawsuit genre either downplayed the importance of the call to heaven and earth in the Prophets,¹⁴¹ or looked for its background,

---

¹³⁷ Gunkel called it the "Gerichtsrede." See Hermann Gunkel and Joachim Begrich, *Einleitung in Die Psalmen, Die Gattungen Der Religiösen Lyrik Isaraels*, 2. Aufl. (Götttingen: Vandenhoeck u. Ruprecht, 1966), 364–65. Originally published in 1926.

¹³⁸ The connection between the Deuteronomic call to heaven and earth and suzerainty treaties was first suggested by G. E. Mendenhall (George E. Mendenhall, *Law and Covenant in Israel and the Ancient Near East* [Pittsburgh, PA: Biblical Colloquium, 1955]). M. Mathias Delcor gives a detailed outline of possible connections in his article "Les Attaches Litteraires, l'origine et La Signification de l'expression Biblique 'Prendre a Temoin Le Ciel et La Terre.'"

¹³⁹ Delcor, "Les Attaches Litteraires, l'origine et La Signification de l'expression Biblique 'Prendre a Temoin Le Ciel et La Terre,'" 11–12.

¹⁴⁰ Pritchard, *Ancient Near Eastern Texts Relating to the Old Testament*, 205.

¹⁴¹ See Michael DeRoche, "Yahweh's Rîb against Israel: A Reassessment of the so-Called 'Prophetic Lawsuit' in the Preexilic Prophets," *Journal of Biblical Literature* 102, no. 4 (December 1, 1983): 572–73.

not in a particular literary form, but in a common understanding of the natural world.[142]

Though both of these questions are appropriate for the purposes of form critics, neither question addresses the role of nonanimal nature in the texts. The content of the texts is used to compare it with other texts, either inside or outside the Bible, but it is not analyzed in its own right. When scholars have paid attention to the content of the passage, their investigations have been hampered by assumptions about the *Sitz im Leben* of the passages. Assuming that the call for witnesses parallels the proceedings of a legal court, scholars have tried to match up the role of the heavens and the earth with a specific role in ancient courts.[143] Hermann Gunkel, in his initial description of the genre, argued that the heavens and earth play the role of judge in the dispute between YHWH and Israel.[144] This designation was deemed unconvincing by many scholars, who offered alternative proposals. What unifies these proposals, however, is that they all reflect a conviction that the writer cannot *really* intend that the heavens and the earth should serve as witnesses. Since they were not deified in ancient Israel, the argument goes, the term must be a poetic way of referring to something else. Scholars have made several suggestions about what this "something else" might be.

The first suggestion is that the call to the heavens and the earth is a meaningless holdover from older forms of speech. Jeffrey Tigay argues that the call to the heavens and the earth is "a vestigial motif that has lost its original significance."[145] Though this invocation served a clear purpose in other Ancient Near Eastern treaties, its presence in the Hebrew Bible is solely the result of the fact that the writers borrowed language. It serves no function in the text as it stands. The "supreme authority" in

---

[142] See Dwight R. Daniels, "Is There a 'Prophetic Lawsuit' Genre," *Zeitschrift Für Die Alttestamentliche Wissenschaft* 99, no. 3 (January 1, 1987): 357.

[143] See Herbert B. Huffmon, "Covenant Lawsuit in the Prophets," *Journal of Biblical Literature* 78, no. 4 (December 1, 1959): 293. For a critique of Huffmon's approach, see Delcor, "Les Attaches Litteraires, l'origine et La Signification de l'expression Biblique 'Prendre a Temoin Le Ciel et La Terre,'" 23.

[144] Gunkel and Begrich, *Einleitung in Die Psalmen, Die Gattungen Der Religiösen Lyrik Isaraels*, 364. For a summary of modern scholarly debate on the role of the heavens and the earth, see Huffmon, "Covenant Lawsuit in the Prophets," 290–92; and Nielsen, *Yahweh as Prosecutor and Judge*, 5–23. Tigay provides a summary of traditional rabbinic interpretations in Jeffrey H. Tigay, *Deuteronomy = [Devarim]: The Traditional Hebrew Text with the New JPS Translation* (Philadelphia, PA: Jewish Publication Society, 1996), 299.

[145] Tigay, *Deuteronomy = [Devarim]*, 52.

the Bible "is the Lord," and the "heaven and the earth ... cannot act independently."[146] At most they are passive tools by means of which God enforces the covenant.[147]

Second, some scholars argue that the heavens and the earth are a poetic stand-in for YHWH. Herbert Huffmon terms the call to the heavens and the earth "a literary device" in which "[YHWH] [asks] a third party to judge between him and Israel."[148] The purpose of the inclusion of the heavens and the earth is to complete the parallel between the Deuteronomic texts and "actual court procedure."[149] Michael DeRoche, who denies that these texts reflect court proceedings, makes an even stronger statement: "The *rîb*-oracles[150] involves only two parties: Israel and [YHWH]."[151] DeRoche argues that these texts describe bilateral relations between YHWH and Israel; in this explanation there is simply no space or reason for the involvement of the heavens and the earth.

A third strategy, a version of the second, is to describe the call to the heavens and the earth as poetic license or hyperbole.[152] Like Tigay's argument, this is to say that the inclusion of the heavens and the earth is meaningless. The writers gave way to religious enthusiasm or love of ornate language, which we as readers ought not to take seriously.

A more promising approach is to argue that the heavens and the earth are metonyms or synecdoches referring to the divine assembly.[153] A metonym is a figure of speech in which an adjunct or attribute stands for the whole, like "suit" for "businessman" or "Hollywood" for the US film industry.[154] A synecdoche is a trope "in which one uses a species term to stand in for a genus, or a genus term for a species."[155] Ernest Wright writes: "Must we not interpret such passages in the light of the Divine

---

[146] Ibid. [147] Ibid. [148] Huffmon, "Covenant Lawsuit in the Prophets," 293.
[149] Ibid.
[150] DeRoche argues that the genre label "prophetic lawsuit" is misleading. The texts, he says, are not modeled on lawsuits, but instead reflect a "personal, bilateral" quarrel. He names the texts *rîb*-oracles, because many of them use the root ריב ("to strive, contend"). See DeRoche, "Yahweh's Rîb against Israel," 574.
[151] Ibid., 572.
[152] See John Skinner, *The Book of the Prophet Isaiah, Chapters I–XXXIX: With Introduction and Notes*, The Cambridge Bible for Schools and Colleges (Cambridge: Cambridge University Press, 1985), 3; and S. R. Driver, *A Critical and Exegetical Commentary on Deuteronomy*, The International Critical Commentary (Edinburgh: T. & T. Clark, 1902), 349.
[153] See Wright, *The Old Testament Against Its Environment*, 36; and Frank Moore Cross, "The Council of Yahweh in Second Isaiah," *Journal of Near Eastern Studies* 12, no. 4 (October 1, 1953): 274–75, n. 3.
[154] See Soskice, *Metaphor and Religious Language*, 57. [155] Ibid.

Assembly, the members of which constitute the host of heaven and earth?"[156] Delcor argues along similar lines: "We believe that heaven and earth or the elements of nature played the role of a true assembly of divine advisors for [YHWH] in the heavenly court."[157] As long as the heavens and the earth are not replaced with some other term – Wright's reference to "*the host* of heaven and earth" leaves it unclear whether he thinks the heavens and the earth themselves participate in the divine council – this line of interpretation leaves open the possibility that the heavens and the earth are powerful persons that aid in YHWH's government of the world.

In each of the examples given above, save the last, scholars dismiss the possibility that the writers of the Hebrew Bible thought that the heavens and the earth were able to hear and respond to summons, and that natural phenomena had an active role to play in the relationship between YHWH and Israel. Though I do not think it is fruitful to try to match the role of the heavens and the earth too closely with any particular role in human courtrooms, it is clear from Deuteronomy 4:26, 30:19, 31:28, and 32:1 that the heavens and the earth observe the formation of the covenants. They are also called on to evaluate Israel's compliance with the terms of the covenant. Dwight R. Daniels makes a helpful contribution here. Daniels writes primarily about the prophetic texts usually grouped under the "prophetic lawsuit" genre, but his argument has consequences for how we understand Deuteronomy as well. Daniels argues that there is no "prophetic lawsuit" genre, and that the summons in the Deuteronomic and prophetic texts do not mimic treaty material.[158] A closer parallel to the prophetic texts, Daniels writes, is Sumerian, Akkadian, and Canaanite incantation texts, specifically ones that include the *zi-pad* formula: "Be adjured by the name of heaven, be adjured by the name of earth!"[159] In these incantations, the heavens and earth are treated as "living entities"

---

[156] Wright, *The Old Testament against Its Environment*, 36.
[157] Delcor, "Les Attaches Litteraires, l'origine et La Signification de l'expression Biblique 'Prendre a Temoin Le Ciel et La Terre,'" 21. See also Cross, "The Council of Yahweh in Second Isaiah," 274–77.
[158] Daniels, "Is There a 'Prophetic Lawsuit' Genre," 355–56.
[159] Ibid., 356. For examples of relevant incantations, see Theodor H. Gaster, "A Canaanite Magical Text," *Orientalia* 11 (1942): 44; Erica Reiner, *Šurpu: A Collection of Sumerian and Akkadian Incantations* (Graz: Im Selbstverlage des Herausgebers, 1958), 31; Markham J. Geller, *Healing Magic and Evil Demons: Canonical Udug-Hul Incantations* (Berlin: De Gruyter, 2015), 301; Tzvi Abusch, "The Socio-Religious Framework of the Babylonian Witchcraft Ceremony Maqlû: Some Observations on the Introductory Section of Text, Part I," in *Riches Hidden in Secret Places: Ancient*

that the person speaking can compel to act on his or her behalf.[160] Daniels's argument is not that the Deuteronomic and prophetic texts reflect incantations *rather than* treaty texts, but instead that both "reflect a common conceptual background regarding the elements of creation"[161]:

> According to this view the universe is not composed of so many inanimate objects subject to the more or less predictable forces of natural laws, but is an intricate web of interrelated (living) entities. It is this conviction that heaven, earth, and the natural phenomena are affected by the behaviour and deeds of mankind that lies behind the appeal to these entities.[162]

According to Daniels, the rationale behind the call to the heavens and the earth in Deuteronomy and the prophetic material is that they are interested parties. Israel's behavior, and that which happens to Israel as a result, will also affect the physical environment. It is unlikely, Daniels writes, that the prophetic texts refer back to the Deuteronomic texts, because the latter probably postdate the prophetic texts.[163] Instead, both texts reflect the idea that YHWH's covenant with Israel affects and to some extent includes the heavens and the earth. Because of this, the heavens and the earth are given responsibilities to monitor Israel's obedience. As interested parties, they are given the task of making known serious breaches of the covenant, and they participate in judging such breaches.[164] In Deuteronomy 11:17, Moses warns Israel that if they fail to keep YHWH's commandments, "the anger of YHWH will burn against you, and he will restrain the heavens, and there will not be rain and the soil will not give its produce," and, in Deuteronomy 28:23, the consequence of faithlessness is that "the heavens above your head will become bronze, and the earth beneath you will become iron." In the words of Harold Fisch, the heavens and the earth "are not passive spectators who testify to the *fact* of a crime having been committed, but rather themselves

---

Near Eastern Studies in Memory of Thorkild Jacobsen, eds. I. Tzvi Abusch and Thorkild Jacobsen (Winona Lake, IN: Eisenbrauns, 2002), 11, 23, 27, 28.

[160] Daniels, "Is There a 'Prophetic Lawsuit' Genre," 357.   [161] Ibid.   [162] Ibid.
[163] Ibid., 355–56. See also Jon D. Levenson, "Who Inserted the Book of the Torah," *Harvard Theological Review* 68, no. 3–4 (July 1975): 203–33. Levenson argues that Deuteronomy 3:29, 4:1–40 and 29:21–28 [22–29]; 30; 31:16–22, 24–29; 31:30; 32:1–44, and probably 29:19[20] were composed by an exilic redactor as a frame for an earlier Deuteronomic corpus.
[164] Fisch, "Analogy of Nature," 165. He is drawing on *Midrash Tanhuma* (cp. Edition). New York: Horeb, 1934, p. 678.

active partners in the Covenant who are bound to come forward publicly when it is violated."[165]

Deuteronomy 32:43: He Will Atone for His Soil

Moses's song in Deuteronomy 32 ends on a note of praise and promise: "Praise, O nations, his people, for he will avenge the blood of his servants and bring revenge on his adversaries and he will atone (וְכִפֶּר) for his soil, his people" (Deuteronomy 32:43). The final words of this song recall two texts that we have already considered: Genesis 47:19, in which the Egyptians equate their own suffering with the suffering of their land, and Leviticus 26:42, in which God promises to remember God's covenant with the patriarchs and the land. An appeal in Deuteronomy 26:15 also resembles this text; the people ask God to "bless your people, Israel, and the soil that you have given us."

The root כפר, "to atone," common in both Leviticus and Numbers, only occurs three times in Deuteronomy, twice in 21:8 and once in 32:43. Both texts mention blood spilled through violence. The issue in chapter 21 is an unsolved murder, "a corpse found ... lying in the field." The verb כִּפֶּר, "to atone," occurs in the declaration of innocence spoken by the elders: "Our hands did not pour out this blood, and our eyes did not see. Atone (כַּפֵּר) for your people Israel, whom you redeem, O YHWH. Do not place innocent blood in the midst of your people Israel" (Deuteronomy 21:8). The narrator declares that, after these words are spoken, "The blood will be covered (וְנִכַּפֵּר) with respect to them [Israel]" (Deuteronomy 21:8). In Deuteronomy 32:43, Moses expresses confidence that YHWH will "avenge the blood of his people." Bloodguilt is not a major theme in Deuteronomy; it is only discussed in relation to the cities of refuge (Deuteronomy 19) and the problem of an unsolved murder (Deuteronomy 21), and is briefly mentioned in one of the curses to be uttered from Mount Ebal (Deuteronomy 27:25). In most of these cases, humans are the carriers of bloodguilt: bloodguilt is "upon you" (עָלֶיךָ, see Deuteronomy 19:10). Deuteronomy 19:13 is less clear about *who* is guilty when innocent blood is spilled; it simply commands that "you are to purge innocent blood from Israel." In contrast to this, the need for atonement on behalf of the land appears to reflect a tradition similar to that of Numbers 35:33, in which blood pollutes the land itself:

---

[165] Ibid., 167. Emphasis in the original.

You shall not pollute the land in which you live, for blood – it pollutes the land. And no atonement can be made (יְכֻפַּר) for the land for the blood spilled in it, except by the blood of the one who spilled it.

Moses's song in Deuteronomy 32 describe the terrible consequences of war – see especially 32:23–25 – consequences that include the slaughtering of many people. Though their blood is hardly innocent blood, the argument of the song being that the people deserve what happens to them, the end result is still a soil drenched in blood. Perhaps the reason Moses assures the people that YHWH will atone for the land is not so much due to slippage between the guilt of the people and the guilt of the land, as to this excess of blood. After the terrors of war, will the land be suitable for YHWH's presence? The song renders this question moot; YHWH will restore both the people and the soil, making of each a fit covenant partner for YHWH.

A NOTE ON IDIOMS AND METONYMY

In this book, I am mostly concerned with two kinds of texts: texts in which nonanimal nature performs some action, and texts in which people or God directly address nonanimal nature. These texts clearly diverge from modern Western language about nonanimal nature, and, when reading them, it is easy to see (though not easy to accurately describe or define) the distance between Western concepts and the concepts of the biblical writers. Conceptual distance, however, is not always noticeable. In her article, "Losing Your Concepts," Cora Diamond argues that loss of concepts if often invisible.[166] We do not necessarily see, when reading old texts or speaking with someone whose culture differs from our own, that we do not share the concepts of our interlocutor. The texts discussed in this work are ones in which the distance between our own concepts and those of the biblical writers are most apparent.

That is not to say that the view of nonanimal nature as alive does not appear in other texts. If my argument is persuasive, we ought to reconsider many of the idioms of the Hebrew Bible. For example, agricultural fertility and infertility are often described as the land giving or not giving its produce,[167] and overgrazing and overpopulation as the land not being able to support its inhabitants.[168] When God's anger "burns against [the]

---

[166] Diamond, "Losing Your Concepts," 266–72.
[167] See, for example, Leviticus 25:19; 26:4; Deuteronomy 11:17.
[168] See Genesis 13:5–6; 36:7.

land," the resulting damage is characterized as "the wounds of the land and its diseases."[169] In 2 Kings 3:19, YHWH commands the people to "pain (תְּכְאִבוּ) every good allotment with stones." Commons phrases for military victory and cessation of hostilities are "the land will be subdued,"[170] and "the land rested from war."[171] In 2 Kings 2:21–22, Elijah is said to "heal" water:

Thus says the YHWH: "I have healed (רִפָּאתִי) these waters and death and bereavement will no longer come from here." The waters have been healed (וַיֵּרָפוּ) until this day, according to the word Elisha spoke. (2 Kings 2:21–22)

These forms of speech may be dead metaphors, or simply idiomatic ways of communication. Or, they may reflect the idea that nonanimal nature is active and alive. It is not possible to prove one or the other; it depends entirely on usage and context. Given that other texts more clearly reflect a personalistic view of nonanimal nature, it is likely that the above expressions also reflect such a worldview.

Equally difficult are so called metonymous uses of the words אֶרֶץ, "earth," and אֲדָמָה, "ground." In Genesis 9:13, is the covenant between "[YHWH] and the earth" really between YHWH and *the earth*, or is the earth a metonym? Or a synecdoche, referring both to the earth and its inhabitants? When Laban asks Jacob to show loyalty to him and to "the land where [he] has sojourned" (Genesis 21:23), does the land mean the physical land, or its inhabitants? How we answer these questions depends in large part on how we conceive of the writers' concepts of nonanimal nature. Though this project first and foremost focuses on strong examples of personalistic nature texts, the presence of such unclear texts should be kept in mind. My argument is not that ancient biblical writers sometimes thought of nonanimal nature as alive and sometimes not, but that the texts included make visible a more general conceptualization of mountains, trees, luminaries, and soil. The fact that many idioms use active language to describe nonanimal nature is further evidence of this, albeit less clear evidence.

CONCLUSION

Nonanimal nature performs a range of actions in the Torah and interacts with humans and God in diverse ways. Some texts highlight the

---

[169] See Deuteronomy 29:26[27], 21[22].
[170] See Numbers 32:22, 29; Joshua 18:1; 1 Chronicles 22:18.
[171] See, for example, Joshua 11:23, 14:15; Judges 3:11, 30; 5:31; 8:28.

interdependence of humans and nonanimal nature, and closely identify the two with each other. In other texts, nonanimal nature witnesses against humans and participates in God's judgment of both individual transgressors and Israel as a whole. Nonanimal nature also has its own relationship with God. In Leviticus we saw that the relationship between YHWH and the land of Canaan predates Israel's entry into that land. In both Genesis and Leviticus, nonanimal nature carries out cultic responsibilities, ones that echo aspects of Israel's cultic life.

My hope in this study is not only to outline how biblical writers thought about other-than-human persons, but also to consider how their thinking might inform how we live in and with the world today. Torah's narration of human interactions with that which is not human is compelling, but also potentially troubling. It is not automatically helpful for addressing contemporary issues – how it informs responses to the ecological crisis depends on our interpretations, on what we do with the text. Two possible interpretations ought to be resisted. The first is to take Torah's emphasis on the responsibilities of nonanimal nature, be it the land, the skies, or the luminaries, as an invitation to abdicate responsibility. If the earth will right itself any time we misbehave, expelling or swallowing miscreants, why worry about climate change and soil erosion? This is both a reckless interpretation and a poor reading on literary grounds. The narratives and precepts of Torah seek to shape Israel into a particular kind of people, molding their relationships to each other, other peoples, their farmlands, more remote areas, and God. Torah does not ease responsibility, it increases it. Israel is expected to act with circumspection in every part of its life; dietary laws, agricultural precepts, and cultic regulations suggest that carelessness is not only unfortunate, but dangerous and destructive. Another way to put this is that the texts of Torah address humans, not skies, not rivers, not soil. It first and foremost sets out *human* responsibilities, but places those in a wider set of responsibilities, relationships, and interactions. This is why the Earth Bible Project's distrust of the tradition that the Bible is "God's book for humans" is misguided.[172] The Bible *is* God's book for humans. This is not anthropocentrism, but a recognition of human particularity: only humans speak human languages, produce written material, and use poetic parallelism. Rather than interpreting nonhuman action and responsibilities as an easy bromide for ecological fears, attending to the behaviors

---

[172] Habel, *Readings from the Perspective of Earth*, 39.

of nonanimal nature in the text suggests we ought to act with a bit of hesitancy. The world is not only for us, nor is it only shaped by us – it is also for other creatures, who mold it in their own distinctive ways, and who have their own concerns, their own lives. Viveiros de Castro writes that the central philosophical problem posed by indigenous thought is "what [other-than-human persons] see and thus are as persons."[173] Practically and ethically, that does not mean that animists are particularly concerned with figuring out what is the most ethical life for a tree or a groundhog. As Harvey writes, "most of the interests, activities, rights, responsibilities, involvements and concerns of animists ... are to do with their own roles and with other humans. They might expect owls, herons, crows and nightjars to be doing whatever it takes to care for country, land, Earth, and life, but the prime duty is to play one's own role fully."[174] If the Torah is read as an exploration of how we play our human role fully, and well, within a larger community of persons, it can help us reflect on how we relate to the rest of the world, as urgent a question as any. Torah does not solve or answer it for us, but it invites us into the conversation.

A second problematic reading would be to use Torah's stories of the responsiveness of the world to human misconduct as a guide for judging the moral standing of other peoples. An abhorrent example is Pat Robertson's claim that the 2010 Haiti earthquake was God's punishment on the Haitians for making "a pact with the devil" in order to rid themselves of the French during the Haitian revolution (Robertson also claimed Hurricane Katrina was sent as divine punishment). On literary grounds, this fails to take into account that natural disasters in the Bible are not obvious signs of anything; they don't self-interpret. Some droughts, like those in Genesis, are not read as divine judgment. Other events, like the plagues in Egypt, are. Knowing which is which is difficult, and requires wisdom, insight, even inspiration. It requires a constant attention to responsibility, particularly our own responsibility, and attunement to how actions produce reverberations and consequences. The Deuteronomic system of curses and blessings is complicated, even challenged, in the narratives and poetry of the Bible; it is not the case that natural disasters are easy, straightforward guides to guilt. A second literary reason to resist such use of the text is that the Bible, in its stories and legal codes, and most especially in its prophetic texts (to which we now turn), is intensely

---

[173] Viveiros de Castro, *Cannibal Metaphysics*, 56.   [174] Harvey, *Animism*, 103.

interested in how the privilege of some undermines the livelihood of others. In particular, its writers are concerned with elite land grabbing, royal control of agriculture, and imperial uses of power. It is not the case that the Bible presents a picture in which anything bad that happens to you is automatically your fault. It takes account of inequalities. This is essential to keep in mind today, because the consequences of climate change, pollution, toxicity, ocean acidification, etc., are not evenly distributed. For example, changes in rain patterns, especially the timing of the onset of the rainy season, are affecting the water level of Malawi's Lake Chilwa Basin.[175] This, in turn, adversely affects the women who depend on the fish in the lake for income. The changes in rain patterns are probably caused by global warming, by carbon emissions. But Malawi's carbon footprint is tiny.[176] It would be perverse to blame Malawi women for the low water levels in Lake Chilwa. The writers of the Bible and its prophets did not receive divine revelation in isolation from the world; they interpreted the world with the information available to them, and we must do the same. This means taking account of science, of what it can say about why some areas experience more extreme weather than others. Again, it is important to think about whom the Bible addresses. Torah repeatedly requires Israel to be self-critical, to watch how they live in the land. It has much less to say about watching how other people live in the land.[177] If we read Torah for self-criticism and self-reflection, with an eye to discerning how we might live better, then it can be a powerful tool in addressing climate change. If we use it to blame others when natural disasters decimate their communities, we use the Bible for violence. Reading the Bible for ways to think and ways to speak about environmental issues is a cooperative endeavor between communities and the text itself, which ideally keeps in view the rest of the world, so that we do not read the Bible in a historical or geographical vacuum. The text provides stories, metaphors, words, prescriptions; it is our responsibility to interpret these and turn them into action appropriate for and necessary to our time.

---

[175] For a discussion on the effects of climate change on women fish-processing groups in Malawi and the effectiveness of current climate change adaptation programs, see Hanne Jørstad and Christian Webersik, "Vulnerability to Climate Change and Adaptation Strategies of Local Communities in Malawi: Experiences of Women Fish-Processing Groups in the Lake Chilwa Basin," *Earth System Dynamics* 7 (2016): 977–89.

[176] See cdiac.ornl.gov/trends/emis/top2014.tot.

[177] There are, of course, the troubling bits about the land spewing out the previous inhabitants in Leviticus 18:24–28.

4

A Sentient World

Personalistic Nature Texts in the Prophets

INTRODUCTION

In the stories and poetry of the Prophets, the kinds of other-than-human persons and the activities they engage in are numerous and diverse, more so than in Torah. The focus shifts from the land as a unit to a plethora of actors – rivers, trees, fields, mountains, stars – all of which interact in complex ways with Israel and with YHWH. In the Former Prophets, the main activity in which other-than-human persons engage is warfare: they serve as military allies to Israel's army. In the Latter Prophets, cooperation between humans and nonhumans often fractures. Fields and mountains mourn and suffer due to human infidelity, and witness to this fact before YHWH. The picture is not entirely bleak, of course; humans and other-than-human persons come together to praise YHWH, and rejoice when they are restored to health. The return of exiles is a source of joy to trees, just as the restoration of agricultural fertility is to humans. The relationship between YHWH and nonanimal nature also grows in intricacy in the Prophets. In most texts, nonanimal nature is, in contrast to humans, a faithful and obedient creature, but some texts portray the sea as rebellious and recalcitrant. The prophetic corpus does not present a picture of other-than-human persons that is bland and one-dimensional, but one in which other-than-human persons are as heterogeneous and complex as human persons.

In Ezekiel, God famously searches for someone "to stand in the breach" (Ezekiel 22:30). This phrase has become a common way of referring to the role of prophets as intercessors, people who stand in the space between YHWH's wrath and YHWH's people.[1] This is how Psalm 106:23 uses the phrase; Moses places himself between God and Israel, and so averts Israel's destruction. The picture is human through and through, humans navigating and negotiating YHWH's dangerous presence. But, in Ezekiel, God asks for something bigger: the request is for someone "to stand in the breach on behalf of *the land*" – the whole land, not just its inhabitants. This is not a neat picture of two camps facing each other, with God on one side and humans on the other, perhaps with one heroic individual in the middle. It is a much messier space, a space of entangled lives, interconnected needs, and surprising acts of resistance and rescue. For example, Ezekiel addresses not only the people of Israel; he also prophesies to the mountains of Israel, the forest of the Negev, the soil of Israel, the mountain of Seir, and the wind. The prophetic writings teem with persons, and their perspectives and needs form a vital part of the narratives. Nature fights, trembles, suffers, receives comfort, and rejoices. The breach between YHWH and Israel is not solely a human issue, but a problem felt by all creatures who share space and place with God's people. Nonanimal nature does not stand idly by, waiting for humans to sort things out, but instead enters the gap, together with prophets, priests, and common people, even with YHWH himself.

In Chapter 3, I treated personalistic nature texts in their canonical order, going through each book of Torah in turn. This would be an impractical approach to the Prophetic books. Instead of five books, the Prophets contain nineteen. Furthermore, personalistic nature texts are numerous; to treat each in detail would require a multi-volume work. Instead, this chapter is divided into five thematic categories, based on recurrent images and vocabulary: (1) war, (2) theophany, (3) address, (4) grief, and (5) joy. The categories roughly sketch the order in which personalistic nature texts appear in the canon, and in broad strokes they suggest a sort of narrative of nonanimal nature through the Prophets.

---

[1] See, for example, Michael Widmer, *Standing in the Breach: An Old Testament Theology and Spirituality of Intercessory Prayer* (Winona Lake, IN: Eisenbrauns, 2015); Patrick D. Miller, "Prayer and Divine Action," in *God in the Fray: A Tribute to Walter Brueggemann* (Minneapolis: Fortress, 1998), 217; Sampson S. Ndoga, "Contemporary Reflections on Ezekiel 22:23–32 as a Depiction of Collective Responsibility of Leaders for National Demise," *Old Testament Essays* 27, no. 1 (January 2014): 247–62; Yochanan Muffs, "Chapter 1: Who Will Stand in the Breach?: A Study of Prophetic Intercession," in *Love & Joy: Law, Language, and Religion in Ancient Israel* (New York, NY: Jewish Theological Seminary of America; Distributed by Harvard University, 1992).

The first category includes texts exclusively from the Former Prophets, while categories four and five only include texts from the Latter Prophets.

WAR

In the Former Prophets, the main context in which nonanimal nature acts is warfare. It fights alongside Israel and mourns Israel's dead. Given that these books concern themselves with the conquest of Canaan and the history of the united and the divided monarchies, this is not surprising; military history and power is a frequent theme in these books. Just like personalistic nature texts in Torah reflect the themes of these books, so here the involvement of nonanimal nature mirrors the preoccupations of the writers of Joshua through Kings. In the Former Prophets, warfare is not only a human activity; humans, gods, and the forces of nature all go to battle together.

The ways in which nonanimal nature engages in war varies between texts. Sometimes nonanimal nature fights like a warrior, while at other times it simply refrains from taking the side of the enemy. In Deborah's victory song in Judges 5, other-than-human persons assist Israel. Her poem lauds the participation of the stars and the Wadi Kishon: "From the heavens they fought; the stars fought from their courses against Sisera. The Wadi Kishon swept them away, the Wadi; the ancient Wadi Kishon" (Judges 5:20–21a). When Israel's army gathers on Mount Tabor, on one side of the Jezreel valley, Sisera commands Jabin's army, stationed on the other side, to charge towards the Kishon. Israel overwhelms their soldiers and charioteers; in her poem, Deborah attributes Israel's victory not solely to their own effort, but to a kind of cosmic chaos, in which water rises up and stars charge down. Instead of two armies facing each other, the poem describes a battle in which Sisera's forces are attacked from every side: Israel in front, the wadi underneath, and the stars above. Soldiers in this battle are not necessarily human; recognizing this, Susan Niditch calls the stars "Yhwh's foot soldiers."[2] The valor of the stars and the wadi is a source of courage for the human poet. After telling her audience of how the stars and the river aided Israel, the poet turns to herself and exclaims: "Walk on, my soul, in strength!" (Judges 5:21b). The poem not only memorializes the defeat of Sisera, but points to the participation of nonanimal nature as a cause for future confidence and action.

---

[2] Susan Niditch, *Judges: A Commentary* (Louisville, KY: Westminster John Knox, 2008), 80.

Judges 5 is the poetic account of a battle narrated in prose in Judges 4. This strategy – combining poetic and prose accounts of the same event – is common in the Hebrew Bible; we have already seen it in Exodus 15, with the Song of the Sea. But this combination of prose and poetry raises an interpretive question: how should we read the two accounts together? What is an appropriate hermeneutic for poetic accounts of battles? Is poetry a reliable guide to how ancient Israelites thought about nature? Or does war poetry exaggerate and embellish the participation of non-animal nature in battles for effect? Both prose and poetry accounts of warfare mention the involvement of nonanimal nature, so the answers to these questions are not decisive for reading all texts. We will study four texts in this section – Judges 5:20-21, Joshua 10:12-13, 2 Samuel 1:21 and 18:8 – and of these 2 Samuel 18:8 is entirely prose, the passages from Judges 5 and 2 Samuel 1 are both poetry, and Joshua 10:12-13 is a mix of poetry and prose. In the latter three texts, the poetic descriptions of battle follow prose accounts of the same events, and the prose narratives are less likely to include references to the participation of nonanimal nature. Dozeman argues that the poetic accounts "provide a commentary on the previous narrative or the larger literary context"; he also says that the poetry "interprets" the prose account.[3] That is not to say that the poetic account is written *in order* to interpret the prose; Dozeman, like most scholars, argues that the poem in Joshua 10, for example, predates the prose narrative.[4] Instead, Dozeman asserts, the author or redactor chose to insert "an older liturgy or poem" because it was considered a suitable commentary on "a related narrative."[5] The poetry answers questions that the prose account does not. Exodus 15 answer the question of how such a small and unarmed group escapes the Egyptian army. Judges 5 addresses similar questions: the poet explains Israel's victory against a bigger army, with more advanced technology, by delineating who fought for Israel and who failed to do so (in Judges 5, Reuben, Gilead, Dan, and Asher are chastised because they did not participate). Judges 5 not only celebrates a victory, but emphasizes that the circle of participants is even wider than the prose account suggests. Israel defeats Sisera not on its own, but with the help of YWHH, the stars, and the

---

[3] Thomas B. Dozeman, *Joshua 1-12: A New Translation with Introduction and Commentary* (New Haven: Yale University Press, 2015), 441. Dozeman compares Joshua 10:12-13 to Exodus 15 (the Song of the Sea), Numbers 21:17 (the Song of the Well), and 1 Kings 8:12-13 (a poem by Solomon).
[4] Ibid.   [5] Ibid.

Wadi Kishon. Murray Lichtenstein writes that Hebrew poetry is "a relational phenomenon"; it "derives from interaction."[6] Lichtenstein is speaking of the interaction between poet and audience, but in this case the interaction is between texts. The poetry does not embellish the prose, nor does the prose correct the poetry. Instead, prose and poetry interact to give a full account of Israel's battles.

In 2 Samuel 8:18, a forest goes to war, the forest of Ephraim, in a verse that brings to mind Tolkien's Ents and Huorns.[7] David's son Absalom has risen up against him, and in an unexpected turn of events (at least for modern readers), David triumphs over Absalom's army because trees ally themselves with his cause: "The battle was scattered there across the entirely face of the earth and in that day the forest consumed more people that the sword" (2 Samuel 18:8). Commentators have spent little time on the verse, despite the intriguing idea of tree soldiers. For example, A. A. Anderson skips it in his detailed commentary on the text, and in his general interpretation, he simply says "even ... nature fought on David's behalf."[8] P. Kyle McCarter rationalizes the verse, suggesting that it means that David's smaller army had a strategic advantage over Absalom's in the forested landscape.[9] The account itself is sparse; no one calls on or commands the forest, and up until this verse it plays no part in the battle. Trees continue to play a part – Absalom dies because his hair is caught in a tree, making him unable to escape Joab and his armor bearers (2 Samuel 18:9, 14–15) – but the narrator does not comment on or marvel at the central role forests play in David's victory. To the writer, it seems, the participation of the forest is matter-of-course, not an enchanting fairytale element, but the sort of thing one would expect to happen in war. The participation of the forest serves to legitimize David's right vis-à-vis his son; even the trees support his claim to the throne. Unlike the battle in Judges, in which legitimization is hardly an issue, here it is crucial; the war

---

[6] M. Lichtenstein, "Biblical Poetry," in *Back to the Sources: Reading the Classic Jewish Texts*, ed. Barry W. Holtz (New York: Summit Books, 1984), 121.

[7] Despite the fact that it is near impossible to read 2 Samuel 18:8 and not picture Tolkien's ents and huorns, Tolkien himself names as inspiration not 2 Samuel, but *Macbeth*: "Their part in the story is due, I think, to my bitter disappointment and disgust from schooldays with the shabby use made in Shakespeare of the coming of 'Great Birnam wood to Dunsinane hill': I longed to devise a setting in which the trees might really march to war" (J. R. R. Tolkien, *The Letters of J.R.R. Tolkien*, ed. Humphrey Carpenter [Boston: Houghton Mifflin, 1981], 211–12).

[8] A. A. Anderson, *2 Samuel* (Dallas, TX: Word Books, 1989), 225, 227.

[9] P. Kyle McCarter, *II Samuel: A New Translation with Introduction, Notes, and Commentary* (Garden City, NY: Doubleday, 1984), 405.

is not between Israelites and their enemies, but between two Davidites: David himself, and David's third son and oldest living heir, a popular leader. Together with the account of David's grief over Absalom and his insistence that Absalom should not be harmed, the participation of the trees provide support for David's right to rule, without implicating David directly in the death of his son.

In Judges 5 and 2 Samuel 18:8, it is nature's liveliness that is cause for wonder, but sometimes other-than-human persons contribute to war by being unusually inactive:

> Then Joshua spoke to YHWH, in the day YHWH set the Amorites before the children of Israel, and he said[10] in the sight of Israel: O sun, be unmoving (דּוֹם) in Gibeon, and moon, in the valley of Aijalon. And the sun did not move (וַיִּדֹּם) and the moon stood still (עָמָד), until he had taken vengeance on his enemies. Is it not written in the scroll of Jashar? The sun stood at the half-point of the heavens and did not hurry to go for a whole day. (Joshua 10:12–13)

Some scholars argue that the sun and the moon are here part of YHWH's entourage, and that they, like the stars in Judges 5, serve alongside YHWH and Israel in a military campaign.[11] Others argue the verbs דָּמַם, "to be silent, motionless," and עָמַד, "to stand," indicate that Joshua and YHWH restrain the sun and the moon from helping the Amorite army. For example, Joseph Blenkinsopp argues that "verse 12b may be an adjuration addressed to the sun and the moon not to take part in the military action."[12] Matthew Michael, going further, suggests that דָּמַם, "to be silent," refers to the silence of death, indicating that YHWH has killed the sun and the moon, who represent rival deities.[13] This reading is unpersuasive. דָּמַם, "to be silent," only rarely refers to death, and עָמַד,

---

[10] Grammatically, the subject of this verb can be either YHWH or Joshua. See Mary Katherine Hom, "A Day Like No Other: A Discussion of Joshua 10:12–14," *The Expository Times* 115, no. 7 (April 2004): 221; and Robert G. Boling, *Joshua: A New Translation* (Garden City, NY: Doubleday, 1982), 283, 287–88. Mary Katherine Hom simply points out the ambiguity, while Boling argues, based on theological grounds, that YHWH must have been the original subject. Boling does not offer any grammatical or lexical evidence to support his claim. Given the current context of the poem, which includes the first verb of verse 13 ("Joshua spoke") and the statement, in verse 14, that "The Lord listened to the voice of a man," I have translated the verb as if Joshua is the subject.

[11] See Dozeman, *Joshua 1–12*, 442; and Hom, "A Day Like No Other," 218.

[12] Joseph Blenkinsopp, *Gibeon and Israel: The Role of Gibeon and the Gibeonites in the Political and Religious History of Early Israel* (Cambridge: Cambridge University Press, 1972), 47.

[13] Michael, "Twilight of the Gods," 70.

A Sentient World

"to stand," is not associated with it at all.[14] The verbs are immediately followed by the particle עַד, "until," which conveys that the stillness of the heavenly bodies is temporary, confined to a specific period of time.

Regardless of how one understands the behavior of the luminaries, it clearly benefits Israel. The writer reports it with appreciation and awe. In contrast to the involvement of the forest of Ephraim in battle, the engagement of the luminaries is sufficiently important to warrant special mention and emphasis. This may be due to the relative importance and power of the sun and the moon as persons. Not considered divinities in ancient Israel, they were still "exceptional beings," in the words of Cooley, and their aid (or nonresistance) in battle conferred a major military advantage.[15]

Matthew Michael argues, in his article "Twilight of the Gods: Hidden Polemics in Joshua 10:12–14," that the references to the sun and the moon serve as polemic against Canaanite solar and lunar cults. He describes the immobilization of the sun and the moon "as Yhwh's military move against the deities that they represent" and, as we've already seen, suggests that the verb דָּמַם, "to be silent," may here refers to the silence of death.[16] Less drastically, Richard Nelson and Thomas Dozeman both argue that the author emphasizes *Joshua's* command to the sun and the moon, rather than the independent action of the luminaries, in order to "demythologize" their participation.[17] Their conclusion is based on no literary evidence except for the fact that Joshua issues the command to the sun and the moon. Dozeman asserts that, without the context of Joshua's command, the poem "presupposes" a solar cult.[18]

---

[14] There are only two cases in which דָּמַם ("to be silent") is clearly associated with death: Psalm 31:18[17] and Jeremiah 8:14.

[15] Cooley, *Poetic Astronomy in the Ancient Near East*, 320.

[16] Michael, "Twilight of the Gods," 66, 70. For a similar reading of Exodus 15 and other texts involving the active engagement of the earth, see Mary K. Wakeman, "Biblical Earth Monster in the Cosmogonic Combat Myth," *Journal of Biblical Literature* 88, no. 3 (September 1969): 313–20. She states that "the earth has mythological connotations as the enemy of God" (Ibid., 320).

[17] Richard D. Nelson, *Joshua: A Commentary* (Louisville, KY: Westminster John Knox, 1997), 145; Dozeman, *Joshua 1–12*, 445. Nelson writes that "calling upon heavenly beings falls considerably outside the horizon of deuteronomistic orthodoxy" (Nelson, *Joshua*, 145).

[18] Dozeman, *Joshua 1–12*, 445. For brief discussions of solar worship, see Ibid., 443–44; and Michael, "Twilight of the Gods," 61–62. For a fuller treatment of solar cults in ancient Israel, see Taylor, *Yahweh and the Sun*.

Inserting Joshua ensures that "the sun and the moon now provide little more than the background to illustrate Joshua's favored status with [YHWH]."[19] Baruch Levine makes a similar claim about the stars in Judges 5. He calls it an example of "theomachy," that is, a struggle among gods, in which "the God of Israel subdue[s] the forces of nature ... and subsequently rule[s] over them."[20]

Much like arguments about the dependence of Genesis 1 on other creation accounts, the claim that Joshua 10:12–14 is polemic is not problematic; it is the conclusions drawn from it that need rethinking. Arguments about polemical texts are filtered through the assumption that a distinguishing feature of Israelite religion is its attitude towards nature. Other ancient Near Eastern religions worship nature, while Israelite writers demythologize it. In this line of argument nature is always a problem for Israelite religion.[21] When nonanimal nature appears in the text as active and engaged, Michael, Dozeman, Nelson, and Levine assume that it is there to guard against various forms of nature worship. They read, either behind the text or hidden in its details, a battle against unacceptable views of nature, sometimes conceptualizing it as a battle between YHWH and nature gods. But, in most of these texts, any sense of opposition between YHWH and nature has been removed (or avoided) either by its writers or redactors. There is no sign that the redactors found the active role of nonanimal nature in itself problematic. As Mary Katherine Hom writes about the sun and the moon in Joshua 10, "if the poetic text was so problematic in the first place, one wonders why a compiler would bother to include it at all."[22] The sun and the moon are at the disposal of Joshua and YHWH in this story, as are the stars, the wadi, the hills, and the trees in the other texts. Hom points especially to the presence of the verb עמד, "to stand," in Joshua 10:13 ("the moon stood"), arguing that it usually carries connotations of obedience.[23] The texts counters Israelite and non-Israelite solar worship by subordinating

---

[19] Dozeman, *Joshua 1–12*, 445.
[20] Baruch A. Levine, *Numbers 21–36: A New Translation with Introduction and Commentary* (New York: Doubleday, 2000), 92.
[21] The most famous example of this line of thinking is the title of von Rad's article on the relationship between creation and soteriology: "The Theological *Problem* of the Old Testament Doctrine of Creation" (emphasis added). See Theodore Hiebert, *The Yahwist's Landscape: Nature and Religion in Early Israel* (New York: Oxford University Press, 1996), 4–29, for a discussion of the history of treating nature as a problem in the Hebrew Bible.
[22] Hom, "A Day Like No Other," 220.   [23] Ibid., 221.

the sun's power to Israel's God. The texts are polemical, but not in a hidden way. They loudly claim that the whole world, including natural forces worshipped by others as gods, responds to and are obedient to YHWH and YHWH's servants. They do not do so by moving the activity of nonanimal nature into the background or by downplaying it – rather the opposite: the poet mentions the stillness of the sun and the moon three times in two verses. Nature is not a problem here, but a faithful promoter of YHWH's causes, and, as long as Israel remains faithful to YHWH, an ally in Israel's wars.

Tikva Frymer-Kensky contrasts Israelite views of nature with those of polytheistic religions. In polytheism, she writes, nature "reflects an interplay of divine forces and personages."[24] In order to ensure agricultural abundance, humans had to plead with, sacrifice to, and appease a host of different gods and forces. If one god proved uncooperative, worshippers could turn to another god for help. In Israel, however, "[n]o such stratagems could operate."[25] YHWH becomes "the master of all nature: all of Israel's wellbeing depends on one God."[26] Frymer-Kensky's argument, considered in its broad lines, does not contradict what I have argued above. The forces of nature are not gods; nature instead is "the creature of God."[27] Frymer-Kensky concludes, however, that this means that "[i]n this monotheistic view, all nature is one unified field ... there are no forces in tension and cooperation."[28] Here she makes similar assumptions to the ones that undergird the arguments of Michael, Dozeman, Nelson, and Levine. To say that YHWH is the sole master of nature does not necessitate the conclusion that nature is "a unified field." Humans too are the creatures of YHWH, and yet humans behave in diverse ways, sometimes obeying YHWH and sometimes not. YHWH does not exercise mastery over creatures by obliterating their ability to act and make choices. "Tension and cooperation" continue to mark Israel's interaction with nature, not because nature is divine, but because humans are only one kind of creature among many.

Taken together, the accounts of war in the Former Prophets present densely populated battlefields. A neatly pitched battle turns into a watery chaos when the river convulses and the stars attack. Absalom's army seeks shelter among the trees, only to find that the trees are enemies. The strength and strategy of the Amonites come to nothing when the sun

---

[24] Tikva Simone Frymer-Kensky, *In the Wake of the Goddesses: Women, Culture, and the Biblical Transformation of Pagan Myth* (New York: Free, 1992), 86.
[25] Ibid.   [26] Ibid., 88.   [27] Ibid., 98.   [28] Ibid.

and the moon refuse to move. But not all battles go in Israel's favor. At the beginning of 2 Samuel, Saul, and Jonathan lie dead on the ground, and David, lamenting, exhorts the hills to mourn: "O mountains of Gilboa, may there be no dew; nor rain upon you, O[29] fruitful fields. For here the shield of the mighty was defiled, the shield of Saul not anointed with oil" (2 Samuel 1:21). Later in the poem, David asks the daughters of Israel to weep over Saul and Jonathan (2 Samuel 1:24), and the dryness of the hills provides a contrast to their tears. Both absence and abundance of water, that is, drought and weeping, respectively, are conventional signs of grief.[30] The earth grieves by becoming parched, humans by shedding tears. By calling to both nonanimal nature and the inhabitants of the land, David summons a diverse community of mourners to mark the death of Saul and Jonathan. Nonanimal nature is not always a terrifying force marshaled to ensure victory; sometimes other-than-human persons are more like neighbors, grief-stricken ones, who share in loss and bereavement.

It is difficult to imagine what it would be like to experience the events of Joshua, Judges, and Samuel. I cannot visualize what the writers of these texts saw or heard, the link between the events encountered and the written texts. What experiences of luminaries, rivers, and trees do the biblical writers interpret in this way? Take, for example, lightning and thunder. Modern Westerners interpret it as discharge between clouds, because we have learned to do so in school and because we have been trained in a specific understanding of cause and effect and impersonal physical forces. The Ojibwe see lightning and call it thunderbirds.[31] Neither of these interpretations of lightning is obvious from experience. Both depend on a combination of worldview and observation. It may seem strange to say that identifying lightning as thunderbirds is based on observation, but that is exactly what Graham Harvey argues. Thunderbirds are neither metaphor nor etiology; lightning and thunder are

---

[29] Reading the *vav* on וּשְׂדֵי ("O fields of ...") as a vocative, following Tod Linafelt, "Private Poetry and Public Eloquence in 2 Samuel 1:17–27: Hearing and Overhearing David's Lament for Jonathan and Saul," *The Journal of Religion* 88, no. 4 (October 2008): 499, n. 6; and Mark S. Smith, *Poetic Heroes: Literary Commemorations of Warriors and Warrior Culture in the Early Biblical World* (Grand Rapids, MI: William B. Eerdmans 2014), 268. See Anderson, *2 Samuel*, 12, 18, for translation and emendation options. Anderson, like Linafelt and Smith, translates the phrase as a vocative.

[30] For the association between the earth's mourning and drought, see Katherine Murphey Hayes, *The Earth Mourns: Prophetic Metaphor and Oral Aesthetic* (Atlanta, GA: Society of Biblical Literature, 2002), 9–10, 13–16.

[31] See Harvey, *Animism*, 38–39.

"recognized as birds because they act in ways that birds, especially birds of prey, act."[32] Like birds, thunder "fl[ies] ... migrate[s] from the south in spring and depart[s] in autumn."[33] The difference between Western interpretations of lightning and Ojibwe ones is not that one is correct and scientific, the other one fanciful. Instead, the two interpretations favor different modes of observation. The Ojibwe prioritize behavior; Western scientists prioritize cause and forces.[34]

This example illustrates that experience and explanation can be linked in many ways. The Bible's foreignness, its removal from Western modernism, consists in part of the ways in which its writers interpret events, the kinds of explanation they provide for what they observe in the world. Sometimes it is possible to glimpse their line of thought. It is not too difficult to imagine how experience informs Deborah's praise of the prowess of the Wadi Kishon. What modern empiricists might refer to as a flash flood, the writers of Judges understand as the wadi's personal assault on Israel's enemies. Or, more precisely, both the biblical writers and modern scientists see a flash flood, but they interpret it, respectively, as the personal activity of the wadi and as an impersonal meteorological phenomenon. The problem is more acute in the case of the text from Joshua 10. What does it mean that the sun and the moon stood still?[35] Flash floods are common, but the sun and the moon never stop in the sky. There is no readily available experience with which to compare the text. The same phrase appears in Habakkuk 3:11, and, in his comments on this text, John Day writes that "[t]he theophany clearly takes the form of lightning and it is surely by its brightness that the sun and the moon are here blotted out."[36] But in Joshua the sun and the moon stand still for the duration of a battle; lightning cannot explain the passage.[37] Yet the

---

[32] Ibid., 39, 107.   [33] Ibid., 38.

[34] To be clear, the difference between modern Western scientific views of the world and that found in the Bible (and in many animistic traditions) is beyond the level of the observable, even the finetuned observations of the natural sciences. Understanding lightning as a personal force, rather than a mechanistic force, is possible, even while also knowing that lightning is an electromagnetic discharge.

[35] For a summary of traditional and contemporary solutions to the question of what it means that the sun and the moon stood still, see Hom, "A Day Like No Other," 217–20; and K. Lawson Younger, *Ancient Conquest Accounts: A Study in Ancient Near Eastern and Biblical History Writing* (Sheffield: JSOT, 1990), 212–13.

[36] John Day, *God's Conflict with the Dragon and the Sea: Echoes of a Canaanite Myth in the Old Testament* (Cambridge: Cambridge University Press, 1985), 108.

[37] Day argues that the parallel between Joshua 10:12–13 and Habakkuk 3:11 "[adds] credence to the view that Josh. 10:12–13 is describing the disappearance of the sun and

difficulty of connecting experience and text is not sufficient justification for assuming that the text is not in earnest in its description of the luminaries. That I am unable to imagine an experience that *I* would interpret as the sun and the moon standing still displays my inability to enter into the mind and perspective of biblical writers. The text bespeaks an understanding of the world that is radically different from the dominant worldview of Western modernity. K. L. Younger recognizes this difference, and concludes by summarizing the little bit of certainty we can have about the text: "What seems to be clear [in Joshua 10] is that celestial bodies participated in the battle which YHWH fought for Israel."[38] What sort of phenomena led the biblical writers to this conclusion is elusive, and searching for a clear, rationalistic explanation for texts like Joshua 10:12–13 is not fruitful. Yet it is undeniably frustrating to be unable to picture the scenario described in the story. As Robert G. Boling writes, "the question of actual relationship between one's experience and confessions of faith will not go away."[39] That frustration is part of the tension of reading personalistic nature texts, and provided we do not assume that modern ways of viewing the world are better, more advanced, the frustration can be a means to greater openness to views of nature that differ from our own. The difficulty of getting to know unfamiliar views of nature sits within Christian and Jewish traditions – it appears on the scene before religions of the book come into contact with other religions and worldviews – and that difficulty has the potential to train us to be humble when judging the "rightness" of traditions that conflict with our experiences of the world.

THEOPHANY

In theophanies, humans and other-than-human persons react to YHWH's presence. One of the most striking aspects of theophanies is the way in which biblical writers use more or less the same language and vocabulary to describe human and nonhuman responses. Mountains, valleys, waves, and trees tremble, melt, and writhe at YHWH's coming, much like humans do. The vocabulary of theophany, even words that permit mechanistic or automatic readings, overlaps substantially with the vocabulary

---

moon as a result of an early morning storm, suggesting a connection with the hail storm alluded to in v. 11" (Ibid.).

[38] Younger, *Ancient Conquest Accounts*, 212.   [39] Boling, *Joshua*, 283.

of fear and reverence. Nature responds in ways not categorically different from humans; it reacts the way all creatures, human and nonhuman, react when they come into close proximity to YHWH.

Kenneth Schmitz argues that nature theophanies posit an "interiority in the cosmos," which "[penetrates] beyond nature as a mere fact into nature as a creature."[40] The awe humans experience in YHWH's presence is not, Schmitz asserts, a uniquely human reaction. When humans tremble before God, they share in a creationwide response, a "joint submission by which nature and history together acknowledge their inner ground."[41] Any interpretation that ignores this, he says, and only attributes interiority to humans, "is a misreading."[42] When biblical writers describe the convulsive joy and fear humans and other-than-humans experience when faced with God, they "[profess] to speak reliably of an interior depth shared by [humanity] and nature."[43]

Schmitz's study begins to fill a lacuna in classical studies of theophany. Though these have, in one sense, given pride of place to nature's response to YHWH, they have done so only to the extent that melting mountains and dripping clouds supply clues to literary genre and ancient Near Eastern parallels. The scholarships of Hermann Gunkel, Jörg Jeremias, Frank Moore Cross, John Day, and Carola Kloos illustrate this. Each of these scholars write about theophany from two related methodological stances: they use form criticism to determine the basic literary form and genre of theophany, and/or they trace the relationship between theophany and Near Eastern myths, paying particular attention to Divine Warrior myths (*Chaoskampf*). Jeremias, Cross, and Kloos may not agree about the exact literary form of theophany (Jeremias posits a two part structure,[44] Cross expands it to a four part framework,[45] while Kloos argues that

---

[40] Kenneth L Schmitz, "World and Word in Theophany," *Faith and Philosophy* 1, no. 1 (January 1984): 67. Fretheim also uses the word "interiority" to describe the relationship between God and the world. He writes "[N]atural phenomenon must be of such a nature that God is able to sustain the close relationship with them that the biblical evidence implies. This relationship suggests that these creatures have a certain inwardness or interiority such that more than external relationships are possible" (Fretheim, *God and World in the Old Testament*, 255).

[41] Schmitz, "World and Word in Theophany," 67.   [42] Ibid.   [43] Ibid.

[44] Jeremias defines theophany as a two part, sequential structure: (1) the coming of the deity, and (2) the reaction of nature. See Jörg Jeremias, *Theophanie: Die Geschichte Einer Alttestamentlichen Gattung* (Neukirchen-Vluyn: Neukirchener Verlag des Erziehungsvereins, 1965), 107–11.

[45] Cross uses Jeremias' basic outline, but expands it into a two part movement, a there-and-back narrative of divine war: (a) The Divine Warrior goes forth to battle against chaos (Yamm, Leviathan, Môt); (b) nature convulses (writhes) and languishes when the Warrior

theophany is a less clearcut literary pattern than Jeremias and Cross suggest[46]), but all of them seek to answer the same question: what are the literary contours of the genre theophany? Nature's response is one aspect of the genre; once that has been determined, the scope of their studies as it relates to nonhuman creatures has been satisfied. Similarly, Gunkel and Day come to divergent conclusions about the source of the genre – Gunkel points to Marduk's victory over Tiamat in the Babylonian epic *Enuma Elish*,[47] while Day points to Baal's victory over Yam[48] – but, again, nature's involvement and the vocabulary used to describe it serve one role in their arguments, that is, to establish a bridge between the Hebrew Bible and other myths.

This study follows Schmitz's lead; I am interested in the *content* of theophany, the ways in which it talks about other-than-human persons. Also helpful is Schmitz's observation that the language used in theophany to describe human and other-than-human reactions to YHWH is similar, sometimes the same. What does vary, however, between one theophany and the next, is the extent to which writers draw their vocabulary of awe and fear from the human sphere or the nonhuman sphere. Both influence each other: poets narrate human fear using storms and earthquakes, and rain showers and eclipses are described with reference to human bodies. Neither serves as the overriding model for the other, but instead the full vocabulary of human and other-than-human agitation is necessary to put words to what it is like to come face to face with YHWH.

---

manifests his wrath; (c) the warrior god returns to take up kingship among the gods, and is enthroned on his mountain; (d) the Divine Warrior utters his voice from his temple, and Nature again responds – the heavens fertilize the earth, animals writhe in giving birth, and men and mountains whirl in dancing and festive glee. See Cross, *Canaanite Myth and Hebrew Epic*, 162.

[46] Kloos argues that Cross exaggerates the extent to which theophany follows a clear pattern. Though the elements that Cross identifies can be found in the Hebrew Bible, she writes that several are not present in Canaanite mythology (especially the "festive glee" of nature). "The motifs are demonstrable," she writes, "but there is not a clear-cut pattern." See Carola Kloos, *Yhwh's Combat with the Sea: A Canaanite Tradition in the Religion of Ancient Israel* (Amsterdam; Leiden: G.A. van Oorschot; Brill, 1986), 46.

[47] Hermann Gunkel, *Creation and Chaos in the Primeval Era and the Eschaton: A Religio-Historical Study of Genesis 1 and Revelation 12*, trans. K. William Whitney Jr. (Grand Rapids, MI: William B. Eerdmans, 2006), 11–12, 75–77.

[48] See Day, *God's Conflict with the Dragon and the Sea*, 4–7. It is anachronistic, in a sense, to say that Day and Gunkel disagree. Day's disagreement with Gunkel was the result of the discovery, in 1929, of the library of Ugarit. Gunkel did not have access to the Baal Cycle and, therefore, could not have come to Day's conclusions.

An example of a theophany that makes clear reference to human bodies is Habakkuk 3:10–11:

The mountains saw you and writhed (יְחִילוּ), a rainstorm of water passed by. The deep gave its voice, the sun raised high its hands. The moon stood still in its height, because of the light of your arrows passing by, because of the brightness of your spear's lightning.[49]

The poet lists a series of responses: seeing and writhing, calling out, raising hands, and standing still. The image is of a great group of creatures who expresses astonishment and fear through human gestures and human limbs. The deep has a voice, the sun has hands, the mountains have eyes to see. Even the verb חִיל, "to writhe," has a human reference: it is associated with fear and the pain of childbirth.[50] The language is metaphorical, but the purpose of this language is to describe with clarity and detail the response of that which is not human.[51] The writers use their own experiences of fear to narrate that of the cosmos. The approximate quality of the language is a necessary consequence of attempting to put words to nature's response to meeting YHWH. Metaphor is necessary both because humans only have direct access to their own interior experiences, and because YHWH is such an undefinable reality. The biblical writers observe a relationship between YHWH and nature and use the language at their disposal to portray it as best they can. By doing so they achieve what Janet Soskice argues is the purpose of much metaphorical

---

[49] Habakkuk 3:8–15 presents several translational difficulties. For a translational approach that relies heavily on parallels between Habakkuk 3 and the Baal cycle, see Francis I. Andersen, *Habakkuk: A New Translation with Introduction and Commentary* (New York: Doubleday, 2001), 312–13. For a different translational approach, one that assumes that Habakkuk 3 instead draws on the language of human kingship, see David Toshio Tsumura, *Creation and Destruction: A Reappraisal of the Chaoskampf Theory in the Old Testament* (Winona Lake, IN: Eisenbrauns, 2005), 164–81.

[50] For instances in which חִיל ("to writhe, travail") describes fear, see Deuteronomy 2:25; Jeremiah 4:19; 5:22; 51:29; Ezekiel 30:16; Joel 2:6; Habakkuk 3:10; and Zechariah 9:5. For examples of the verb being used in the context of childbirth, see Deuteronomy 32:18; Isaiah 45:10; 51:2; 54:1; 66:7; and Job 39:1. Isaiah several times takes advantage of the connection between fear and childbirth; see Isaiah 13:8; 23:4–5; 26:17. See also Micah 4:10. Though חִיל is primarily used with human subjects, other examples of its use to describe trembling or writhing in nature include Jeremiah 51:29; Ezekiel 30:16; Zechariah 9:5; Psalm 29:8–9, 77:17 [16], 97:4, 114:7; and 1 Chronicles 16:30.

[51] According to Rudolf Otto, even human experiences of divine presence are so mysterious and unlike other human experiences that "metaphor and symbolic expression" necessarily form a part in any description of them. See Rudolf Otto, *The Idea of the Holy: An Inquiry into the Non-Rational Factor in the Idea of the Divine and Its Relation to the Rational*, trans. John W. Harvey (London: Oxford University Press, 1970), 12.

language: they provide us access to a referent and a relationship we otherwise would not be able to talk about or put into descriptive language.[52]

Several theophanies avoid humanoid descriptions of other-than-human persons. These are interesting for the ways in which their vocabulary bleeds into descriptions of human terror found elsewhere. Joel 2:10 and 4:15–16 are good examples:

Before him the earth trembles (רָגְזָה), the heavens shake (רָעֲשׁוּ), the sun and the moon are dark (קָדָרוּ)[53] and the stars gather in (אָסְפוּ) their brightness. (Joel 2:10)

The sun and the moon are dark (קָדָרוּ) and the stars gather in (אָסְפוּ) their brightness. YHWH roars from Zion and from Jerusalem he gives his voice; the heavens and the earth shake (וְרָעֲשׁוּ). But YHWH is a refuge for his people, and a stronghold for the children of Israel. (Joel 4:15–16)[54]

The only verb borrowed from a human context is אָסַף, "to gather," which usually describes harvesting produce or gathering together people. The other verbs, most obviously רָגַז, "to tremble," and רָעַשׁ, "to shake," sound much like the sort of language a moderner would use to describe tectonic disturbances. In biblical Hebrew, רָעַשׁ, "to shake," is more or less reserved for nonhuman subjects, but רָגַז, "to tremble," also describes human fear and awe.[55] Similarly, the verb קָדַר, "to be dark, to mourn," whose subjects are the sun and the moon in Joel, refers to mourning when its subject is human.[56] The verb depicts both the physical experience of

---

[52] See Soskice, *Metaphor and Religious Language*, 124–32. Soskice helpfully distinguishes between "referring and defining," and argues that this distinction lies "at the very heart of metaphorical speaking" (Ibid., 140). The biblical writers do not define the relationship between YHWH and nonanimal nature, but they do attempt to describe it.

[53] The NRSV and the ESV both translate the Qal Perfect forms of the root קדר in these verses as "to be darkened," as in "The sun and the moon are darkened." This translation is possible, but, given that קָדַר is a simple stative verb, it would make more sense to translate it as "to be dark." The translation "to be darkened" suggests a greater degree of passivity on the parts of the sun and the moon than what is present in the Hebrew text.

[54] Other texts also associate darkness with YHWH's coming, but do so with language that is less suggestive of the direct involvement of the luminaries themselves. See, for example, Isaiah 13:10.

[55] See Exodus 15:14; Deuteronomy 2:25; 28:65; Isaiah 32:10–11; Jeremiah 33:9; Joel 2:1; and Habakkuk 3:16.

[56] See, for example, Jeremiah 8:21; and Psalm 35:14; 38:7[6]; 42:10[9]. Jeremiah 4:28 uses קָדַר, "to be dark," in parallel with אָבַל, "to mourn." Other roots are also used to express the parallel between human mourning and disturbances in nature; see, for example, Amos 8:7–8: "YHWH has sworn by the pride of Jacob: If I ever forget any of their deeds ... On account of this, will not the land tremble (תִּרְגַּז), and all who live in it mourn (וְאָבַל), and all of it go up like the Nile, and be tossed up and sink like the Nile of Egypt?"

darkness and the affective experience of grief. Such multivalent language extends beyond Joel. Micah 1:4 says that "The mountains will melt (וְנָמַסּוּ) under him, the valleys will split open, like wax before the fire, like water poured down a descent." The Niphal of the verb מָסַס, "to melt," is common in stories of human terror and alarm: "Our heart melted (וַיִּמַּס), and we could no longer stand before you" (Joshua 2:11).[57] Perhaps even describing human experiences of meeting YHWH is so difficult that it requires drawing on more than everyday emotions and terms. How do I feel when YHWH arrives? I feel like the storm clouds, like the moon in eclipse, like the tremors of a quake, like rock blistering into lava.

These examples show how inappropriate it is in biblical texts to distinguish between active and affective response and mechanistic processes. Much like the Ojibwe call lightning birds because birds and lightning behave in similar ways, so biblical writers use the same language to narrate human and nonhuman fear. From this point of view, fear and awe are behaviors, not primarily internal attitudes. As Theodore Hiebert writes, speaking of the poet's fear in Habakkuk 3, human awe in the face of YHWH participates in the larger response of the cosmos: "The poet is part of the entire creation which shudders at the appearance of the divine warrior."[58] When humans cower and are petrified before YHWH, they are not doing something characteristically human; they participate in an experience and a behavior that spans the whole created world. They are one creature among many who thrill and quail at the presence of God.

If nature is afraid of YHWH, does that mean that it is God's enemy? The short answer is no. Fear in God's presence is not unique to God's enemies, but is rather a common and appropriate response to encountering the divine. The fear of YHWH (יִרְאַת יהוה) characterizes YHWH's followers, and is positively valued throughout the Hebrew Bible. To the psalmist, "the fear of YHWH" is the beginning of wisdom (Psalm 111:10), and Isaiah argues that such fear is a source of delight to God's servant (Isaiah 11:3).[59] Terror or dread (פַּחַד) more often belongs to

---

[57] See also Joshua 5:1; 7:5; Isaiah 8:6; and Ezekiel 21:12[7]; in most of these texts the immediate subject is the heart of a person or people group, as in "our heart melted" (Joshua 2:11).

[58] Theodore Hiebert, *God of My Victory: The Ancient Hymn in Habakkuk 3* (Atlanta, GA: Scholars, 1986), 115. See also Ezekiel 38:19–20, in which humans are only one item on a long list of creatures (fish, birds, animals, creeping things, and humans) that shake because of YHWH's words.

[59] "The fear of YHWH" is a particularly prominent theme in Proverbs. In Proverbs, "the fear of YHWH" is "the beginning of knowledge" (Proverbs 1:7), "hatred of evil"

YHWH's enemies, but it too can have positive valences. In Genesis 31:42, Jacob describes YHWH as "the dread of Isaac (פַּחַד יִצְחָק),"[60] and in Isaiah 60:5, פַּחַד, "dread," is included in a list of joyful responses to the return of the exiles.[61] In call narratives, fear during encounters with God is common. When Isaiah sees God's throne in the temple, his immediate response is "woe is me" (Isaiah 6:5), Ezekiel falls on his face when he sees God's chariot (Ezekiel 1:28), Moses hides his face at the burning bush for fear of seeing God (Exodus 3:6), and Israel asks Moses to speak to them instead of God, "lest we die" (Exodus 20:19). In Habakkuk 3, the poet speaks of his own fear at YHWH's approach using terms reminiscent of those with which he described nature's response: "I hear and my insides trembled (וַתִּרְגַּז), at the sound my lips tingled. Rottenness entered my bones, and beneath me my steps[62] trembled (אֶרְגָּז/יִרְגָּזוּ)" (Habakkuk 3:16). Habakkuk is not afraid that he himself will be punished. He looks with anticipation to "the day of calamity [coming] upon the people who attack us" (Habakkuk 3:16). YHWH's coming is awesome and appalling to both those who benefit from it and to those who do not. In Joel 2, nature's devastation at YHWH's appearance is followed by assurance: "Do not be afraid, O soil, be glad and rejoice" (Joel 2:21a). Hiebert describes fear in theophany texts as "the deep dread of the worshiper of [YHWH] at the recognition of his awful power."[63] Rudolf Otto aptly calls this fear "creature-feeling" or "creature-consciousness."[64] It is "the emotion of a creature, abased and overwhelmed by its own nothingness in contrast to that which is supreme above all creatures."[65] Terror is not first and foremost an anticipation of punishment or violence, but rather a recognition of YHWH's incomparable majesty and power.

(Proverbs 8:13), "the beginning of wisdom" (Proverbs 9:10), "a fountain of life" (Proverbs 14:27), and "instruction in wisdom" (Proverbs 15:33). It is credited with prolonging life (Proverbs 10:27), and it is better than treasure (Proverbs 15:16).

[60] See also Genesis 31:53.
[61] Isaiah 60:5 reads: "Then you will see and be radiant. Your heart will feel dread (פָּחַד) and expand (רָחַב). For the multitude of the sea will be turned over to you, the wealth of the nations will come to you." See also Psalm 36:1, in which the poet chastises the wicked because they do not feel dread of God (פַּחַד אֱלֹהִים), and Psalm 119:120, 161.
[62] Reading the MT אֲשֶׁר (relative particle, "that, which") as אֲשֻׁרַי, the dual form of the noun אֶשֶׁר ("step"). For a discussion of translation options for Habakkuk 3:16, see Hiebert, *God of My Victory*, 51.
[63] Ibid., 113. See also Cross, *Canaanite Myth and Hebrew Epic: Essays in the History of the Religion of Israel*, 156.
[64] Otto, *The Idea of the Holy*, 10.
[65] Ibid. Otto elsewhere uses the lovely phrase "plenitude of being (*Seinsfülle*)" to describe YHWH's superiority. See Ibid., 21.

One creature stands out as a potential enemy of God: the sea. In Habakkuk 3, the poet asks: "Were you angry with the rivers, O YHWH? Or was your anger against the rivers? Or your wrath against the sea?" (Habakkuk 3:8a). While some commentators have asserted that the implied answer to this question is "no," Theodore Hiebert answers in the affirmative.[66] A rhetorical question prefixed with a plain interrogative *hey* usually implies a negative answer (for a positive answer, לֹא, "no, not," is added to the interrogative), but Hiebert cites several instances in which this is not the case.[67] He also points out that the structure of the psalm requires a positive answer to the question "were you angry with the rivers?"[68] The center of the poem narrates YHWH's coming as a warrior, a section framed by verses 3:8 and 3:15. The latter verse, "You trod (דָּרַכְתָּ) on the sea with your horses, foaming the great waters," is reminiscent of verse 3:12, in which God tramples the nations: "In your indignation you march (תִּצְעַד) on the earth, in your anger you trampled (תָּדוּשׁ) the nations" (Habakkuk 3:12). The verbs are different in the two verses, but they appear to be based on the same image: "the triumphant warrior with his feet on the back of the conquered foe."[69] Together, the two images prove YHWH's prowess as a military leader by offering examples of humiliated adversaries. The sea is also YHWH's enemy in Isaiah 50:2 and Nahum 1:4; both poems state that YHWH "rebukes" (גָּעַר) the sea. These passages, then, in contrast to other texts we have looked at,

---

[66] See also Day, *God's Conflict with the Dragon and the Sea*, 105. For commentators who assert that the answer to the question is no, see Sigmund Olaf Plytt Mowinckel, "Zum Psalm Des Habakuk," *Theologische Zeitschrift* 9, no. 1 (January 1953): 14; Umberto Cassuto, *Biblical and Oriental Studies*, vol. 2 (Jerusalem: Magnes, Hebrew University, 1973), 11, 13; and John D. W. Watts, *The Books of Joel, Obadiah, Jonah, Nahum, Habakkuk, and Zephaniah* (Cambridge: Cambridge University Press, 1975), 149.

[67] Hiebert, *God of My Victory*, 102. Hiebert cites Job 20:4, Jeremiah 31:10 (probably intending 31:20, since 31:10 does not have an interrogative *hey*), and Genesis 3:11. The last is uncertain support for his claim, as it need not be read as a rhetorical question, but can also be taken as a request for information ("have you eaten from the tree about which I commanded you, 'Do not eat from it'?") – the question need not imply a specific answer. He references the BDB entry on the interrogative, which includes the option that the interrogative *hey* is "used in questions which, by seeming to make doubtful what cannot be denied, have the force of an impassioned or indignant affirmation." Cited in the entry are Genesis 27:36, 1 Samuel 2:27, 1 Kings 16:31, 21:19, and Jeremiah 31:20 (Brown et al., *The Brown-Driver-Briggs Hebrew and English Lexicon* [Peabody, MA: Hendrickson, 1996], 210). See also Wilhelm Gesenius, *Gesenius' Hebrew Grammar*, ed. E. Kautzsch (Oxford: The Clarendon, 1910), para. 150e.

[68] Hiebert, *God of My Victory*, 102. See also Andersen, *Habakkuk*, 316–17.

[69] Hiebert, *God of My Victory*, 116. Hiebert argues that this is the image evoked in the final line of the poem as well, "he makes me thread on my heights" (Habakkuk 3:19c).

describe situations in which one part of nature is in rebellion against God. In the words of Jon Levenson, "we have a sense of the Sea as a somewhat sinister force that, left to its own, would submerge the world and forestall the ordered reality we call creation."[70] In some biblical passages, such as Genesis 1 and Exodus 15, the recalcitrant waters of Canaanite and Babylonian myth have become creatures obedient to YHWH. In Habakkuk 3:8–15, Isaiah 50:2, and Nahum 1:4, the relationship between God and the sea remains tense and conflictual.

The role of the sea reflects a dynamic found in myths about the battle between Baal, Yamm, and Leviathan, in which Baal defeats the monsters of chaos.[71] In the Hebrew Bible, in contradistinction to Canaanite myth, this conflict is not between God and other divinities, but between God and one particularly rebellious creature.[72] Levenson's contribution on "the persistence of evil" is helpful here. Levenson argues that the rebellion of the sea shows that creation is "inherently unsafe" and "precarious."[73] Not all creatures are safe company for Israel, and Israel survives only through "God's vigilance."[74] Levenson's argument contrasts with Frymer-Kensky's claim that, in the Hebrew Bible, "all nature is one unified field … there are no forces in tension and cooperation."[75] Though YHWH is unified and one, the world of creatures is full of *both* tension and cooperation. Biblical writers do not in these texts express concern that YHWH will be defeated by other deities, but instead that he will forget or abstain from restraining those creatures that threaten Israel's wellbeing, be it forces of nature or imperial armies.[76] Historical experience confirms that sometimes YHWH not only permits the ongoing existence of enemies, but even allows enemies to defeat Israel.[77] The recalcitrant sea is a nonhuman version of such enemies; it is not a god,

---

[70] Jon D. Levenson, *Creation and the Persistence of Evil: The Jewish Drama of Divine Omnipotence* (Princeton, NJ: Princeton University Press, 1994), 15.

[71] Though almost all commentators claim that Habakkuk 3 draws on Ba'al material, see Tsumura, *Creation and Destruction*, 164–81, for an argument to the contrary. Tsumura refutes the common assertion that the *Chaoskampf* motif is present in the Hebrew Bible.

[72] See, for example, Cassuto's comments on the sea in Habakkuk 3 (*Biblical and Oriental Studies*, 2:5).

[73] Levenson, *Creation and the Persistence of Evil*, 17.   [74] Ibid.

[75] Frymer-Kensky, *In the Wake of the Goddesses*, 98.

[76] Other stories suggest concern about the relative power of YHWH vis-à-vis other gods. See, for example, the stories in 1 Samuel 5, in which the ark of YHWH is placed in the temple of Dagon, only to "defeat" his image.

[77] Levenson argues that descriptions of God's power over the sea appear most often in contexts in which the writer worries about the power of Israel's human enemies. He cites Psalm 74 and Isaiah 51:9–11.

but a creature that could, if YHWH gave it free rein, annihilate Israel and undo God's promises to her.

The language of God's domination of the sea resembles the language of God's judgment of Israel's enemies and of Israel herself. The root גער, "to rebuke," which Day calls "a ... technical term for the divine conflict with the sea,"[78] appears not only in texts in which God rebukes the sea, but also in texts in which God rebukes Israel or her adversaries.[79] More generally, the verb is used when someone in authority disciplines another person who has acted inappropriately or aggressively.[80] Habakkuk's words for anger, including חָרָה, "to be angry," אַף, "anger," עֶבְרָה, "wrath," and זַעַם, "to be indignant," occur in situations of interpersonal conflict and when God disciplines humans. Scholars usually explain the similarities in the language of theophany, *Chaoskampf*, and God's judgment of the nations by positing a tendency in the Bible to historicize mythic material.[81] Israel's neighbors focused on mythic patterns and mythic enemies, but Israel, with its interest in history, morphed these mythic monsters into historic, human enemies.[82] Just as Baal/YHWH battles against the sea, so YHWH battles against the nations. As a general explanation, this is convincing, but the relationship between the nations as enemies and the sea as enemy has not been sufficiently interrogated. The whole weight of the comparison, in most explanations, lies on the verbal phrase "battles against." The similarity is in God's actions, not in the recipients of that action. But Israel applies the Canaanite myth to historical enemies not only because YHWH battles against both the sea and peoples, but because the nations, the sea, and Israel are all sometimes

---

[78] Day, *God's Conflict with the Dragon and the Sea*, 127. Day cites Job 26:11; Psalm 18:16 [15] (also found in 2 Samuel 22:16), 104:7; Isaiah 17:13; and Nahum 1:4.

[79] God rebukes Israel (or promises to stop rebuking Israel) in Isaiah 54:9 and Malachiah 2:3, and the nations in Isaiah 17:3 and Psalm 9:6 [5].

[80] Jacob rebukes Joseph in Genesis 37:10; in Jeremiah 29:27, Zephaniah is encouraged to rebuke Jeremiah; YHWH rebukes Satan in Zechariah 3:2; and God promises to rebuke the locust in Malachi 3:11.

[81] See Day, *God's Conflict with the Dragon and the Sea*, 88–139; Kloos, *Yhwh's Combat with the Sea*, 158–90; Carol L. Meyers, *Exodus* (Cambridge: Cambridge University Press, 2005), 120. Technical terms reflect this explanation. God's judgment of the nations is called *Völkerkampf*, in parallel with *Chaoskampf* (Day, *God's Conflict with the Dragon and the Sea*, 125–38).

[82] See, for example, Anderson, *Creation versus Chaos*, 30. For a critique of history as the main characteristics of Israelite religion, over against the mythic focus of other Ancient Near Eastern religions, see James Barr, "Revelation Through History in the Old Testament and in Modern Theology," *Interpretation* 17 (1963): 193–205. Barr contests the claim that history is the primary form of revelation in the Hebrew Bible.

defiant and bellicose creatures. It is not necessary to say with Day that the sea is a kind of demon in the Hebrew Bible.[83] The designation "demon" implies a natural/supernatural divide, which obfuscates rather than clarifies the role of the sea. The sea is not a mystical being, but a personal force, just as human enemies are personal forces. Both the nations and the sea are sometimes aggressors; the similarity between them lies in how they behave towards Israel and God. Rather than a unique demonic antagonist, the ocean is only one adversary among several.

The sometimes inimical relationship between YHWH and the sea sounds troubling in light of the contemporary ecological devastation of oceans, lakes, and rivers. Peter Trudinger writes that, in the classic *Chaoskampf* myth, the earth "in the form it is encountered now, is dead, and in its original mode of being, was hostile to God and inimical to harmony and order."[84] Though he argues that the Old Testament portrayal of the sea is more nuanced than this – sometimes it appears as God's loyal servant, sometimes as God's enemy – he writes that when it appears in the context of *Chaoskampf*, it is "always the villain, fit only for death."[85] Habel and Avent, in an essay suggestively titled "Rescuing Earth from a Storm God," claim that YHWH's appearance in a storm in Psalm 29 is "destructive" and betrays "a theocentrism that exalts the power of God at the expense of the Earth community."[86] But all this looks less ecologically suspect if the ancient context is kept in mind. Ancient Israelites were not able, as we are now, to disrupt and destroy oceans. Oceans and lakes can be terrifying and dangerous; anyone who has been out in a boat during a storm will have firsthand knowledge of this. If viewed as persons, rather than mechanical forces, it takes no great leap of imagination to understand why writers of the Hebrew Bible portray bodies of water as combative and threatening.

It is also important to keep in mind that worldviews often praised for their ecological sensitivity, such as animistic traditions, rarely posit a bland

---

[83] Day, *God's Conflict with the Dragon and the Sea*, 189.
[84] Peter L. Trudinger, "Friend or Foe? Earth, Sea and Chaoskampf in the Psalms," in *Earth Story in the Psalms and the Prophets*, ed. Norman C. Habel, The Earth Bible 4 (Sheffield: Sheffield Academic, 2001), 30. Trudinger writes about the earth, not the sea, because in the *Enuma Elish* the whole world is created out of the dead body of Tiamat, a water goddess.
[85] Ibid., 41.
[86] Norman C. Habel and Geraldine Avent, "Rescuing Earth from a Storm God: Psalms 29 and 96–97," in *The Earth Story in the Psalms and the Prophets*, ed. Norman C. Habel, The Earth Bible 4 (Sheffield: Sheffield Academic, 2001), 50.

harmony between all aspects of nature. The same beliefs praised by scholars who suspect God's rebuke of the sea include recognition of competitive and conflictual relationships, as well as methods for dealing with them.[87] The most obvious is that between hunter and prey, but there are closer parallels to YHWH's conflict with the sea. The Ojibwe considers both thunder and lakes (or lake beings) as persons, but they seek to maintain respectful and positive relationships with Thunderers (or Thunder Birds), while their relationship with the lake beings is aggressive.[88] Humans and Thunderers ally themselves against the lake aggressors, towards whom they have a "shared hostility."[89] That the writers of the Hebrew Bible understand elements of nonanimal nature as persons does not mean that all relationships between humans, animals, nonanimals, and YHWH are amicable. In animist traditions, relationships with other-than-human persons include many of the possibilities of human relationships – they can be friendly, cooperative, and harmonious, or they can be antagonistic and frightening. This need not be ecologically troubling. If the world is populated with both human and other-than-human persons, it is important to know not just to whom to relate, but the quality of your relationship with each person. Interacting with a sometimes bellicose sea requires a different kind of relationship than interacting with a friend. The sea as an enemy only becomes really problematic when it is put in the context of the modern objectification and commodification of all that is not human. In this context, the sea as an enemy can serve as justification for unbridled resource extraction and pollution.[90] In the context of the Hebrew Bible, the trope of the sea as an enemy does not justify destruction and ecological irresponsibility.[91] Instead, God's control over the sea provides a reminder and assurance of God's power. In a world that is sometimes

---

[87] Veronica Brady names Aboriginal and indigenous views of the earth as one inspiration for the Earth Bible Project (Habel, *Readings from the Perspective of Earth*, 16).

[88] Harvey, *Animism*, 22, 39. For more on the water being(s) in Ojibwe tradition, see Theresa S. Smith, *The Island of the Anishnaabeg: Thunderers and Water Monsters in the Traditional Ojibwe Life-World* (Moscow, ID: University of Idaho, 1995), 95–125.

[89] Harvey, *Animism*, 39.

[90] Harvey contrasts aggressive relationships in animism with the depersonalized aggression of modern objectifications of the world. Writing about shamans, he stresses that "shamanic engagement with potential, alleged or actual aggressors is of a piece with everything else that is central to shamans and their communities" (Ibid., 150). Aggressive relationships between humans and other-than-human persons is not a deviation from animism, but part and parcel of it: "Shamanic aggression and defence is animist. It is a relational engagement with subjects, agents, persons ... shamans aggress without depersonalising or objectifying their opponents" (Ibid.). See also Viveiros de Castro, *Cannibal Metaphysics*, 74.

[91] See, for example, Ellen Davis' argument that the statement in Revelation 21:1 that "the sea is no more" is not a sign of a "tradition that is phobic with respect to any aspect of the

hostile to human safety and need, these texts assure the reader that YHWH is more powerful than all creatures, and capable of protecting God's people.

ADDRESS

A distinct feature of Israelite prophetic writings is that YHWH and YHWH's prophets do not address humans exclusively. Other-than-human nature is also summoned to listen. The heavens, the earth and its soil, forests and their trees, mountains, the wind – the divine word goes out to all of them. They receive oracles of judgment and consolation, and are called on to witness YHWH's judgment and mercy towards Israel. The responsiveness of creation to YHWH's word also serves as a sign of YHWH's power; Israel's God is a god who can command the waters and the winds.

This feature of prophetic literature is usually called apostrophe.[92] Apostrophe is a literary device in which one "[turns] away from one's [primary] audience to address a person, city, nation, or other inanimate object."[93] We have already seen an example of apostrophe in David's lament for Saul and Jonathan: "O mountains of Gilboa, may there be no dew ..." (2 Samuel 1:21).[94] Apostrophe is a subset of the vocative case; all apostrophes are vocative, but not all vocatives are apostrophe.

---

created order," but instead "signals and epitomizes the disintegration of the empire's political and cultural dominance" (Ellen F. Davis, *Biblical Prophecy: Perspectives for Christian Theology, Discipleship, and Ministry* [Louisville, KY: Westminster John Knox, 2014], 134). For the inhabitants of "the Roman province of Asia," Davis writes, "Roman power always materialized in the form of naval and merchant ships coming over the western horizon" (Ibid.). John's vision of the end of the sea does not support unrestrained extraction and use of resources, but instead protests against the empire's unchecked commerce and consumption.

[92] See Linafelt, "Private Poetry and Public Eloquence in 2 Samuel 1"; Joseph Blenkinsopp, *Isaiah 40–55: A New Translation with Introduction and Commentary* (New York: Doubleday, 2000), 250; Jack R. Lundbom, *Jeremiah: A New Translation with Introduction and Commentary* (New York: Doubleday, 1999), 267; Carol L. Meyers and Eric M. Meyers, *Zechariah 9–14: A New Translation with Introduction and Commentary* (New York: Doubleday, 1993), 238. Apostrophe is so characteristic of prophetic speech that Jonathan Culler, writing of the use of apostrophe in European postenlightenment poetry, calls apostrophe a "prophetic voice" (Jonathan Culler, "Apostrophe," in *The Pursuit of Signs: Semiotics, Literature, Deconstruction*, An Augmented Edition [Ithaca, NY: Cornell University Press, 2001], 139, 142).

[93] Jack R. Lundbom, *The Hebrew Prophets: An Introduction* (Minneapolis, MN: Fortress, 2010), 204.

[94] For a discussion of apostrophe in David's lament, see Linafelt, "Private Poetry and Public Eloquence in 2 Samuel 1."

For example, God's call to Abraham in Genesis 22:11 ("Abraham, Abraham") is not apostrophe, because Abraham is the primary addressee. Apostrophe is a means by which a writer puts his or her primary audience into a position of overhearing speech to a second audience, shifting the relationship between speaker and addressee.[95]

Apostrophe sometimes makes use of fictive addressees, but the trope works equally well with fictive and nonfictive audiences. When speaking of prophetic oracles to other-than-human persons, scholars often use language like "imaginary" and "real" audiences for nonhuman and human audiences, respectively.[96] But, as Jonathan Culler points out, apostrophe as a trope says nothing about the animicity of its addressee: "The animicity enforced by the apostrophe is independent of any claims made about the actual properties of the object addressed."[97] Culler studies European postenlightenment poetry, and, therefore, has good reason to believe that lines like "O wild West Wind" ought not to be taken as indication that the poet (in this case Shelley) believes in the personhood of the wind. The same assumption cannot be made with confidence when assessing apostrophe in the Hebrew Bible. Biblical writers did not draw as clear a line between objects and subjects as modern Westerners. The fact that nonanimal nature serves as a *secondary* audience in the Hebrew Bible is not sufficient evidence to conclude that it is not a genuine audience. The plethora of personalistic nature texts suggest otherwise. Apostrophe is only one indication that biblical writers thought that nonanimal nature possessed personhood. This trope makes clear that nature's personhood extends to conversation; nonanimal nature can hear and respond to divine and human words.

Culler's work on apostrophe has further application to prophetic texts, so I will summarize it briefly. Culler organizes his exposition on apostrophe into four levels of reading, each of which offers a different perspective

---

[95] Culler states that what distinguishes apostrophe from other tropes is that "it makes its point by troping not on the meaning of a word but on the circuit or situation of communication itself" (Culler, "Apostrophe," 135).

[96] See, for example, Otto Kaiser, *Isaiah 1–12: A Commentary*, 2nd ed. (Philadelphia, PA: Westminster, 1983), 11; and Lundbom, *Jeremiah*, 265. Moshe Greenberg contrasts "the real audience" with the "the ostensible addressee of the oracle" (Moshe Greenberg, *Ezekiel 1–20: A New Translation with Introduction and Commentary* [Garden City, NY: Doubleday, 1995], 131). Apostrophe can also be addressed to absent human audiences, as is sometimes the case in oracles against foreign nations. See, for example, Isaiah 47:1; Jeremiah 50:42; and Psalm 137:8.

[97] Culler, "Apostrophe," 141.

on the relationship between the speaker and the addressee.[98] On the first level of reading, which Culler rejects, apostrophe is an expression of passion. There is only one subject, the speaker him- or herself, whose exclamation to a second subject signifies nothing more than "metonymically, the passion that caused it."[99] This is how many biblical scholars treat both apostrophe and figurative speech in general; statements such as "Jubilate, O heavens, and rejoice, O earth" (Isaiah 49:13) and "the trees of the field will clap their hands" (Isaiah 55:12) stand in for the exuberance of the poet. On the second level of reading, Culler argues that apostrophe is an attempt "to make the objects of the universe potentially responsive forces."[100] By using this trope, poets suggest that the universe is not a mute assortment of materials, but a world of "sentient" persons.[101] In other words, the speaker addresses the world, or some element of the world, as a subject capable of participating in dialogue. This is an accurate description of how apostrophe functions in the Bible. Apostrophe signals that Israel's prophetic tradition not only concerns itself with YHWH's relationship with Israel, but also that it is attentive to God's interaction with the rest of nature. On the third level of reading, apostrophe transforms the speaker him- or herself. By addressing nature as another "you," the poet claims the power of one who can speak to nature and becomes, in turn "one to whom nature might ... speak."[102] On this level of reading, apostrophe is about "vocation," about the writer becoming a poet, a prophet.[103] This is also operative in the biblical prophets. Addressing the mountains or the waters is not an everyday occurrence; outside oracles, people only address nonanimal nature three times in the Prophets: Joshua addresses the sun and the moon in Joshua 10:12, David addresses the hills of Gilboa in 2 Samuel 1, and in Hosea 10:8, the people of Israel plead with the mountains and hills: "Cover us! ... Fall on us!" The prophet, by speaking to nonanimal nature, takes on the role of God's messenger. Because God has the power to speak to the wind, the prophet is able to do so too. Apostrophe, in this

---

[98] Culler does not define what he means by "levels" of reading. What distinguishes each level of reading, however, is how the interpreter treats the subjects and objects of apostrophe. It seems that "levels," to Culler, indicate different ways interpreters and critics have theorized the ability of apostrophe to posit speaking subjects and listening objects.

[99] Culler, "Apostrophe," 138. Jack Lundbom, contra Culler, writes that apostrophe "is used to emphasize a point, heighten grief, or express indignation" (Lundbom, *The Hebrew Prophets*, 204).

[100] Culler, "Apostrophe," 139.   [101] Ibid., 149.   [102] Ibid., 142.   [103] Ibid.

explanation, not only accentuates the subject position of the nonhuman world, but also confirms the prophet in his or her role as God's servant.

Finally, on the fourth level, Culler argues that apostrophe is a form of interiorization and solipsism, by which the poet "peoples the universe with fragments of the self."[104] Culler only considers postenlightenment authors; when he calls apostrophe the act of naming "as a *you* something which in its empirical state cannot be a you," he can be reasonably sure that the poets he covers would concur with him about what can and cannot "in its empirical state ... be a you."[105] But, in the Hebrew Bible, apostrophe is exactly *not* an instance of self speaking to self, but instead the human manifestation of a dialogue that exists between God and nonanimal creatures, a dialogue into which humans are sometimes invited.

Culler discusses at length the embarrassment apostrophe causes literary critics, and their means of avoiding the trope, methods that resemble the ways in which biblical scholars deal with apostrophe. Culler notes that the primary way in which literary critics approach apostrophe is denial and avoidance. Most works of literary criticism, even studies of poets who frequently use apostrophe, simply ignore the form of speech altogether.[106] This is a common approach in biblical studies as well. For example, Robert Carroll, in his Jeremiah commentary, offers no comment on the address to the heavens in Jeremiah 2:12 and the call to the earth in 6:19.[107] When critics articulate reasons for ignoring apostrophe, they resemble arguments in biblical scholarship concerning figures of speech that address nonhuman nature. In modern poetry, apostrophe is considered insignificant because it has been borrowed from classical poetry; it is "an inherited element now devoid of significance."[108] In classical poetry it is also insignificant, this time because it is considered a stereotyped genre element.[109] The first explanation echoes arguments about traces and borrowed material in biblical studies; just as Post-Enlightenment poets borrowed forms from classical poetry, so biblical authors borrowed genres and forms of speech from ancient Near Eastern traditions. The second finds its twin in form criticism; the presence of

---

[104] Ibid., 146.
[105] Ibid., 146. Culler lists "the earth" as an example. Although Culler does not question his certainty about what can and cannot "in its empirical state ... be a you," he does argue that one function of "post-enlightenment poetry ... [is] to overcome the alienation of subject from object" (Ibid., 143).
[106] Culler, "Apostrophe," 135–37.
[107] Robert P. Carroll, *Jeremiah: A Commentary* (Philadelphia, PA: Westminster, 1986).
[108] Culler, "Apostrophe," 136.   [109] Ibid.

certain tropes is due to the requirements of genre, rather than to any intentional meaning-making on the part of the writer.

Biblical writers primarily use apostrophe in three ways: First, in judgment oracles; second, in oracles of restoration; and third, to signal YHWH's power. In judgment oracles, nonanimal nature is called on to act as witness or audience to YHWH's dispute with Israel. In some texts, nonanimal nature alone is addressed, though more commonly the call to nature is part of an inclusive call to the whole world: peoples, animals, and nonanimals. Examples of the latter abound, and include both texts that use the merism "the heavens and the earth" to indicate the whole cosmos, as well as texts that place human audiences in parallel with nonhuman ones. An example of a merism can be found in Isaiah 1:2, in the opening call of the book:

Hear, O heavens (שָׁמַיִם), and give ear, O earth (אֶרֶץ), for YHWH has spoken. I brought up children and raised [them]; but they – they have rebelled against me.
(Isaiah 1:2)

A merism is a literary device in which two contrasting parts are used to represent the whole: "young and old," "thick and thin," etc.[110] This is probably how the opening lines of Isaiah should be read. The call to the heavens and the earth is not to them as two as distinct domains, but instead a call to the whole cosmos.[111] That is not to say that Isaiah does not *really* address the heavens and the earth or that they stand in for human subjects. Merisms are inclusive forms of speech; when Isaiah calls on the heavens and the earth, he calls on the heavens, the earth, and everything in and between them. To reduce this to humans only would be to reduce radically the scope of the figure of speech. Isaiah claims as his audience not only Israel, not only humans, but the whole world, human and nonhuman.

Another means by which biblical writers widen their audience beyond the human is parallelism. In Isaiah 34:1, Jeremiah 6:18–19, and Micah 1:2 the earth stands in parallel with the nations:

Draw near to hear, O nations; pay attention, O peoples. Let the earth and its fullness hear (הָאָרֶץ וּמְלֹאָהּ), the world (תֵּבֵל) and all its offspring. (Isaiah 34:1)

Therefore, hear O peoples, and know, O assembly, what is in them.[112] Hear, O earth (הָאָרֶץ)! Look, I am about to bring evil to this people, the fruit of their plans. (Jeremiah 6:18–19a)

---

[110] See Lundbom, *The Hebrew Prophets*, 187.
[111] For a clear example of the use of the heavens and the earth as a merism, see Genesis 1:1.
[112] The pronominal suffix refers back to Jeremiah 6:13: "From the least to the greatest of them, all of them use violence for gain, and from prophet to priest, all of them act deceptively."

Hear, O peoples, all of [you];[113] pay attention, O earth and its fullness (אֶרֶץ וּמְלֹאָהּ), and let the Lord YHWH be a witness against you, the Lord from his holy temple.
(Micah 1:2)

In these texts the nouns that refer to groups of people and to the earth (and its fullness) can be read simply as synonyms. By this interpretation, the call to the earth, which follows the call to humans in all three texts, is a case of poetic variation, and "earth" metonymously refers to human inhabitants. This reading is unlikely because it ignores the inclusiveness of the call, which is contextually important in each of these texts. In Isaiah 34, the list of judgments that follow involve nonhuman nature alongside humans. Not only will YHWH's wrath against the nations produce piles of decomposing corpses ("Their slain will be cast out, the stench of their corpses will go up" [Isaiah 34:3a]), but nature itself will decay: "All the host of the heavens will rot and the heavens will be rolled up like a scroll and all their host wither like the withering of the leaf of the vine, or a withering fruit from a fig tree" (Isaiah 34:4). The nations and nonanimal nature are named together in this judgment oracle because YHWH's wrath will affect both.[114] This is also the case in Micah 1. YHWH will "tread on the high places of the earth," and "the mountains will melt" and the "valleys split open" (Micah 1:3–4). The cause of this disturbance of the land is "the rebellion of Jacob . . . and sins of the house of Israel" (Micah 1:5). Though the earth itself has not erred, God's anger affects it. The opening of the judgment oracle is addressed to all those who will experience YHWH's coming in judgment, which in this case include high places, mountains, valleys, and humans.

In Jeremiah 6 the case is a little different. One of the central themes of this chapter is Judah's failure to listen to prophetic warnings. In 6:10, the prophet asks "To whom shall I speak and give warning, that they may hear?," only to conclude that the people's ears are closed. The call to the nations and the earth in 6:18–19 follows directly on the heels of the people's declaration "We will not listen!" (Jeremiah 6:17). Judah's rejection of Jeremiah's words precipitates his call to the whole world. Since "holding it in" (Jeremiah 6:11) is not an option, the prophet turns away from Judah in order to speak to the rest of the cosmos, detailing the judgment that is about to come. In this case the world is not so much an

---

[113] The BHS has כֻּלָּם, "all of them." Contextually, the shift from a plural imperative to a third person plural does not make sense.

[114] Human and ecological destruction also follow the call to heaven and earth in Isaiah 1:2. See, especially, Isaiah 1:7–8.

interested party, though it often serves that role in Jeremiah, but a witness to the fact that Judah has been warned.

The line between population and land is sometimes even more difficult to draw. In Jeremiah 22:29–30, the prophet addresses himself to the earth:

Land, land land (אֶרֶץ אֶרֶץ אֶרֶץ)! Hear the word of YHWH. Thus says YHWH: record this man as childless, a man [who] will not prosper during his days. For none of his offspring will succeed in sitting on the throne of David or rule again in Judah. (Jeremiah 22:29–30)

The triple call to the land can be either a call to the physical land only, a call to the land and its inhabitants, or a call to the population only. Carroll argues that the triple address introduces "an incantatory act," and is "addressed to the land itself."[115] Verse 30 proscribes Coniah's claim on the throne, as well as his offspring's, and recruits the land to uphold this injunction.[116] Fretheim thinks the words are addressed both to the land and to its inhabitants. He too emphasizes Coniah's claim to the throne, saying that the king is "stripped of any relationship to the land of Israel; he no longer has a homeland."[117] Both Carroll and Fretheim conclude that the land itself is addressed (with or without its inhabitants), because they interpret the text as a reconfiguration of the relationship between Coniah and the territory of Judah.[118] Brueggemann, on the other hand, does not think "Land, land, land" is vocative at all. Instead he reads it as a dirge addressed to the population of the land, in which "land, land, land" forms the content.[119] This interpretation is unlikely. Though Jeremiah 22:29 is unusual in placing the subject before the verb – contrast it with, for example, Isaiah 1:2: שִׁמְעוּ שָׁמַיִם, "hear, O heavens"[120] – this is

---

[115] Carroll, *Jeremiah*, 440–41.   [116] Ibid., 441.

[117] Terence E. Fretheim, *Jeremiah* (Macon, GA: Smith & Helwys, 2002), 232.

[118] This project looks at nonanimal nature, but it should be noted that biblical writers also address materials that have been manipulated by humans. For example, compare Jeremiah 22:29–30 to 1 Kings 13:2: "He proclaimed against the altar by the word of YHWH. He said: O Altar! Altar! Thus says YHWH: Look, a son will be born of the house of David, Josiah will be his name, and he will sacrifice on you the priests of the high places, who send up smoke on you, and they will burn human bones on you." Keeping in mind that the sharp dualism between culture and nature is a modernist concept, it is possible that just like the hills could be addressed as persons, so manipulated stones could be addressed as subjects. For a discussion of the ability of culturally produced objects to act as persons, see Gell, *Art and Agency*.

[119] Walter Brueggemann, *To Pluck Up, to Tear Down: A Commentary on the Book of Jeremiah 1–25* (Grand Rapids, MI: William B. Eerdmans; Handsel, 1988), 197.

[120] See also Jeremiah 6:19.

likely caused by the triple repetition of the word אֶרֶץ, "land." The oracle to Jeroboam's altar in 1 Kings 13:2, "Altar, altar, thus says YHWH," follows a similar sentence structure, and other examples of the subject preceding the imperative of שְׁמַע, "to hear," exist.[121]

While the addressee of texts like Jeremiah 22:29–30 is ambiguous, other texts more clearly address nonanimal nature as an audience distinct from humans. In Jeremiah 2:12–13, the prophet goads the heavens to respond to Judah's faithlessness:

Be appalled (שֹׁמּוּ), O heavens; on account of this, be horrified (וְשַׂעֲרוּ), be very dry (חָרְבוּ), an utterance of YHWH. For my people have committed two evils: They have forsaken me, a spring of living water, in order to hew for themselves cistern, broken cisterns that are not able to [hold] water. (Jeremiah 2:12–13)

In her book *The Earth Mourns: Prophetic Metaphor and Oral Aesthetic*, Katherine Hayes writes that texts that call on nonanimal nature to mourn tend to use "words with both a physical and literal, and psychological and figurative meaning."[122] In Jeremiah 2:12–13, the roots שׁמם, "to be desolate, appalled," and שׂער, "to be horrified," can take either human or nonhuman subjects. שָׁמֵם, "to be desolate, appalled," refers either to the desolation of landscapes and cities,[123] or to human emotional desolation, to horror and disbelief.[124] שָׂעַר, "to be horrified," is a less common verb, occurring only four times, and, except in this case, it describes human fear.[125] The verb חָרֵב "be desolate/dry" is the only verb that always describes landscape or city devastation. The multivalence of the vocabulary of Jeremiah 2:12–13 is similar to that of theophany, and suggests that human and nonhuman grief, like fear, are related to each other.

Notice, however, that the writer does not simply use the language of human emotion. As Hayes says, the language has both physical *and* psychological characteristics. In the case of Jeremiah 2:12–13, the horror of the skies is linked to dryness, following the common coupling of mourning and drought in the Hebrew Bible.[126] Just as with shaking and

---

[121] See, for example, Genesis 23:15; 27:8; Deuteronomy 4:1; and Ezekiel 16:35.
[122] Hayes, *The Earth Mourns*, 2.
[123] See, for example, Genesis 47:19; Leviticus 26:22, 31, 34-35, 43; and Isaiah 33:8.
[124] See, for example, Leviticus 26:32; 2 Samuel 13:20; 1 Kings 9:8; and Isaiah 52:14. Leviticus 26 is particularly interesting in this context, in that it parallels human and landscape desolation.
[125] See Deuteronomy 32:17 and Ezekiel 27:35 and 32:10.
[126] Hayes cites Psalm 102:5 [4]: "My heart has been struck like grass and dried up." She writes that "[h]ere is an explicit example of the application of the physical meaning "to dry up" to a psychological context of grieving" (Hayes, *The Earth Mourns*, 14–15).

trembling in theophany, here the writer connects an observable event, namely drought, with affect and personalistic response. The passage is not so much as example of anthropomorphism as it is evidence of a way of thinking that draws broad lines of continuity between human experiences of the world and the experiences of nonanimal nature.

Sometimes it is more difficult to understand the precise connection between event and address, even for passages whose imagery is physical and material. In Zechariah 11:1–3, the prophet addresses a word of doom to Lebanon, its cypresses, and its oaks:

Open up, O Lebanon, your doors, and let a fire devour your cedars. Wail (הֵילֵל), O cypress, for [the] cedar has fallen, for the mighty are devastated. Wail (הֵילִילוּ), O oaks of Bashan, for the thick forest has gone down. (Zechariah 11:1–3)

The "realism" of these verses lies not in the overlap between physical and psychological language, but in the phenomenon of logging and forest clearing. Trees, just like humans, can have their land taken away, can suffer, and can die. In fact, the verbs that here denote the destruction of Lebanon elsewhere refer to the destruction of cities and their inhabitants.[127] The verb ילל, "to wail" or "to howl," takes both human and nonhuman subjects (such as gates [Isaiah 14:31] and ships [Isaiah 23:1, 14]), though human subjects are by far the more common.[128] What differentiates this verb from the mourning language of Jeremiah 2:12–13 is that it does not carry both physical and psychological meanings; it has no clear relationship with observable behaviors of trees. The writer is, nonetheless, concerned with real trees.[129] Just as humans wail at their own destruction, so the prophet here calls on trees to lament the end of their life.

It is not clear why the trees of Zechariah suffer destruction. Carol and Eric Meyers argue that deforestation is a necessary part of God's eschatological plan.[130] The returned exiles will be so numerous that they will

---

[127] See Exodus 32:28; Leviticus 26:30; Numbers 16:35; Isaiah 15:1; Jeremiah 20:4; and Ezekiel 32:12.

[128] For human subjects, see Isaiah 15:2; 23:6; 52:5; Jeremiah 4:8; 25:34; 47:2; Ezekiel 21:17 [12]; Hosea 7:14; and Joel 1:5. For nonhuman subjects, see Isaiah 14:31 and 23:1.

[129] Contra David Petersen, who argues that the trees symbolize "the fate of foreign nations" (David L. Petersen, *Zechariah 9–14 and Malachi: A Commentary* (Louisville, KY: Westminster John Knox, 1995), 80).

[130] Mark Boda makes a similar suggestion, but one that takes into account the negative tone of Zechariah 11:1–3. He writes: "[I]t may be that these regions were not open to receiving exiles, and thus are threatened with the judgment of God on their vegetation" (Mark J. Boda, *The Book of Zechariah* [Grand Rapids, MI: William B. Eerdmans, 2016], 640). Boda finds his own argument unpersuasive, and concludes

settle in the forested hills of Lebanon and use fires to clear land there.[131] They also suggest that the trees do double duty as symbols for empire; the oracle foresees "the eschatological resettlement of Israel, and ... symbolize[s] the demise of the existing world order."[132] The fact that the trees of Lebanon were an important financial resource for the empires of the Near East lends support to the Meyers' symbolic reading, as does the existence of other texts in the Hebrew Bible that associate the destruction of trees with victory over enemies.[133] But not all texts assign parallel fates to military enemies and trees. Isaiah names trees as beneficiaries of Babylon's downfall: "Even the cypresses rejoice because of you, the cedars of Lebanon: 'Since you have lain down, the logger does not go up against us'" (Isaiah 14:8). Nothing conclusive can be said about Zechariah based on a single text in Isaiah, but this text shows at the very least that not all biblical writers thought that the end of empire and the return of the exiles would come at the cost of trees. In Isaiah 14, Babylon's fall results in less logging, not more. Zechariah 9–14 is an unusually convoluted and difficult text, and the oracle to the trees is only one of its puzzles.[134] For the purpose of this project, the central point is that the writer assumes that trees, like humans, grieve and mourn when their life is threatened and annihilated; Zechariah 11:1–3 is sensitive to the suffering of trees. The language of human grief provides a portal by which the prophet can explore the response of trees to fire and deforestation.

The use of human experience as a guide or entry point to the experience of other-than-human persons is a common feature of animist traditions. Viveiros de Castro, who studies Amerindian peoples, has coined the term "perspectivism." He defines it as an ontology in which "the world is inhabited by different sorts of subjects or persons, human and nonhuman, which apprehend reality from distinct points of view,"

---

that the trees are either a cipher for "illicit members of the Davidic line ruling in Yehud," and/or foreign military powers (Ibid., 644).

[131] Meyers and Meyers, *Zechariah 9–14*, 240, 245. Judah's return to the land is promised in Zechariah 10:6–12. In 10:10, the prophet writes that the people will be settled in Gilead and Lebanon, "until there is no room for them" (literally: "and there will not be found for them").

[132] Ibid., 245.

[133] For a description of the importance of trees as a financial resource, see Nielsen, *There Is Hope for a Tree*, 161. For texts in which the destruction of trees is associated with victory over enemies, see Amos 2:9 and Isaiah 14:8.

[134] A major crux in Zechariah 11 is the identity of the shepherd(s) in Zechariah 11:4–17. This passage tends to draw attention away from Zechariah 11:1–3, which most commentators treat only briefly.

according to "their respective characteristics and powers."[135] Perspectivism is the idea that all persons experience the world in similar ways, but do so by means of different bodies. Anne-Christine Hornborg elaborates:

All beings have in common a system of categories (a classificatory system), but how they embody these categories depends on which body they inhabit (they have, for example, a category for food, but this category is embodied as maggots for the hawk and beaver meat for the Mi'kmaq).[136]

Scholars usually use perspectivism to elucidate human–animal and human–spirit relations, but it is also a useful lens for rethinking the application of affective language to nonanimal nature.[137] Perspectivism does not depend on bodily similarities (it does not, for example, only apply to mammals), but names an *a priori* assumption that persons experience the world in similar ways, by means of similar categories. The categories which humans and nonhumans share in the Hebrew Bible are primarily ones having to do with emotions – fear, mourning, happiness – and physical events, like earthquakes and droughts, are interpreted by means of these shared categories. Perspectivism is a useful alternative to anthropomorphism. Calling something anthropomorphism is to claim that human attributes are imposed on something that is not human. Humanness is the baseline, and the term depends on the premise that the application of human characteristics to nonhumans is counterfactual. Perspectivism differs in two respects. People who hold a perspectivistic ontology do not take human experience as the definitive one. It is simply the one to which humans have access, and through which the experience of other bodies can be guessed.[138] Second, perspectivism does not carry associations of fictiveness or inappropriateness. It is not that perspectivist animists first see an animal or a tree, and then impose on it human characteristics. Instead, perspectivist interactions with the world are predicated on the idea that all persons encounter the world in ways appropriate to their bodies. When Jeremiah calls on the heavens to "be appalled … be horrified," the writer does not anthropomorphize the skies, but instead gives voice to the conviction that the whole created order bemoans transgression against YHWH. The wailing of the trees in Zechariah 11 affirm that all persons value their lives. Each part of the created order responds differently, depending on their "bodies" (used

---

[135] Viveiros de Castro, "1. Cosmologies" and *Cannibal Metaphysics*.
[136] Hornborg, *Mi'kmaq Landscapes*, 34. Hornborg uses Viveiros de Castro's category to talk about the Mi'kmaq, an Algonquian-speaking group that lives in Eastern Canada.
[137] See Viveiros de Castro, *Cannibal Metaphysics*, 56. [138] Harvey, *Animism*, 39, 170.

loosely in relation to the skies). While humans wail, wear sackcloth, and throw dust on their heads, the heavens grow dark and withhold moisture. The biblical writers may not be able to hear the keening of the trees, but they assume its presence. They use their own experiences of grief as guides to the grief of other creatures. Human experience can only ever be an approximate guide, hence the multivalence and openness of metaphor, but it is better than no guide at all. These texts do not betray a naive anthropomorphism or an escape into rhetorical fancy, but a concerted effort to observe and respect the perspective of all persons, be they human, animal, or other-than-animal.

Though humans can only guess at the feelings and experiences of nonanimal nature, it is a mark of YHWH's power that YHWH can converse with vast creatures like oceans and skies, as well as more down-to-earth ones, like grain. When used as a marker of YHWH's power, what matters is not *what* YHWH says to nature, but *that* YHWH speaks to nature and that it obeys. For example, in Isaiah and Amos, YHWH's ability to command the waters confirms his authority:

I am YHWH ... who says to the deep, "Be dry! I will dry up your rivers." (Isaiah 44:24b, 27)

The maker of the Pleiades and Orion, the one who turns deep darkness into morning, and darkens the day into night. The one who calls to the waters of the sea and pours them out on the face of the earth; YHWH is his name. (Amos 5:8)

And the Lord YHWH of hosts, who touches the earth and it melts and all who live in it mourn, and all of it goes up like the Nile and sinks like the Nile of Egypt; who builds in the heavens his steps and founds his vault upon the earth, who calls to the waters of the sea and pours them out upon the face of the earth; YHWH is his name. (Amos 9:5–6)[139]

In some of the theophany texts we have looked at, the waters are rebellious creatures in need of chastisement. In Isaiah 44:27, and Amos 5:8 and 9:5, the writers pass over the character of the waters in order to foreground and celebrate YHWH's capacity to summon them. This is the

---

[139] In Amos 7:4, God also calls to "a contender of fire." Amos 5:8, 7:4, and 9:6 all use the verb קָרָא, "to call, summon." Marlow connects the three texts: "In three places in Amos, YHWH summons (קרא) parts of his creation to act in judgment against the people" (Marlow, *Biblical Prophets and Contemporary Environmental Ethics*, 136). I do not treat Amos 7:4 in any detail, because of the translational difficulties that surround the verse, especially the phrase "a contender of fire" (לָרִב בָּאֵשׁ). See Francis I. Andersen and David Noel Freedman, *Amos: A New Translation with Introduction Notes and Commentary*, The Anchor Bible 24A (New York: Doubleday, 1989), 746–47, for a discussion of possible translations.

point at which the problems with calling address to nonanimal nature "imaginary" become most clear. If nonanimal nature cannot be addressed, cannot be commanded, it is poor proof of YHWH's abilities.

YHWH's commands to nonanimal nature are not always so grand. Sometimes YHWH displays YHWH's saving action by summoning plants, specifically grain, to provide for human bodily needs:

And I will save you from all your uncleanness and I will call to the grain and I will multiply it and I will not set on you a famine. (Ezekiel 36:29)

It may seem like the difference between making stars and multiplying grain is considerable. Amos 5:8 and 9:5–6 describe cosmic structures and larger-than-human creatures. The image is of a god who controls and commands it all, the whole universe. YHWH's claim in Ezekiel is tiny in comparison: "I'll talk to the grain." Hosea's promises of restoration connect the two extremes. YHWH talks to the heavens and sets in motion a creationwide call-and-response; a conversation that begins in the skies finds its way to "the grain and the wine and the oil," and to Jezreel, a specific, geographical location:[140]

And in that day, I will answer, an utterance of YHWH, I will answer the heavens and they will answer the earth and the earth will answer the grain and the wine and the oil, and they will answer Jezreel. And I myself will sow [them][141] in the land, and I will have compassion on *Lo-Ruhamah* [she will find no compassion], and I will say to *Lo-Ami* [not my people], you are my people, and it will say: My God. (Hosea 2:23–25 [21–23])[142]

---

[140] Hosea first introduces Jezreel as a place of violence and bloodshed. The prophet names his oldest son in commemoration of "the blood of Jezreel" (Hosea 1:4). In Hosea 2:23–24 it is transformed into a place of peace and plenty. The name means "God sows"; Fretheim writes that "the images of 'sowing' is suggestive of a new beginning, leading to new growth and prosperity" (Terence E. Fretheim, *Reading Hosea-Micah: A Literary and Theological Commentary* [Macon, GA: Smyth & Helwys, 2013], 33). Davis points out that Jezreel is "the richest agricultural district in the land" (Davis, *Scripture, Culture, and Agriculture*, 137).

[141] Literally, "her."

[142] The wording of this text is unique in the Hebrew Bible, but echoes a passage from the Baal cycle: "For a message I have, and I will tell you, a word and I will repeat to you: The word of tree and the whisper of stone, the converse of Heaven to Hell, of Deeps to Stars" (KTU 1.1 III:12–14; this translation is from Mark S. Smith, *The Ugaritic Baal Cycle*, Supplements to Vetus Testamentum 55 [Leiden: E. J. Brill, 1994], 159–60). Smith writes that, while the lines in the Baal cycle lack temporal and geographic specificity, Hosea transforms this "message of divine fertility bestowed upon the universe" into a word for a specific time and place in Israel (Ibid., 178). See also Smith, *The Early History of God*, 73–75.

God's ability to command nonanimal nature is not abstract; YHWH displays power by commanding nature to meet specific, material needs. Sometimes, like in Amos 9:1–6, YHWH upends cosmic structures in order to intimidate and discipline. Other times, YHWH speaks to nonanimal creatures in order to restore agricultural fertility and verdure. In the case of Hosea, this provision of food then enables a "planting" of people. Here it is nonanimal creatures that behave in characteristically human ways – they talk – while humans behave like plants – they are sown. It is in their quasivegetative state that Israel receives God's new mercy, that they again become God's people. Neither in Amos nor Hosea does the logic of the text permit God's summons to nonanimal nature to be fictive or figurative. The writers do not go into detail about the exact form of divine communication with nonanimal nature, but its presence is the premise on which their claims rest. Nonanimal nature can be spoken to. YHWH has the power to enter into such conversation. YHWH's summons to the universe and to its disparate parts prove YHWH's preeminence. It is only in a universe populated by numerous persons, only some of whom are human, that such a claim convinces and persuades.

Before leaving the topic of address, we turn to Ezekiel, because the book of Ezekiel makes distinct use of address. YHWH repeatedly commands the prophet to prophesy to features of nonanimal nature. In Ezekiel 6:2, YHWH commands Ezekiel to prophesy against "the mountains of Israel"; in 7:2, to "the soil of Israel"; in 21:2 [20:46] against "the south" and "the forest of the field of Negev"; in 21:7 [21:2] against "Jerusalem ... the sanctuaries ... the soil of Israel"; in 35:2 against "the mountain of Seir"; and in 36:1, to "the mountains of Israel" again. These oracles, like the book of Ezekiel itself, move from prophecies of doom and condemnation to promises of restoration and peace.

Brad Kelle argues that Ezekiel does not primarily refer to the land as a metonym or metaphor for its inhabitants, but instead "as the physical site of God's destructive activity."[143] The first oracle addressed to nonanimal nature, Ezekiel 6:1–7, is representative:

The word of YHWH came to me, saying: Mortal, set your face against the mountains of Israel and prophecy against them.[144] You are to say: Mountains

---

[143] Brad E. Kelle, "Dealing with the Trauma of Defeat: The Rhetoric of the Devastation and Rejuvenation of Nature in Ezekiel," *Journal of Biblical Literature* 128, no. 3 (September 2009): 476.

[144] Ezekiel three times addresses mountains. In 6:2 and 36:1, he addresses the mountains of Israel. In 35:2, he addresses the mountain of Seir. For parallels between Ezekiel 6, 35,

of Israel, hear the word of the Lord YHWH. Thus says the Lord YHWH to the mountains and to the hills and to the ravines and to the valleys: Look! I am bringing against you a sword, and I will destroy your high places. Your altars will be desolate and your incense altars will be broken and I will make your slain fall before your idols. And I will set the corpses of the children of Israel before your idols, and I will scatter your bones round about your altars. In all your dwelling places, cities will be waste, and the high places desolate, so that your altars will be waste and desolate, your idols broken and destroyed, your incense altars hewn, and your work wiped out. The slain will fall in your midst, and you will know that I am YHWH. (Ezekiel 6:1–7)

Scholars have pointed out that Ezekiel's rhetoric is unusual in portraying the land not as an innocent sufferer, but as a guilty party.[145] For example, in Ezekiel 7:3, the prophet says to the soil of Israel: "Now the end is upon you, and I will let loose my anger against you, and I will judge you according to your ways, and I will repay you for all your abominations." In an age of ecological crisis, climate change, and unprecedented extraction of natural resources, the response to this aspect of Ezekiel is often horror. Keith Carley writes that "Earth has no compassionate advocate in this prophetic tradition," and Kalinda Rose Stevenson describes the earth in Ezekiel as "battered."[146] Brad Kelle, in contrast, explains the violent conflict between the land and YHWH as an extension of Priestly theology:

[The] rhetorical shaping suggests that Ezekiel employs his distinctive nature motif in order to integrate the people's trauma and defeat into the narrative plot line of priestly theology characterized by concern for [YHWH]'s sovereignty and holiness, thus rendering it understandable as part of a larger divine plan.[147]

---

and 36, see Moshe Greenberg, *Ezekiel 21–37: A New Translation with Introduction and Commentary* (New York: Doubleday, 1997), 723.

[145] See Kelle, "Dealing with the Trauma of Defeat," 471; Julie Galambush, "God's Land and Mine: Creation as Property in the Book of Ezekiel," in *Ezekiel's Hierarchical World: Wrestling with a Tiered Reality* (Atlanta, GA: Society of Biblical Literature, 2004), 98–102.

[146] See Keith Carley, "Ezekiel's Formula of Desolation: Harsh Justice for the Land/Earth," in *The Earth Story in Psalms and Prophets*, ed. Norman C. Habel, The Earth Bible 4 (Sheffield: Sheffield Academic, 2001), 154; and Kalinda Rose Stevenson, "If Earth Could Speak: The Case of the Mountains against YHWH in Ezekiel 6:35–36," in *The Earth Story in Psalms and Prophets*, ed. Norman C. Habel, The Earth Bible 4 (Sheffield: Sheffield Academic, 2001), 171. Habel stresses the silence of the earth: "the lands have no voice, no advocate, no venue for crying out against the injustice they experience" (Norman C. Habel, "The Silence of the Lands: The Ecojustice Implications of Ezekiel's Judgment Oracles," in *Ezekiel's Hierarchical World: Wrestling with a Tiered Reality* (Atlanta, GA: Society of Biblical Literature, 2004), 140).

[147] Kelle, "Dealing with the Trauma of Defeat," 472.

Ezekiel, Kelle argues, attributes the devastation of Judah not to the military activity of the empire but to YHWH's direct action.[148] He writes that Ezekiel sets the war and the ruin of the land within the context of the covenant curses and blessings of Leviticus 26.[149] Judah is not destroyed because YHWH is weak, but because the people and the land have broken the covenant. YHWH's reputation is key: divine holiness explains God's judgment on Judah, and also provides the rationale for its eventual restoration.[150]

Kelle argues that this framing of the exile is "a means of dealing with the trauma of the past and the present," and persuasively captures the function of the rhetoric for the human audience.[151] More important for this project, however, is how Ezekiel's oracles to nonanimal nature reflect a personalistic understanding of land, landscape features, and plants. The book of Ezekiel draws heavily on Leviticus, and we saw in the last chapter that Leviticus speaks of the land as an active being.[152] The land in Leviticus relates to both its inhabitants and YHWH, and YHWH's presence requires it to maintain cultic purity. Just as the people are responsible for their failures to uphold the covenant, so the land is responsible when it fails to maintain purity and observe sabbath. This is true even if its failure stems from human interference. As shocking as this seems to modern ecological sensibilities, the corollary of a personalistic, relational view of nonanimal nature is that nonanimal nature can fail in much the same ways that humans fail. That biblical writers can imagine hostility between YHWH and the land, or between YHWH and the sea, or between YHWH and the forests of the Negev is a sign that they take seriously the ability of nonanimal nature to interact and make choices. This is not the hostility of dualistically opposed forces, forever locked in a battle for supremacy, but the hostility between YHWH and creatures in rebellion, creatures who for one reason or another are no longer fit company for God. The language of YHWH's fury against the land resembles that of

---

[148] Ibid., 485, 489.
[149] Ibid., 480. See also Christopher J. H. Wright, *The Message of Ezekiel: A New Heart and a New Spirit*, The Bible Speaks Today (Leicester, UK: InterVarsity, 2001), 94.
[150] See, for example, Ezekiel 36:22–23.
[151] Kelle, "Dealing with the Trauma of Defeat," 481.
[152] For a discussion of the relationship between Ezekiel and Leviticus 17–26 (the Holiness Code), within which almost all references in Leviticus to the land as an active being are found, see Michael A. Lyons, *From Law to Prophecy: Ezekiel's Use of the Holiness Code* (New York: T & T Clark, 2009).

YHWH's fury against Israel; both have failed to uphold their covenant responsibilities and both must face judgment.[153]

When Ezekiel turns to comfort, his words to the land are no less extravagant than those addressed to the people. The language is baroque, repetitive, and lengthy, a passionate promise that the land will receive agricultural fertility, human and animal inhabitants, and a restored reputation. I quote at length, because summary or description fails to capture the intimate and insistent assurance of the text:

> Therefore, prophesy concerning the soil of Israel and say to the mountains and to the hills, to the ravines and to the valleys, thus says the Lord YHWH: Look! In my jealousy and in my wrath I will speak, because you have carried the disgrace of the peoples. Therefore, thus says the Lord YHWH: I myself swear,[154] the nations that surround you, they will carry their disgrace. But you, O mountains of Israel, you will put out your branches and you will carry your fruit for my people Israel, for they are near to coming. For look, I am for you and I will turn to you and you will be tilled and you will be sown. I will multiply human[s] upon you, all the house of Israel, all of it, and the mountains will be inhabited and the dry places will be built. I will multiply human[s] and cattle upon you and they will be many and fruitful. And I will make you inhabited like your former times and I will do good to you like your first time and you will know that I am YHWH. I will lead upon you human[s], my people Israel, and they will possess you and you will be to them a possession and you will not again be bereaved of them.[155] Thus says the Lord YHWH: because they are saying concerning you: "You devour human[s] and you are bereaved of your peoples," therefore you will not again devour human[s] and of your peoples you will not again be bereaved. An utterance of the Lord YHWH. And I will not let you hear the disgrace of the peoples, and the reproach of the peoples you will not again bear and your peoples you will not again cause to stumble. An utterance of the Lord YHWH. (Ezekiel 36:6–15)

The movement from judgment to promises of restoration is not unique to Ezekiel. What is unique is the extent to which the land itself is caught up in this dynamic, not as an innocent bystander, but as a key participant. Change the nouns in Ezekiel 6 and 36, and it would sound much like

---

[153] See, for example, Ezekiel 5:13–17.
[154] Literally, "I myself lift my hand." Verses 36:6–8 turn on four uses of the verb נשׂא, "to carry, lift." First the soil of Israel carries disgrace. This condition is transformed by a second "lifting": YHWH lifts his hand and makes a vow. YHWH's vow results in the nations, not Israel, carrying the disgrace they have heaped on the soil. In verse 8, the land of Israel will carry fruit for the returning exiles.
[155] "Bereave" translates the Piel of שׁכל. Greenberg writes: "The point is not that parents shall no longer be bereft of their children, but that the country shall never again be depopulated and thus subject to seizure by its neighbors" (Greenberg, *Ezekiel 21–37*, 721). See also 2 Kings 2:19 and 2:21–22, in which Elisha heals the land from bereavement.

oracles directed at Judah in Isaiah and Jeremiah. Speaking of the land in Leviticus, Jonathan Morgan argues that the relationship between YHWH and the land is most accurately described as a covenant.[156] Ezekiel's oracles to the land evince a similar reading of Leviticus. The judgment and restoration of the land is not so much Ezekiel's innovation as an extension of Leviticus' insistence that the land has a unique relationship with God, a relationship that includes the responsibility to present itself as a suitable habitation for YHWH.

I have spoken of the land and its inhabitants as separate groups in the writings of Ezekiel, and that is somewhat misleading. For example, in Ezekiel 6, the prophet, addressing the mountains of Israel, says "your slain" and "your bones" (Ezekiel 6:4, 5). Moshe Greenberg argues that this indicates a shift in reference: in verse 3, "your" refers to the mountains, whereas at the end of verse 4 and in verse 5, "your" refers to the people.[157] This distinction is unnecessary. Equally unnecessary is Milgrom's insistence that Ezekiel's transformation of the phrase "I will multiply you" from Leviticus 26:9 into "I will multiply upon you" in Ezekiel 36:10–11 turns a "natural promise" into "a forced image."[158] Though Ezekiel distinguishes between mountains, ravines, animals, and people, these together form one community whose members are related by kinship ties. For example, Ezekiel 36:12 likens inhabitants to the land's children. Restoration of the land includes the return of human and animal inhabitants. There is no healing for the land that does not include those who live on it. It is a modern habit to draw a clear line between people, animals, and land, but in Ezekiel these are all part of a differentiated whole.

GRIEF

The prophets frequently report that nonanimal nature grieves. Nine times in the Latter Prophets do we read that the earth mourns (Isaiah 24:4; 33:9; Jeremiah 4:28; 12:4, 11; 23:10; Hosea 4:3; Joel 1:10; and Amos 1:2). This is particularly common in Jeremiah; four out of the nine occurrences appear in this book. The sorrow of the earth is not an isolated

---

[156] Morgan, "Transgressing, Puking, Covenanting," 178. Morgan cites Leviticus 26:42 as evidence.

[157] Greenberg, *Ezekiel 1–20*, 131.

[158] Jacob Milgrom, "Leviticus 26 and Ezekiel," in *The Quest for Context and Meaning: Studies in Biblical Intertextuality in Honor of James A. Sanders*, eds. Craig A. Evans and Shemaryahu Talmon (Leiden: Brill, 1997), 59.

event, but instead partakes of a wider expression of dismay. Humans faint, fish and animals languish, plants wither, and the earth mourns. As with theophany, the passages in question draw no clear line between affective response and physical event. Aridity, the loss of animal life, and famine are all signs of the earth's grief.

Isaiah 24:4–7, 11b and Jeremiah 4:28 are representative:

The earth mourns (אָבְלָה) and withers (נָבְלָה), the world languishes (אֻמְלְלָה) and withers (נָבְלָה), the heights, the people of the earth. The earth is polluted beneath its inhabitants, for they have transgressed laws and overstepped statutes; they have broken an everlasting covenant. Therefore a curse devours the earth and her inhabitants are held guilty. Therefore the inhabitants of the earth dwindle, and few humans remain. The new wine mourns (אָבַל), the vine languishes (אֻמְלְלָה), all who are merry sigh … the rejoicing of the earth has departed (גָּלָה).[159] (Isaiah 24:4–7, 11b)

Because of this, the earth mourns (תֶּאֱבַל), and the heavens above darken (וְקָדְרוּ). For I have spoken, I have purposed, and I have not relented, and I will not turn back. (Jeremiah 4:28)

Katherine Hayes argues that the biblical language of mourning is closely associated with the language of drought.[160] She focuses her attention on the verb אָבַל, "to mourn," which occurs in all nine mourning passages. The Akkadian cognate of the verb is *abālu*, which means "to dry up."[161] The two verbs used in parallel with אָבַל, "to mourn," in the Isaiah passage, namely נָבֵל and אָמַל, mean "to wither" and "to be weak/to languish," respectively. The former is rarely used with human subjects, except to compare them to withering plants. The few times it appears outside this context, it expresses physical and mental exhaustion, even despair.[162] The latter is associated with human and nonhuman loss of offspring and fruit.[163] The association

---

[159] Note that Isaiah also uses the verb גָּלָה, "to uncover, remove, go into exile," to describe the people going into exile (See Isaiah 5:13).
[160] See also Fretheim, *Reading Hosea-Micah*, 38.   [161] Hayes, *The Earth Mourns*, 13.
[162] See Exodus 18:18; 2 Samuel 22:46; Psalm 18:46 [45].
[163] See 1 Samuel 2:5, Jeremiah 15:9, and Joel 1:10–12. The BDB writes that the Pulal of אָמַל, "to languish," is associated with loss of fertility. Brown et al., *The Brown-Driver-Briggs Hebrew and English Lexicon*, 51. The verb contrasts previous fertility with current bereavement ("she who bore seven languishes," see Jeremiah 15:9), and it applies equally to human, animal, and plant fruitfulness. The verb does not describe the kind of barrenness faced by the women of Genesis, but instead experiences of reversal from plenty to absence and lack. This accords with Delbert Hillers' claim that in passages about drought, the stress is "on the *absence* of persons or things that should normally be there" (Delbert R. Hillers, "Roads to Zion Mourn (Lam 1:4)," *Perspective* 12, no. 1–2 [1971]: 124; emphasis in original).

between mourning and drought recurs in Isaiah 33:9, Jeremiah 12:4, 23:10, Joel 1:10, and Amos 1:2. Jeremiah, Joel, and Amos add a final verb to the vocabulary of grief and drought, namely יָבֵשׁ, "to dry up."[164] Like נָבֵל, "to wither," the verb most frequently describes the drying up of plants or bodies of water, and it takes human subjects primarily when humans are compared to grass. That said, it is also used for certain bodily injuries – withered hands, dry bones, parched skin (see 1 Kings 13:4; Ezekiel 37:4; Zechariah 11:17; Proverbs 17:22; Lamentations 4:8). The point is that the duality mourning/drought does not align neatly with a human/earth duality. The biblical writers are not comparing a human emotion with a meteoric phenomenon, using the first as a metaphor for the second. Instead, bodily, meteoric, and emotive language intertwine. Human grief has physical and emotional aspects; so does the grief of the land.

The association between aridity and mourning is not random, but builds on observations and experience. Hayes points to parallels between mourning rituals and drought:

[T]he mourning rituals alluded to throughout the Hebrew Bible offer a number of parallels to the state of the earth in periods of drought. In these rituals the mourner fasts, strips off clothing, shaves the head, bows down toward the ground and sits on it, and pours dust or ashes over the head and body. So in a state of drought the earth "fasts," or is deprived of water; plants and trees wilt and droop toward the ground; the vegetative covering withers and is shed; and dust is everywhere.[165]

In other words, mourning rituals and drought share structural similarities. They look alike. Perspectivism is again helpful. The *a priori* supposition that the earth is capable of a similar range of emotions as humans guides the interpretation of weather and plant death: if the earth acts in ways characteristic of a person in grief, it is likely that the earth is grieving.

Cultural background also shapes biblical writers. Delbert Hillers explains the association between drought and mourning by reference to mythic materials, specifically Anath's mourning over the death of Baal.[166] Baal's death causes drought throughout the world, which is only alleviated when Anath defeats the god of death, Môt. Hillers' article provides additional support for Hayes' argument. Some of the funerary rituals

---

[164] See Jeremiah 12:4, 23:10; Joel 1:10; and Amos 1:2.
[165] Hayes, *The Earth Mourns*, 15–16. Hayes cites Koehler and Baumgartner's translation of אָבַל. They translate it as "'observ[ing] the mourning rites,' whether the reference is to people or to the earth" (Ibid., 16, n. 26). See Ludwig Köhler and Walter Baumgartner, *The Hebrew and Aramaic Lexicon of the Old Testament* (Leiden: E. J. Brill, 1994), 6–7.
[166] Hillers, "Roads to Zion Mourn," 128.

Hayes associates with drought are performed by the god El: he sits on the ground and "pours dust of mourning on his head; earth of mortification on his pate."[167] More importantly, Hillers offers proof for a general cultural association between drought and mourning. He writes that it is not necessary that the authors of these texts knew the Baal cycle or intended to reference the myth.[168] The association between mourning and drought may have become a more general cultural association. As such, it shaped the choices of the writers of the prophetic books.

Hayes labels the earth's mourning a use of metaphor and personification. She writes that, in these texts, "earth assumes a persona."[169] Saying that the texts use metaphor is accurate, as long as it is carefully qualified; saying that the earth "assumes a persona" is less helpful. The language is figurative, to the extent that it is borrowed from the realm of human emotion, but that does not mean that the passages "personify" the earth. It was not inert and then enlivened by means of metaphor. Instead the language is descriptive and interpretive. It is descriptive in that it builds on observations of the land: it is dry, dusty, agricultural yields are diminishing, etc. It is interpretive in that it explains this in personalistic terms. The assumption that the land is personalistic undergirds and produces these texts. The earth is not static until prophetic writers come along and attribute feelings to it. These texts are the product of writers and communities who ask, when faced with drought and famine, what the cause is, and answer that question in terms of personal causation.

The mourning of the land is closely related to the state of its human inhabitants. Hayes writes that a common feature of these nine passages is that they use "parallel structures" to "relate and contrast the fate or state of the human community with the fate or the state of the earth."[170] Sometimes the earth mourns together with humans. In Isaiah 24, the grief of nonanimal nature precedes verses that foretell the end of human mirth: "The mirth of the timbrel has ceased; the noise of the exultant has ended" (Isaiah 24:8a). In Jeremiah, the writer imputes the earth's mourning to human transgression. In 12:10–11, for example, the writer contrasts the cruelty and inattentiveness of humans with the earth's dismay:

Many shepherds have destroyed my vineyard, they have trampled my portion. They have made my desirable portion a desolation. He has made it a desolation.

---

[167] *I AB vi*. See James B. Pritchard, ed., *The Ancient Near East: An Anthology of Texts and Pictures* (Princeton, NJ: Princeton UniversityPress, 2011), 126.
[168] Hillers, "Roads to Zion Mourn," 131.   [169] Hayes, *The Earth Mourns*, 2.
[170] Ibid.

It mourns to me, desolate. All the earth is made desolate, for no one takes it to heart. (Jeremiah 12:10–11)[171]

Human action has caused desolation and destruction. Further proof of human perfidy is their inattentiveness to the suffering of other creatures. The earth is left with no option but to cry directly to YHWH. Marilyn Strathern writes that one consequence of understanding the world as a multiplicity of persons is that all human interpretations "[encounter] ... counter-interpretations."[172] In Jeremiah, the earth's mourning stands as a counterinterpretation to prevailing interpretations of the exile. Jeremiah aligns himself with the earth's interpretation over against the interpretations of the leaders and the people of Jerusalem. Hosea also explains the condition of the earth as a result of human failures. This time the prophet highlights a series of lacks: no truth, no loyalty, no knowledge, attributes that Israel ought to possess. The absence of truth, loyalty, and knowledge adversely affects the earth, its animals, birds, and fish:

Hear the word of YHWH, O children of Israel, for YHWH has a dispute with the inhabitants of the earth, for there is no truth and no loyalty and no knowledge of God in the earth ... Therefore the earth mourns and all who dwell in it languish. With the animals of the field and the birds of the heavens, even the fish of the sea – they perish together. (Hosea 4:1–3)

These texts do not, like Ezekiel, blame the land for its sorrows. The land itself has not transgressed. Still, the passages have given ecologically minded scholars pause. Is it fair that the land, with its plants and animals, should suffer because of human failings?[173] Scholars have posed this question in tones ranging from musing[174] to outraged.[175] Though it

---

[171] See also Jeremiah 12:4: "How long will the earth mourn and the vegetation of every field dry up? Because of the evil of those who dwell in it, it is swept away, animals and fowl. For they say: he does not see our end." Jeremiah 7:20 emphasizes the total reach of YHWH's wrath: "Therefore, thus says the Lord YHWH: Look, my anger and my wrath will be poured out upon this place. Upon the humans and upon the cattle and upon the trees of the field and upon the fruit of the soil, and it will burn and will not be extinguished."
[172] Marilyn Strathern, *Partial Connections*, updated ed. (Walnut Creek, CA: AltaMira, 2004), 23, quoted in Viveiros de Castro, *Cannibal Metaphysics*, 62, n. 23.
[173] See, for example, Habel's response to the burning of the forest of Negev in Ezekiel: "[W]hat has the forest done to deserve this disaster? Why should the trees, the habitat for creatures of the field, suffer such a fire at God's hands?" (Habel, "The Silence of the Lands," 134).
[174] See, for example, Bauckham, *Bible and Ecology*, 101.
[175] See, for example, the essays by Carley, Stevenson, and Wurst in Norman C. Habel, ed., *The Earth Story in Psalms and Prophets* (Sheffield: Sheffield Academic, 2001). Wurst, writing about Jeremiah, calls the relationship between YHWH and the earth "a record of ... assault and battery" (Ibid., 172).

certainly isn't "fair," fairness is beside the point. Ellen Davis says about the intertwining of marriage and agricultural metaphors in Hosea that the people and the land "are bound together in their well-being, 'for better, for worse.'"[176] The world is not interconnected and interdependent only when it is convenient or pleasant for it to be so. It is a modern conceit to imagine that human wellbeing and human suffering can be isolated from the wellbeing of the rest of the world.[177] Even the most human-centered judgments in the Prophets, such as military sieges, affect the whole land. Sieges sometimes led to such horrors as parents eating their children; they also had profound effects on vegetation and animals, to the point of causing permanent changes in the landscape.[178] We have seen repeatedly that biblical writers describe human and nonhuman experiences with overlapping language: both humans and the earth tremble at YHWH's coming; humans, the heavens, and the earth are addressed by YHWH and must pay attention; humans and nonhumans mourn and rejoice, sometimes together, sometimes not. That the earth suffers because of human sin is the dark side of the much celebrated interconnection and interdependence of humans and the world in the Hebrew Bible.[179] Though terrifying and disturbing, this connection between human action and

---

[176] Davis, "The Pain of Seeing Clearly," 88. See also Marlow, *Biblical Prophets and Contemporary Environmental Ethics*, 193–94.

[177] Christoph Uehlinger blames modern specialization for the bifurcation of what he calls "social sin" and ecological disaster. He argues that, for people who feel on their bodies the effects of empire and dictatorship, the connection between human behavior and environmental degradation is perfectly comprehensible (Christoph Uehlinger, "The Cry of the Earth: Biblical Perspectives on Ecology and Violence," in *Ecology and Poverty*, Concilium [London: SCM, 1995], 47).

[178] For a general description of ancient siege warfare, see Israel Eph'al, *The City Besieged: Siege and Its Manifestations in the Ancient Near East* (Jerusalem: Hebrew University Magnes, 2013); and Erika Bleibtreu, "Five Ways to Conquer a City," *Biblical Archaeology Review* 16, no. 3 (May 1990): 37–44. For a description of permanent landscape changes, see O. Ackermann, H. J. Bruins, and A. M. Maeir, "A Unique Human-Made Trench at Tell Eṣ-Ṣâfī/Gath: Anthropogenic Impact and Landscape Response," *Geoarchaeology* 20, no. 3 (2005): 303–27. For a discussion of the practice of taking fruit trees hostage as a tactic to shorten sieges, see Jacob L. Wright, "Warfare and Wanton Destruction: A Reexamination of Deuteronomy 20:19–20 in Relation to Ancient Siegecraft," *Journal of Biblical Literature* 127, no. 3 (September 1, 2008): 423–58.

[179] The interconnectedness of the whole created realm may be the most lauded and remarked on aspect of the ecological thought of the biblical writers. See, for example, the preface of Bauckham, *Bible and Ecology*; Fretheim, *God and World in the Old Testament*, xvi; Marlow, *Biblical Prophets and Contemporary Environmental Ethics*, 120; Davis, *Scripture, Culture, and Agriculture*, 19; Morgan, "Transgressing, Puking, Covenanting," 178.

nonhuman suffering is ethically important. One way to think about the current ecological crisis is as a failure to understand the consequences of human behavior on the rest of the world. There are certainly aspects of the biblical text that are difficult to harness for ethical reflection, a prime example being Ezekiel's repeated claim that the land is devastated so that "they shall know that I am YHWH."[180] Despite this, the biblical insistence that human action has profound influences on animal and nonanimal nature displays not callous indifference to ecological issues, but astute observation. Human action affects all other creatures, whether it is fair or not. The earth's mourning in the Prophets gives voice to the suffering of nonanimal nature, and chastises humans for putting other creatures through pain, adversity, and death.

JOY

If the mourning of the earth goes hand-in-hand with judgment oracles against Judah and Israel, then the companion to oracles of restoration and words of comfort is nature's joy. The theme is particularly prominent in the second half of Isaiah; between chapters 35 and 64, the prophet repeatedly exhorts the heavens and the earth, mountains and trees, dry places and the sea, to rejoice in YHWH's deliverance.[181]

Associated with the joy of nonanimal nature is moisture, growth, and fertility. Mourning and drought belong together; deliverance takes the form of rain and dew and extravagant verdure. For example, in Isaiah 35:1–2, the writer weaves together language of joy and plant growth:

The wilderness and the dry place will exult, the desert will rejoice and blossom like the crocus. It will bloom abundantly, and rejoice with joy and jubilation. The glory of Lebanon will be given to it, the majesty of Carmel and Sharon. They themselves[182] will see the glory of YHWH, the majesty of our God. (Isaiah 35:1–2)

Isaiah's words of comfort in the verses that follow (35:3–4) address points of human weakness and exhaustion: weak hands, stumbling knees, and

---

[180] See, for example, Ezekiel 6:14; 29:9; 32:15; 33:29; and 35:15.
[181] For a summary of how restoration of nonanimal nature intertwines with restoration of humans, and how each serve as a metaphor for the other, see Patricia K. Tull, "Persistent Vegetative States: People as Plants and Plants as People in Isaiah," in *The Desert Will Bloom: Poetic Visions in Isaiah* (Leiden: Brill; SBL, 2009), 27.
[182] Isaiah prefaces the finite verb with a technically superfluous independent personal pronoun (הֵמָּה יִרְאוּ), in order to emphasize the subject of the verb.

anxious hearts. It is to people who are bone-tired from fear and need that YHWH comes to deliver: "Say to those of anxious heart ... Look, your God!" (Isaiah 35:4). Arid places also know want. They are the near equivalent of humans worn down by distress and hardship, and Isaiah promises them consolation:

For YHWH has comforted (נִחַם) Zion, he has comforted (נִחַם) all her dry places and he has made her wilderness like Eden, and her dry places like the garden of YHWH. Gladness and rejoicing will be found in her, praise and the sound of song.
(Isaiah 51:3)[183]

To the prophet the transformation of dry places into gardens is an instance of YHWH *comforting* dry places. The verb is the same as the verb in Isaiah's famous "Comfort, O comfort, my people" (Isaiah 40:1). Here the language tying together humans and nonhumans focuses less on shared characteristics and more on their common relation to YHWH: both are recipients of consolation and restoration. The logic recalls Genesis 1, in which humans, animals, plants, and luminaries, even the skies, the dry land, and the waters, owe their existence to God's "let there be ...." In both texts, YHWH extends similar care towards humans and other-than-humans, taking into account their unique bodies and needs.

Joint experiences of restoration also include mutual joy. Isaiah beckons the heavens and the earth to rejoice because YHWH has restored Judah: "Jubilate, O heavens, and rejoice, O earth, let the mountains break forth in jubilation. For YHWH has comforted his people, and he has had compassion on his afflicted" (Isaiah 49:13).[184] The writer does not explain why the heavens, the earth, and the mountains should rejoice because YHWH has comforted his people, but it accords with ideas of nonanimal wellbeing in prophetic writings and elsewhere. In Genesis 2, the land cannot produce vegetation without the help of humans, and Leviticus 26:42 implies that God's covenant with Jacob, Isaac, and Abraham is also a covenant with the land. In the prophetic corpus, a common source of suffering for the land is depopulation.[185] To be without people is a kind of barrenness, much like being without vegetation. Jeremiah, in fact, narrates the return of inhabitants and animals to Israel using the language of plant growth: "Look, the days are coming, an oracle of YHWH, when I will sow the house of Israel and the house of Judah with

---

[183] See also Isaiah 52:9.   [184] See also Isaiah 44:23; 49:13; 52:9.
[185] See, for example, Isaiah 6:11–12; Jeremiah 4:23–26; 21:6; 32:43; 33:10; Ezekiel 33:28; Zephaniah 3:6; and Zechariah 7:14.

human seed and with animal seed" (Jeremiah 31:27). A restored land in the prophetic imagination is not a pristine wilderness, far away from people and their cities, but a land teeming with every kind of inhabitant: humans, animals, birds, fish, insects, and plants.[186] Jeremiah promises the land that it will be full of noise and bustle:

> Again will be heard in this place about which you say: "It is a waste, without a human, without an animal," in the cities of Judah and the streets of Jerusalem, the desolate places without a human and without an inhabitant and without an animal, the voice of joy and the voice of rejoicing and the voice of bridegroom and the voice of bride, the voices of those who sing, "Praise YHWH of hosts, for YHWH is good, for his loyalty is eternal," bringing praise [into] the house of YHWH. For I will restore the fortunes of the land as at first, says YHWH. (Jeremiah 33:10–11)[187]

Just as YHWH's judgment of Israel and Judah inevitably and unavoidably affects the wellbeing of the land, so the land is comforted when its people are comforted. Humans, animals, plants, and the land form an interdependent community, internally differentiated but indivisible in terms of welfare and flourishing. This explains why hills, mountains, and trees should greet the return of the exiles with the enthusiasm described in Isaiah 55:12: "For you will go out with rejoicing and in peace you will be brought in. The mountains and the hills will burst into jubilation before you, and all the trees of the field will clap their hands." At the heart of this text is the conviction that all aspects of creation need each other and rejoice at being together. When considering the horrors of present day ecological devastation, it can sometimes seem as if the world would be better off without humans, without us. This thought is foreign to prophetic hope. The trees will clap their hands, not because humans are the most important creature, but because humans, animals, plants, and lands desire each other and depend on each other for wellbeing, flourishing, and joy.

Despite the interdependence of creatures, biblical writers acknowledge that humans sometimes exploit nonanimal nature. In two texts, nonanimal nature rejoices over the end of empire and its extractive practices: "The whole earth is at rest and quiet. They break forth in shouts of joy.

---

[186] See also Jeremiah 33:10–11.
[187] See also Isaiah 62:4: "No longer will it be said about you: forsaken! And about your land it will no longer be said: desolate! For it will be declared about you: My joy is in her, and about your land: Married, for YHWH delights in you and your land will be married."

Even the cypresses rejoiced because of you, the cedars of Lebanon: Since you have lain down, the logger does not go up against us" (Isaiah 14:7–8).[188] The demise of the king of Babylon, who has ruthlessly oppressed humans, lands, and plants, is occasion for creationwide rejoicing. The writer singles out cypresses in particular, probably because the timber of Lebanon was one of the commodities most coveted by the successive empires of the Near East.[189]

Jeremiah also records creation's joy at the fall of Babylon, but in more general terms: "Heaven and earth and all that is in them will jubilate over Babylon, for the devastators come against her from the north" (Jeremiah 51:48). Not every form of human habitation is cause for joy for nonanimal nature. Certain forms, in particular those represented by empire, hurt land and vegetation. When the prophets invite the earth and its mountains to "break forth in jubilation" (Isaiah 49:13) at the return of the exiles, it is because the exiles are expected to uphold a different relationship with the land. Recall Leviticus: its writers insist that Israel will only remain in the land if it respects the land's covenant obligations to YHWH.

If Leviticus extends covenant observance beyond humans, the prophets do the same with righteousness, salvation, and peace. These are not exclusively human terms, or human experiences, but rather embrace all creatures. In Isaiah 44–45, the prophet addresses three audiences in turn: Judah/Jacob, Cyrus, and the heavens and the earth.[190] In the final

---

[188] See also Habakkuk 2:8 and 17. Habakkuk cries "alas" for a series of oppressors, "the one who multiplies that which is not his own," "the one who gains evil by violence for his house," "the one who builds the city by bloodshed," and "the one who makes his companion drink," and summarizes their crimes as "human bloodshed and violence to the earth." J. J. M. Roberts writes that Habakkuk's summary "suggest a ... profound understanding of the evils of wars of conquest. Such conflicts do violence to the ecology of the countryside, the culture of the city, and the well-being of even those inhabitants of the conquered territory who survive the bloodshed" (J. J. M. Roberts, *Nahum, Habakkuk, and Zephaniah: A Commentary* [Louisville, KY: Westminster/John Knox, 1991], 120).

[189] See Nielsen, *There Is Hope for a Tree*, 161–62.

[190] Joseph Blenkinsopp describes Isaiah 44:24–45:8 as a unit, with two distinct audiences: "a Judean audience" and "Cyrus" (Blenkinsopp, *Isaiah*, 245). Isaiah 45:8, he says, is simply a "brief hymn" (Ibid.). As evidence of the importance of the oracles to Judah and Cyrus, he points to the repetition of "[YHWH] who made all things, [YHWH] who has done all these things" in 44:24 and 45:7 (Ibid.). Brevard Childs also focuses exclusively on Cyrus as addressee, and does not consider why the heavens and the earth are also summoned (Brevard S. Childs, *Isaiah* [Louisville, KY: Westminster John Knox, 2001], 354). Other scholars, however, have pointed out that the calls to the heavens and the earth in 44:23 and 45:8 serve as an *inclusio* (see, for example, Claus Westermann, *Isaiah 40–66: A Commentary* [Philadelphia: Westminster, 1969], 163), suggesting that there are in fact *three* audiences, not two. Addition evidence is the fact that Isaiah 45:8 ends

address, righteousness and salvation are indistinguishable from plants germinating, sprouting, and bearing fruit:

Drip, O heavens, from above, and let the clouds stream righteousness. Let the earth open (תִּפְתַּח),[191] so that salvation may bear fruit, and let it cause righteousness to sprout also. I, YHWH, have created it. (Isaiah 45:8)

Righteousness, like joy, finds its expression in moisture and fruitfulness. Weather and agricultural terms, like "drip," "stream," "bear fruit," and "sprout," comingle with nouns like "righteousness" and "salvation." Just as the infidelity of Judah and Israel has led to cosmic mourning, expressed primarily in terms of drought and ecological devastation, so righteousness is associated with lush, well watered landscapes. Note, however, that righteousness does not precede fruitfulness; the prophet does not promise rain as a reward for good behavior. Instead the earth itself participates in the restoration of salvation by opening up and giving itself over to the gestation of righteousness. The verse is a crescendo variation on Genesis 1:11: "Let the earth sprout vegetation ..." In Genesis 1, the earth aids YHWH in the creation of plants; here it participates in YHWH's reestablishment of right relations within creation.

Interpreters struggle with putting words to the precise connection between rain and righteousness. John Goldingay's commentary on Isaiah is representative. Goldingay contrasts Cyrus, whose agency is "literal and immediate," with the heavens and the earth, whose agency is "intermediate and metaphorical," and claims that the language, in the latter case "is thus ... more that of myth than that of history ... Metaphorical and mythic language is used to describe what is to happen as a reality in the realm of political events."[192] And yet he ends on an ambiguous statement:

---

with the statement "I, YHWH, has created it"; the addresses to Jacob, Cyrus, and the heavens and the earth all include, in other words, a statement that confirms YHWH's power to create. Exegetically, there is little reason to call Jacob and Cyrus "audiences," but exclude the heavens and the earth from this category.

[191] Goldingay, referencing Moshe Goshen-Gottstein, notes that the LXX translates this verb as ἀνατειλάτω, "grow," perhaps to avoid associations with the story of Korah in Numbers 16. If this text does reference Numbers 16, or Exodus 15, the writers may use the verb פקד, "to open," to signal the drastic change in the participation of the earth. It does not open to punish, but to allow salvation to grow.

[192] John Goldingay, *The Message of Isaiah 40–55: A Literary-Theological Commentary* (London: T&T Clark, 2005), 272. See also Goldingay's statements that "Yhwh bids the heavens to do what will be *concretely real* in the person of Cyrus" (Ibid.; emphasis added), and "Perhaps we are to assume that the language constitutes a more poetic version of the commission to heavenly aids [like angels and the heavenly army] and earthly agents such as Cyrus, who have responsibility to see that Yhwh's right purpose is put into effect" (John

"Heaven and earth *are and/or stand for* the heavenly and earthly agents through whom Yhwh's purpose is achieved."[193] Are the heavens and the earth tools or agents? Goldingay hesitates. Isaiah 45:8 suggests not only that the heavens and the earth are personal beings, but that they have influence over such abstract concepts as righteousness and salvation. In modern Western thought, morality and ethics are human concerns; we do not attribute righteousness to animals, fields, mountains, or clouds. In the texts studied so far, the land responds to human activity. Faithful living produces rains in their time, plentiful harvest, and healthy flocks. Failure to observe cultic responsibilities leads to drought, famine, and war. It is this pattern that prompts scholars to call the land a barometer of Israel's relationship with YHWH.[194] But, the land is not simply a barometer. Isaiah shows us a land with the power to contribute to conditions that make righteous life and salvation available to humans.

This need not be metaphoric or abstract. Because human righteousness and deliverance take concrete form in the Hebrew Bible, and involve agricultural, economic, familial, and political aspects of life, it is likely that righteousness practiced by nonanimal nature is also tangible and material. First, it is the task of all creatures, be they animals or plants, to be fruitful. The heavens and the earth do not themselves procreate, but they aid the fecundity of other creatures. By being fruitful, the land lives out the life ordained for it at creation.[195] Second, the land partners with YHWH to save Israel. The heavens and the earth contribute to Jacob's salvation in ways as concrete as does Cyrus; the difference between the two is not that one is metaphorical and the other realistic, the one mythic and the other historic, but that they contribute in different ways.[196] Cyrus issues decrees, provides military support, and so on; the heavens and the earth provide food, places to live, spaces in and with which to enact Torah.[197] In Isaiah,

---

Goldingay and David F. Payne, *A Critical and Exegetical Commentary on Isaiah 40–55*, vol. II [London; New York: T&T Clark, 2006], 29). For another text that pairs political leaders and the land as sources of righteousness, see Psalm 72:1–3.

[193] Goldingay, *The Message of Isaiah 40–55*, 273 (emphasis added).

[194] See Milgrom, *Leviticus*, 1777, 1580; and Kay, "Human Dominion Over Nature in the Hebrew Bible," 217. See also Christopher Wright's description of the land as "covenantal thermometer" (Wright, *Old Testament Ethics for the People of God*, 77, 96).

[195] See Genesis 1:11–12, 22, 28.

[196] Patricia Tull writes that Isaiah emphasizes humanity's absolute dependence on plant lives. See Tull, "Persistent Vegetative States," 21–22.

[197] Randi Rashover argues that land tenure is an essential part of the religious life of ancient Israelites. The family land holding system was essential, she says, for proclaiming divine

righteousness and justice are not moral qualities, but inhabitants of the land: "Justice will dwell in the wilderness, righteousness will live in the fertile field" (Isaiah 32:16). Far from being products of human effort alone, they depend on the generous hospitality of Israel's landscapes, both sown and unsown.

Isaiah is not unique in attributing righteousness to nonanimal nature, nor is he the only prophet to point in particular to precipitation and fruitfulness. Joel speaks of "rain for righteousness":

Do not be afraid, O soil, be glad and rejoice. For the YHWH has done great things. Do not be afraid, O animals of [the] field, for the pastures of the wilderness will be green, for the tree will carry its fruit and the fig and the vine will give their strength. O children of Zion, rejoice and be glad in YHWH your God, for he has given you the early rain for righteousness,[198] and he has brought down on you rain, early rain and later rain, like before. (Joel 2:21–23)

In Joel, YHWH provides rain for righteousness for all creatures: the soil, animals, and people. The prophet speaks words of consolation to each of them in turn; the absence of righteousness is not a human problem, but a creationwide one. The book of Joel starts with an extended description of ecological devastation, caused by a locust swarm as powerful as any army. The locust has eaten everything (Joel 1:4), destroying vines and fig trees (1:7, 12); there are no grain and drink offerings to present to YHWH (1:9, 13), fields are devastated, the ground mourns, the grain harvest, both wheat and barley, is destroyed (1:10–11), together with pomegranate,

---

sovereignty and guarding against idolatry and economic disorder (Randi Rashkover, "Reasoning through the Prophetic: A Reading of Isaiah 61, Leviticus 25 and Luke 4:16," *The Journal of Scriptural Reasoning* 6, no. 1 [2006], http://jsr.shanti.virginia.edu/back-issues/vol-6-no-1-may-2006-scripture-and-democracy/reasoning-through-the-prophetic-a-reading-of-isaiah-61-leviticus-25-and-luke-416/). See also Wright, *God's People in God's Land*.

[198] John Watts writes that the "rain for righteousness" symbolizes "teaching being the sowing of truth to bring about a rich harvest" (Watts, *The Books of Joel, Obadiah, Jonah, Nahum, Habakkuk, and Zephaniah*, 26), taking the reference to rain figuratively (Watts' reading is based, in part, on the Vulgate's translation of the phrase as "teacher of righteousness"). The NRSV translated the phrase "rain for your vindication," which ties the phrase to drought as a consequence of transgression. Crenshaw translates לִצְדָקָה "the early rain in its season," based on the pattern of Egyptian *ma'at*. *Ma'at* refers to "the structure of the universe ... in an orderly fashion-in its season" (James L. Crenshaw, *Joel: A New Translation with Introduction and Commentary* [New York: Doubleday, 1995], 154–55). Margaret Barker, using more modern terminology, writes that the meaning of the word is "almost the same as sustainability" (Margaret Barker, *Creation: A Biblical Vision for the Environment* [London: T & T Clark, 2010], 144). The parallel with Isaiah 45:8 should caution interpreters against dismissing too quickly an association between literal rain and righteousness in the sense of right living.

palm, and apple trees (1:12); seeds have shriveled up, animals sigh, sheep suffer punishment (1:17–18), fire has devoured pasturage and uncultivated trees (1:19–20), and the wild animals are so thirsty they call out to YHWH (1:20). This is the situation that Joel's oracles of consolation address. The soil has every reason to be afraid, so have the animals, the pastures, the trees, the fig, and the vine, together with the "children of Zion," whose entire food supply has failed. The opening picture of Joel is one of complete devastation: there is nothing to eat, nothing to feed one's animals with, nothing to offer to YHWH in the temple.

Between this wreckage and the ensuing consolations sits a call for repentance: "Even now, an oracle of YHWH, return to me with your whole heart, and with fasting, and weeping, and lament ... Who knows? He might turn and relent, and leave behind a blessing: a grain offering and a drink offering for YHWH, your God" (Joel 2:12, 14). The devastation is not bad luck or random weather, but a result of the people's failure to ... Joel is not specific, but he is unambiguous about the fact that the famine should make the people feel ashamed (Joel 2:19, 27). Just as Joel is unspecific about what the people have done, so he fails to describe any actual repentance. After the call to fast and pray, he writes: "Then YHWH became jealous for his land and took pity on his people" (2:18). Perhaps it is a sort of literary ellipses, in which the call to repentance assumes the place of a narrative of repentance. Or maybe not. YHWH becomes jealous on behalf of the devastated landscape, and feels bad for the people. Rather than assuming a repentance that isn't there, perhaps the "rain for righteousness" is just what it sounds like, a shower to restore the people to just living. The soil, animals, and trees need not rest their confidence on the ability of the people to repent, an ability the writers of the Hebrew Bible often doubt, but can trust wholly in YHWH. YHWH will send righteousness on the land, and they themselves will respond with abundant gifts. All that is left to humans is to rejoice to find themselves in such munificent company.

In Zechariah too, a seemingly abstract concept, שׁלוֹם, "wellbeing" or "peace," is connected with abundant harvests, which humans receive as a gift given by plants, soil, and skies:[199]

---

[199] Biblical writers often write about rain and plant yield using the language of giving. See, for example, Leviticus 25:19; 26:4; Deuteronomy 11:17; and Ezekiel 34:26–27. When rain or fruit are absent, the vocabulary shifts to restraint. See 1 Kings 8:35–36, and Haggai 1:10–11.

For there will be a sowing of wellbeing (זֶרַע הַשָּׁלוֹם).²⁰⁰ The vine will give its fruit and the earth will give its produce, and the heavens will give its dew. And I will cause the remnant of this people to inherit all these things. (Zechariah 8:12)

The presence or absence of wellbeing is a recurrent theme in Zechariah 1–8. Zechariah 6:13 promises that the king and a priest will share "peaceful council (עֲצַת שָׁלוֹם)," Zechariah 8:10 describes how, in past days, there was no "safety from the foe (שָׁלוֹם מִן־הַצָּר)," and 8:16 and 19 exhort the people to make "judgments of wellbeing (מִשְׁפַּת שָׁלוֹם)" and to love "truth and wellbeing (וְהַשָּׁלוֹם אֱמֶת)." Considered in the context of these verses, 8:12 describes a turning point: the land that was characterized by a lack of wellbeing will now, by means of a sowing, be full of it. This shift comes about not primarily by means of human work – the sowing of wellbeing precedes the exhortations to the Yehudite audience in 8:16 and 19. Instead, the shift is a result of divine promise: YHWH promises not to deal with the people "as in the former days" (Zechariah 8:11). YHWH pledges seed, and the resulting abundance, an overflowing of gifts from the vine, the earth, and the heavens, forms the context in which the Yehudites will behave differently towards each other. Having received peace from the world around them, having inherited good things from it, they are now expected to give good things to each other: truth, wellbeing, and good judgment. They are to imitate the generosity of YHWH and of YHWH's world, instead of plotting against each other and loving false oaths (Zechariah 8:17). Because they will have festivals of joy and happiness, they are to love truth and peace. As in Isaiah, other-than-human persons facilitate and make possible human wellbeing and justice. Righteousness is not a human moral achievement, but a

---

²⁰⁰ The construct chain זֶרַע הַשָּׁלוֹם has given translators pause. The BDB suggests the phrase is corrupt and offers אֶזְרְעָה שָׁלוֹם ("I will sow peace") as an alternative. Mark Boda, however, writes that the noun זֶרַע, "seed," can refer to the act of sowing, as it does in Genesis 8:22 and Leviticus 26:5 (Boda, *The Book of Zechariah*, 490). Boda argues that the construct relationship should be read as a genitive of effect, and renders it "a sowing time that will yield prosperity" (Ibid., 488, 490). Similarly, Carol and Eric Meyers translate it "a prosperous sowing" (Carol L. Meyers and Eric M. Meyers, *Haggai; Zechariah 1–8: A New Translation with Introduction and Commentary*, The Anchor Bible 25B [Garden City, NY: Doubleday, 1987], 409). Ralph L. Smith suggests "For they will sow in peace," but does not offer syntactical evidence to support his translation (Ralph L. Smith, *Micah-Malachi*, Word Biblical Commentary 32 [Waco, TX: Word Books, 1984], 234). Smith's translation is not possible without emending the text; the translations of Boda and the Meyers are. I have chosen a more literal rendering, "a sowing of wellbeing," to draw attention to the word הַשָּׁלוֹם, "the peace," a key concept in Zechariah 1–8.

cooperative venture between humans and other-than-human persons, a venture that more often than not begins with humans accepting peace and wellbeing as gifts from that which is not human, from YHWH and YHWH's land.

CONCLUSION

Nonanimal nature is busy in the Prophets! Stars go to battle, hills perform mourning rituals, fields grieve over droughts and locust attacks, mountains convulse in YHWH's presence, ravines receive oracles. The emotional life of other-than-human persons is equally diverse; they feel fear, dread, grief, joy, and exultation. No longer are the people of Israel preparing for life in the land. Instead these books narrate the, often messy, reality of living with God in the hills, valleys, ravines, and plains of the land promised to their ancestors. Other-than-human persons experience this new reality too – for them the challenge is often to *be* that land, to enact and to weather God's exacting expectations. They too are judged and disciplined, they too are promised restoration and health.

The writer P. D. James ends a 2008 novel with a bleak reflection on the world of the twenty first century: "the earth," she writes, is "a dying planet where millions of people [are] constantly moving like a black stain of human locusts, invading, consuming, corrupting, destroying the air of once remote and beautiful places now rancid with human breath..."[201] James' reflection is part and parcel of a larger cultural suspicion, the sense that humans have become a blight, a planetary diseases, and that "remote and beautiful places" are better off without us. A nihilistic response to climate change, it is the corollary to the idea that climate change has always been inevitable, given human nature. With enough time, and enough fire power, we were always going to make the planet burn. From this point of view, there's little to do but to lie down and die – that is, if you want to save the planet.

The biblical writers are rarely interested in "remote and beautiful places." There are a few exceptions of course (the divine speeches of Job 38–41 are a prime example), but most landscapes in the Bible are inhabited. Vast deserts or bustling cities, villages or pasture lands, the writers of the Bible concern themselves with places in which humans live or which they move through. This should not be mistaken for

---

[201] P. D. James, *The Private Patient* (New York: Alfred A. Knopf, 2008), 348.

anthropocentrism, for excessive attention to human concerns. In fact, the preference for inhabited landscapes goes hand in hand with the prophetic attention to other-than-human persons. The prophets do not ask themselves how to preserve remote nature – national parks are far in the future – but how to live well with others, be it humans, animals, plants, mountains, or skies. Cities are not bad news to the prophets; they do not pine for pristine wilderness. Instead they desire mutual flowering, communities of soil, plants, animals, and humans in supportive and beneficial relationships. Their attention to nonanimal nature, in particular to its emotional life, arises out of this desire. Far from imposing human characteristics on that which is not human, the biblical writers consider how Israel must live in order to be a source of joy to its fields, and not a source of mourning. The cypresses of Lebanon gloat over Babylon's downfall; if they are to respond differently to the return of the exiles, if Isaiah's vision of a forest chorus of applause is to be realized, Israel and Judah cannot live like their imperial overlords. They must be good neighbors to trees and fields, rivers and ravines, mountains and valleys. Landscapes do not always rejoice at human presence in the Bible, but a terrain denuded of its inhabitants is only ever a partial solution to human exploitation. According to the prophets, the land experiences population loss as bereavement, not as ecological liberation.

It is difficult now to imagine humans as good news for other-than-human persons, but this is the challenge the prophetic corpus sets for us. We must live in such a way so as not only to stave off ecological apocalypse, but so that animals, trees, and pasture lands may be pleased to host us, to live alongside us. This is more demanding than splitting land into parks that must be preserved, and cities and suburbs that can be exploited. It is certainly more demanding than geoengineering fixes that allow us to go on as usual. It even goes beyond responses that at the moment seem farfetched, like a drastic reduction in CO_2 emissions, though this is certainly a necessary aspect of what the prophetic call requires in the present context. Of course, this sense of challenge, of insurmountable odds, is familiar to the prophets. Joel and P. D. James speak of environmental destruction in similar terms: "invading, consuming, corrupting, destroying" – this is James; Joel's list includes invading, laying waste, splintering, stripping. Both authors lay the ultimate responsibility at the feet of humans, James directly, Joel indirectly. What makes Joel different from James is that he imagines a return (or a turn) to a different world. It is possible to repent: "And who knows? Perhaps [YHWH] will turn and relent, and leave behind a blessing" (Joel 2:14).

We are past the point where climate change is avoidable; we cannot return to a pristine past (if such a thing is even real). All we can do is to try to limit the scope, and the prophetic corpus can help us to do this. Instead of asking us to engage in wilderness preservation and environmental protection, it calls on us to be good neighbors. Or, to doctor Harvey's words a little, the prophets "insist not only on the inevitability but also the great value of human entanglements with all life."[202] They ask us to live in such a way that this entanglement is not only good for us, but good for other-than-human persons as well.

P. D. James does not end the book on her nightmare description of human locust. Her character realizes that this is only one of several human possibilities: just as she is "part of [the world's] corruption," so she is "part of its splendors and its joys."[203] The latter faintly echoes Ezekiel's promise to the hills of Judah:

But you, O mountains of Israel, you will put out your branches and you will carry your fruit for my people Israel, for they are near to coming. For look, I am for you and I will turn to you and you will be tilled and sown ... I will make you inhabited like your former times and I will do good to you like your first time and you will know that I am YHWH. (Ezekiel 36:8–11)

Here is what the Bible asks of us: to prepare ourselves so that we might be good and pleasant gifts to our lands, to its hills, rivers, and ravines, so that when YHWH promises our lands that "you [will be] inhabited like your former times," our lands respond with joy.

---

[202] Harvey, *Animism*, 179.   [203] James, *The Private Patient*, 348.

5

An Articulate World

Personalistic Nature Texts in the Writings

INTRODUCTION

This chapter is about personalistic nature texts in the Writings. I have tried, in the two previous chapters, to be more or less comprehensive, discussing, or at least referencing, every personalistic nature text in the Torah and the Prophets. This chapter is different. Many of the personalistic nature texts in the Writings belong to categories discussed in the Prophets chapter, and to analyze each of them would be repetitive and tedious. For example, the Book of Psalms contains several theophanies.[1] Though these theophanies have some unique features (there is more skipping and fleeing, among other things),[2] the questions they raise in respect to the activity of nonanimal nature are more or less the same as prophetic theophanies. Instead of aiming for comprehensiveness, this chapter concerns itself with aspects of the life of nonanimal nature that have not yet been explored. In the Psalms, I will look at the articulateness of nonanimal nature, a theme that is more prominent in the Psalms than in other biblical books. The motif of nonanimal nature as judge will form the bulk of the discussion of the Book of Job. Though nonanimal nature has served as both witness and judge in other texts, a distinctive feature of the Book of Job is that its characters explicitly debate how this relates to human conduct and suffering. Finally, I turn to the Song of Songs in order

---

[1] See Psalms 18:8–16 [7–15]; 29:5–9; 68:8–9 [7–8]; 77:17–19 [16–18]; 97:3–4; 104:32; 114:3–8.
[2] See Psalms 29:5–9 and 114:3–8.

DECLARATION IN THE PSALMS

The Book of Psalms is a noisy book. Humans cry and beg and pray and praise, but their voices are only part of the din: "The heavens declare [YHWH's] righteousness" (Psalm 50:6); "The sources of the morning and evening jubilate" (Psalm 65:9 [8]); "The pastures of the wilderness drip and the hills gird themselves with joy ... They shout, even sing" (Psalm 65:13–14 [12–13]); "The floods have lifted up, O YHWH, the floods have lifted up their voice, the floods have lifted up their pounding" (Psalm 93:3) – if you imagine the book as a record of voices trying to get God's attention, the resulting sound is big and raucous, more like the sound of every instrument of an orchestra playing at once than a human choir. The poets borrow vocabulary from the realm of the human voice – verbs like סָפַר ("to recount"), נָגַד (Hiphil: "to declare"), רָנַן ("to sing for joy"), רוּעַ (Hiphil: "to shout"), שִׁיר ("to sing"), and יָדָה (Hiphil: "to confess, give thanks")[3] – but applies it in unfamiliar ways. In the psalms, being human or even having vocal cords (or a throat, for that matter) is no prerequisite for partaking in YHWH's throng. In fact, the psalmists revel in noisy, happy verbs, distributed liberally among human and nonhuman subjects: הָלַל (Piel: "to praise"), רָעַם ("to roar, thunder"), מָחָא ("to clap"), גִּיל ("to rejoice"), שָׂמַח ("to be glad"), and עָלַז ("to exult") are popular.[4] It is sometimes difficult to imagine what these verbs mean when their subjects are things like mountains and breakers, but what *is* clear is that prayer and praise in the Psalter is creationwide; all persons, human and otherwise, are invited to join the cacophony.

Paul Santmire writes that the theme of nature's praise of YHWH is "one of the least understood themes in the Old Testament."[5] The reason it has given interpreters trouble is not that it is particularly obscure or cryptic, but that interpreters have considered it in isolation from other personalistic

---

[3] See Psalms 19:2 [1]; 50:6; 65:9 [8], 14 [13]; 97:6; 145:10.

[4] See Psalms 69:35 [34]; 89:6 [5]; 96:11–13; 97:1; 98:7–8; 148:3–9.

[5] H. Paul Santmire, *The Travail of Nature: The Ambiguous Ecological Promise of Christian Theology* (Philadelphia, PA: Fortress, 1985), 198–99. Santmire goes on to say that while nature's praise might imply a "'primitive' animism or panpsychism," this "should not be allowed to obscure the coherent theological assumption: that the glories of nature are enjoyable and pleasing to [YHWH]" (Ibid., 199). There is no reason to consider YHWH's enjoyment of nature more theologically "coherent" than nature's enjoyment of YHWH.

nature texts. Viewed on its own, nature's praise of YHWH looks like an anomaly, as if the mountains and the coastlands suddenly wake up in the Psalter after a canon-long slumber. For example, Fretheim writes:

> The praise of God on the part of nature is a theme that never occurs in narrative material. Found only in poetry, it is almost exclusively associated with hymnic literature, primarily in the Psalter and Second Isaiah.[6]

This is true as far as it goes. But Fretheim goes on to say that the genre specificity of nature's praise gives credence to the idea that "we have here to do with poetic license or poetic fancy ... or the language of personification."[7] He himself rejects this argument, stating that it "[closes] off several interpretive possibilities."[8] More specific exegetical arguments, however, can be marshaled to argue that nature's praise is more than poetic exaggeration. First, nature acts outside of the Psalter and Second Isaiah. Its activity takes different forms, forms I have explored in Chapters 3 and 4, but the Psalter stands in continuity with the larger canon when it ascribes deliberate behavior and emotions to mountains, trees, and waterways. Second, human praise is also concentrated in hymnic material, especially in the Psalter. A look at the roots הלל, "to praise," and ידה, "to give thanks," the two roots that most explicitly name praise and adoration, show that they occur primarily (though not exclusively) in the psalms.[9] Nature's praise occurs in hymnic material, because hymnic material, more than any other genre in the Hebrew Bible, is concerned with praise. As we have seen in earlier chapters, the activity of nature tends to mirror the themes of specific biblical books. In Genesis through Deuteronomy, personalistic nature texts focus attention on the land as character, the land being a central concern in these books. In Joshua and Judges, the luminaries and rivers partake in battle, because

---

[6] Terence E. Fretheim, "Nature's Praise of God," in *God and the World in the Old Testament: A Relational Theology of Creation* (Nashville, TN: Abingdon Press, 2005), 255.

[7] Ibid.   [8] Ibid., 256.

[9] The Piel form of verb הָלַל, "to praise," with YHWH as its object occurs a total of one hundred and ten times. Eighty-four of these occurrences are in the Psalter. Five are in the Prophets, and twenty-one in the Writings. Of the occurrences in the Writings, the bulk are found in hymnic material, introduction to hymnic material, and descriptions of priestly duties in Chronicles (see, for example, 1 Chronicles 16:36; 29:13; 2 Chronicles 5:13; 7:6; 20:21). The same pattern holds true for the Hiphil form of the verb יָדָה, "to give thanks, praise," with YHWH as the object. It occurs ninety-six times, sixty-four times in the Psalter. It occurs once in Torah, four times in the Former Prophets, six times in the Latter Prophets, four times in Ezra and Nehemiah, and sixteen times in Chronicles. The context for its use in Chronicles mirrors that of הָלַל.

conquest is at the heart of these stories. In the Prophets, the heavens and the earth share in prophetic grief over Israel and Judah's rebellion. In the Psalter, a book oriented towards praise, nature's praise is brought to the fore.

In most psalms, nature's praise is stated matter-of-factly. It is not explained or explored, only described or elicited. The one exception is Psalm 19, which opens with a meditation on how nature speaks about YHWH:

> The heavens recount the glory of God,
> and the firmament proclaims his handiwork.
> Day to day pours forth speech,
> and night to night declares knowledge.
> There is no speech, nor are there words;
> their voice is not heard.
> Yet their line[10] goes out through all the earth,
> and their words to the end of the earth.
> (Psalm 19:2–5a [1–4a])

The two parts of this psalm, the second half of which extols the excellence of torah (Psalm 19:8–15 [7–14]), were considered by early historical and form critics as independent and unrelated psalms.[11] More recently scholars have demurred, arguing that the psalm intentionally contrasts or compares nature's speech, the sun (19:5b-7[4b-6]), and torah.[12] Attention to the psalm's unity has turned conversations towards issues of natural theology and revelation. In this discussion, Karl Barth and James Barr represent two extreme positions. James Barr argues that Psalm 19, in

---

[10] This noun and suffix (קָוָּם, "their line") is often emended to קוֹלָם, "their voice." See, for example, Nancy L. DeClaissé-Walford, Rolf A. Jacobson, and Beth LaNeel Tanner, *The Book of Psalms* (Grand Rapids, MI: William B. Eerdmans, 2014), 205. Dahood argues that the original text should be retained, but that the noun should be translated "sound," based on parallels with Psalm 40:2 [1]; 52:11 [9]; and Job 17:13 (Mitchell J. Dahood, *Psalms. The Anchor Bible* [Garden City, NY: Doubleday, 1966], 121–22). See also William P. Brown, *Seeing the Psalms: A Theology of Metaphor* (Louisville, KY: Westminster John Knox, 2002), 83; 237, n. 2.

[11] See, for example, Hermann Gunkel, *Ausgewählte Psalmen*, 4. verb. Aufl. (Göttingen: Vandenhoeck & Ruprecht, 1917), 17–24; and Artur Weiser, *The Psalms: A Commentary* (Philadelphia, PA: Westminster, 1962), 197–204.

[12] For an early dissent to the two-psalm theory, see Dahood, *Psalms*, 121. For more recent arguments for the unity of the psalm, see Jeffrey L. Cooley, "Psalm 19: A Sabbath Song," *Vetus Testamentum* 64, no. 2 (2014): 177–95; James Alfred Loader, "What Do the Heavens Declare? On the Old Testament Motif of God's Beauty in Creation," *HTS Theologiese Studies* 67, no. 3 (2011): 1–8; and Benjamin D. Sommer, "Nature, Revelation, and Grace in Psalm 19: Towards a Theological Reading of Scripture," *Harvard Theological Review* 108, no. 3 (July 2015): 376–401.

its entirety, meditates on natural theology, while Karl Barth reads the psalm as a repudiation of the same. Each interpretation hinges on the extent to which they think the voice of the heavens is directed to and intelligible to humans.

Barr writes that both parts of Psalm 19 celebrate "universally available and accessible" divine instruction.[13] In the first part, "everyone on earth" receives the voice of the heavens.[14] The second part extols the kind of wisdom a parent passes on to a child, rather than any specific legal framework.[15] In Barr's interpretation, the communication of "day to day" and "night to night" is generally intelligible to humans. The speech of heaven is *for* humans; it is one of God's chosen methods of revelation.

Barth, on the other hand, writes that "there can be no invitation or summons to natural theology, to a biblical doctrine which underlies, makes possible and justifies natural theology."[16] The point of the opening lines of Psalm 19 is not that the heavens communicate God's glory to humans, but that "the cosmos is ... mute."[17] The speech of night and day is entirely inaccessible to humans, and only through YHWH "speaking and acting in Israel" do persons come to know anything about God.[18] In his reading, the first stanza of the psalm warns people against looking to the heavens for knowledge of YHWH. Only God's revealed word can provide access to God.

Though these readings are mirror images of each other, they are inadequate for the same reasons. First, neither reading takes account of both the "is" and "is not" of metaphorical speech.[19] Barr focuses solely

---

[13] James Barr, *Biblical Faith and Natural Theology: The Gifford Lectures for 1991, Delivered in the University of Edinburgh* (Oxford: Clarendon Press, 1993), 88.

[14] Ibid., 87–88. [15] Ibid., 88.

[16] Karl Barth, *Church Dogmatics*, ed. Thomas F. Torrance and G. W. Bromiley, trans. G. W. Bromiley, vol. 1.2 (Peabody, MA: Hendrickson, 2010), 107.

[17] Ibid., 1.2:112. See also Hans-Joachim Kraus: "*Die Schöpfung hat keine Anrede für Menschen;* mit ihren Aussagen, ihren Selbstaussagen ist sie dem Menschen *nicht* zugewandt" (H. Berkhof and Hans-Joachim Kraus, *Karl Barths Lichtœlehre* [Zürich: Theologischer Verlag, 1978], 24. Emphasis in original). Declaissé-Walford interprets verses 19:2–3 [1–2] along similar lines as Kraus: "Verse 2 emphasizes that creation speaks a message about God ...; v. 3 denies that the message can be interpreted" (DeClaissé-Walford, Jacobson, and Tanner, *The Book of Psalms*, 207).

[18] Barth, *Church Dogmatics*, 1.2:112.

[19] For a discussion of the "is" and "is not" of metaphorical speech, and how interpretation of metaphor requires taking stock of each, see Ricœur, *The Rule of Metaphor*, 247–49. James Alfred Loader repeatedly calls the speech of nature in Psalm 19 "paradoxical" because it is inaudible (see Loader, "What Do the Heavens Declare?," 1, 5, 6, 8). This too misses the metaphor. It is not paradoxical that other-than-human creatures speak, or that

on the "is": the heavens declare the glory of God, and everyone can "hear" their declaration. Barth focuses only on the "is not": "there is no speech, nor are there words." An adequate reading of Psalm 19 must take account of both. The heavens genuinely communicate, but they do so using nonhuman means of communication.

Second, neither scholar considers in detail the fact that the opening lines of the psalm describe speech that is not primarily for humans. In this they are not unique. Most commentators on this psalm make one of two assumptions: either the communication of the cosmos is directed at and intelligible to humans, and is therefore meaningful, or it is not for humans, and is therefore meaningless.[20] For example, Benjamin Sommer writes that if the heavens "provide no information to humanity," their speech is "[pointless]," since "no person hears or sees their message."[21] Here human intelligibility arbitrates the importance of nonhuman speech, a stance that shapes the whole of Sommer's interpretation. The main question in Psalm 19, he writes, is "to what extent does knowledge of the divine originate from human observation of the natural world, and to what extent must this knowledge depend on a gift from God?"[22] The poem is about how *humans* come to know God. In nature, God is disclosed "constantly and impersonally," while in torah, "God as person conveys teaching or demands to a human being or human community."[23] Another way to state the central question of the psalm, according to Sommer, is "whether and to what extent a connection between God and a human being or a human community must involve covenant and law."[24] The activity of nonanimal nature, its own relationship with YHWH, has been largely erased from Sommer's interpretation. The same is true in James Alfred Loader's article, "What Do the Heavens Declare?,"

---

they do so by means radically different than those employed by humans. It is simply difficult to write about such speech in nonmetaphorical language.

[20] A related assumption that governs these interpretations is that communication is either completely open and accessible, or entirely opaque. Animist conversations with nonhuman beings tend to be organized instead by degrees of communication. For example, Descola writes that the Achuar organize the world by means of a hierarchy of intelligibility, "according to the levels of the exchange of information that is reputed to be possible" (Descola, *Beyond Nature and Culture*, 6). Humans can speak to some nonhuman creatures with more ease than with others. Mountains are better able to speak to other mountains than they are to humans. See also Harvey, *Animism*, 105, for a discussion on the limits on conversations between humans and plants.

[21] Sommer, "Nature, Revelation, and Grace in Psalm 19," 393.

[22] Ibid., 377. Sommer, like Barth and Barr, is concerned with the possibility (or not) of natural theology. Sommer's argument resembles Barth's.

[23] Ibid., 390.   [24] Ibid.

though Loader's focus is different from Sommer's. Loader explores how the speech of nature relates to visual phenomena, concluding that "the days and nights divulge something that cannot be heard, which only leaves the possibility that this be observed visually."[25] The form of speech is measured by human faculties; since we cannot hear the words, but are able to look at the sky, the "words" must be visual. Loader offers the following "dynamic translation" of verse 2 [1]: "The heavens reflect the beauty of God."[26] The heavens no longer speak; they are only a mirror in which humanity can see God's reflection. Somehow a psalm that does not mention humans at all until verse 8 [7] has become all about humanity and its relationship to YHWH.

The claim that the heavens declare God's glory by their visual display is common. Sommer argues that the knowledge passed between day and night can be attained through "observing" and "watching" nature, Ḥakham writes that it is the "appearance of the heavens and their hosts" that testifies to YHWH's greatness, and Robert Alter comments that the heavens speak using "the language of images."[27] It does seems likely that, in Psalm 19, the aspect of the heavenly conversation to which humans have access is visual. But that is not to say that the conversation is *only* visual. The heavens talk to themselves; the fact that humans can derive testimony of YHWH from their conversation is an auxiliary benefit. Moreover, the "visual display" interpretation does not take account of the diversity of nonanimal speech in the Psalter. In Psalm 77, it is the sound of the heavens, presumably in thunder, that awes the psalmist: "The clouds poured out water, the skies gave voice" (Psalm 77:18 [17]). In Psalms 93 and 98, the poet listens to crashing waves: "The floods have lifted up, O YHWH, the floods have lifted up their voice; the floods have lifted up their pounding"; "Let the sea thunder and its fullness ... let

---

[25] Loader, "What Do the Heavens Declare?," 3.
[26] Ibid., 5. See also Amos Ḥakham's comment on the same verse: "The psalmist means to say here that the appearance of the heavens and their hosts testifies to the greatness of God who created them ... People who look at the firmament are astonished by the wisdom with which it was formed, and they say: 'How great is the handiwork of God'" (Amos Ḥakham, *The Bible: Psalms with the Jerusalem Commentary*, ed. Israel V. Berman, vol. 1 [Jerusalem: Mosad Harav Kook, 2003], 133). Ḥakham's commentary on 19:3 [2] is less anthropocentric: "Each night expresses to the next night those words of wisdom which should be recited to the glory of the creator" (Ibid., 1:134).
[27] Sommer, "Nature, Revelation, and Grace in Psalm 19," 390; Ḥakham, *The Bible: Psalms with Jerusalem Commentary*, 1:133; Robert Alter, *The Book of Psalms: A Translation with Commentary* (New York: W. W. Norton, 2007), 60. Alter is quoting the poet H. N. Bialik.

the floods clap their hands" (93:3; 98:7–8). The psalmists' observations are not easily reduced to one kind of sensory stimulus. The claim that the heavens speak and the waves roar comes from careful observation of the world, coupled with a conviction that articulate persons inhabit the world, only some of whom are human. "The heavens recount the glory of God" does not "have to be" visual. The heavens speak their own mysterious language. Some of what they say is available to humans, to those who are alert and pay attention. But the psalmist does not claim full knowledge. The "is" and "is not" of the poet's language signal restraint. Like wisdom's elusiveness in Job, the psalmist has "heard a rumor about it" (Job 28:22). To define that "rumor" too closely, to limit it to visual displays of natural beauty, is to domesticate and restrict the rich language of the psalms.

Another thing to consider is that conversations involving nonanimal nature are not limited to praise. Nature's praise is part of a complex account of communication between God, humans, and other-than-humans. For example, the psalmists frequently claim that God speaks to nature, to various effects and purposes. Theophany accounts often include God's voice causing widespread reactions:

> The voice of YHWH breaks the cedars, YHWH breaks the cedars of Lebanon.
> He makes them skip like a calf, Lebanon and Sirion like a young wild ox ...
> The voice of YHWH makes the wilderness writhe,
> YHWH makes writhe the wilderness of Kadesh.
> The voice of YHWH makes oaks writhe and strips bare the forest.
> And in his temple the whole of it[28] says "glory!"
>
> (Psalm 29:5–9)[29]

Brown, Driver, and Briggs, in a comment on the verb רקד, "to skip," write that the word here describes the movement of trees in lightning, reducing the reaction of the trees, the wilderness, Lebanon, and Sirion to the sharp, flickering light of thunderstorms.[30] In their defense, the theophany account in Psalm 29, much like a number of theophany accounts in the Psalter, can and should be read as accounts of storms. But that is

---

[28] "Of it," translating a third person suffix on כָּל, "all," is usually deleted as a dittography of the ending of הֵיכָלוֹ ("his temple"). For an argument in favor of maintaining the suffix, see Dahood, *Psalms*, 179.

[29] See also Psalms 18:14–16 [13–15]; 42:8 [7]; 46:7 [6]; 77:17–18 [16–17]. Note that not all theophanies mention God's voice or word. Sometimes the sight of God is enough to send creation into convulsions, as is the case in 97:4.

[30] "*he ... made them skip like calves* (trees, by lightning)" (Brown et al., *The Brown-Driver-Briggs Hebrew and English Lexicon*, 955).

An Articulate World

not all there is to say. The storm account builds to verse 9: "And in his temple the whole of it says "glory!" It is difficult to know what "the whole of it" refers to: the whole temple, the whole world, the cedars and oaks of the preceding verses? Either way, the skipping and writhing result in praise, in adoration that potentially arises from the "mouths" of the bucking trees. God's voice comes with overwhelming strength; in response, everything and everyone shout back "glory!"

Some psalms frame God's interaction with creation as command. The creation account in Psalm 104, for example, attribute the flight of the waters to God's rebuke:

[YHWH] founded the earth on its pillars; it will never totter.
He made the deep cover it like a garment; the waters stood above the mountains.
From your rebuke they fled, from the voice your thunder they took flight.
They went up the mountains and down into the valleys,
To the place that you founded for them.
You set a boundary that they will not cross;
Never will they return to cover the earth.

(Psalm 104:5–9)

The waters here are like a flock of livestock, running here and there according to the herding of God. They bolt across the landscape, eventually settling into the pen that YHWH has built for them. Similarly, in Psalm 147, frost and thaw arrive because "[YHWH] sends out his word" (Psalm 147:15–18), which the psalmist compares to God's proclamation to Israel: "He declares his word to Jacob, his statutes and judgments to Israel" (Psalm 147:19). In Psalm 78, YHWH directs the skies to rain down manna: "He commanded the skies above; he opened the doors of heaven" (78:23), and, in 107:25, he controls the wind "He spoke and raised up the stormy wind; it lifted up its waves."[31] Psalm 148 describes the stormy wind (רוּחַ סְעָרָה, the same words as in 107:25) as "the one who does his word" (Psalm 148:8), and in one text, other-than-human persons are God's couriers: "He makes winds his messengers, blazing fire his servants" (Psalm 104:4). Added to these are texts that claim that God speaks judgment to the whole world, not just to humans, as in Psalm 50:1–6 and 76:9 [8]. The first of these, Psalm 50, even includes a sort of call-and-response: YHWH "calls to the heavens above and to the earth," and the heavens echo back God's message by "[declaring] his righteousness" (Psalm 50:4, 6). If theophanies resemble verbal interaction in which

---

[31] See also Psalm 89:10 [9], which praises God for being able to still the waves of the sea.

one person or group of persons overwhelms others by their roar, these latter texts come closer to the sharing of directives between a superior and a subordinate group. When God speaks, creation takes notes, sometimes even spreading God's word.

When it is humans who address nonanimal nature, they do so almost exclusively to elicit praise: "Let the heavens and the earth praise [YHWH], the seas and all that creep in them" (Psalm 69:35 [34]).[32] These invocations are not different from the invocation that address human audiences; all are invited to join in praising their creator. The psalmists only divert from this pattern twice, in order to ask nonanimal nature for more specific information. In Psalm 68, the poet asks the mountains of Bashan why they are envious of Zion (68:17 [16]), and in Psalm 114, the psalmist asks the sea, Jordan, and the mountains why they flee at God's coming (Psalm 114:5–6). Together the invocations to praise and these two latter texts suggest that YHWH's presence is desirable to other-than-human persons, but also frightening, a set of emotions that parallel human responses to God's nearness.

All this goes to show that the speech of and to nonanimal nature in the Psalter cannot be reduce to visual (or auditory) sensory experiences whose aim is to reveal God to humans. The declaration of day to day and the praises of the heavens are part of a larger conversation between God and the world, a conversation in which humans sometimes participate. Much like human speech, conversations in the Psalter take multiple forms. Some cases are rather one-sided, like when God roars and everything melts, topples, writhes, and shakes. Sometimes there is more mutuality, though a mutuality conditioned by the unequal relationship between creature and creator, like when God directs the heavens and the earth to produce certain kinds of weather and they respond. When the psalmists speak to other-than-human persons, it is to address them as fellow worshippers, calling on them to praise YHWH and rejoice in YHWH's justice. To reduce this cacophonous interaction to only that which humans can observe, or to covert messages for humans, is to turn the articulateness of creation into a code system and a cipher.

In his article "Creation's Praise of God: A Proposal for a Theology of the Non-Human Creation," Dominic Coad identifies the theological misstep common to interpretations that privilege human intelligibility:

---

[32] See also 89:6 [5]; 96:11–12; 97:1; 148:3–10.

> Much theological engagement ... has focused on the question of how humanity is to relate to non-human creation. An orthodox theology of nature ... will begin with a different question: it will ask what relation the non-human world has to God.[33]

Coad is not writing specifically about the Psalter, but his point is, nonetheless, helpful. Returning again to Psalm 19, when it is read with attention to nonanimal nature's relationship to God, it becomes clear that the heavens, the firmament, the day, and the night do not speak to humans. They are speaking among themselves, telling each other about God: "Day to day pours forth speech, and night to night declares knowledge." This is consistent with other psalms that narrate the discursive abilities of nonhuman creatures. Sometimes they speak to each other, as in Psalm 42:8 [7] ("deep calls out to deep"), often they turn to God, as in Psalm 145:10 ("all your works praise you"), and, most common of all, they rejoice together in YHWH, as in Psalms 65:9 [8], 13–14 [12–13]; 89:13 [12]; 93:3; and 98:7.[34] In none of these examples are humans the primary recipients of nature's communication. Instead, humans overhear an interchange between YHWH and various parts of the world. At most, humans sometimes participate in this interchange by adding their own praise. Humans are a secondary audience to nature's adoration of YHWH, not its raison d'être.

Parallels within the Psalter support the claim that day and night speak to other days and nights, not to humans. Loader points out that Psalm 19:3a is a near parallel to Psalm 145:4a; "day to day pours forth speech" has a similar structure as "generation to generation praises your works." Scholars interpret the second verse as elders passing on the knowledge of YHWH to younger people. For example, Nancy Declaissé-Walford writes that 145:4 "states a firm intention to proclaim to others [YHWH's] attributes."[35] Kraus writes: "In a living tradition the praise should be repeated from one generation to another."[36] This is also the sense in which "day to day pours forth speech" and "night to night declares

---

[33] Dominic Coad, "Creation's Praise of God: A Proposal for a Theology of the Non-Human Creation," *Theology* 112, no. 867 (May 1, 2009): 182.
[34] The psalmist also often exhorts nonanimal nature to turn to God in praise. See Psalms 69:35 [34]; 89:6 [5]; 98:7–9; 148:3–10.
[35] DeClaissé-Walford, Jacobson, and Tanner, *The Book of Psalms*, 993.
[36] Hans-Joachim Kraus and Hilton C. Oswald, *Psalms 60–150* (Minneapolis, MN: Ausburg Fortress, 1989), 548. Kraus notes the syntactical parallel with Psalm 19:3, but does not comment on it. See also Dahood, *Psalms*, 336. Dahood compares 145:4 to Psalm 22:31–32 [30–31]: "Offspring will serve him; YHWH will be spoken off to future generation. They will go and they will declare his righteousness to a people unborn, that he has done it."

knowledge." Nonhuman creatures share what they know of YHWH with each other: Psalm 19 describes something like nonanimal nature's practice of theology, one that is only minimally accessible to humans.

Does this mean I agree with Barth? By no means! Though humans are not the primary audience for the declarations of the heavens, this need not mean that those declarations are meaningless to human onlookers. In fact, Psalm 19 associates the declarations of nonanimal nature with a word that is most definitely for humans, namely torah, the topic of the second half of the psalm: "The torah of YHWH is complete, restoring the self" (19:8 [7]). Though historical critical scholars have traditionally maintained that this is the start of a new psalm, the vocabulary of verses 1–7 [1–6] and 8–15 [7–14] overlaps substantially.[37] The first half uses vocabulary usually associated with the Torah (including מְסַפְּרִים, ["recount"], מַגִּיד ["proclaim"], יַבִּיעַ אֹמֶר ["pour forth speech"], דַּעַת יְחַוֶּה ["declare knowledge"], דְּבָרִים ["words"], and מִלֵּיהֶם ["their words"]), while the second half applies the attributes of the sun to YHWH's law (מְשִׁיבַת נָפֶשׁ ["renewing life"],[38] בָּרָה ["bright"],[39] מְאִירַת ["enlighten"], נִזְהָר ["be warned" or "bedazzled"[40]]). The evidence suggests that the two stanzas have either been put together on purpose, or were written by one poet.[41] Somehow the declarations of the heavens and the sun's trek across the skies relate to human torah observation.

A loose connection could be established between the two parts by claiming that the first half deals with words appropriate to nonanimal nature, while the second half looks at specifically human words. The two parts meditate on how different creatures throughout the world praise God. A more common proposal is to state that nonanimal nature, and the sun in particular, is either a source of illumination, just like torah, or a model for human behavior.[42] Humans should be as eager to observe

---

[37] See Sommer, "Nature, Revelation, and Grace in Psalm 19," 385, 389–90.
[38] The expression מְשִׁיבַת נָפֶשׁ ("renewing life") is a frequent epitaph of ancient sun deities. See Ibid.
[39] In the Hebrew Bible, the adjective בָּרָה ("pure") is used both for purity of conduct and the brightness of the sun. See Song of Songs 6:10 for the latter. The adjective also occurs in Ugaritic literature to describe the sun. See Ibid.
[40] The verb זָהַר has two meanings: to warn and to shine. In verse 19:12 [11] the poet is likely punning on the verb. As Sommer writes, "the poet takes warning from the commandments ... but he is also 'enlightened' or 'bedazzled' by them" (Ibid.).
[41] See Dahood, Psalms, 121.
[42] For parallel sources of illumination, see Mark Smith, "'Seeing God' in the Psalms: The Background to the Beatific Vision in the Hebrew Bible," Catholic Biblical Quarterly 50 (1988): 171–83; and Jon D. Levenson, "The Theologies of Commandment in Biblical

torah as the sun is to run its course. These are both plausible readings of the psalm, but Jeffrey Cooley provides a more satisfying solution. Cooley looks at the psalm through the lens of Priestly writings, especially Genesis 1.[43] In Genesis 1, the sun, moon, and stars are not, according to Cooley "mere cogs in a giant celestial machine," but instead "conscious agents."[44] Like humans, the sun and the moon are given responsibility to distinguish and to rule (Genesis 1:14–15). The consequence of this, Cooley writes, is that "the outcome of obedience to God's will for ... celestial ... persons exceeds their own selves."[45] Much like human obedience and disobedience have consequences beyond the human, so celestial obedience affects noncelestial beings. Cooley focuses specifically on the ability of humans to keep the cultic calendar, though it is difficult to separate the calendar from other aspects of torah.[46] Sacrifice, purity laws, and agricultural regulations are all tied to calendric concerns, so it is not necessary to restrict the domain affected by the luminaries to sabbath and festival observance. The larger point is that human obedience is only possible within an obedient cosmos. Without the declarations of the skies, without the sun making a distinction between day and night and marking the seasons, humans cannot fulfill their own cultic obligations. Torah observance is, in the words of Cooley, "a collective effort."[47] The heavenly declarations of adoration are not *for* humans, but they affect humans and are noticeable, to a certain extent, by humans. They are meaningful words, spoken among nonhuman persons, whose effects are felt by humans and nonhumans alike. Human disobedience

---

Israel," *The Harvard Theological Review* 73, no. 1/2 (1980): 29. For the sun as a model for torah piety, see Brown, *Seeing the Psalms*, 97; Robert B. Coote, "Psalm 19: Heavenly Law and Order," in *From Biblical Interpretation to Human Transformation: Reopening the Past to Actualize New Possibilities for the Future. A Festschrift Honoring Herman C. Waetjen*, ed. Douglas R. McGaughey and Cornelia Cyss Crocker (Salem, MA: Chora Strangers, 2006), 92; and Fisch, "Analogy of Nature," 171–72.

[43] For connections between Psalm 19 and the Priestly corpus, see Cooley, "Psalm 19: A Sabbath Song," 180–83. See also David Clines' claim that the background of Psalm 19:1–7 is Genesis 1 (David J. A. Clines, "Tree of Knowledge and the Law of Yahweh, Psalm 19," *Vetus Testamentum* 24, no. 1 [January 1974]: 12–13).

[44] Cooley, "Psalm 19: A Sabbath Song," 183.   [45] Ibid., 184.

[46] Cooley overreaches when he writes that "the astral bodies exist for the express and sole purpose of making the calendar of [YHWH]'s temple functional" (Ibid.). Humans are not created solely in order to do the tasks they are assigned in Genesis 1, and neither are the sun, the moon, and the stars. Both humans and luminaries are declared "good" or "beautiful" (טוֹב); they exist not simply to carry out their respective functions, but because God takes pleasure in each.

[47] Ibid., 190.

makes the land mourn; cosmic obedience facilitates a human life of integrity (Psalm 19:14 [13]).[48]

The praise of nonanimal nature is offered in adoration of the creator; in this it is just like the praises of Israel. Though nature's praise does not exist for the benefit of humans, it is not isolated and independent. It takes place within the same meshwork in which Israel lives and acts. In the previous chapter I argued that human action inevitably affects nonhumans, for good or for ill. The reverse is also true. The actions of nonhuman beings affect humans, in this case in positive ways. The declarations of the skies and the jubilation of the forest contribute to a world in which humans too can enact faithfulness. The interdependence of the world works in every direction; each creature, human, animal, and nonanimal, affects the lives of other creatures.

In his book *A New Heaven and a New Earth: Reclaiming Biblical Eschatology*, Richard Middleton writes that worship is not a uniquely human vocation: "[A]ll creatures in heaven and on earth are called to worship God."[49] This is abundantly clear in the book of Psalms, in which humans are one creature among many offering praises to YHWH. The situation is not unlike what we saw in theophany. When humans tremble at YHWH's coming, they take part in creationwide fear and awe. When humans sing and rejoice before God, they are one voice among many. Middleton goes on to ask *how* nonhuman creatures praise God. "Certainly not verbally or with emotions," he writes. "Rather, mountains worship God simply by being mountains ... [a]nd stars worship God by being stars."[50] This is part of the picture, but it smacks of rationalization. I have argued that the declarations of the heavens are not for humans, but that humans nonetheless have some access to them. That is not to say that this access is easy or universal. The psalmist knows something about creation's praise because the psalmist has been paying attention. The poets of the Psalter have practiced and trained their ears and eyes to observe the worship of nonhuman beings. And the text of the Psalter does not permit the comfortable conclusion that creation's praise is "certainly not [verbal] or [emotional]." The psalmists bear witness to an articulate and exuberant world. It speaks and feels joy. Its words are not

---

[48] "Then I shall act with integrity (אֵיתָם) and be free of great transgression." The verb אֵיתָם is from the root תמם ("to be complete"), but this particular form of the first person imperfect is unique. See Gesenius, *Gesenius' Hebrew Grammar*, para. 67p.

[49] J. Richard Middleton, *A New Heaven and a New Earth: Reclaiming Biblical Eschatology* (Grand Rapids, MI: Baker Academic, 2014), 40.

[50] Ibid.

human words, and its joy is the kind of joy appropriate to mountains, billows, and fields. Provided humans are not the measure of all things, these words and this joy are real. In the Psalter the world is not mute; it is sonorous, humming with voices.

JOB'S NEGOTIATION WITH HIS PLACE

In the Book of Job, an innocent sufferer confronts God, demanding a hearing. With good reason, most scholars argue that the theme of the book is human suffering, how it relates to righteousness and conduct, and God's role in doling out reward and judgment. Having agreed on something, scholars go on to immediately differ on the next important question, that is, *what* exactly does the book say about the relationship between righteousness and suffering? Hakham simply claims that "problems of the doctrine of reward and punishment" are central to Job.[51] James Crenshaw is a bit more specific: "At issue in the book of Job is the existential question, "Why does innocent suffering exist?"[52] David Clines disagrees with both Hakham and Crenshaw, writing that the main question in the book of Job is not "*Why* suffering" or "Whether there is such a thing as *innocent* suffering," but "In what way am I supposed to suffer? Or, What am I to do when I am suffering?"[53] The differences between these interpretations (and others) come down to how readers deal with a number of cruxes in the book. In the words of Carol Newsom, "From Gregory the Great to Maimonides to Aquinas to Calvin to Fohrer, commentators have pondered over such issues as why God rebukes the friends but not Elihu, whether Job's words in the dialog are or are not blasphemous, what the divine speeches do to resolve the issues raised in the book, and the significance of the restoration of Job."[54] The purpose of this

---

[51] Hakham, *The Bible*, 1:x.
[52] James L. Crenshaw, *Reading Job: A Literary and Theological Commentary* (Macon, GA: Smyth & Helwys, 2011), 2.
[53] David J. A. Clines, *Job 1–20*, Word Biblical Commentary (Waco, TX: Word Books, 1989), xxxviii. Seow interprets the theme of Job along similar lines. The Book of Job "is not," he writes, "ultimately about theodicy" (C. L. Seow, *Job 1–21: Interpretation and Commentary* [Grand Rapids, MI: William B. Eerdmans, 2013], 108). The book does not explain why people suffer, or why God allows suffering. Instead, he argues, "the book is ... about theology, or more specifically, how one speaks of God in the face of chaos" (Ibid.).
[54] Carol A. Newsom, *The Book of Job: A Contest of Moral Imaginations* (Oxford: Oxford University Press, 2003), 3.

section is to investigate what attention to personalistic nature texts may contribute to discussions of the Book of Job. My main claim is that Job's words are addressed not only to God, but also to his land. Job imagines himself standing before two judges; the primary one is God, but beside God stand his land and his fields, who are able, like YHWH, to attest to Job's innocence or guilt.

The Book of Job has featured prominently in recent debates about the Bible and ecology, but scholars have focused almost exclusively on the divine speeches in Job 38–41.[55] The dialogs between Job and his friends rarely enter the conversation.[56] I have argued in earlier chapters that human innocence and guilt is never an isolated issue in the Hebrew Bible, but connects with human relations with other-than-human persons. Especially important is the relationship with land. A little noticed feature of Job's dialog with his friends is that Job's standing before God is worked out in part through his standing before his land, most often referred to as his "place" (מָקוֹם). On the one hand, his friends argue that the land participates in God's judgment of Job and reveals his guilt. If Job were to repent, not only would his relationship with God be restored, but so, also, would his relationship with his land. Job, on the other hand, claims innocence vis-à-vis his land, and calls on the earth to witness to the violence done to him. The Book of Job examines and debates earlier traditions on the connections between righteousness, habitation in the

---

[55] See, for example, Kathryn Schifferdecker, *Out of the Whirlwind: Creation Theology in the Book of Job*, Harvard Theological Studies 61 (Cambridge, MA: Harvard University Press, 2008); Kathryn Schifferdecker, "Of Stars and Sea Monsters: Creation Theology in the Whirlwind Speeches," *Word & World* 31, no. 4 (September 2011): 357–66; Fred Gottlieb, "The Creation Theme in Genesis 1, Psalm 104 and Job 38–42," *Jewish Bible Quarterly* 44, no. 1 (January 2016): 29–36; Kathleen M. O'Connor, "Wild, Raging Creativity: The Scene in the Whirlwind (Job 38–41)," in *God So Near: Essays on Old Testament Theology in Honor of Patrick D. Miller* (Winona Lake, IN: Eisenbrauns, 2003), 171–79; Karen Pidcock-Lester, "'Earth Has No Sorrow That Earth Cannot Heal': Job 38–41," in *God Who Creates: Essays in Honor of W. Sibley Towner* (Grand Rapids, MI: William B. Eerdmans, 2000), 125–32; Carol A. Newsom, "The Moral Sense of Nature: Ethics in the Light of God's Speech to Job," *The Princeton Seminary Bulletin* 15, no. 1 (1994): 9–27. Schifferdecker includes a chapter on creation theology in the prolog, epilog, and dialogs in order to set up her argument. An exception is Brian Doak's *Consider Leviathan: Narratives of Nature and Self in Job* (Minneapolis, MN: Fortress, 2014), which deals in detail with the plant and animal vocabulary of the dialogs.

[56] Job's first speech, in Job 3, is an exception. See, for example, Eun Suk Cho, "Creation in the Book of Job: An Exegetical Essay on Job 3 from a Korean Perspective," *The Asia Journal of Theology* 17, no. 1 (April 2003): 26–76; and Detlev Tönsing, "The Use of Creation Language in Job 3, 9 and 38 and the Meaning of Suffering," *Scriptura* 59 (1996): 435–49.

land, agricultural fecundity, and exile. It is a book not only about the connection between human faithfulness and suffering, or about human relations with the divine, but also about the entanglement of human lives in the life of the world.

Suffering takes many forms in the Book of Job. One is alienation from one's place. Against the background of the tradition that a righteous life is rewarded with long life in the land, Job and his friends argue over the stability of human ties with their dwelling places.[57] Job compares human mortality to the life of a wage worker (Job 7:1-2). Just as wage workers lack a permanent relationship with a specific plot of soil, so death erases all connection between a person and his or her land: "He will not again return to his house, and his place (מְקֹמוֹ) will no longer recognize him" (7:10). Bildad restricts this fate to those "who forget God": "If he is swallowed up from his place, it will deny him: 'I have not seen you'" (Job 8:18). Zohar also argues that the fleetingness Job attributes to all human life, including the instability of the tie between a person and his place, only applies to the godless; he will disappear like a dream, and "the eye that gazed on him will not do so again and not again will his place see him" (Job 20:9).[58] Instead of the cross-generational bond between a human family and a plot of land, Job and his friends (for different reasons) envision a complete severance.[59]

Job and his friends also debate the tradition that a righteous life produces agricultural fecundity and harmony between farmer and land.[60] Eliphaz tells Job that, if he accepts God's chastening, he will not only be safe from famine and sword (Job 5:20), but he will live in peace with animals and stones: "For with the stones of the field will be your covenant (בְרִיתֶךָ), and the animals of the field will be at peace (הָשְׁלְמָה) with you" (Job 5:23). Zophar threatens with the opposite. The wicked will not enjoy friendship with the world, but instead "the heavens will reveal his iniquity

---

[57] See, for example, Deuteronomy 4:1; 25:15; Exodus 20:12; and Proverbs 3:1-2; 4:10; 9:10-11.
[58] Job and his friends mention place, dwelling, and possession of land again and again, though most of the mentions do not qualify as personalistic nature texts. See, for example, Job 8:6; 11:14; 12:6; 18:17; 21:28; 22:8.
[59] The bond between a person and a plot of land is normally maintained through progeny. This is especially clear in texts that address situations in which someone dies without male heirs. See, for example, Ruth 4:5 and Numbers 27:4; 36:3-4. For a discussion of progeny as a form of afterlife, see Jon D. Levenson, *Resurrection and the Restoration of Israel: The Ultimate Victory of the God of Life* (New Haven, CT: Yale University Press, 2006), especially chapter 6 "Individual Mortality and Familial Resurrection."
[60] See, for example, Leviticus 26:3-5; and Deuteronomy 28:3-5, 8, 11-12.

and the earth will raise itself up against him" (Job 20:27). Job counters that his experience belies the reassurance (and threat) of his friends. He complains that "even the clods of the wadi are sweet" to the wicked (Job 21:33). The world used to be on Job's side – "My steps were washed in curds, and the stone poured out streams of oil for me" (Job 29:6) – but now all he can do is to call on the earth to witness to his suffering: "O earth, do not cover my blood and let there be no place for my outcry (זַעֲקָתִי)" (Job 16:18). In Job's final words, he does not claim innocence before God, but before his field: "If my soil has cried out (תִזְעָק) against me ..." (Job 31:38).[61] Neither Job nor his friends question that the relationship between humans and their land ought to be marked by responsibility and mutuality, and they agree that nonanimal nature serves as witness to human righteousness or lack thereof. What distinguishes Job from Eliphaz, Bildad, and Zophar is that he maintains that the current rupture with his place is not a reliable indicator of his innocence or guilt. Job asserts that he has *not* given the field cause to cry out against him. In return for his equitable treatment of his soil, he asks that the earth cry out not against him, but on his behalf, serving as an ally in his case against God.

The words of Job and his friends contain multiple echoes of texts concerned with the relationship between humans, their land, and righteousness. I will highlight affinities that emphasize the active participation of land in judgment and restoration. The most concentrated set of echoes occurs in Job's final oath in 31:38–40b:

If my soil (אַדְמָתִי) has cried out (תִזְעָק) against me and its furrows cried together; if I have eaten (אָכַלְתִּי) its strength (כֹּחָהּ) without payment and I have made the throat (נֶפֶשׁ) of its lord breathe [its last] (הִפָּחְתִּי): instead of wheat may thorns (חוֹחַ) come forth, and instead of barley, weeds (בָאְשָׁה).

The oath recalls the language and ideas of Genesis 2–4. The noun נֶפֶשׁ, "throat, self, soul," and the root נפח, "to breathe," occur in the creation of humanity in Genesis 2:7. The verb and noun forms of the root אכל,

---

[61] Most scholars argue that verses 31:35–37 were originally Job's final words, and that 31:38–40b were at some point transposed to their present location. See, for example, David J. A. Clines, *Job 21–37*, Word Biblical Commentary (Nashville, TN: Thomas Nelson, 2006), 973; Michael B. Dick, "Job 31, the Oath of Innocence, and the Sage," *Zeitschrift Für Die Alttestamentliche Wissenschaft* 95, no. 1 (1983): 31–53, 35–36; John C. Holbert, "The Rehabilitation of the Sinner: The Function of Job 29–31," *Zeitschrift Für Die Alttestamentliche Wissenschaft* 95, no. 2 (1983): 231. I will discuss possible explanations for the current location of verses 38–40b below.

"to eat," are key words in both Genesis 2 and 3, and the noun אֲדָמָה, "ground," occurs fourteen times in Genesis 2–4.[62] Job's words for weeds are not the ones used in Genesis 3:18 (קוֹץ וְדַרְדַּר, "thorn and thistle"), but the idea is the same: transgression makes the ground uncooperative. Most striking is the connection between Job's oath and YHWH's words to Cain. Job uses the same root to describe the soil's outcry, זעק, as God does when speaking of Abel's blood ("the blood of your brother calls out [צֹעֲקִים] to me"; Genesis 4:10), and both Job and God refer to produce as the strength of the ground (כֹּחָהּ, "its strength"; see Genesis 4:12). The root זעק, "to cry out," is common, but using כֹּחַ, "strength," to refer to produce is not; it occurs only in these two texts and, possibly, in Hosea 7:9.[63] Together these affinities suggest that Job is gesturing toward a well-known network of ideas. Genesis 2–4 establish a connection between transgression, scant agricultural yield, and exile. If Job, like Adam and Eve, has eaten that which he ought not, then he deserves the hostility of his fields.

The affinities between The Book of Job and Genesis do not stand alone, but are intertwined with connections to Deuteronomy and prophetic literature. In 16:18–19, Job speaks directly to the earth, and, in the process, alludes to the role of the heavens in judgment: "O earth, do not cover (תְּכַסִּי) my blood and let there be no place (מָקוֹם) for my outcry (לְזַעֲקָתִי). Even now, look, my witness is in the heavens, and my advocate is on high." The verse recalls Abel's blood calling out to God, as well as the disclosure of uncovered blood in Isaiah 26:21 and Ezekiel 24:7–8.[64] Job, Isaiah, and Ezekiel all use the verb כָּסָה, "to cover." The protest of innocent blood is here mingled with the idea of the heavens and the earth as witnesses, found in Deuteronomy and the prophets.[65] In Deuteronomy, the heavens and the earth witness to the fact that, should Israel transgress against YHWH, they will "quickly perish from the land" (Deuteronomy

---

[62] For the centrality of אכל, "to eat" or "food," in Genesis 2–3, see Carol Meyers, "Food and the First Family: A Socioeconomic Perspective," in *The Book of Genesis: Composition, Reception, and Interpretation*, ed. Craig A. Evans, Johl N. Lohr, and David L. Petersen (Leiden: Brill, 2012), 137–57.

[63] Hosea 7:9a reads: אָכְלוּ זָרִים כֹּחוֹ, "foreigners devour his strength." כֹּחַ, "strength," might here refer to foreign armies eating the agricultural produce of Israel, or it might be a metaphor for some other form of imperial consumption. See also Joel 2:22, which uses the noun חַיִל, "strength, wealth, army" to refer to the fruit of vines and fig trees.

[64] See Seow, *Job 1–21*, 738, and Clines, *Job 1–20*, 389.

[65] See Deuteronomy 4:26; 30:19; 31:29; 32:1; Isa. 1:2; Jer. 2:12; Mic. 6:1–2; and Ps. 50:4–7. For the connection between Job and witnessing texts, see Habel, *The Book of Job*, 274; and Clines, *Job 1–20*, 388.

4:26; see also 30:19–20). Zophar draws on the same tradition when he says that "the heavens will reveal [the wicked one's] iniquity, and the earth will rise up against him" (Job 20:27). To describe the consequence of this earthly and celestial uprising, Zophar employs the language of exile: "The produce of his house will depart (יִגֶל), torrents (נִגָּרוֹת) in the day of his anger (בְּיוֹם אַפּוֹ)" (Job 20:28).[66] The Qal of the verb גָּלָה can mean either "to uncover," "to depart," or "to go into exile." Translators usually choose a neutral translation here, one without historic overtones, like "depart" or "be carried away."[67] The phrase בְּיוֹם אַפּוֹ, "the day of his anger," occurs only in two other places – once in Psalm 110:5, in reference to God striking foreign kings, and once in Lamentations 2:1, in reference to the destruction of Israel and Judah – but the "day of YHWH" is a day of judgment in Isaiah, Joel, Amos, and Obadiah.[68] English translators must choose whether to highlight or mute the resonances between the Book of Job and the history of Israel and Judah, but the Hebrew text presents both possibilities. The two readings are there, on the text's surface, gesturing simultaneously towards the misfortunes of individuals and the misfortunes of nations.

The evocation of earlier traditions in the Book of Job are often imprecise and gestural; exact quotes are rare.[69] For example, Bildad's metaphor of the wicked as a spreading plant in Job 8 uses language familiar from a number of other texts: "If he is swallowed (יְבַלְּעֶנּוּ)[70] from his place (מִמְּקוֹמוֹ), it will deny him: 'I have not seen you'" (Job 8:18). The verb בָּלַע, "to swallow," occurs several times to describe the earth swallowing people as a form of discipline,[71] and the Prophets use the verb in texts

---

[66] The relationship between the first and second cola of this verse is unclear. The NRSV translates it "The possessions of their house will be carried away, dragged off in the day of God's wrath," turning the noun נִגָּרוֹת ("flowing water") into a verb.

[67] See KJV and NRSV. The JPS chooses to associate this verse with the flood, due to the noun נִגֶּרֶת, "torrent": "His household will be cast forth by a flood, spilled out on the day of His wrath." To do so requires translating נִגֶּרֶת twice ("by a flood" and "spilled out" both translate the noun), and disregarding the Masoretic pointing, which divides the verse after בֵּיתוֹ, "his house."

[68] See Isaiah 13:6, 9; Joel 1:15, 2:1, 11, 31; Amos 5:18–20; and Obadiah 15.

[69] Job 9:8 is identical to Isaiah 44:24c, and Job 12:9b is identical to Isaiah 41:20c. See Seow, *Job 1–21*, 41.

[70] The Piel of בָּלַע ("to swallow") is active, but has an indefinite subject; hence the passive translation in English. See Bruce K. Waltke and Michael Patrick O'Connor, *An Introduction to Biblical Hebrew Syntax* (Winona Lake, IN: Eisenbrauns, 1990), para. 4.4.2.

[71] See Exodus 15:12; Numbers 16:30–34; 26:10; Deuteronomy 11:6; and Psalm 106:17.

detailing experiences of conquest and exile.[72] Bildad's words do not neatly parallel any one of these texts. The place does not itself swallow the wicked: the subject is unspecified. It is unclear whether the author intentionally references earlier traditions like Numbers 16, or whether the verb בָּלַע, "to swallow," has entered the general vocabulary of judgment and consequence.

Job and his friends repeatedly use the word מָקוֹם, "place." Nowhere in the Torah and Prophets is this noun the subject of an active verb, unlike אֲדָמָה, "ground," and אֶרֶץ, "earth." It tends to refer to a specific place, like a city, town, or well,[73] to clean and unclean "places,"[74] or to the place YHWH will choose for the temple.[75] The only texts in which מָקוֹם, "place," is the subject of an active verb are Job 7:10, 8:18, 20:9, and Psalm 103:16.[76] In Job, the issue in each text is the extent to which a place will remember and acknowledge its inhabitants:

> As a cloud vanishes and goes away,
> So the one who goes down to Sheol does not come up.
> He will not again return to his house,
> Nor will his place again remember him.
> (Job 7:9–10)

> If he [the wicked] is swallowed from his place,
> It will deny him: I have not seen you.
> (Job 8:18)

> The eye that gazed on [the wicked] will do so no more,
> His place will not again behold him.
> (Job 20:9)

Interestingly, the word מָקוֹם, "place," is sometimes used in the psalms to distinguish between the fate of the wicked and that of the righteous. For example, Psalm 37 promises that the righteous will live long and securely in the land (Psalm 37:3, 9, 11, 22, 29, 34), while the wicked will disappear from his place: "A little while longer, and the wicked will not be. You will look diligently at his place (מְקוֹמוֹ), but he will not be" (Psalm 37:10). Psalm 37 promotes a worldview not unlike that of the friends:

---

[72] See Isaiah 49:19; Jeremiah 51:34; Hosea 8:7; see also Lamentations 2:2, 5, 8, 16.
[73] See, for example, the use of מָקוֹם in Genesis 19–22.
[74] This is the common use of מָקוֹם in Leviticus.
[75] This is the primary use of the מָקוֹם in Deuteronomy.
[76] Psalm 103:15–16 reads: "As for mortals, their days are like grass; like a flower of the field, so they flourish. For a wind passes over it and it is not; its place no longer recognizes it."

YHWH rewards the righteous, the righteous inherit the land, and their children need never beg (see, especially, 37:25). As already stated, the theme of alienation from land in the Book of Job combines language from several traditions. In the case of מָקוֹם, "place," the traditions of personal relationship with land and longevity as reward for a righteous life are combined with the psalmic contrast between the righteous and the wicked. Job and his friends do not so much quote earlier traditions as buttress their claims by using traditional vocabulary and evocations of paradigmatic experiences of suffering in Israelite history.[77] According to Job's friends, the wicked live short lives, and at their deaths they are immediately forgotten and disavowed by their place (Job 8:18, 20:9). Job, however, uses the same tradition to argue that all human life is short ("my life is breath" [Job 7:7]) and destined for forgetfulness and obscurity (Job 7:10). It is not only the wicked who are forgotten by their place, Job argues, but everyone, the wicked and the good. Together Job and his friends echo Israel's traditions in order to test established ideas against Job's misfortune and pain.

The above connections between the Book of Job and other biblical books do not exhaust the intertextuality of the text. Scholars have long recognized that Job shares language with Lamentations, Deutero-Isaiah, and the Book of Psalms.[78] The overlap between Isaiah's description of the Suffering Servant and the Book of Job is particularly strong.[79] These connections have prompted scholars to wonder about the relationship between the Book of Job and the exile. Is Job a stand-in for Israel, or some part of Israel, and the book a protest against the traditional idea that the exile was YHWH's righteous judgment on Israel and Judah? Some, like Habel, say no: "There is no evidence that [Job] represents Israel, a prophetic class within Israel, or a righteous remnant."[80] David Wolfers,

---

[77] Jennie Barbour writes that Qohelet, though not obviously tied to Israelite history, is shaped by a "historical habit of imagination" (Jennifer Barbour, *The Story of Israel in the Book of Qohelet: Ecclesiastes as Cultural Memory* [Oxford: Oxford University Press, 2012], 3). The same could be said about the Book of Job.

[78] For outlines of thematic and linguistic ties between Job, Lamentations, Deutero-Isaiah, and Psalms, see Seow, *Job 1–21*, 41; and Hakham, *The Bible*, 1:xix–xxii.

[79] See Gunnel André, "Deuterojesaja Och Jobsboken: En Jämförande Studie," *Svensk Exegetisk Årsbok* 54 (1989): 33–42; Jean Bastiaens, "The Language of Suffering in Job 16–19 and in the Suffering Servant Passages in Deutero-Isaiah," in *Studies in the Book of Isaiah: Festschrift Willem A M Beuken* (Louvain: Leuven University Press; Peeters, 1997), 421–32; S. Terrien, "Quelques Remarques Sur Les Affinités de Job Avec Le Deutéro-Esaïe," in *Volume Du Congrès*, Supplements to Vetus Testamentum 15 (Leiden: E. J. Brill, 1966), 295–310.

[80] Habel, *The Book of Job*, 41.

on the other end of the spectrum, writes that "the true occasion for the writing of the Book of Job was as a contribution to ... a debate over the significance of the destruction of the kingdoms of Israel and Judah by successive Assyrian monarchs."[81] Habel and Wolfers represent false alternatives. Job does not have to be *either* a suffering innocent individual *or* a cipher for Israel. More helpful is Jean Charles Bastiaens' approach; he writes that Deutero-Isaiah and Job "share a common 'language of suffering.'"[82] The Book of Job and Deutero-Isaiah reflect on suffering, individual and communal, using traditional language of pain. Much of this language stems from experiences of imperial practices of conquest, destruction, and exile. In the Hebrew Bible, exile is not religiously neutral, but receives theological interpretation and weight. Israel and Judah are deported not because of the military might of empires, but because they fail to uphold their responsibilities towards YHWH, other humans, and their land. It is difficult to know when the author of Job intentionally evokes the exile, and when he or she simply draws on stock vocabulary of suffering. Regardless of how scholars evaluate the intentionality of the author, the end product is a text that resonates with scriptural traditions on the relationship between humans and their land, especially with texts that treat the disintegration of this relationship.

One piece of evidence that suggests intentional echoes between the character Job and the national experience of Israel and Judah is the use of theologically freighted words by Job, his friends, and even the narrator. Eliphaz uses the words בְּרִית, "covenant," and שָׁלַם, "to pay, be complete, be at peace," in Job 5:23, promising Job that he will be in covenant (בְּרִית) with stones, and at peace (הָשְׁלְמָה) with wild animals. The vocabulary clearly makes translators uncomfortable. JPS translates the verse "For you will have a pact with the rocks of the field, and the beasts of the field will be your allies." The NRSV reads: "For you shall be in league with the stones of the field, and the wild animals shall be at peace with you." Both translate בְּרִית as "covenant" when the relationship in question is between God and humans.[83] The reluctance to translate בְּרִית here as "covenant" obscures the references within the book of Job to the larger history of Israel. Similarly, the narrator describes Job's restoration as

---

[81] David Wolfers, *Deep Things Out of Darkness: The Book of Job, Essays and a New English Translation* (Grand Rapids, MI: William B. Eerdmans, 1995), 69.
[82] Bastiaens, "The Language of Suffering in Job 16–19 and in the Suffering Servant Passages in Deutero-Isaiah," 421.
[83] See, for example, the JPS and NRSV translations of Genesis 6:18 and Exodus 2:24.

return from captivity: "YHWH turned the captivity of Job" (וַיְהוָה שָׁב אֶת־שְׁבוּת אִיּוֹב [Job 42:10]).⁸⁴ Most scholars avoid translating the verse with such clear historical resonance; it can also be translated "YHWH restored the fortunes of Job," though this latter usage is uncommon.⁸⁵ Regardless of translation choices, it is unlikely that the author of Job and early audiences of the book would not think of the exile when reading this verse. Similarly, as strange as a covenant with stones sounds, it is unlikely that Eliphaz's words in 5:23 would not bring to mind the fact that Israel's covenant with YHWH is set within a relationship with their land and its animals.⁸⁶

What makes the Book of Job unusual is not its dependence on traditional language, but the use to which it puts such language. The relationship between human righteousness and land tenure outlined in Genesis, Leviticus, and Deuteronomy, is, in the Prophets, used primarily to condemn human misconduct.⁸⁷ Micah and Isaiah call on nonanimal nature as witnesses (Micah 1:2; Isaiah 1:2), and Jeremiah speaks again and again of the mourning of the land (Jeremiah 4:28; 12:4, 11; 23:10). Job, however, puts the tradition to work for himself. He uses it to insist on his innocence. His current alienation from his place, his failed harvests, and the death of his children are not reliable indicators of his guilt, he argues, and calls on the earth to confirm his innocence. The fact that humans and nonhumans alike are turned against Job is, in Job's view, an injustice. The wind that knocks over the house in which Job's children are feasting is not a natural disaster, it is an outrage, an undoing of the moral

---

⁸⁴ The consonantal text reads שבית, corrected to שבות in the marginal *qere*. For another verse brimming with theological vocabulary, see Elihu's enigmatic saying in 37:13: "Whether for correction (לְשֵׁבֶט), for his land (לְאַרְצוֹ), or for loyalty (לְחֶסֶד), he makes it happen."

⁸⁵ For a defense of translating this verse with reference to exile, see Wolfers, *Deep Things Out of Darkness*, 103. Contra Wolfers, see David J. A. Clines, *Job 38–42*, Word Biblical Commentary 18B (Nashville, TN: Thomas Nelson, 2011), 1228. A second case in which the noun שְׁבִית is usually translated as "fortunes" is Psalm 126:1: "When YHWH restored the fortunes of Zion, we were like those who dream."

⁸⁶ Seow points out that both the stones and the animals are "of the field" (הַשָּׂדֶה). This parallelism leads him to conclude that the poet images a radical peace with the whole world. The stones are the "counterparts to the wild creatures – the one inanimate, the other animate" (Seow, *Job 1–21*, 446).

⁸⁷ I am not here making a claim about the chronological priority of the Torah vis-à-vis the Prophets. Rather, the Torah texts speak about the tradition in abstract, as regulations to be put into use in the future, while the Prophets presuppose this tradition in their calls for the heavens and the earth to witness, and in the image of the mourning land. In terms of the dating of Job, the current consensus date is in the Persian period, in the late sixth to mid-fifth century. See Ibid., 41; Ḥakham, *The Bible*, 1:xvii–iii; Clines, *Job 1–20*, lvii.

fabric of the cosmos. This may explain why Job ends by insisting that he has not mistreated his fields. Scholars have long claimed that Job's final words are not, as in the canonical text, 31:38–40b, but instead verses 31:35–37:[88]

Oh, that I had someone to listen to me (here, my signature; may the Almighty answer me), the scroll written by my adversary. I would carry it on my shoulder, I would bind it to myself, a crown. I would declare to him an account of my steps, like a noble I would approach him.

These words certainly have a ring of conclusion. But if Job is considered from the angle of the involvement of land in judging human conduct, then Job ending on an appeal to his soil is not impossible or out of context. Exile and alienation from your land are paradigmatic forms of discipline in the Hebrew Bible, though traditions differ in their portrayals of the involvement of the land in exile. In Leviticus, the land vomits out its inhabitants. In Deuteronomy, Moses warns the people that the heavens and the earth observe their lives and that they will not live long on the land if they transgress against YHWH. In Jeremiah, Joel, and Hosea the land mourns to YHWH, and in Ezekiel the land is judged alongside its inhabitants. Micah even invites the people to "plead [their] case before the mountains" (Micah 6:1), though in this case the prophet assumes the people's guilt and YHWH's innocence. The Book of Job, in a sense, does what Micah suggests. Job pleads his case not before the mountains, but before his soil. His last ditch effort to prove his innocence is directed not at YHWH, but at his fields. Perhaps, since YHWH has not answered him, his fields will speak out on his behalf. Having failed, it seems, to catch YHWH's attention, Job turns to his secondary judge. The oath in 31:38–40b is not of a kind with the other oaths Job utters in chapter 31. In the other oaths, Job insists that he is innocent of various actions: walking with that which is worthless (Job 31:5), turning away from the path (Job 31:7), being enticed by women (Job 31:9), oppressing his servants (Job 31:13), ignoring the plight of the poor (Job 31:16), and trusting in wealth (Job 31:24). He calls down punishments on himself if he is found guilty of any of these, but the punishment is not enacted by the wronged parties. Job's final oath differs because the soil has authority, like YHWH, but to a lesser degree, to pass judgment on Job. The final

---

[88] See Dick, "Job 31, the Oath of Innocence, and the Sage," 35; Georg Fohrer, "The Righteous Man in Job 31," in *Essays in Old Testament Ethics (J Philip Hyatt, in Memoriam)* (New York: Ktav, 1974), 3; Clines, *Job 21–37*, 933, 973.

oath is not just a claim of innocence, but an appeal to an other-than-human person to come to Job's aid.

The divine speeches in Job 38–41 do little to settle Job's dispute with his place, and his innocence is neither confirmed nor denied. Instead, God presents Job with a world that is for the most part unconcerned with him and his troubles. It is too big, too old, too powerful to pay attention to Job. None of the creatures so lovingly cataloged in Job 38–41 are particularly attuned to human righteousness, with the possible exception of the dawn (Job 38:13). This world does not exist to cater to human needs; it lives its life before God, in its own boisterous company.

Though the majority of the divine speeches deal with animals, the opening poem (Job 38:1–38) speaks of "cosmic geographies and meteorologies."[89] It takes us back to the time of Genesis 1, to God's founding of the world: "Where were you when I founded the earth ... when the morning stars sang together, when the heavenly beings shouted for joy?" (Job 38:4, 7). Unlike Psalm 19, Job 38:7 leaves no room for questions about human intelligibility and natural theology. Humans were not there to hear the stars sing or to join in their praise! Like the land's relationship with God in Leviticus, here creation's adoration of YHWH predates human worship. And, unlike Genesis 1, in which the rule of the sun, moon, and stars serve in part to order the human cultic calendar, here the world is not focused on human ways of life. The stars sing for their own sake and for God's sake; that's it.

What about the rebellious sea of the Psalms and the Prophets? "Who shut up the sea with doors, when it burst out from the womb? – when I made a cloud its clothing, and darkness its swaddling band, and proscribed my statute for it, and set bar and doors, and said: 'So far you may come, but no further, and here is set [a boundary] for your majestic waves'" (Job 38:8–11).[90] Though God sets definite limits for the sea here, the text betrays little concern that the sea might swallow up Israel or rebel against its maker.[91] The sea is a lively infant, whom God swaddles and firmly puts

---

[89] Doak, *Consider Leviathan*, 191.
[90] The Hebrew of the clause of Job 38:11 is unclear. According to Habel, a literal translation would be "here he will set on the pride of your waves." Despite the unclear Hebrew, Habel argues that the meaning is unambiguous: "The sense is clearly that the waves break at a set limit" (Habel, *The Book of Job*, 521).
[91] Abigail Pelham writes about Job 38:8–11 that "[t]he parent, in restricting the child, has the child's interests at heart. The child is not restricted primarily so that he or she will not encroach on the space of the 'someone else' who really matters. Rather, it is the child who is at the center of the parent's attention. So it is with God and the sea" (Abigail Pelham,

to bed. "Now stay put," – the text seems to speak of a captivated and exasperated parent of a toddler that refuses to sleep, not of a great cosmic warrior going to battle against his enemy.[92] It is a domestic scene; the sea, and then the weather, are under God's parental care: "Has the rain a father, or who has begotten the drops of dew? From whose womb did the ice come forth, and who has given birth to the frost of heaven?" (Job 38:28–29). Whether you answer the first question ("has the rain a father?") yes or no, the implication is the same: only God provides care for the rain and the frost, only God is big and powerful and maternal enough to be kin, be it biological or adoptive, to the great weather systems. God even teaches the stars where to go, and how to exercise their rule: "Can you bind the bonds of the Pleiades, or loosen the cords of Orion? Can you bring forth the Mazzaroth in its time, or lead the Bear with its children? Do you know the statute of the heavens, or can you set its authority in the earth?" (Job 38:31–33). Job can do none of this, of course, but God can and does. The world is nursery and school room for God's great and terrifying creations, and humans are nowhere in sight.[93]

And this world responds to God's care with joy and ready obedience: "Can you raise your voice to the clouds, so that an abundance of water covers you? Can you send out the lightning and they go, saying to you 'here we are' (הִנֵּנוּ)?" (Job 38:34–35; see also 38:12–13). Though God takes pride in the wildness and fearlessness of the creatures catalogued in Job 38–41, this is still a world ready to do God's word. Long before Abraham, to whom God said "go," and who also responded to God's call with "here I am (הִנֵּנִי)" (Genesis 12:1; 22:1), the clouds, lightning, stars, and sea crowded eagerly around God, waiting for God's care and commandment.

In the divine speeches, God does not deny the general principle that Job and his friends have debated at length, namely that human land tenure is tied to righteousness. In fact, Job's restoration includes renewed agricultural wealth. But the divine speeches orient this human–land community

---

Contested Creations in the Book of Job: The-World-as-It-Ought-and-Ought-Not-to-Be (Leiden: Brill, 2012), 177).

[92] Rebecca S. Watson writes that "the depiction of God's protective care of the newborn sea represents the antithesis of the *Chaoskampf*, both in its appreciation of the need to nurture this great body of water and in the assumption of God's unchallenged parenting and ordering of the world, before which the sea stands not in antagonism but in infantile dependence." See Rebecca S. Watson, *Chaos Uncreated: A Reassessment of the Theme of "Chaos" in the Hebrew Bible* (Berlin: de Gruyter, 2005), 278.

[93] The only mention of humans in Job 38 emphasizes their absence: Job 38:26 speaks of rain falling on "no-man's land (אֶרֶץ לֹא אִישׁ)" and "a wilderness without human life (מִדְבָּר לֹא־אָדָם בּוֹ)."

within a larger context, one that gives no thought to humans. It is not only Job who has "a place" (מָקוֹם) in the world; so does the dawn (Job 38:12), and so does darkness (Job 38:19). Many creatures live here, fearsome, wild, and proud, and, as Kathleen M. O'Connor says, "God glories in [them]."[94] In the divine speeches, the world as a whole is not a dial that turns in response to human action. The poems do not give precise shape to the connection between the responsiveness of the other-than-human creatures with whom humans share everyday life and the indifference of the ostrich and the sea. Instead, the conditions of human land tenure, especially as they relate to righteousness, are set within an unpredictable world. The common denominator between the human–land community, the leviathan, the war horse, and the ostrich is not that each and every creature responds predictably to human behavior, but that each is under YHWH's care. In different ways, Job and YHWH both challenge traditional notions of the extent to which righteousness produces long life on the land. Job presents his own experience as a counter-case, insisting that both YHWH and his soil recognize the injustice of his suffering. YHWH presents Job with the rest of the world. The cosmos does not revolve around humans or human behavior. Humans must act responsibly towards the nonhuman creatures with which they live, but that does not mean that every event and change in the cosmos results from or responds to humans and their choices. The human–land community is one community among many, each of which has its own needs and ways of living, and each of which is known and valued by YHWH.

BOUNDARIES AND BLISS

When I describe this project to people, be it in casual conversation, at academic conferences, or in the classroom, it usually is only a matter of time before someone asks "so if mountains and rivers are persons, what distinguishes humans from other kinds of persons?" This is a reasonable question and an interesting one; in the Bible, what are the marks of humanness, if it is not a monopoly on interiority, emotion, and consciousness? Still, I mistrust how quickly that question crops up, and how predictably. And often, right behind it lies another, less helpful question: "How are we special?" Thinking about the possibility of other-than-human persons makes us nervous, not only because it is such a foreign

---

[94] O'Connor, "Wild, Raging Creativity," 174.

idea, not only because it bumps us right out of our position at the center of the world, but also because it makes our conduct so much worse. If the world really is full of persons, with their own lives and concerns, what have we done? So we go back to thinking about humans and our specialness. But we need to practice thinking differently, to dwell not on our specialness, but on the permeability and fluidity of the boundaries between humanness and plantness, for example, between mammals and minerals. A perfect place to go to practice is the Song of Songs, a book that delights in dissolving boundaries. Here is no nervous defense of human uniqueness; in the Song, bliss is the reward for those whose bodies bleed across distinctions, those who give themselves to be plant and animal and architecture, and in these moments of blurring and blending, offer themselves to another in love and trust.

Given how quickly people become uneasy when I talk about ways in which nonanimal nature is like us, you would think the Song would be a disturbing text, but it isn't. The Song revels in fading human bodies into gardens and gardens into human bodies, continually destabilizing the reader's ability to tell one from the other, and yet it manages to put off the nagging "how are we special?" The text triggers joy; its obvious eroticism, clear to most people when they first encounter the text, is delicious and delightful. "A cluster of henna is my lover to me, in the vineyards of Ein Gedi" (Song 1:14); it would seem churlish, and besides the point, to ask what distinguishes humans from henna blossoms. The Song sidesteps our fear; it "draws us after it" (paraphrasing Song 1:4) into its lush world, and we imagine ourselves as palm trees before we have had time to worry. Its disregard for boundaries shows us that putting aside human specialness can be exquisite, that beyond our obsession with ourselves is a more satisfying way to live in the world.

I am not the first to explore how the Song blurs the boundaries between humans and other-than-humans. For example, scholars have argued that the woman in the Song is presented as the land of Israel, especially in the poems in Song 4:1–7, 6:4–7, and 7:2–7 [1–6]. By means of native plant species, livestock, and place names, the body of the woman becomes the landscape of ancient Palestine.[95] I will not pursue this particular line of inquiry, but will instead focus on how the woman and

---

[95] Athalya Brenner, "The Food of Love: Gendered Food and Food Imagery in the Song of Songs," *Semeia* 86 (1999): 109; Elaine T. James, *Landscapes of the Song of Songs: Poetry and Place* (New York: Oxford University Press, 2017), 118–50; Davis, *Scripture, Culture, and Agriculture*, 169–75.

the man compare each other to trees and vegetation, and on why these comparisons are often part of invitations to and descriptions of moving through and inhabiting the landscape. Again and again, the lovers call to each other to come, to go out into the field, and to explore the vineyards, only to move to speak of each other in terms reminiscent of the places they have just invoked. Metaphor and nature walks blend into each other; the lovers are in a garden, the lovers are gardens, the lovers eat from the garden.

Though the lovers compare each other to myrrh and henna in Song 1:13–14, they only begin to seriously make use of plant imagery in chapter 2, starting with the famous line: "I am a rose of Sharon, a lily of the valley" (Song 2:1). The woman declares herself a flower, the man echoes her description ("like a lily among briers, so is my darling among the daughters," Song 2:2), and the woman then turns attention onto the man: "Like an apple tree among the trees of the forest, so is my beloved among the sons. In his shade I delight to sit, and his fruit is sweet to my palate" (Song 2:3).[96] This image is one of rest and enjoyment, and its simile is out in the open: "Like an apple tree...." But this quiet image quickly gives way to comings and goings, and to texts in which the boundary between metaphor and literal land becomes difficult to draw.[97] In a tightly organized section running from 2:8–14, the man invites the woman into a springtime landscape. The section begins and ends with lines that compare the man and the woman to animals, in each case using the keyword קוֹל, "voice." In 2:8–9, the woman compares the man to a gazelle; in 2:14, the man compares the woman to a dove. The gazelle is on the mountains, but approaches the window of the woman's house; the dove is on a cliff and the man begs to hear its voice and see its form. These descriptions frame the man's invitation to the woman in 2:10 and 13 "to arise" (קוּם) and "to go" (הָלַךְ), which again frame a meditation on the land in springtime: "Winter has passed, the rain has gone away.

---

[96] It is not clear which tree the woman is referring to. Traditionally rendered "apple," it may also refer to an apricot or a quince tree. Cheryl Exum discusses the possible candidates in terms of archeological evidence, before concluding in a general way that "the tree is here distinguished from others by its shelter and its sweet fruit" (J. Cheryl Exum, *The Song of Songs: A Commentary* [Louisville, KY: Westminster John Knox, 2005], 114).

[97] I am indebted to Elaine T. James for this observation and for the shape of my argument throughout this section. Her book *Landscapes of the Song of Songs: Poetry and Place*, "considers the way that the poetry of the biblical Song of Songs draws on human experience in landscapes, and how it creates experiences of landscapes" (James, *Landscapes of the Song of Songs*, vii).

Buds appear in the land, the time for song[98] has arrived, and the voice of the dove is heard in our land. The fig tree has put forth its early figs, and the vines in blossom give of fragrance" (2:11–13). The movement of the whole section is towards this scene. On each end the man and woman are shy, distant animals, hidden on mountaintops and in cliff sides. By means of imperative verbs in 2:10 and 13, the man invites the woman to wander with him (or so it seems; he does not say what they will do together once she accepts his invitation) through a budding, agricultural landscape. In this case, the vegetation is not a cipher for their bodies but a place where they can meet. The lily and the apple tree become two lovers on a springtime walk among the early evidence of a bountiful fruit harvest.

The play between lovers as verdure and verdure as a meeting place for lovers continues in chapter 4. The poem in 4:12–15 resembles 2:11–13, in that its garden is not necessarily a metaphor, though it might be. The opening line contains a grammatical ambiguity, probably an intentional one. It can either be translated "A locked garden is my sister, bride, a locked well, a sealed spring" or "A locked garden, O my sister, bride, a locked well, a sealed spring"[99] (Song 4:12). The ambiguity arises because the statement could either be a predicate clause which compares the woman to a locked garden (in Hebrew, a predicate clause is verbless, unlike English, which uses a form of "to be"), or "my sister, bride," could be vocative, in which case the man is describing a garden to the woman. After a luscious list of the garden's fruits ("an orchard of pomegranate with excellent fruit, henna and nard, nard and saffron, cane and cinnamon, with every spice tree, myrrh and aloes, with every choice perfume"

---

[98] The noun זָמִיר can also mean "pruning" (the word is a homonym). The writer exploits the double meaning to express both a sense of joy and festival, and to heighten the poem's connection with a particular time in the spring. See Exum, *The Song of Songs*, 121.

[99] See James, *Landscapes of the Song of Songs*, 58. James argues that both translation possibilities are viable, stating that the text is "evocative and multiply significant," but that the second option, that the garden is a garden, has gone unexplored in scholarship (Ibid., 63). The NRSV, KJV, and JPS translations all choose the first option, as do Ariel and Chana Bloch in their 1998 translation (Ariel A. Bloch and Chana Bloch, *The Song of Songs: A New Translation with an Introduction and Commentary* [Berkeley, CA: University of California Press, 1998], 79). This translation goes hand in hand with the assumption that the garden symbolizes the woman's sexuality, which is currently unavailable (see Ibid., 176; and the notes on verse 4:12–16 in Adele Berlin, Marc Zvi Brettler, and Michael A. Fishbane, eds., *The Jewish Study Bible* [New York: Oxford University Press, 2004]). Exum writes that this verse "identifies the woman as the metaphor's referent" (Exum, *The Song of Songs*, 174). Robert Alter chooses the second option, though he too equates the garden with the woman's body (Alter, *Strong as Death Is Love*, 27).

(Song 4:13–14), the woman picks up the description and turns it into an invitation: "Wake, O north [wind], and come, O south [wind], breathe on my garden, let its perfumes flow, that my beloved may come to his garden and eat its excellent fruit" (Song 4:16). The invitation exploits the possibility that the preceding poem is a metaphor for the woman, but also the earlier theme of the landscape as a place where the lovers find each other. It also picks up an image from 2:3: much like the woman has enjoyed the man's fruits, so now she invites him to enjoy the fruits of the garden. To see this poem *either* as a metaphorical depiction of the woman *or* a nonmetaphorical description of a luxurious garden is unnecessary; the man and the woman playfully evoke both these possibilities. The man's response to the woman is another example of this: "I have come to my garden, I have gathered my myrrh and my frankincense, I have eaten my honeycomb with my honey, I have drunk my wine with my milk" (Song 5:1). Sexual consumption or a really good meal? The man and the woman compare each other to plants to speak of their pleasure in each other; they also describe their pleasure in places they both know. They love each other and they love the fields, vineyards, and gardens in which they work, wander, embrace, and eat.

This same ambiguity crops up in 6:1, when the chorus of women asks where they might find the man: "Where has your beloved gone, most beautiful of women? Where has he turned, that we might seek him with you?" She replies: "My beloved has gone down to his garden, to the terraces of balsam, to graze in the garden, to pick lilies. I am my beloved's and my beloved is mine, who grazes among the lilies" (Song 6:2). The exchange recalls the woman's earlier statement that she is a lily of the valley, but that comparison is not made here. Instead she describes the man either grazing in the garden like a sheep or as a shepherd pasturing his flocks in the garden.[100] Her statement could be a sexual boast or a sensuous description of the man in the landscape. At the end of the poem the man does something similar, saying "I went down to the nut garden, to see the green shoots, to see if the vine has opened, if the pomegranate has blossomed" (Song 6:11). It is as if the poet is drunk with her skill; having picked up the reference to lilies in 2:1, she now recalls the springtime landscape of 2:11–13. But this time the man is not declaring the coming of spring, but looking for it. After the exuberance of 4:16–5:1,

---

[100] The verb רָעָה, "to graze, to pasture," allows both possibilities. James writes that the poem "plays with this double vision of the human caretaker, who is also metaphorically a sheep in need of care" (James, *Landscapes of the Song of Songs*, 37).

in which the man comes and eats, and the certainty of 6:2, in which the man is in the garden, gathering lilies, this verse is more tentative: the man is looking for signs of spring, to see if it has arrived. Though the verb רָאָה, "to see," is common in the Song, this is the first time its object is a landscape; the woman will soon invite the man on another walk through the land "to see" its budding. The verb serves to delay and to further action, to both postpone and promote pleasure: is springtime here yet, it is time for love? Let us go into the fields to see, reply the lovers, making of the delay a moment to be together.

Before this happens, however, the man describes the woman as a palm tree, in a text that parallels the woman's comparison of the man to an apple tree in 2:3: "Your stature resembles a date palm, and your breasts – clusters. I said: I will climb into the palm, I will seize the fruit stalks. May your breasts be like clusters of the vine, and the scent of your nose like apples" (Song 7:9 [8]). It is the man's turn to enjoy the woman-as-tree. The man, however, does not sit down in the shade of the date palm, but climbs right up. (Perhaps his actions differ from the woman's because he compares the woman to a tree that is considerably taller than an apple tree; date palms often grow to over 20 meters in height – if he wants dates, climbing is the only way.)[101] In the excitement of the climb, his metaphor multiplies, and the woman becomes not only a date palm but a grape vine and, like the man, an apple tree. This text returns decisively to the metaphor of the man and woman as vegetation and as eatable fruit, but then immediately turns back to the landscape as a meeting place for the lovers:

Come, my beloved, let us go to the field, let us spend the night among the henna blossoms.[102] Let us go early to the vineyards, let us see if the vine has budded, if the grape blossoms have opened, if the pomegranates are in bloom. There I will give you my love. (Song 7:12–13 [11–12])

The man and woman are looking for signs of spring; they go to see if vine and pomegranate have budded. The excursion comes with a promise; the woman says she will "give [her] love" to the man among the buds and flowers. This seems explicit enough, but then her love becomes food and

---

[101] The comparison holds even though we do not know what kind of tree to which the woman compares the man in 2:3. Though apple trees vary greatly in height, the tallest are about 10 meters. Quince trees grow to 5–8 meters and apricots to 8–12 meters.
[102] Alternatively, "in the villages." The plural of the two nouns, כָּפָר ("village") and כֹּפֶר ("henna"), is the same. See Exum, *The Song of Songs*, 240.

fruit: "The mandrakes[103] give off fragrance, and over our doors is every excellent [fruit] – new and old, my love, I have hidden away for you" (Song 7:14 [13]). The pleasure of a spring landscape, the pleasure of sex, and the pleasure of fruits all blend into one; the woman is a bower, is a lover, is a host putting out delicacies for her guest. It is like the opening of Gwendolyn MacEwen's famous poem "Sunday Morning Sermon": "The cat sits on the fence, turning into a bird, turning into a river, turning into an antelope."[104] Rather than splitting apart the different strands of the woman's identity, the poem invites us to keep them together; in this keeping together lies its bliss.[105]

All of the above texts may be read as improvisations on the last verses of the Song's first chapter: "Look[106] at you, my darling: beautiful! Look at you: beautiful! Your eyes are doves. Look at you, my beloved: beautiful! Delightful indeed! Indeed, our bed is green; the rafters of our house are cedar, our beams are cypress" (Song 1:15–17). This early poem is domestic and stationary. All through the Song the lovers invite each other to come, to run, to turn, to seek; here they are together, enjoying each other's beauty, as the room around them turns into a forest of sussurating, fragrant trees. The adverb אַף, "and, also, indeed," ties together the woman's contemplation of the man's beauty with the lushness of their

---

[103] The mandrakes, הַדּוּדָאִים, can also be translated "love fruits." James writes that "the actual plant referenced by "love-fruits" is not entirely certain," that is, it may not be mandrakes at all, "but its sexual associations are apparent etymologically, which is corroborated by the biblical story of Reuben collecting these 'love-fruits' to enhance Rachel's fertility" (James, *Landscapes of the Song of Songs*, 50; referencing Genesis 30:14–17).

[104] Gwendolyn MacEwen, *The Selected Gwendolyn MacEwen* (Toronto: Exile Editions, 2007), 266.

[105] Alicia Ostriker writes that the lovers are "virtually interchangeable with [their environment]" (Alicia Ostriker, "A Holy of Holies: The Song of Songs as Countertext," in *A Feminist Companion to the Bible* 6 (Second Series), ed. Athalya Brenner and Carole R. Fontaine, [Sheffield: Sheffield Academic, 2000], 43), but, as Roland Boer points out, the majority of interpretations focus almost entirely on the lovers; the "interchange" is one-directional, aiming to relate the plant imagery to "love and/or sex between human beings" (Roland Boer, "Keeping It Literal: The Economy of the Song of Songs," *The Journal of Hebrew Scriptures* 7 [2007]: 7).

[106] The particle הִנֵּה, here translated "look" is not connected with sight as such, but with attention. James, citing Robert Kawashima, writes that the word "has no essential reference to vision. Instead, it is a deictic marker for interiority – specifically, the awareness of the other that 'flashes across a character's consciousness' as internal speech" (James, *Landscapes of the Song of Songs*, 123, citing Robert S. Kawashima, *Biblical Narrative and the Death of the Rhapsode* [Bloomington, IN: Indiana University Press, 2004], 93). James translates הִנְּךָ as "Here you are!" which may be more accurate, but also more awkward; I have stuck with the more traditional "look," extended to "look at you" when the particle occurs with a second person suffix.

bed, a lushness expressed as verdure. Out of this little domestic scene flows a rush of poetry, in which the man and the woman meet in gardens, become gardens, become trees, eat the fruit of trees, wait for spring. At the conclusion of the poem, the woman sits in a garden while the man longs for her: "You who dwell in gardens: friends listen for your voice. Let me hear it!" (Song 8:13). She is a woman again, sitting in a garden, but also a little bit a dove, cooing in springtime. The man is again a man, but also a gazelle: "Flee, my love, and be like a gazelle, or like a fawn on the balsam mountains" (Song 8:14). The poem ends not on the notes of satisfied love found in the bedroom of 1:15–17 and the sated conclusion to chapter 4, but on a new dispersal, more movement. The man is again on the mountain, and the woman in the garden, ready to start back at the beginning, the woman entreating: "Draw me after you, let us run" (Song 1:4).

The Song's movement between lovers-as-gardens and lovers-in-gardens does not meet my criteria for personalistic nature texts, but it shows that continuities between humans and other-than-human creatures operate in multiple ways. The personalistic portrayal of nonanimal nature is not an isolated literary trope, but part of the overall fabric of the Bible's world. One way to read the Song is as an exploration of the many images of restoration in the Prophets, most of which describe bountiful agriculture and luxuriant landscapes where previously were desert and desolation (see Isaiah 41:17–20; Jeremiah 31:12; Joel 2:18–19). For example, the Song could be seen as an image of Ezekiel's vision of a repopulated landscape:

But you, O mountain of Israel, you will put out your branches and you will carry your fruit for my people of Israel, for they are near to coming. For look, I am for you and I will turn to you and you will be tilled and you will be sown. I will multiply humans upon you ... and the mountains will be inhabited and the dry places built. I will multiply humans and cattle upon you and they will be many and fruitful. (Ezekiel 36:8–11b)

Several scholars have argued that the Song responds to and redeems Genesis 2–3, restoring the relationships that are broken there.[107] That interpretation is helpful, but should be expanded. The Song does not

---

[107] For an extended discussion of the correspondences between the garden in Genesis 2–3 and Song of Songs, see Francis Landy, *Paradoxes of Paradise: Identity and Difference in the Song of Songs* (Sheffield: Almond, 1983), 183–265; and Ellen F. Davis, "Reading the Song Iconographically," in *Scrolls of Love: Ruth and the Song of Songs*, ed. Peter S. Hawkins and Lesleigh Cushing Stahlberg (New York: Fordham University Press, 2006), 172–84.

respond only to a couple of chapters, but to a long tradition in which humans, the land, vegetation, and animals suffer and fight, sometimes sharing each other's burdens, but often causing each other pain.[108] The Prophets respond with visions of restoration; the Song goes one step further. It imagines a world free of this dynamic, of the recurring cycles of transgressions and judgment, invasion and drought, exile and return. The Song speaks of eager, famished longing and sated bliss, but always between lovers who want one other. Neither of them is resistant or tepid, neither looks to other lovers, like the Prophets accuse Israel of doing (see, for example, Jeremiah 2:25; Ezekiel 16:15; and Hosea 2:9 [7]). If the Song is read in continuity with the Prophets, it shows YHWH and Israel as lovers walking together through a garden, two people astounded at each other's beauty and the pleasures of their bodies, each a verdant tree at one moment, a shy and graceful animal the next. The Song imagines a peace outside the constant failures of people, outside the vagaries of history and empires, somehow outside of time but also inside it, within the joy two lovers find in each other.[109]

In addition to the emphatic blending of humans, animals, plants, and land, the Song contains one clear personalistic nature text. In 4:16, right in the middle of the poem that commentators usually identify as the structural center of the book (Song 4:9–5:1), the woman turns to the winds: "Wake, O north [wind], and come, O south [wind], breathe on my garden, let its perfumes flow, that my beloved may come to his garden and eat its excellent fruit." The first verb, an imperative of עור, "to wake up, to

---

[108] For a commentary that pays close attention to the Song's use of scriptural allusions, see Ellen F. Davis, *Proverbs, Ecclesiastes, and the Song of Songs* (Louisville, KY: Westminster John Knox, 2000).

[109] Traditionally, both Jews and Christians have read the Song allegorically, identifying the lovers as YHWH and Israel, or as Christ and the church (or some variation thereof; the individual soul sometimes stands in for Israel/the church). Modern scholarship has for the most part moved away from this approach, insisting that the lovers are human, and the Song is essentially a secular love song. A prime example of this is Michael V. Fox's *The Song of Songs and the Ancient Egyptian Love Songs* (Madison, WI: University of Wisconsin Press, 1985). Martti Nissinen, however, points out that, for ancient texts, "the distinction between sacred and secular texts is difficult, if not impossible, to maintain" (Martti Nissinen, "Song of Songs and Sacred Marriage," in *Sacred Marriages: The Divine-Human Sexual Metaphor from Sumer to Early Christianity*, ed. Martti Nissinen and Risto Uro [Winona Lake, IN: Eisenbrauns, 2008], 196). Or, in the words of James, "The earliest audiences for the Song did not assume that the Song could be restricted to a single (literal) meaning, but recognized that its theological potential was directly linked to its literary form as erotic poetry" (James, *Landscapes of the Song of Songs*, 12).

wake someone up" picks up the key verb of one of the Song's refrains: "I place you under oath, O daughters of Jerusalem, by the gazelle or the doe of the field, do not wake (תָּעִירוּ) and do not rouse (תְּעוֹרְרוּ) love, until it is willing" (Song 2:7; see also 3:5 and 8:4; with variation in 5:8–9). Right at the center of the poem, the woman asks for the help of the winds to rouse love. Of course, in 4:16, it is the winds that she rouses; they do not wake love, but blow on the garden that the man may come. Still, the word play and the central position of the poem suggest an answer to a question the refrain implies: when is the time to awaken love? For the woman that time is now. To do so she calls not on the chorus of women that she addresses in the refrain, nor on her brothers (see Song 1:6) or mother (see Song 1:6; 3:4; 6:9; 8:1–2, 5), but on the powerful north and south winds. Here nonanimal nature is not witness, soldier, or sufferer, but matchmaker; its breath spreads the garden's fragrance across the land, declaring that love is willing.

CONCLUSION

In this chapter I have probed different ways the Bible expresses and reflects on the relationship between humans and the rest of nature. In the Psalter, humans overhear a conversation that is not for them, and observe adoration that points away from humans, and away from nonanimal nature, towards YHWH. This is a joyous situation, and much celebrated by Israel's poets. Unease only enters in when interpreters try to untangle what any of this has to do with humans and human–divine interactions. The poets of the Psalter have no such anxiety; they seem perfectly happy to find that their own praises are only a small part of the chorus lauding YHWH.

The situation is different in the Book of Job. Job and his friends are very concerned with how nonhumans relate to humans. They claim, in different ways, that nonanimal nature is responsive to human action, or at least ought to be. Job points to his suffering at the hands of both humans and nonhumans as an instance of injustice. To Job, there is no such thing as a natural disaster; the wind that kills his children, the death of his animals, and the failure of his fields go against the moral fabric of the cosmos. Job is innocent, and nonanimal nature ought to respond accordingly. In the divine speeches, God's presentation of the world aligns more closely with the psalmist's view of nonanimal nature, though the picture is not necessarily comforting. Outside of Job's attention is a whole world that does not care about Job. Or, as Habel puts it, "[i]f the observable world is characterized by diversity, ambiguity, and possibility, the cosmic design in its grand totality must be even more complex."[110] Job is not wrong to assert that the state of his place, of his fields and their soil, is intimately connected and responsive to Job's choices and Job's standing before God. But this is only part of the picture. Job and his fields are a tiny slice of the created world. Humans are ignorant of most of this world, just as most of this world is ignorant of humans.

Finally, in the Song of Songs, humans, plants, and animals blend together in dizzying pleasure. Where both Psalm 19 and Job assume a certain distance between humans and the world's nonhuman inhabitants, the Song envisions an amorous coexistence, a dream of a world in which humans and landscapes do not stand in judgment of, grieve, or misunderstand each other, but instead promote and participate in each other's desires and joys, the garden feeding the lovers its fruit, the lovers tending and admiring the vineyard's blossoms. The Song is not only a crescendo but also a reprieve, a space to flee to imagine for a while that things are different. This reprieve is not escapism, however, but practice: practice for approaching the world with affection, tenderness, awe, and delight.

The Book of Psalms, Job, and the Song of Songs each, in their own way, removes humans from the center of the cosmos, an experience that ranges from wonderful to terrifying. The activity of nonanimal nature in the Hebrew Bible extends beyond cozy interdependence and harmonious affiliation. The profusion of persons, all of them created by YHWH, in a chaos of abundance, makes for an untidy world. That untidiness sometimes takes the form of the exuberance of the Psalter and the rowdy joy of the Song, but other times it takes the form of randomness and pain. The world is not a thermometer or mirror of human righteousness; it is a cacophonous community of persons, whose interactions and communications are sometimes friendly, sometimes hostile, sometimes indifferent, but never wholly patterned and predictable.

It is tempting to want to nail down *the* biblical perspective on nature, the overarching attitude that spans the entire canon. But what Job, the Song, and the Psalter show is that the biblical writers are continually thinking and rethinking the relationship between humans and all that is not human. Their attitudes towards and interactions with nature are not static; it is an ongoing process of getting to know each other. From the

---

[110] Habel, *The Book of Job*, 60.

most painful aspects of the canon to its most joyful, the biblical writers struggle with the tradition handed down to them, measuring it against their daily interactions with winds, wadis, henna blossoms, and doves. They consider and reconsider different levels of intimacy, ranging from the aspects of the world that are beyond us and largely inaccessible to us to those that we feel under our skin. And we can be part of that process, that dynamic engagement with canon and world. If personalistic nature texts are to be useful for ethical reflection and action, it is not enough that we read them. We have to enter into conversation with them with the same passion as Job and his friends, with the hope and openness of the Song, with the curiosity of the psalmists. And we can't do so in locked, air-conditioned rooms – we need both the words of the text and the landscape around us. That landscape will not be the same as the landscape encountered by the biblical writers, and the challenges that face us now are different from theirs. But their ability to stay in close relationship to the words of their tradition and the places where they live: that is a useful model. If we learn how to be those kinds of readers, we might find ourselves a little less the enemy and blight of the creatures with which we share the world. Perhaps we might in time be able to exchange hostility for words of endearment, for a confident assurance that were we to whisper to our landscapes, our forests, our gardens, our seas, "I am my beloved's and my beloved is mine," they would whisper back, "Look at you, my darling: beautiful! ... Look at you, my beloved: beautiful! Delightful indeed."

6

Conclusion

Befriending the World

We do not have to live as if we were alone.
— Wendell Berry, *It All Turns on Affection*[1]

The world that meets us in the Bible is, to use Jeffrey Cohen's lovely phrase, a world of "companionable landscapes."[2] In this world you can be *with* mountains, trees, rivers, and soil, not just *on* them. In this world, Israel lives in the hollow of the land's mouth, a rich, intimate place – oozing with milk and honey – and a precarious one: the land might swallow you or spit you out, then grieve like a mother bereaved over your absence. This is a world attuned to "all things' togetherness," presenting creation as if it were a big family reunion, complete with the joy, chaos, and all out fights that can accompany extended time with kin.[3] It is messy, there are so many persons to consider and respect, but it is not lonely. Here we are among "our relations," to borrow from the great Winona LaDuke.[4]

In this final chapter, I begin by suggesting some further avenues for research, topics on which attention to other-than-human persons might shed light. Second, I return to Cora Diamond in order to investigate how we evaluate the relative worth of one set of concepts over against others,

---

[1] Wendell Berry, *It All Turns on Affection: The Jefferson Lecture and Other Essays* (New York: Counterpoint, 2012).
[2] Jeffrey Jerome Cohen, *Stone: An Ecology of the Inhuman* (Minneapolis, MN: University of Minnesota Press, 2015), 3.
[3] Torsten Hägerstrand, "Geography and the Study of Interaction between Nature and Society," *Geoforum* 7 (1976): 334.
[4] Winona LaDuke, *All Our Relations: Native Struggles for Land and Life* (Cambridge, MA: South End, 1999).

and to ask whether it is even possible to choose between concepts. I then put the work of two modern artists – Patricia Johanson and Jules Renard – into conversation with biblical texts, focusing in particular on how each express relations between human and other-than-human persons. Finally, I consider possible roles religious communities might play in addressing climate change, and what joys await us if we become intimate with the world.

AVENUES FOR FURTHER STUDY

Personalistic nature texts are not an isolated phenomenon within the Bible, but part of its larger textual world. Given that, what areas within biblical studies could benefit from this work? Here I suggest three topics, namely theological anthropology, architecture and artifacts as presented in biblical texts, and iconographic exegesis of the archaeological record of ancient Israel.

Theological Anthropology

What is a human being? I suggested in Chapter 5 that we should avoid the question "how are we special?" and I stand by that. But we need to ask questions that come close: What is a human being? How does a human being live? How *should* a human being live? How do you know a human being when you see one, and what should you do when you've recognized one? One of the destabilizing aspects of reading about animism is that it makes clear that defining humanness is by no means an easy endeavor, but also that it is essential to know *how* to be human: "most of the interests, activities, rights, responsibilities, involvements and concerns of animists ... are to do with their own roles and with other humans. They might expect owls, herons, crows and nightjars to be doing whatever it takes to care for country, land, Earth, and life, but the prime duty is to play one's own role fully."[5] Theological anthropology is important because it can help clarify for us what it is to play our role fully, what it is to be properly human. The Bible should have much to offer here. I have focused on ways in which humans and other-than-humans are alike in the Hebrew Bible, but that is not to say that the Bible does not differentiate between kinds of persons. Its writers do not mistake humans for rocks, or

---

[5] Harvey, *Animism*, 103.

forests for people. The question is on what they base their distinctions, what purposes those distinctions serve, and how they are maintained.

Cora Diamond's reflections on the concept of the human being suggest we should look not for an abstract definition of humanness (for biblical equivalents to the species designation *Homo sapiens*), but instead look at how humans in the Bible live and interact: "Grasping a concept (even one like that of a human being, which is a descriptive concept if any are) is not a matter just of knowing how to group things under that concept; it is being able to participate in life-with-the-concept."[6] In this case we can only participate in life-with-the-concept through reading; if you want to know what the concept of a human being meant to the writers of the Hebrew Bible, you need to look to ways of life described in the biblical text. One of the promises of widening the circle of what counts as a person in the Hebrew Bible is that it can shed light on practices that, from a modern perspective, are opaque. Examples include bodily practices and the legal codes that govern them, such as how you cut your hair, what you wear and what you eat, whom you can have sex with and when, how you slaughter an animal, which animals you may *not* slaughter. These, I suspect, serve in part to maintain humanness, to sustain a particular kind of personhood in relation to YHWH. Comparisons with contemporary animist societies support this hunch. In a 1979 article, Anthony Seeger, Roberto da Matta, and Eduardo Viveiros de Castro argued that humanness is not a given in Brazilian indigenous societies: it must be made or fabricated, and bodily practices are the means of doing so.[7] Istvan Praet, in a more recent book, builds on their insight: "Amazonian Indians never take humanity for granted. Being human – being 'one of us' – is not so much a safe premise as a never-ending effort that has to be kept up through the continuous sharing of food, the gradual acquisition of bodily ornaments, and much else."[8] Rather than using categories such as personhood, agency, and consciousness to determine what humans are, instead we should look at what humans do in the Bible, what their responsibilities are, what kinds of actions and skills are most emphasized and most regulated. I expect that the question of humanness will have to be further divided into questions about what it is to be an

---

[6] Diamond, "Losing Your Concepts," 266.
[7] Anthony Seeger, Roberto Da Matta, and Eduardo Viveiros de Castro, "A Construção Da Pessoa Nas Sociedades Indigenas Brasileiras," *Boletim Do Museu Nacional (Rio de Janeiro)* 32 (1979): 2–19.
[8] Praet, *Animism and the Question of Life*, 20.

Israelite human and how Israelites are different from other peoples. If Israel's legal framework works in part to maintain humanness, what does that mean for how they view non-Israelites? Is there a general humanness in the Bible, and, if so, what are its characteristics?

Architecture and Artifacts in Biblical Texts

One way to build on this study is to look at what distinguishes one kind of person from another; a second approach is to further problematize the boundary between persons and things, this time by looking at humanmade artifacts. Speaking of Maori meeting houses, Harvey writes:

> It is typical of animist life ways that the transformation of living persons from trees to "artefacts" is not experienced as a destruction of life and personhood, nor their consequent transformation into artificiality. Human artefacts not only enrich the encounter between persons, but are often themselves experienced as autonomous agents. In "art" not only do humans express themselves, so too do those persons who are transformed.[9]

Keeping in mind that the sharp dualism between culture and nature is a modernist concept, the distinction I have implicitly drawn in my criteria for personalistic nature texts between "nature" and humanmade objects is probably artificial. It is possible that ancient Israelites, like the animists whom Harvey describes, maintained social relationships with what we would think of as humanmade objects. There is some evidence for this in the text. In a few cases, artifacts are addressed in ways that resemble addresses to nonhuman nature, such as the man of God's proclamation to an altar in 1 Kings 13:2 and the psalmist's call to gates in Psalm 24:7 and 9. Like the ground, the gates of Zion mourn in Isaiah 3:26 (see also Jeremiah 14:2), while in Lamentations it is the roads to Zion that grieve (Lamentations 1:4). Lamentations also include an extended personified portrait of Jerusalem (Lamentations 1); though clearly an example of the common presentation of cities as women in the ancient Near East, the text might also be studied from the perspective of social relations between humans and their architecture. Also significant might be the detailed descriptions of the Temple and its furnishings found in Exodus 25–30, 36–40 (these texts technically describe the wilderness tabernacle), 1 Kings 6, and Ezekiel 40–46 (a visionary temple), in particular the prevalence of plant and garden imagery. The abundance of fragrant wood, palm trees,

---

[9] Harvey, *Animism*, 56–57.

pomegranates, and hybrid beings in the Temple's furnishings bring to mind the boundary blurring of Song of Songs. The Song itself may be a helpful source here, as it compares its lovers to walls, towers, and shields, not only to plants and animals. Finally, objects, much like people, can be clean and unclean, even holy. How do these states of objects relate to the topic of this book? What about humans and objects mean that both can be "infected" with holiness and its opposite? Alfred Gell's *Art and Agency* would be a good place to begin addressing these questions, as well as the writings of scholars in thing theory and object oriented ontology, such as Bruno Latour, Graham Harman, Tim Ingold, W. J. T. Mitchell, and Jane Bennett.[10]

Iconographic Exegesis and Archeology

The work of Othmar Keel and the Fribourg School have brought attention to the importance of nontextual remains, to the images and iconography of the ancient Near East. In this study, I have restricted myself to textual evidence only; another source of data is the archeological record of ancient Israel, its paintings, pottery decorations, seals, amulets, mosaics, statuary, ivories, etc. I do not expect that a survey of ancient Israelite images will turn up images of anthropomorphized trees; the difference between an animist and a nonanimist in how they see a mountain or river is not visual, but relational – the "body" of an oak tree looks the same whether you think it is a person or not.[11] It has the same shape, the same colors, the same position in the landscape. Instead of looking for such images, a fruitful avenue of research might be to compare anthropological studies on art made by animist peoples – for example, Maori

---

[10] Gell, *Art and Agency*; Bruno Latour, *We Have Never Been Modern*, trans. Catherine Porter (Cambridge, MA: Harvard University Press, 1993); Graham Harman, *Tool-Being: Heidegger and the Metaphysics of Objects* (Chicago, IL: Open Court, 2002); Ingold, *Being Alive: Essays on Movement, Knowledge and Description*; W. J. T. Mitchell, *Picture Theory: Essays on Verbal and Visual Representation* (Chicago, IL: University of Chicago Press, 1995); Bennett, *Vibrant Matter: A Political Ecology of Things*.

[11] The one example of anthropomorphic tree images I have found is of an Egyptian tree goddess. She is represented as a tree with an arm and a breast, or as a tree with the torso of a person coming out of the tree. See Silvia Schroer, *Die Ikonographie Palästinas/Israels Und Der Alte Orient: Eine Religionsgeschichte in Bildern*, vol. 3: Die Spätbronzeit (Fribourg: Academic Press Fribourg, 2005), 272–75. These images are at most tangentially related to this project. First, because they are from Egypt, not Israel, and, second, because they represent a goddess, whose iconography include tree imagery, rather than trees as such.

meeting houses – to see how artistic expressions, architecture, decoration, etc., function within their societies and whether any parallels can be drawn with biblical and archeological material. Andrew Gell's warning that it "is an error to imagine that 'culture' in some general sense ... is responsible for the visual style of artefacts" should be kept in mind.[12] There is no such thing as "animist" art, a style consistent across different cultures with animist beliefs and practices. As Gell writes, "Culture may dictate the practical and/or symbolic significance of artefacts, and their iconographic interpretation; but the only factor which governs the visual appearance of artefacts is their relationship to other artefacts in the same style."[13] A place to start might be to look at plant imagery, which is plentiful, cataloging where it occurs, on what kind of object, how it relates to other symbols with which it occurs, etc.[14] Mountain, sun, star, and storm imagery may also be interesting. Such a project would require methodological innovation; the congruence and correlation between images and an extensive worldview like animism is not obvious. Benjamin Sommer's study of divine embodiment, *The Bodies of God and the World of Ancient Israel*, might be a helpful guide, as an example of a study that mines texts and images in order to investigate ancient Israelite concepts.[15]

WHAT IS THE GOOD OF A CONCEPT?

In this book I have investigated how ancient Israel interacted with non-animal nature, and how their concepts of nonanimal nature differ from our own. Throughout the underlying assumption has been that their concepts are in some way better than ours, or at least that their concepts of other-than-human persons might help us respond more adequately to the environmental crisis. But how do we evaluate the relative worth of one concept against another? And, even if we can evaluate concepts, is it possible to choose between them?

Cora Diamond begins her essay "Losing Your Concepts" by observing that "No principles of classification are forced on us by the nature of ethics; we shape what ethical discussion is in part by what we choose to bring together, by the pattern of resemblances and differences in ethical

---

[12] Gell, *Art and Agency*, 216.   [13] Ibid.
[14] Of particular interest might be the "YHWH and his asherah" pithos inscription found at Kuntillet Ajrud.
[15] Benjamin D. Sommer, *The Bodies of God and the World of Ancient Israel* (Cambridge: Cambridge University Press, 2009).

thought that we trace and display."[16] But much of her essay is about the inadequacy of the category *choice*; her criticism of the effect of empiricism on moral philosophy is that it leads us to "represent all goods as goods which are either chosen by individuals for themselves or imposed on us through an accident of birth and education or the choice of others."[17] Family relations illustrate why this understanding of the good of a concept is inadequate: I can choose whether or not to betray my parents or mistreat my children, but I cannot choose whether loyalty to family is good or not – the idea that "betraying one's parents should be a horror ... is in the life of *our* words"; it is not "subject to choice."[18] The human weight of "certain sorts of relationships between parents and their ... children" is "already settled" if we are able to imagine a world, one that we can choose if we want to, in which parents bear no responsibility towards their children and vice versa.[19] To think that such a choice is available is already to have lost the concept of family that makes betrayal reprehensible.

We cannot simply choose between concepts, according to Diamond, because description and categorization are not the same. To be able to point out a member of the species *Homo sapiens* is not the same as being able to describe and live with the concept of a human being.[20] The latter (description and living with) depends on a particular kind of recognition, which Diamond illustrates using Leo Tolstoy's *War and Peace*:

> There is a great scene in *War and Peace* in which Pierre's life is saved. He is brought as prisoner before General Davoût, who, when he first looks up from the papers on his writing table, sees Pierre, who is standing before him, only as the present prisoner, the present circumstance to be dealt with; but something in Pierre's voice make him look at him intently. At that moment, "an immense number of things passed dimly through both their minds." ... In that second look, human relations between the two men are established; and it is that look which saves Pierre's life.[21]

The difference between Davoût's two ways of looking at Pierre is not one of classification; he does not, in the first case, fail to see that Pierre is a member of the species *Homo sapiens*. Instead, he fails to see Pierre as a human being. This changes when "something in Pierre's voice [makes] him look at him intently." The resulting recognition restores Pierre to

---

[16] Diamond, "Losing Your Concepts," 255.   [17] Ibid., 272.
[18] Ibid. Emphasis in the original.   [19] Ibid.   [20] Ibid., 266.
[21] Ibid., 264, referring to: Leo Tolstoy, *War and Peace*, trans. Louise Maude and Aylmer Maude (Oxford: Oxford University Press, 2010).

humanness in Davoût's eyes, and prompts him to acknowledge Pierre as someone towards whom he has certain responsibilities and commitments: he must treat him like one treats a human being.

Diamond's second example, taken from Primo Levi's writing about his experience in Auschwitz, shows what happens when recognition does not take place:

> Levi the prisoner in Auschwitz is brought before Pannwitz, a chemist in a supervisory position at the Buna factory where some Auschwitz prisoners worked. If Levi's credentials as a chemist are accepted, he will be assigned to work at Buna, he will not be destroyed by horrendous physical labor in the cold, he will be far more likely to survive the "selections." Pannwitz sits at the writing table, Levi stands before him: and the look that passes between them "was not one between two men."[22]

I think we find ourselves in a similar situation – we don't know how to look at that which is not human in a way that makes possible the giving and receiving of recognition. I am unsure about the exact moral weight and practical consequence of this, because to look at a tree in search of recognition requires concepts whose way of life differ drastically from my own. I am convinced, however, that our current form of looking is damaging, and of that there is ample proof. Is it as bad as the look that Pannwitz gives Levi? Even suggesting that possibility makes me feel queasy. Humans to me feel so much more important than trees. But thinking of it in those terms (which are more important: humans or trees?) is, I think, a sign of my conceptual loss. The two need not be separate; by looking at a tree or a mountain or a river in a certain way, I not only live out a particular understanding of the value of trees, but also an understanding of what it is to be human. In that sense, the question "so if mountains and rivers are persons, what distinguishes humans from other kinds of persons?" is as urgent as the question of similarities between humans and the rest of the world. The question need not devolve into concerns with our specialness, but instead can open up ways to consider what sort of humans we need to be if we are to look at trees and mountains in a way that recognizes them and leaves room for them to recognize us in turn.

Recall, however, Diamond's claim that concepts are not like goods on a shelf, that we can choose between at will. We cannot just wake up and choose to see differently. If choosing to value and recognize the world *or not* was present to us as an abstract choice, we would already have

---

[22] Ibid., 265, quoting Primo Levi, *"If This Is a Man" and "The Truce"* (Harmondsworth: Penguin Books, 1979), 111.

forfeited the concept of the world as valuable. And yet our present concepts of the nonhuman world are clearly inadequate, unable to motivate us to action that is proportional to the magnitude of the climate crisis. We urgently need to change. Still, I do not think we start from zero. The concepts of the Bible are far removed from our own, but I do not think we are so far away as to have no sense of the value of the world or of its manifold lives. The longing present in the work of anthropologists writing on animism suggests otherwise; they see something in animists that appears good to them, desirable, and right.[23] They know enough to want to live with animist concepts. Their longing suggests that such concepts are not completely gone from modernist worldviews – maybe they are simply dormant (or in a coma), buried deep, deep somewhere. Maybe if we commit ourselves, if we are patient and careful, we might coax them out of sleep and learn to live with them again.

Whether this is possible depends in part on how far we have to travel, and on the quality of our distance from personalistic ways of interacting with the world. Diamond distinguishes between two accounts of conceptual loss. According to the first, represented by Alastair MacIntyre, our conceptual loss is real and actual; when philosophers speak of the loss of concepts (moral concepts, in MacIntyre's case), they offer a true portrait of the world.[24] According to the second account, represented by Stanley Cavell, philosophers are writing philosophy *as if* they have forgotten what morality and moral thought are like, but "it is not that [they have] lost it so much as that [they] cannot or will not acknowledge or recognize what [they know]."[25] Summarizing the difference between these two stances, Diamond writes that MacIntyre and Cavell, respectively, represent "those, on the one hand, who say that we have *actually lost* concepts central to moral life, and those, on the other, who point out that some or many philosophers write *as if* we inhabit a world from which those concepts have vanished."[26]

Those who believe our conceptual loss is actual differ on how it relates to our language and our experiences. MacIntyre argues that, because the background conditions that supported the concept of

---

[23] I discuss this longing in Chapter 2, in the section entitled "Personalistic Nature Texts and Patience."
[24] Diamond, "Losing Your Concepts," 255.
[25] Ibid. Both MacIntyre and Cavell are responding to the writing of Charles Stevenson, but through their accounts of his work they are making more general points about conceptual loss and its relationship to philosophy.
[26] Ibid., 256. Emphasis in the original.

morality no longer exist, "we have certain words and use them, but are unable to give them a truly intelligible use."[27] Duke Maskell, however, argues that we are incapable of using older vocabulary "with conviction, so we are unable to make fully intelligible to ourselves experiences that those words would help us to articulate, and actions that they would enable us to justify."[28] It is the difference between using words confidently without realizing that they no longer have content (in this account our loss is invisible to us), and using words without conviction, without believing in our own language, which makes us unable to make sense of our experiences. For MacIntyre a part of the language has died; for Maskell it is "not dead … but asleep"; the words we use still have potency, but they have fallen out of "respectable speech."[29] John Berger, however, disagrees with both MacIntyre and Maskell. He argues that it is not that we have words, but use them poorly; we have lost words entirely. He writes: "There are large sections of the English working and middle class who are inarticulate as the result of wholesale cultural deprivation. They are deprived of the means of translating what they know into thought which they can think."[30] What Berger's villagers need is not MacIntyre's background conditions or Maskell's conviction, but a return to the vocabulary of their traditions. They need help to become articulate again.

Tradition is key for MacIntyre, Maskell, and Berger. It is one of the things that bind together their accounts of conceptual loss, and it is also the source of hope in their writing:

> For all three … the deprivation of not being able to *name things properly* (with the result, that one's thoughts cannot properly be thought, are misexpressed or not expressed at all) – that deprivation is tied to lack of connection with cultural traditions. It appears, though, that the very fact that they have experiences and commitments which require for their expression a vocabulary which they lack depends on their retaining some connection with those traditions.[31]

Tradition is the benchmark; we used to be more able to "name things properly" than we are now. Something lingers, however, in that people have experiences tied to traditions, but are not able to think or speak those experiences. The gesture towards tradition leaves open the

---

[27] Ibid., 258. [28] Ibid., 257–58. [29] Ibid., 257.
[30] Ibid., 258, quoting John Berger, *A Fortunate Man* (New York: Pantheon Books, 1982), 98–99.
[31] Diamond, "Losing Your Concepts," 259. Emphasis in the original.

possibility that we can regain our words, that we can again make them adequate to our "experiences and commitments."

This bit of hope is the segue to the second kind of account of conceptual loss, the *as-if* accounts. Diamond summarizes Stanley Cavell's argument:

> [Philosophers do] not suffer from incapacity to use moral vocabulary in [their] ordinary life ... but from an incapacity that shows itself in reflection on that use. What [they lack] the capacity for is itself a particular kind of use of the moral vocabulary. To be able to say: "This is what it is *like* to use these concepts" is itself a use, a philosophically reflective use, of the concepts ... In philosophical reflection on morality, we need to be able to make plain how saying things to others is connected with responsibility and commitment; and that is what [philosophers] cannot do.[32]

The difference between MacIntyre's and Cavell's accounts is that MacIntyre believe philosophers offer an accurate portrait of the world when they say we have lost the concept of morality, while Cavell thinks they suffer from an inability that is peculiar to philosophical discourse. Concepts aren't lost; what we have lost is the ability to reflect on them in a certain way, to evaluate and to speak of what kinds of life certain concepts make possible. In Cavell's account, the concepts are a little less lost. It is still problematic, deeply so, that we lack the ability to reflect on concepts, but the concepts themselves continue to be part of everyday life. We have lost one way of interacting with them, but we have not lost them entirely.

The distinction between MacIntyre and Cavell may seem considerable, but Diamond argues that it is less so than appears on first blush. She contrasts two explorations of conceptual loss in the writing of Iris Murdoch. In the first, she sounds like MacIntyre: "We have suffered a general loss of concepts, the loss of a moral and political vocabulary ... We can no longer see man against a background of values, of realities, which transcend him. We picture man as a brave naked will surrounded by an easily comprehended empirical world."[33] In the essay "The Idea of Perfection," she sounds more like Cavell; she argues that the problem is not "a *general* loss of concepts" but a loss peculiar to philosophers, due to

---

[32] Ibid., 261. Emphasis in the original. Again, Cavell is specifically writing about Charles Stevenson, but doing so to make a general point.

[33] Ibid., 260, quoting Iris Murdoch, "Against Dryness: A Polemical Sketch," in *Revisions, Changing Perspectives in Moral Philosophy*, ed. Stanley Hauerwas and Alasdair C. MacIntyre (Notre Dame: University of Notre Dame Press, 1983), 46.

their philosophy of mind: "Given our philosophy of mind, some values are, as far as modern ethics is concerned, no longer capable of expression; the moral experience of ordinary people cannot be illuminated by a vocabulary used in the ways available to modern philosophy."[34] Murdoch's thoughts cohere, according to Diamond, because, for Murdoch, philosophy is "both the guide and mirror of its age."[35] The philosophy of mind which Murdoch blames in her second account of conceptual loss is both cause and mirror of a "picture of the human personality which our culture in general has inherited from the Enlightenment."[36] Central to this picture is the idea of humans as autonomous rational agents, whose actions are based on rational choices. This idea is blind to the inadequacy of "choice" as a description of how we live with concepts.

Murdoch's attention to philosophy of mind brings us full circle; we are back to Chapter 2, to a humanity that is defined by agency, by the ability to make plans in the mind and then carry them out in the world. To locate the essence of what it is to be a person in the mind, in the brain, hampers our ability to use moral vocabulary well, because it makes of morality a shopping experience: you can choose which responsibilities and moral concepts to value and which to ignore in much the same way you choose between breakfast cereals. From this point of view, defining humanness by rational choice is to take a limited view of what it is to be human. But this same view of agency also gives a limited view of what other-than-human persons are and can be, and, as such, makes us unable to relate well to them. Whatever trees are, they are not autonomous rational agents; if we make rational choice the litmus test of what it is to be a person, we restrict the circle of beings with whom we may share mutual recognition.

Diamond, in contrast to Murdoch, argues that what makes it difficult for us to recover moral concepts is not our philosophy of mind, but our philosophy of language. Specifically, she is concerned with the equation of description and classification. For Diamond, the problem is not primarily that we think of humans as rational agents, but that we do not know the difference between living with the concept of *Homo sapiens* and the concept of human beings. We mistake definition for relationship, classification for the ability to behave appropriately and adequately towards

---

[34] Diamond, "Losing Your Concepts," 262. This is Diamond's summary of Murdoch, not a quote from her writing.
[35] Ibid.   [36] Ibid.

others. Having defined what a human being is, we think we automatically know how to be one. Fortunately, both Diamond's and Murdoch's explanations are useful: we are unable to relate well with other-than-human persons because of how we understand minds *and* language. Our language prioritizes categorization, making us unable to express what it is for humans and trees, mountains, rivers, soil, and winds to recognize and relate to each other (we are better at "what is that?" than "how ought I to relate to that?"). Our philosophy of mind encourages us to live as if we are the only ones here.

Diamond only hints at what it would mean to recover concepts, but we can draw inferences from her writing. I do not think we can or should choose between the accounts offered by MacIntyre, Maskell, Berger, Cavell, and Murdoch; instead, we should mine them for different ways of restoring what we have lost or building something we may not ever have had. It is not an easy task. We are deeply habituated to the Cartesian split, to mind/body dualism, and struggle to think of creatures without brains as persons. Even when we experience that "the world comes, and comes to bring [us] out," as Buber says, we cannot articulate that experience.[37] When we do try to talk about it, we do so with little conviction, but much embarrassment: it sounds so sentimental and naive. What language we do have is bleached and weak – it cannot undergird and motivate action. Against this mountain of difficulty, we can borrow from each of the writers Diamond surveys. From MacIntyre we can take the fact that our words become meaningless when they no longer resonate with a wider background. To say, for example, that the ground mourns, makes little sense if we are sure that only humans, or at most, humans and animals, really suffer. From Maskell we get the sense that our language has lost its connection to experience and action; if we no longer believe or know how to say that land has a responsibility to observe sabbath, it cannot form our sense of responsibility towards other-than-humans or motivate action on climate change. Berger contributes the sense that our inadequate language makes us unable to think or speak our experiences; it is not just that the words have become meaningless, the words we need are simply not there. The Bible might help us become articulate again, its language a tutor in how to speak about that which is not human. Murdoch, via Cavell, shows that the difference between the language of people in general and the discourse of philosophy

---

[37] Buber, *I and Thou*, 32.

are not separate issues; how we think about minds, about language, affects our concepts and how we live.

The upshot of all this is that we need to go at conceptual loss from more than one angle. We both need a vocabulary, or a new relationship with the one we already have, and we need ways of living that can make real again the background against which such language is intelligible. Throughout this book I have pointed to contemporary animists as people from whom we might learn a different way of interacting with the world, and I would encourage everyone to spend time with writers like Winona LaDuke and Linda Hogan. It is vital to remember that there are plenty of contemporary animists, many of whom are excellent writers and poets; the sense that animism is a thing of the past is part and parcel of the convenient and violent notion that indigenous peoples are a thing of the past. So, when I now offer a couple of examples of people who are not animists, I do so as a form of training wheels, as examples that require less drastic leaps of imagination and responsiveness. Think of these as stepping stones, as a way to start. The social world that the authors of the Bible assume in their writings often feels like it is always just over the hill: far away animists know how to do it, so did premodern peoples, but for us modern city dwellers, it is always the knowledge of someone else. Yet, as Diamond writes of the philosophers and cultural critics whose work she canvases, "the intention of these works nevertheless requires that the reader not have wholly lost the old conceptual life."[38] If that is the case, perhaps some among us are less lost than the rest. If "person" is no more a category than Diamond's "human being," but instead a way of interacting, then we need people who know how to interact well with persons, human and otherwise. Here I will point to two examples, one an artist, the other a poet. The landscapes that Patricia Johanson build and nurture can introduce us to a way of life that assumes different concepts than the modern mind/body, nature/culture dualisms: her spaces make possible life with the concept in a way that most modern landscapes do not. The poet Jules Renard can help us with vocabulary. His poems are not as foreign as the Bible, but they show a deep connection with the world around him, as well as a desire for closer kinship with it. Together, Johanson and Renard can help us build tradition, build background, and build language, so that perhaps we can recover a concept of the world that is more relational, more social, and more equitable towards humans and nonhumans alike.

[38] Ibid., 275.

LIVING TOGETHER: PATRICIA JOHANSON AND JULES RENARD

Patricia Johanson makes large scale public art with the aim of creating habitats for humans, wildlife, and plants.[39] Johanson's art builds on her close relationship with one place, Buskirk, New York, which has been her home her entire adult life. Her intimacy with this place has grown into a commitment to local knowledge that affects all her work; it has given her "a sense of the local that can be translated to the unfamiliar places where she is commissioned to make public art."[40] Whenever Johanson undertakes a project, she begins by getting to know the place in which she will be working, researching the location and talking to local residents, naturalists, scientists, and so on:

> I never design until I have discovered the meaning of the place. Each place has a unique set of conditions, and we need an intimate understanding of what it has been, is now, and will become in the future, in order to create a design that is more than a willful act.[41]

Johanson's language about place resembles the language of agrarians. For example, Wendell Berry writes that,

> For the good farmer ... the place where knowledge is applied is minutely particular, not *a* farm but *this* farm, *my* farm, the only place exactly like itself in the world. To use it without intimate, minute particular knowledge of it, as if it were *a* farm or *any* farm, is ... to violate it, to do it damage, finally to destroy it.[42]

Wes Jackson insists that global, environmental problems will only be solved if we "become native to our ... place," and he urges universities to teach students how "to return home, or to go some other place, and dig in."[43] Johanson's projects ask those who interact with them "what it would mean to *come home* to the places we inhabit."[44] Johanson begins her art by turning to people who are intimate with a place, so that she herself can become intimate with it; her work then invites others to participate in this coming to know a place.

---

[39] For pictures and descriptions of Johanson's projects, see "Patricia Johanson," accessed September 15, 2016, http://patriciajohanson.com/ and Caffyn Kelley, *Art and Survival: Patricia Johanson's Environmental Projects* (Salt Spring Island, BC: Islands Institute, 2006).
[40] Kelley, *Art and Survival*, xii.   [41] Ibid., 19.
[42] Berry, "Whose Head Is the Farmer Using? Whose Head Is Using the Farmer?," 28. Emphasis in the original.
[43] Wes Jackson, *Becoming Native to This Place*, The Blazer Lectures (Lexington, KY: University Press of Kentucky, 1994), 2–3.
[44] Kelley, *Art and Survival*, 19. Emphasis in the original.

Conclusion: Befriending the World 211

Fair Park Lagoon, August 2016,
©Michael Barera[45]

An example is Johanson's project for Fair Park Lagoon in Dallas. Before Johanson's work, the lagoon was "a stagnant, dangerous eyesore in the middle of the city."[46] Fertilizers from surrounding lawns caused frequent algal blooms, and the pond could not sustain plant and animal life.[47] People avoided the pond because it was unpleasant and dangerous. Johanson planted the pond with various water plants, and the shore with grasses. She created sculptural elements based on native plants; these stabilized the shoreline, created habitats, and formed paths, perches, and bridges. Once the pond was planted, she introduced various species of fish. Walter Davis, the director of the adjacent Dallas Museum of Natural History, describes the changes caused by Johanson's intervention:

---

[45] CC BY-SA 4.0 (https://creativecommons.org/licenses/by-sa/4.0), CC BY-SA 3.0 (https://creativecommons.org/licenses/by-sa/3.0) or GFDL (www.gnu.org/copyleft/fdlhtml), from Wikimedia Commons.
[46] Ibid., 20.
[47] Fertilizer runoff from the surrounding park has continued to be a problem, with algae blooms damaging the water quality of the lagoon. Public access to Johanson's sculptures has also become a problem; the city has installed fences around them. For a discussion of the current state of Fair Park Lagoon, see Jon Revett's article "The Fair Park Lagoon, and the Fate of Fair Park," Glasstire: Texas Visual Art, http://glasstire.com/2017/10/02/the-fair-park-lagoon-and-the-fate-of-fair-park/ (accessed July 30, 2018).

Today the lagoon teems with life ... A kingfisher visiting for the first time in decades signals that the water is clear enough for this master fisherman to spot minnows swimming beneath the surface. A pair of least bitterns ... moved in the first year ... Ducks and turtles sun themselves on emergent parts of the sculpture, safe from predatory dogs and enthusiastic children. These plants and animals are not captives held for the enjoyment of human spectators. Most have chosen to live in the lagoon because it provides food and shelter for themselves and their offspring.[48]

The prophets speak repeatedly of the mourning of the land – "the earth mourns and all who dwell in it languish; the animals of the field and the birds of the heavens, even the fish of the sea – they perish together" (Hosea 4:3) – and it takes only a small stretch of the imagination to connect this biblical theme with Fair Park lagoon. The lagoon had become stagnant, unhealthy, and barren, and had been abandoned by its inhabitants. Johanson's work effects that which YHWH promises in Ezekiel: "I will multiply upon you humans and animals, they will multiply and be fruitful" (Ezekiel 36:11). By carefully and lovingly tending to the lagoon, Johanson comforts it in its mourning, and invites back to it those who have been exiled. This welcome extends to humans, plants, animals, birds, fish; as in Ezekiel, the community addressed is one in which no clear divisions separate human and other-than-human persons.

In the poetry of Jules Renard, attention and relationship go hand in hand. His collection of prose poems, *Histoires Naturelles*, was inspired by the landscape, animals, and people of his childhood home in Le Morvan, and of the area of Chaoumont where he lived as an adult.[49] Most of the poems are about animals and insects (for example, "The Hen," "The Water-Flies," "The Nanny-Goat," "The Worm"), but he also includes poems about garden flowers, the moon, and the landscape more generally. A common feature of Renard's poems is that they combine careful observation of behavior with a desire to connect and interact. For example, in the poem "The Mouse," he reports how the sound of his pen against paper creates a bond between him and a mouse:

As I sit beneath the lamp, writing my daily page, I hear a faint noise.
If I stop, it stops. It starts again as soon as my pen scratches the paper.
It's a mouse waking up.
...

---

[48] Ibid., 24–25.
[49] Jules Renard, *Histoires Naturelles*, trans. Richard Stokes (Richmond, UK: Oneworld Clasics, 2010).

Conclusion: Befriending the World

Each time I set down my pen, the silence alarms her. Each time I put pen to paper,
  she thinks perhaps that another mouse is somewhere near, and feels assured.
Then I lose sight of her. She's under my table, between my feet. She moves from
  one chair leg to the next. She brushes against my clogs, nibbles the wood, or,
  boldly climbs onto them.
I mustn't move my leg or breathe too deeply – otherwise, she'd scamper off.
But I must continue to write and, for fear she might abandon me to my solitude,
  I scribble signs, I doodle, no matter what, daintily, the way she nibbles.[50]

Renard adjusts his actions to retain the company of the mouse. He "[scribbles] ... [doodles] ... daintily, the way she nibbles," so that the mouse will stay with him. His actions are not what we would usually refer to as ecological; he is not seeking a solution to poor water quality or lack of biodiversity. What he does do is pattern his movements on the movements of the mouse. At the very least, it is a metaphor for ecological engagement. It is not unlike the levitical mirroring of farmer, animal, and field. Leviticus 19:19 enjoins farmers not to "breed mixed animals, sow your field with mixed seed, or wear clothes of mixed fiber." No mules, no hybrid plants, no cotton–polyester blends. The rule is the same whether you are talking about animal husbandry, crop choices, or human clothing; each sphere of life reflects the others, so that human bodies, animal bodies, and plant bodies recall each other. Leviticus 19:9 says not to reap the corners of your field; 19:27 makes the same suggestion for the farmer's hair: "do not trim the corner of your temples; do not cut the corner of your beard." This likeness across "haircuts" establishes a relationship between the farmer and the farmer's land; the farmer's head is like the farmer's field – you cannot look at one without thinking of the other. Leviticus 19 reminds me of a childhood delight in coming to school in an identical outfit as my best friend. The mirroring (both the levitical one and the childhood one) are not embarrassing erasures of the self, but bodily reminders and enactments of relationship. And relationships involve us in responsibilities. If we were to seek the companionship of the ocean with the same dedication as Renard seeks the companionship of the mouse and Leviticus seeks companionship with fields, we could not use them as a dumping site for mining waste, drill oil in areas with vulnerable fish populations, or subjugate large areas of land to monoculture cultivation.[51]

---

[50] Ibid., 101.
[51] It should be noted that monoculture cultivation could be read as in keeping with Leviticus' emphasis on not sowing mixed seeds. Keep in mind, however, that the biblical prophets condemn excessively large fields (see Isaiah 5:8).

In a poem titled "A Family of Trees," Renard wonders what he must do to be adopted by a copse. As with the mouse, he assumes that intimacy will only be possible if he learns from the trees:

It was having crossed a sun-baked field that I encountered them.
...
From afar, they seem impenetrable. As soon as I approach, their trunks separate. They greet me with caution. I can rest, refresh myself, but I sense they're watching me, distrustfully.
They live together as a family, the oldest in the middle, and the little ones, the ones whose first leaves have just been born, just about everywhere, but never too far away.
They take a long time to die, and their dead are left standing till they crumble to dust.
They stroke each other with their long branches, to make sure they are all there, like blind people. They gesticulate angrily if the wind wears itself out attempting to uproot them. But among themselves they never quarrel. They murmur only in agreement.
I feel they should be my real family. I shall quickly forget the other one. Little by little, these trees will adopt me, and to deserve it, I'm learning what I must know:
I know already how to watch the scudding clouds.
I know also how to stay in one place.
And I almost know how to be silent.[52]

Renard's poetic treatment of animals and plants is often described as anthropomorphizing, and justly so. His flowers speak ("THE ROSE: Do you think I'm beautiful? THE HORNET: I'd have to look at your petticoat. THE ROSE: Enter"), and he calls the jay "The Deputy Prefect of the fields."[53] But most of his poems are more subtle than that; though he compares poppies to soldiers, the poem "The Poppies" is a meditation on how poppies, wheat, and cornflowers grow together.[54] The cornflower is the "compatriot" of poppies because they flourish together at the edge of fields, not because Renard imagines them to be human.[55] Describing the trees as a family is only inappropriate if one insists that humans and plants cannot be covered by the same linguistic terms. Recent research in forestry shows that some plants *do* interact as families: they avoid root competition with genetically related plans, and parent plants can

---

[52] Ibid., 167.   [53] Ibid., 117, 151.   [54] Ibid., 120.
[55] Renard is also making a visual pun on the French flag. That fact does not lessen the accuracy of his observation.

recognize their offspring and share nutrients with them through the root system.⁵⁶ Renard is not humanizing trees; instead he attempts to adopt their point of view in order to enter their fellowship. Like biblical writers who observe drought and conclude that the land must be mourning, Renard combines what he can see and experience of trees with his own experiences of belonging. It is an imaginative act whose purpose is to get to know creatures that are not human, to gain their trust. It assumes, like Leviticus' concern for the land's need for sabbath, that nonhuman creatures can welcome or dismiss human presences. In order to be adopted by the land, to gain its acceptance, Israel must "[learn] what [it] must know"; it must become familiar with the land's form of life, and it must respect its needs and obligations. If Israel fails to do so, it will be expelled from the land's company. Both Leviticus and Renard begin with the assumption that the right of welcome belongs to the trees, to the land; if humans are to share life with these creatures, they must pattern their lives on the life of the land.

Renard speaks of nonhuman creatures as persons, but Johanson does not; or, if she does so, she keeps it to herself. Despite this difference, both Renard and Johanson model a minute attention to the world, one that resembles the dependence on close observation in the Bible's personalistic portrayals of nature. They are considerate of the needs, wants, and desires of the varied communities of creatures with whom they share space. The poetry of Renard and the art of Johanson teach us careful, intimate, and engaged interaction with nonhuman creatures, both animal and nonanimal, and do so without requiring that we first acquire a perfect understanding of how animists view the world, or of why the writers of the Bible address mountains and luminaries. They help us on the way to becoming worthy companions for the creatures with whom we live.

Cavell writes of language that it "is not only an acquirement but a bequest; ... we are stingy in what we attempt to inherit."⁵⁷ His statement intimates a kind of mission in our use of language, a political purpose. And he gives us leave to be more greedy, more ambitious. Cavell would have us read poetry, and I second that, but would add that the Bible is another rich source, another inheritance. Reading poetry and participating in art can open our eyes to aspects of the biblical text that have gone unnoticed, can make us hungry for its language. It can make us less

---

⁵⁶ Michael Pollan, "The Intelligent Plant," *The New Yorker*, December 23, 2013, 95; 96; 105, www.newyorker.com/magazine/2013/12/23/the-intelligent-plant.

⁵⁷ Cavell, *The Claim of Reason*, 189.

awkward, less concerned with dignity. Rather than hemming and hawing in embarrassment over the Bible's romping mountains and belligerent rivers, we should wade in with eagerness, ready to receive whatever the Bible, and the world, will grant us.

RELIGIOUS COMMUNITIES AND CLIMATE CHANGE

In *Creation and the Persistence of Evil: The Jewish Drama of Divine Omnipotence*, Jon Levenson writes about aspects of creation that are hostile to humans and the ways in which God restrains them so that we are not destroyed.[58] The sea is kept at bay, locked behind doors or swaddled in swaddling clothes, the Leviathan is broken or domesticated, the foundations of the earth are sunk deep so that its tottering will not be too violent. A precarious balance, a situation in which our dependence on YHWH never diminishes, an ordered world but only just. In a yet to be published article, cultural anthropologist Christine Folch analyzes the rationale for climate change denial in conservative Christian primary and secondary school curriculum. She concludes that climate change is threatening to Evangelical worldviews because it undermines any firm sense of the orderliness of creation and of the place of humanity within it: "Because the earth has been perfectly designed by God for people ... the idea that humans can rupture planetary cycles through their use of resources flies in the face of orderly design."[59] Though I certainly do not wish to add fuel to the fire of climate change denial, it is easy to sympathize with the emotion behind the resistance of Evangelical Christians – it is painful to face the fact that God may leave us to the Leviathan, to the rising oceans, to the hot winds. "Who shut up the sea with doors when it burst forth?" (Job 38:8) ... it is terrifying to think that perhaps this time, the answer is "no one." And emphasizing the personhood of other-than-humans at this point may seem strange. Though humans have set in motion climate change, it is some of the Bible's most powerful other-than-human persons that now threaten to swallow us. Is now really a good time to consider the personhood of the heavens, the earth, and the sea?

---

[58] Jon D. Levenson, *Creation and the Persistence of Evil*.
[59] Christine Folch, "Resisting Climate Change, Learning Skepticism: US Evangelical Science Education and Nature" (Unpublished paper, n.d.).

In Amitav Ghosh's book *The Great Derangement: Climate Change and the Unthinkable*, Ghosh suggests that religious communities have a unique opportunity to lead climate activism. Religious networks are already there, ready to be mobilized, they are cross-national, they recognize "intergenerational, long-term responsibility," and they do not "partake of economists ways of thinking and are therefore capable of imagining nonlinear change."[60] His turn to religious communities makes me blanch – it feels about as realistic as a friend's comment that the church is her best hope for political change in the US, to which my immediate response was "you must not have been to church in a while." Ghosh is not talking about churches specifically, but maybe he is right. Maybe religious communities are the most ready, the most suited to action at this time. For one thing, sticking to communities for whom the Hebrew Bible is Scripture, Christian and Jewish communities know what it is to build futures on slim or nebulous hopes, on the keening yet exhilarating demand that God show up. The anticipation of God's deliverance is always, to some extent, a hope against hope, not a calculation based on political realism, on projections of market economies, or on longitudinal studies. And at our best, we live by those hopes, we shape our life by them. "Even now, an oracle of YHWH, return to me with all your heart, and with fasting, weeping, and lamentations," writes Joel, "tear your hearts, and not your garments, return to YHWH, your God. For he is gracious and compassionate, slow to anger and abounding in faithfulness, and relenting from disaster. Who knows, he might turn and relent, and leave behind him a blessing: a grain offering and drink offering for YHWH, your God" (Joel 2:12–14). Perhaps God will turn, will relent from disaster, and leave behind enough that we may eat and bless, enough that we may again bring the world to God in praise and thanksgiving.

Joel calls for repentance, but repentance has come to sound like an individual matter, a question of being sorry. Even if it is given a more active turn, say, for example, if we try to get church and synagogue attenders to live in smaller houses, drive electric cars, and eat less meat, the focus is still on individual action and responsibilities. This isn't bad – we do need to rethink individual consumption – but it is far from sufficient. In his study of the shift from water to steam in nineteenth century Britain, *Fossil Capital: The Rise of Steam Power and the Roots*

---

[60] Amitav Ghosh, *The Great Derangement: Climate Change and the Unthinkable* (Chicago, IL: University of Chicago Press, 2016), 160.

of Global Warming, Andreas Malm argues that climate change is not the result of human activity in general. Not even Western consumers can shoulder that blame, he says. Climate change is the result of capitalist industry and its imperative to control labor for maximum profit. If carbon dioxide emissions are to go down, corporations need to change: oil companies, mass producers, those who pull the strings of capitalism. This then is the Leviathan against which Ghosh would pit religious communities. The repentance needed is only incidentally about individual behavior, and more about to whom we lend our strength, whether voluntarily or by force. In Isaiah, the rulers of the people boast of a terrible deal: "We have cut a covenant with death, and with Sheol we have made a pact" (Isaiah 28:15). What the leaders hope for is protection from the storm: "When the deluging scourge passes over, it will not come to us." If Malm is right, most of us were never asked if we wanted this deal with death; it was chosen for us. And the deluge is not likely to pass us by if we wait for those in charge to choose responsibility: "As in all crises of capitalism, this one presents a welter of opportunities for those in clover, and *après moi, le deluge*."[61] Repentance in this context will have to look a lot like resistance, a refusal to make covenants with those who would burn our world for money. "Go and stop the smoke!" writes Malm, admitting that this "might seem like an exceedingly improbable event."[62] To do this we will need every resource in our religious traditions. This study highlights only one such resource, the Bible's attention to the lives of persons who are not human, some of which are the very ones now threatening human cities and our fields. We need not only to save ourselves, but all these others, multitudes and multitudes of lives. Some of them might be much better equipped to deal with climate change than we are, and, in moments of despair, it is easy to think that they would be better off without us. But this is not the biblical hope:

> I will make them and the areas around my hill a blessing. I will bring down rain in its time, rains of blessing they will be. The trees of the field will give their fruit and the earth will give its produce and they will be safe upon their soil. And they will know that I am YHWH when I break the bars of their yoke and deliver them from the hand of those who enslave them. (Ezekiel 34:26–27)

---

[61] Andreas Malm, *Fossil Capital: The Rise of Steam-Power and the Roots of Global Warming* (London: Verso, 2016), 391.
[62] Ibid., 394.

THE PROMISE OF DELIGHT

The personalistic portrayals of fields and rivers in the Hebrew Bible hold out the promise that if we look hard enough, we might find companions and friends all around us. We might find ourselves adopted by trees. It is a promise of enjoyment, of new relationships. Timothy Morton criticizes the tendency of ecological discourse to focus on limits to the exclusion of pleasure:

> [W]hat bothers me is that the language of limits edits questions of pleasure and enjoyment out of the ecological picture ... If interconnectedness implies radical intimacy with other beings, then we had better start thinking about pleasure as a coordinate of the ecological thought. We must take a new path, into the vast mesh of interconnection. Who lives there?[63]

The world is not a complicated but mute machine whose workings humans must attend to in order not to overtax or break it. The world is full of persons, only some of whom are humans; attention might lead to interaction, friendship, conversation. Wendell Berry writes that "The *primary* motive for good care and good use is always going to be affection, because affection involves us entirely."[64] What personalistic nature texts suggest is that human affection towards the land will be met with affection in return. Isaiah promises Israel that mountains and trees will celebrate the return of the exiles: "The mountains and hills will break into song before you, and all the trees of the field will clap their hands" (Isaiah 55:12). At a time when humanity looks like a burden that the rest of creation must bear, the idea of trees and hills rejoicing at the return of a people is both strange and breathtaking. It hints at the pleasure of shared life, of friends meeting after a long time apart, of renewed intimacy after a period of alienation. Linda Hogan writes about her experience of being loved by the world:

> Some of the religious say the five senses are thieves
> So let's say I am stolen
> Because my senses are all awake
> And like the tree I can lose myself
> Layer after layer
> All the way down to infinity
> And that's when the world has eyes and sees.
> The whole world loves the unlayered human.[65]

---

[63] Timothy Morton, *The Ecological Thought* (Cambridge, MA: Harvard University Press, 2010), 37.
[64] Berry, *It All Turns on Affection*, 32–33. Emphasis in the original.
[65] Linda Hogan, excerpt from "Eucalyptus" in *Dark. Sweet.: New & Selected Poems*. Copyright (c) 2014 by Linda Hogan. Reprinted with the permission of The Permission Company, Inc. on behalf of Coffee House Press, www.coffeehousepress.org.

Hogan describes herself as "stolen," the passive verb here referring to a sort of sensual self-abandonment, but also to being the object of theft – someone else is acting. This act of "[losing]" herself, she claims, is not a one-directional, esthetic enjoyment of a world that can say nothing in return. "The whole world loves the unlayered human," she promises, an invitation to anyone who will follow her. Personalistic nature texts suggest that one reason to pursue ecological justice is that, by our actions, we might gain the welcome of other-than-human persons. We might be able to say, with Isaiah, "the wilderness and the dry land will exult, the desert will rejoice and blossom like the crocus. It will bloom abundantly, and rejoice with joy and jubilation" (Isaiah 35:1). Personalistic nature texts hold out the promise that if we pay attention, if we act with circumspection, respect, and love, we might be met by a host of friends, a community that extends beyond our humanness, beyond our limited knowledge.

Bibliography

Abusch, Tzvi. "The Socio-Religious Framework of the Babylonian Witchcraft Ceremony Maqlû: Some Observations on the Introductory Section of Text, Part I." In *Riches Hidden in Secret Places: Ancient Near Eastern Studies in Memory of Thorkild Jacobsen*, edited by I. Tzvi Abusch and Thorkild Jacobsen, 1–34. Winona Lake, IN: Eisenbrauns, 2002.
Ackermann, O., H. J. Bruins, and A. M. Maeir. "A Unique Human-Made Trench at Tell Eṣ-Ṣâfī/Gath: Anthropogenic Impact and Landscape Response." *Geoarchaeology* 20, no. 3 (2005): 303–27.
Alter, Robert. *Strong as Death Is Love: The Song of Songs, Ruth, Esther, Jonah, and Daniel: A Translation with Commentary*. New York: W. W. Norton & Company, 2015.
   The Book of Psalms: A Translation with Commentary. New York: W. W. Norton & Company, 2007.
Andersen, Francis I. *Habakkuk: A New Translation with Introduction and Commentary*. New York: Doubleday, 2001.
Andersen, Francis I., and David Noel Freedman. *Amos: A New Translation with Introduction Notes and Commentary*. The Anchor Bible 24A. New York: Doubleday, 1989.
Anderson, A. A. *2 Samuel*. Dallas, TX: Word Books, 1989.
Anderson, Bernhard W. *Creation versus Chaos: The Reinterpretation of Mythical Symbolism in the Bible*. New York: Association Press, 1967.
André, Gunnel. "Deuterojesaja Och Jobsboken: En Jämförande Studie." *Svensk Exegetisk Årsbok* 54 (1989): 33–42.
Arneth, Martin. *Durch Adams Fall Ist Ganz Verderbt . . . : Studien Zur Entstehung Der Alttestamentlichen Urgeschichte*. Göttingen: Vandenhoeck & Ruprecht, 2007.
Arnold, Bill T. *Genesis*. Cambridge: Cambridge University Press, 2009.
Barbour, Jennifer. *The Story of Israel in the Book of Qohelet: Ecclesiastes as Cultural Memory*. Oxford: Oxford University Press, 2012.

Barker, Margaret. *Creation: A Biblical Vision for the Environment.* London: T & T Clark, 2010.
Barr, James. *Biblical Faith and Natural Theology: The Gifford Lectures for 1991, Delivered in the University of Edinburgh.* Oxford: Clarendon Press, 1993.
——— "Man and Nature: The Ecological Controversy and the Old Testament." In *Ecology and Religion in History*, edited by David Spring and Eileen Spring, 48–75. New York: Harper and Row, 1974.
——— "Revelation through History in the Old Testament and in Modern Theology." *Interpretation* 17 (1963): 193–205.
Barth, Karl. *Church Dogmatics.* Edited by Thomas F. Torrance and G. W. Bromiley. Translated by G. W. Bromiley. Vol. 1 & 2. Peabody, MA: Hendrickson, 2010.
Barton, John. "Reading the Prophets from an Environmental Perspective." In *Ecological Hermeneutics: Biblical, Historical and Theological Perspectives*, edited by David G. Horrell, Cherryl Hunt, Christopher Southgate, and Francesca Stavrakopoulou, 46–55. London: T & T Clark, 2010.
Basso, Keith H. *Wisdom Sits in Places: Landscape and Language among the Western Apache.* Albuquerque: University of New Mexico Press, 1996.
Bastiaens, Jean. "The Language of Suffering in Job 16–19 and in the Suffering Servant Passages in Deutero-Isaiah." In *Studies in the Book of Isaiah: Festschrift Willem A M Beuken*, edited by M. Vervenne and J. Van Ruiten, 421–32. Louvain: Leuven University Press, 1997.
Bauckham, Richard. *Bible and Ecology: Rediscovering the Community of Creation.* London: Darton, Longman & Todd, 2010.
——— *Living with Other Creatures: Green Exegesis and Theology.* Waco, TX: Baylor University Press, 2011.
Bennett, Jane. *Vibrant Matter: A Political Ecology of Things.* Durham: Duke University Press, 2010.
Berger, John. *A Fortunate Man.* New York: Pantheon Books, 1982.
Berkhof, H., and Hans-Joachim Kraus. *Karl Barths Lichterlehre.* Zürich: Theologischer Verlag, 1978.
Berlin, Adele, Marc Zvi Brettler, and Michael A. Fishbane, eds. *The Jewish Study Bible.* New York: Oxford University Press, 2004.
Berry, Wendell. *It All Turns on Affection: The Jefferson Lecture and Other Essays.* New York: Counterpoint, 2012.
——— "Whose Head Is the Farmer Using? Whose Head Is Using the Farmer?" In *Meeting the Expectations of the Land: Essays in Sustainable Agriculture and Stewardship*, edited by Wes Jackson, Wendell Berry, and Bruce Colman, 19–41. San Francisco: North Point, 1984.
Bird-David, Nurit. "'Animism' Revisited: Personhood, Environment, and Relational Epistemology." *Current Anthropology* 40, no. S1 (1999): S67–91.
Bleibtreu, Erika. "Five Ways to Conquer a City." *Biblical Archaeology Review* 16, no. 3 (1990): 37–44.
Blenkinsopp, Joseph. "Creation, the Body, and Care for a Damaged World." In *Treasures Old and New: Essays in the Theology of the Pentateuch*, 36–54. Grand Rapids, MI: William B. Eerdmans, 2004.

Gibeon and Israel: The Role of Gibeon and the Gibeonites in the Political and Religious History of Early Israel. Cambridge: Cambridge University Press, 1972.

Isaiah 40–55: A New Translation with Introduction and Commentary. New York: Doubleday, 2000.

Bloch, Ariel A., and Chana Bloch. *The Song of Songs: A New Translation with an Introduction and Commentary.* Berkeley: University of California Press, 1998.

Blocher, Henri. *In the Beginning: The Opening Chapters of Genesis.* Leicester: Inter-Varsity, 1984.

Boda, Mark J. *The Book of Zechariah.* Grand Rapids, MI: William B. Eerdmans, 2016.

Boer, Roland. "Keeping It Literal: The Economy of the Song of Songs." *The Journal of Hebrew Scriptures* 7 (2007).

Boling, Robert G. *Joshua: A New Translation.* Garden City, NY: Doubleday, 1982.

Bonhoeffer, Dietrich. *Creation and Fall: A Theological Exposition of Genesis 1–3.* Edited by Martin Rüter, Ilse Tödt, and John W. de Gruchy. Translated by Douglas S. Bax. Vol. 3. *Dietrich Bonhoeffer Works.* Minneapolis: Fortress, 1997.

Brenner, Athalya. "The Food of Love: Gendered Food and Food Imagery in the Song of Songs." *Semeia* 86 (1999): 101–12.

Brichto, Herbert Chanan. *The Names of God: Poetic Readings in Biblical Beginnings.* New York: Oxford University Press, 1998.

Brown, Francis F., Charles A. Briggs, S. R. Driver, and Wilhelm Gesenius. *The Brown-Driver-Briggs Hebrew and English Lexicon.* Peabody, MA: Hendrickson, 1996.

Brown, William P. *Seeing the Psalms: A Theology of Metaphor.* Louisville, KY: Westminster John Knox, 2002.

The Ethos of the Cosmos: The Genesis of Moral Imagination in the Bible. Grand Rapids, MI: William B. Eerdmans, 1999.

The Seven Pillars of Creation: The Bible, Science, and the Ecology of Wonder. Oxford; New York: Oxford University Press, 2010.

Brueggemann, Walter. *To Pluck up, to Tear down: A Commentary on the Book of Jeremiah 1–25.* Grand Rapids, MI: William B. Eerdmans; Handsel, 1988.

Buber, Martin. *I and Thou.* Translated by Ronald Gregor Smith. Edinburgh: T. & T. Clark, 1950.

Carley, Keith. "Ezekiel's Formula of Desolation: Harsh Justice for the Land/Earth." In *The Earth Story in Psalms and Prophets*, edited by Norman C. Habel, 143–57. The Earth Bible 4. Sheffield: Sheffield Academic, 2001.

Carroll, Robert P. *Jeremiah: A Commentary.* Philadelphia, PA: Westminster, 1986.

Cassuto, Umberto. *A Commentary on the Book of Genesis.* Jerusalem: Magnes, Hebrew University, 1961.

Biblical and Oriental Studies. Vol. 2. Jerusalem: Magnes, Hebrew University, 1973.

Cavell, Stanley. *The Claim of Reason: Wittgenstein, Skepticism, Morality, and Tragedy*. New York: Oxford University Press, 1999.
Childs, Brevard S. *Isaiah*. 1st ed. Louisville, KY: Westminster John Knox, 2001.
The Book of Exodus; a Critical, Theological Commentary. Philadelphia, PA: Westminster, 1974.
Cho, Eun Suk. "Creation in the Book of Job: An Exegetical Essay on Job 3 from a Korean Perspective." *The Asia Journal of Theology* 17, no. 1 (April 2003): 26–76.
Clines, David J. A. *Job 1–20*. Word Biblical Commentary. Waco, TX: Word Books, 1989.
Job 21–37. Word Biblical Commentary. Nashville, TN: Thomas Nelson, 2006.
Job 38–42. Word Biblical Commentary 18B. Nashville, TN: Thomas Nelson, 2011.
"Tree of Knowledge and the Law of Yahweh, Psalm 19." *Vetus Testamentum* 24, no. 1 (January 1974): 8–14.
Coad, Dominic. "Creation's Praise of God: A Proposal for a Theology of the Non-Human Creation." *Theology* 112, no. 867 (May 1, 2009): 181–89.
Coats, George W. *Rebellion in the Wilderness; the Murmuring Motif in the Wilderness, Traditions of the Old Testament*. Nashville, TN: Abingdon, 1968.
Cohen, Jeffrey Jerome. *Stone: An Ecology of the Inhuman*. Minneapolis, MN: University of Minnesota Press, 2015.
Collins, Billie Jean. "Necromancy, Fertility and the Dark Earth: The Use of Ritual Pits in Hittite Cult." In *Magic and Ritual in the Ancient World*, edited by Paul Mirecki and Marvin Meyer, 224–41. Leiden: E. J. Brill, 2002.
"Purifying a House: A Ritual for the Infernal Deities (1.68)." In *The Context of Scripture: Vol. 1: Canonical Compositions from the Biblical World*, edited by William W. Hallo and K. Lawson Younger, 168–71. Leiden: Brill, 2003.
Cooley, Jeffrey L. *Poetic Astronomy in the Ancient Near East: The Reflexes of Celestial Science in Ancient Mesopotamian, Ugaritic, and Israelite Narrative*. History, Archaeology, and Culture of the Levant 5. Winona Lake, IN: Eisenbrauns, 2013.
"Psalm 19: A Sabbath Song." *Vetus Testamentum* 64, no. 2 (2014): 177–95.
Coote, Robert B. "Psalm 19: Heavenly Law and Order." In *From Biblical Interpretation to Human Transformation: Reopening the Past to Actualize New Possibilities for the Future. A Festschrift Honoring Herman C. Waetjen*, edited by Douglas R. McGaughey and Cornelia Cyss Crocker. Salem, MA: Chora Strangers, 2006.
Crenshaw, James L. *Joel: A New Translation with Introduction and Commentary*. New York: Doubleday, 1995.
Reading Job: A Literary and Theological Commentary. Macon, GA: Smyth & Helwys, 2011.
Cross, Frank Moore. *Canaanite Myth and Hebrew Epic: Essays in the History of the Religion of Israel*. Cambridge, MA: Harvard University Press, 1973.

"Song of the Sea and Canaanite Myth." In *Canaanite Myth and Hebrew Epic: Essays in the History of the Religion of Israel*, 1–25. Cambridge, MA: Harvard University Press, 1973.

"The Council of Yahweh in Second Isaiah." *Journal of Near Eastern Studies* 12, no. 4 (October 1, 1953): 274–77.

Culler, Jonathan. "Apostrophe." In *The Pursuit of Signs: Semiotics, Literature, Deconstruction*, An Augmented Edition, 135–54. Ithaca, NY: Cornell University Press, 2001.

Dahood, Mitchell J. *Psalms. The Anchor Bible*. Garden City, NY: Doubleday, 1966.

Daniels, Dwight R. "Is There a 'Prophetic Lawsuit' Genre." *Zeitschrift Für Die Alttestamentliche Wissenschaft* 99, no. 3 (January 1, 1987): 339–60.

Davidson, Richard M. "The Divine Covenant Lawsuit Motif in Canonical Perspective." *Journal of the Adventist Theological Society* 21, no. 1–2 (January 1, 2010): 45–84.

Davis, Ellen F. *Biblical Prophecy: Perspectives for Christian Theology, Discipleship, and Ministry*. Louisville, KY: Westminster John Knox, 2014.

"The Pain of Seeing Clearly: Prophetic Views of the Created Order." In *Biblical Prophecy: Perspectives for Contemporary Ministry*, 83–110. Interpretation: Resources for the Use of Scripture in the Church. Louisville, KY: Westminster John Knox, 2014.

Proverbs, Ecclesiastes, and the Song of Songs. Louisville, KY: Westminster John Knox, 2000.

"Reading the Song Iconographically." In *Scrolls of Love: Ruth and the Song of Songs*, edited by Peter S. Hawkins and Lesleigh Cushing Stahlberg, 172–84. New York: Fordham University Press, 2006.

Scripture, Culture, and Agriculture: An Agrarian Reading of the Bible. Cambridge: Cambridge University Press, 2009.

Day, John. *God's Conflict with the Dragon and the Sea: Echoes of a Canaanite Myth in the Old Testament*. Cambridge; New York: Cambridge University Press, 1985.

DeClaissé-Walford, Nancy L., Rolf A. Jacobson, and Beth LaNeel Tanner. *The Book of Psalms*. Grand Rapids, MI: William B. Eerdmans, 2014.

Delcor, M. "Les Attaches Litteraires, l'origine et La Signification de l'expression Biblique 'Prendre a Temoin Le Ciel et La Terre.'" *Vetus Testamentum* 16, no. 1 (January 1, 1966): 8–25.

Deloria, Vine. *God Is Red: A Native View of Religion*. Golden, CO: Fulcrum, 1994.

Deloria, Vine, Jr., and Daniel Wildcat. *Power and Place: Indian Education in America*. Golden, CO: Fulcrum, 2001.

DeRoche, Michael. "Yahweh's Rîb against Israel: A Reassessment of the so-Called 'Prophetic Lawsuit' in the Preexilic Prophets." *Journal of Biblical Literature* 102, no. 4 (December 1, 1983): 563–74.

Descola, Philippe. *Beyond Nature and Culture*. Translated by Janet Lloyd. Chicago, IL: University of Chicago Press, 2013.

The Ecology of Others. Translated by Geneviève Godbout and Benjamin P. Luley. Paradigm 42. Chicago, IL: Prickly Paradigm, 2013.

Diamond, Cora. "Losing Your Concepts." *Ethics* 98, no. 2 (1988): 255–77.
Dick, Michael B. "Job 31, the Oath of Innocence, and the Sage." *Zeitschrift Für Die Alttestamentliche Wissenschaft* 95, no. 1 (1983): 31–53.
Dillard, Annie. "Teaching a Stone to Talk." In *Teaching a Stone to Talk: Expeditions and Encounters*, 85–94. New York: Harper & Row, 1982.
Doak, Brian. *Consider Leviathan: Narratives of Nature and Self in Job*. Minneapolis, MN: Fortress, 2014.
Douglas, Mary. *Leviticus as Literature. Oxford*. New York: Oxford University Press, 1999.
Dozeman, Thomas B. *Joshua 1–12: A New Translation with Introduction and Commentary*. New Haven, CT: Yale University Press, 2015.
Driver, S. R. *A Critical and Exegetical Commentary on Deuteronomy*. The International Critical Commentary. Edinburgh: T. & T. Clark, 1902.
Ebach, Jürgen. *Genesis 37–50*. Freiburg: Herder, 2007.
Eph'al, Israel. *The City Besieged: Siege and Its Manifestations in the Ancient Near East*. Jerusalem: Hebrew University Magnes, 2013.
Erdrich, Louise. *Books and Islands in Ojibwe Country*. Washington, DC: National Geographic, 2003.
Exum, J. Cheryl. *The Song of Songs: A Commentary*. Louisville, KY: Westminster John Knox, 2005.
Feder, Yitzhaq. *Blood Expiation in Hittite and Biblical Ritual: Origins, Context, and Meaning*. Writings from the Ancient World Supplements 2. Atlanta, GA: Society of Biblical Literature, 2011.
Fisch, Harold. "Analogy of Nature: A Note on the Structure of Old Testament Imagery." *The Journal of Theological Studies* 6, no. 2 (October 1955): 161–73.
Fisk, Bruce N. "Gaps in the Story, Cracks in the Earth: The Exile of Cain and the Destruction of Korah in Pseudo-Philo (Liber Antiquitatum Biblicarum)." In *Of Scribes and Sages Volume 2, Later Versions and Traditions*, edited by Craig A. Evans, 20–33. London: T&T Clark International, 2004.
Fohrer, Georg. "The Righteous Man in Job 31." In *Essays in Old Testament Ethics: (J Philip Hyatt, in Memoriam)*, 1–22. New York: Ktav, 1974.
Folch, Christine. "Resisting Climate Change, Learning Skepticism: US Evangelical Science Education and Nature." Unpublished paper, n.d.
Fox, Michael V. *The Song of Songs and the Ancient Egyptian Love Songs*. Madison, WI: University of Wisconsin Press, 1985.
Frazer, James George. *The Golden Bough: A Study in Magic and Religion*. Vol. 11. London: MacMillan and Co., 1925.
Fretheim, Terence E. *Creation, Fall, and Flood: Studies in Genesis 1–11*. Minneapolis, MN: Augsburg, 1969.
   Creation Untamed: The Bible, God, and Natural Disasters. Grand Rapids, MI: Baker Academic, 2010.
   God and World in the Old Testament: A Relational Theology of Creation. Nashville, TN: Abingdon, 2005.
   Jeremiah. Macon, GA: Smith & Helwys, 2002.

"Nature's Praise of God." In *God and the World in the Old Testament: A Relational Theology of Creation*, 249–68. Nashville, TN: Abingdon, 2005.

Reading Hosea-Micah: A Literary and Theological Commentary. Macon, GA: Smyth & Helwys, 2013.

"The Plagues as Ecological Signs of Historical Disaster." *Journal of Biblical Literature* 110, no. 3 (1991): 385–96.

Frymer-Kensky, Tikva Simone. *In the Wake of the Goddesses: Women, Culture, and the Biblical Transformation of Pagan Myth*. New York: Free, 1992.

Galambush, Julie. "God's Land and Mine: Creation as Property in the Book of Ezekiel." In *Ezekiel's Hierarchical World: Wrestling with a Tiered Reality*, 91–108. Atlanta, GA: Society of Biblical Literature, 2004.

Garuba, Harry. "Explorations in Animist Materialism: Notes on Reading/Writing African Literature, Culture, and Society." *Public Culture* 15, no. 2 (2003): 261–85.

Gaster, Theodor H. "A Canaanite Magical Text." *Orientalia* 11 (1942): 41–79.

Gell, Alfred. *Art and Agency: An Anthropological Theory*. Oxford: Clarendon Press, 1998.

Geller, Markham J. *Healing Magic and Evil Demons: Canonical Udug-Hul Incantations*. Berlin: De Gruyter, 2015.

Gesenius, Wilhelm. *Gesenius' Hebrew Grammar*. Edited by E. Kautzsch. Oxford: The Clarendon, 1910.

Ghosh, Amitav. *The Great Derangement: Climate Change and the Unthinkable*. Chicago, IL: University of Chicago Press, 2016.

Glucklich, Ariel. *The End of Magic*. Oxford: Oxford University Press, 1997.

Goldingay, John. *The Message of Isaiah 40–55: A Literary-Theological Commentary*. London: T&T Clark, 2005.

Goldingay, John, and David F. Payne. *A Critical and Exegetical Commentary on Isaiah 40–55*. Vol. II. London: T&T Clark, 2006.

Gottlieb, Fred. "The Creation Theme in Genesis 1, Psalm 104 and Job 38–42." *Jewish Bible Quarterly* 44, no. 1 (January 2016): 29–36.

Greenberg, Moshe. *Ezekiel 1–20: A New Translation with Introduction and Commentary*. Garden City, NY: Doubleday, 1995.

Ezekiel 21–37: A New Translation with Introduction and Commentary. New York: Doubleday, 1997.

Gunkel, Hermann. *Ausgewählte Psalmen*. 4. verb. Aufl. Göttingen: Vandenhoeck & Ruprecht, 1917.

Creation and Chaos in the Primeval Era and the Eschaton: A Religio-Historical Study of Genesis 1 and Revelation 12. Translated by K. William Whitney Jr. Grand Rapids, MI: William B. Eerdmans, 2006.

Gunkel, Hermann, and Joachim Begrich. *Einleitung in Die Psalmen. Die Gattungen Der Religiösen Lyrik Isaraels*. 2. Aufl. Götttingen: Vandenhoeck u. Ruprecht, 1966.

Guthrie, Stewart. *Faces in the Clouds: A New Theory of Religion*. New York: Oxford University Press, 1993.

Habel, Norman C., ed. *Readings from the Perspective of Earth*. Sheffield: Sheffield Academic, 2000.

The Birth, the Curse and the Greening of Earth: An Ecological Reading of Genesis 1–11. Sheffield: Sheffield Phoenix, 2011.
The Book of Job: A Commentary. Philadelphia, PA: Westminster, 1985.
"The Silence of the Lands: The Ecojustice Implications of Ezekiel's Judgment Oracles." In *Ezekiel's Hierarchical World: Wrestling with a Tiered Reality*, 127–40. Atlanta, GA: Society of Biblical Literature, 2004.
Habel, Norman C., and Geraldine Avent. "Rescuing Earth from a Storm God: Psalms 29 and 96–97." In *The Earth Story in the Psalms and the Prophets*, edited by Norman C. Habel, 42–50. The Earth Bible 4. Sheffield: Sheffield Academic, 2001.
Hägerstrand, Torsten. "Geography and the Study of Interaction between Nature and Society." *Geoforum* 7 (1976): 329–34.
Ḥakham, 'Amos. *The Bible: Psalms with the Jerusalem Commentary*. Edited by Israel V. Berman. Vol. 1. Jerusalem: Mosad Harav Kook, 2003.
Hallowell, A. Irving. "Ojibwa Ontology, Behavior, and World View." In *Readings in Indigenous Religions*, edited by Graham Harvey, 18–49. London: Continuum, 2002.
Hamilton, Victor P. *The Book of Genesis: Chapters 18–50*. Grand Rapids, MI: William B. Eerdmans, 1995.
Harman, Graham. *Tool-Being: Heidegger and the Metaphysics of Objects*. Chicago, IL: Open Court, 2002.
Harvey, Graham. *Animism: Respecting the Living World*. London: Hurst & Co., 2005.
Hayes, Katherine Murphey. *The Earth Mourns: Prophetic Metaphor and Oral Aesthetic*. Atlanta, GA: Society of Biblical Literature, 2002.
Hegel, Georg Wilhelm Friedrich. *Lectures on the Philosophy of Religion*. Translated by Peter Crafts Hodgson and J. M. Stewart. Vol. I. Berkeley, CA: University of California Press, 1984.
Hiebert, Theodore. *God of My Victory: The Ancient Hymn in Habakkuk 3*. Atlanta, GA: Scholars, 1986.
The Yahwist's Landscape: Nature and Religion in Early Israel. New York: Oxford University Press, 1996.
Hillel, Daniel. *The Natural History of the Bible: An Environmental Exploration of the Hebrew Scriptures*. New York: Columbia University Press, 2006.
Hillers, Delbert R. "Roads to Zion Mourn (Lam 1:4)." *Perspective* 12, no. 1–2 (1971): 121–34.
Hogan, Linda. *Dwellings: A Spiritual History of the Living World*. New York: W. W. Norton & Company, 1995.
Dark. Sweet.: New & Selected Poems. Minneapolis, MN: Coffee House, 2014.
Holbert, John C. "The Rehabilitation of the Sinner: The Function of Job 29–31." *Zeitschrift Für Die Alttestamentliche Wissenschaft* 95, no. 2 (1983): 229–37.
Hom, Mary Katherine. "A Day like No Other: A Discussion of Joshua 10:12–14." *The Expository Times* 115, no. 7 (April 2004): 217–23.
Hornborg, Anne-Christine. *Mi'kmaq Landscapes: From Animism to Sacred Ecology*. Aldershot: Ashgate, 2008.

Houston, Walter J. "Towards an Integrated Reading of the Dietary Laws of Leviticus." In *The Book of Leviticus: Composition and Reception*, 142–61. Leiden: Brill, 2003.
Huffmon, Herbert B. "Covenant Lawsuit in the Prophets." *Journal of Biblical Literature* 78, no. 4 (December 1, 1959): 285–95.
Ingold, Tim. *Being Alive: Essays on Movement, Knowledge and Description*. London: Routledge, 2011.
——— "Being Alive to a World Without Objects." In *The Handbook of Contemporary Animism*, edited by Graham Harvey, 213–25. Durham: Acumen, 2013.
Jackson, Wes. *Becoming Native to This Place*. The Blazer Lectures. Lexington, KY: University Press of Kentucky, 1994.
Jackson, Wes, Wendell Berry, and Bruce Colman. *Meeting the Expectations of the Land: Essays in Sustainable Agriculture and Stewardship*. San Francisco: North Point, 1984.
James, Elaine T. *Landscapes of the Song of Songs: Poetry and Place*. New York, NY: Oxford University Press, 2017.
James, P. D. *The Private Patient*. New York: Alfred A. Knopf, 2008.
Janzen, J. Gerald. *Abraham and All the Families of the Earth: A Commentary on the Book of Genesis 12–50*. Grand Rapids, MI: William B. Eerdmans, 1993.
Jeremias, Jörg. *Theophanie: Die Geschichte Einer Alttestamentlichen Gattung*. Neukirchen-Vluyn: Neukirchener Verlag des Erziehungsvereins, 1965.
Jørstad, Hanne, and Christian Webersik. "Vulnerability to Climate Change and Adaptation Strategies of Local Communities in Malawi: Experiences of Women Fish-Processing Groups in the Lake Chilwa Basin." *Earth System Dynamics* 7 (2016): 977–89.
Kaiser, Otto. *Isaiah 1–12: A Commentary*. 2nd ed. Philadelphia, PA: Westminster, 1983.
Kawashima, Robert S. *Biblical Narrative and the Death of the Rhapsode*. Bloomington, IN: Indiana University Press, 2004.
Kay, Jeanne. "Human Dominion over Nature in the Hebrew Bible." *Annals of the Association of American Geographers* 79, no. 2 (June 1989): 214–32.
Kelle, Brad E. "Dealing with the Trauma of Defeat: The Rhetoric of the Devastation and Rejuvenation of Nature in Ezekiel." *Journal of Biblical Literature* 128, no. 3 (September 2009): 469–90.
Kelley, Caffyn. *Art and Survival: Patricia Johanson's Environmental Projects*. Salt Spring Island, BC: Islands Institute, 2006.
Kloos, Carola. *Yhwh's Combat with the Sea: A Canaanite Tradition in the Religion of Ancient Israel*. Amsterdam: G. A. van Oorschot, 1986.
Knierim, Rolf P., and George W. Coats. *Numbers*. The Forms of the Old Testament Literature 4. Grand Rapids, MI: William B. Eerdmans, 2005.
Koch, Klaus. "The Old Testament View of Nature." *Anticipation* 25 (January 1979): 47–52.
Köhler, Ludwig. *Vom Hebräischen Lexikon*. Leiden: E. J. Brill, 1950.
Köhler, Ludwig, and Walter Baumgartner. *The Hebrew and Aramaic Lexicon of the Old Testament*. Leiden: E. J. Brill, 1994.

Kraus, Hans-Joachim, and Hilton C. Oswald. *Psalms 60–150*. Minneapolis, MN: Ausburg Fortress, 1989.
Kriegs, Jan Ole, Gennady Churakov, Martin Kiefmann, Ursula Jordan, Jürgen Brosius, and Jürgen Schmitz. "Retroposed Elements as Archives for the Evolutionary History of Placental Mammals." *PLOS Biology* 4, no. 4 (March 14, 2006): e91.
LaDuke, Winona. *All Our Relations: Native Struggles for Land and Life*. Cambridge, MA: South End, 1999.
Landy, Francis. *Paradoxes of Paradise: Identity and Difference in the Song of Songs*. Sheffield: Almond, 1983.
Laroche, Emmanuel. *Catalogue Des Textes Hittites*. Paris: Klincksieck, 1971.
Latour, Bruno. *We Have Never Been Modern*, translated by Catherine Porter. Cambridge, MA: Harvard University Press, 1993.
Leveen, Adriane. *Memory and Tradition in the Book of Numbers*. New York: Cambridge University Press, 2008.
Levenson, Jon D. *Creation and the Persistence of Evil: The Jewish Drama of Divine Omnipotence*. Princeton, NJ: Princeton University Press, 1994.
   Resurrection and the Restoration of Israel: The Ultimate Victory of the God of Life. New Haven, CT: Yale University Press, 2006.
   "The Theologies of Commandment in Biblical Israel." *The Harvard Theological Review* 73, no. 1/2 (1980): 17–33.
   "Who Inserted the Book of the Torah." *Harvard Theological Review* 68, no. 3–4 (July 1975): 203–33.
Levi, Primo. *"If This Is a Man" and "The Truce."* Harmondsworth: Penguin Books, 1979.
Levine, Baruch A. *Numbers 1–20: A New Translation with Introduction and Commentary*. New York: Doubleday, 1993.
   Numbers 21–36: A New Translation with Introduction and Commentary. New York: Doubleday, 2000.
Lichtenstein, M. "Biblical Poetry." In *Back to the Sources: Reading the Classic Jewish Texts*, edited by Barry W. Holtz, 105–28. New York: Summit Books, 1984.
Linafelt, Tod. "Private Poetry and Public Eloquence in 2 Samuel 1:17–27: Hearing and Overhearing David's Lament for Jonathan and Saul." *The Journal of Religion* 88, no. 4 (October 2008): 497–526.
Lindell, Kristina. "Himmelens Andar." In *Kammu - Om Ett Folk i Laos*, edited by Håkan Lundström and Jan-Olof Svantesson, 40–48. Lund: Lunds universitetshistoriska sällskap, 2006.
Loader, James Alfred. "What Do the Heavens Declare? On the Old Testament Motif of God's Beauty in Creation." *HTS Theologiese Studies* 67, no. 3 (2011): 1–8.
Lohfink, Norbert. "The Strata of the Pentateuch and the Question of War." In *Theology of the Pentateuch: Themes of the Priestly Narrative and Deuteronomy*, translated by Linda M. Maloney, 173–226. Minneapolis, MN: Fortress, 1994.
Lubbock, John. *The Origin of Civilization and the Primitive Condition of Man: Mental and Social Condition of Savages*. New York: D. Appleton and Company, 1874.

Lundbom, Jack R. *Jeremiah: A New Translation with Introduction and Commentary.* New York: Doubleday, 1999.
  The Hebrew Prophets: An Introduction. Minneapolis, MN: Fortress, 2010.
Lyons, Michael A. *From Law to Prophecy: Ezekiel's Use of the Holiness Code.* New York: T & T Clark, 2009.
MacEwen, Gwendolyn. *The Selected Gwendolyn MacEwen.* Toronto: Exile Editions, 2007.
Malm, Andreas. *Fossil Capital: The Rise of Steam-Power and the Roots of Global Warming.* London: Verso, 2016.
Marlow, Hilary. *Biblical Prophets and Contemporary Environmental Ethics: Re-Reading Amos, Hosea, and First Isaiah.* Oxford: Oxford University Press, 2009.
McCarter, P. Kyle. *II Samuel: A New Translation with Introduction, Notes, and Commentary.* Garden City, NY: Doubleday, 1984.
Mendenhall, George E. *Law and Covenant in Israel and the Ancient Near East.* Pittsburgh, PA: Biblical Colloquium, 1955.
Merwe, Christo H J van der. "Lexical Meaning in Biblical Hebrew and Cognitive Semantics: A Case Study." *Biblica* 87, no. 1 (2006): 85–95.
Meyers, Carol. "Food and the First Family: A Socioeconomic Perspective." In *The Book of Genesis: Composition, Reception, and Interpretation*, edited by Craig A. Evans, Joel N. Lohr, and David L. Petersen, 137–57. Leiden: Brill, 2012.
Meyers, Carol L. *Exodus.* Cambridge: Cambridge University Press, 2005.
Meyers, Carol L., and Eric M. Meyers. *Haggai; Zechariah 1–8: A New Translation with Introduction and Commentary.* The Anchor Bible 25B. Garden City, NY: Doubleday, 1987.
  Zechariah 9–14: A New Translation with Introduction and Commentary. New York: Doubleday, 1993.
Michael, Matthew. "Twilight of the Gods: Hidden Polemics in Joshua 10:12–14." *Hebrew Studies* 55 (2014): 59–72.
Middleton, J. Richard. *A New Heaven and a New Earth: Reclaiming Biblical Eschatology.* Grand Rapids, MI: Baker Academic, 2014.
  The Liberating Image: The Imago Dei in Genesis 1. Grand Rapids, MI: Brazos, 2005.
Midrash Tanhuma (cp. Edition). New York: Horeb, 1934.
Milgrom, Jacob. "Leviticus 26 and Ezekiel." In *The Quest for Context and Meaning: Studies in Biblical Intertextuality in Honor of James A. Sanders*, edited by Craig A. Evans and Shemaryahu Talmon, 57–62. Leiden: Brill, 1997.
  Leviticus: A New Translation with Introduction and Commentary. New York: Doubleday, 1991.
  Numbers = [Ba-Midbar]: The Traditional Hebrew Text with the New JPS Translation. Philadelphia, PA: Jewish Publication Society, 1990.
Miller, Patrick D. "Prayer and Divine Action." In *God in the Fray: A Tribute to Walter Brueggemann*, 211–32. Minneapolis, MN: Fortress, 1998.
Mitchell, W. J. T. *Picture Theory: Essays on Verbal and Visual Representation.* Chicago, IL: University of Chicago Press, 1995.

Morgan, Jonathan. "Land, Rest & Sacrifice: Ecological Reflections on the Book of Leviticus," 2010. https://ore.exeter.ac.uk/repository/handle/10036/119945.
"Sacrifice in Leviticus: Eco-Friendly Ritual or Unholy Waste." In *Ecological Hermeneutics: Biblical, Historical, and Theological Perspectives*, edited by David Horrell, Cherryl Hunt, Christopher Southgate, and Francesca Stavrakopoulou, 32–45. London: T & T Clark, 2010.
"Transgressing, Puking, Covenanting: The Character of Land in Leviticus." *Theology* 112, no. 867 (May 1, 2009): 172–80.
Morrison, Kenneth M. "Animism and a Proposal for a Post-Cartesian Anthropology." In *The Handbook of Contemporary Animism*, edited by Graham Harvey, 38–52. Durham, UK: Acumen, 2013.
Morton, Timothy. *The Ecological Thought*. Cambridge, MA: Harvard University Press, 2010.
Mowinckel, Sigmund Olaf Plytt. "Zum Psalm Des Habakuk." *Theologische Zeitschrift* 9, no. 1 (January 1953): 1–23.
Muffs, Yochanan. "Chapter 1: Who Will Stand in the Breach?: A Study of Prophetic Intercession." In *Love & Joy: Law, Language, and Religion in Ancient Israel*. New York: Jewish Theological Seminary of America; Distributed by Harvard University Press, 1992.
Murdoch, Iris. "Against Dryness: A Polemical Sketch." In *Revisions, Changing Perspectives in Moral Philosophy*, edited by Stanley Hauerwas and Alasdair C. MacIntyre. Notre Dame: University of Notre Dame Press, 1983.
Ndoga, Sampson S. "Contemporary Reflections on Ezekiel 22:23–32 as a Depiction of Collective Responsibility of Leaders for National Demise." *Old Testament Essays* 27, no. 1 (January 2014): 247–62.
Nelson, Maggie. *The Argonauts*. Minneapolis, MI: Graywolf, 2015.
Nelson, Richard D. *Joshua: A Commentary*. Louisville, KY: Westminster John Knox, 1997.
Nelson, Richard K. "The Watchful World." In *Readings in Indigenous Religions*, edited by Graham Harvey, 343–64. London: Continuum, 2002.
Newsom, Carol A. *The Book of Job: A Contest of Moral Imaginations*. Oxford: Oxford University Press, 2003.
"The Moral Sense of Nature: Ethics in the Light of God's Speech to Job." *The Princeton Seminary Bulletin* 15, no. 1 (1994): 9–27.
Niditch, Susan. *Judges: A Commentary*. Louisville, KY: Westminster John Knox, 2008.
Nielsen, Kirsten. *There Is Hope for a Tree: The Tree as Metaphor in Isaiah*. Sheffield: JSOT, 1989.
Yahweh as Prosecutor and Judge: An Investigation of the Prophetic Lawsuit (Rîb-Pattern). Sheffield: Dept. of Biblical Studies, University of Sheffield, 1978.
Nissinen, Martti. "Song of Songs and Sacred Marriage." In *Sacred Marriages: The Divine-Human Sexual Metaphor from Sumer to Early Christianity*, edited by Martti Nissinen and Risto Uro, 173–218. Winona Lake, IN: Eisenbrauns, 2008.

Noth, Martin. *Numbers: A Commentary.* Old Testament Library. Philadelphia, PA: Westminster, 1968.

O'Connor, Kathleen M. "Wild, Raging Creativity: The Scene in the Whirlwind (Job 38–41)." In *God So Near: Essays on Old Testament Theology in Honor of Patrick D. Miller,* 171–79. Winona Lake, IN: Eisenbrauns, 2003.

Olson, Dennis T. *Numbers.* Interpretation: A Bible Commentary for Teaching and Preaching. Louisville, KY: John Knox, 1996.

Ostriker, Alicia. "A Holy of Holies: The Song of Songs as Countertext." In *A Feminist Companion to the Bible* 6 (Second Series), edited by Athalya Brenner and Carole R. Fontaine, 37–54. Sheffield: Sheffield Academic, 2000.

Otto, Rudolf. *The Idea of the Holy: An Inquiry into the Non-Rational Factor in the Idea of the Divine and Its Relation to the Rational.* Translated by John W. Harvey. London: Oxford University Press, 1970.

"Patricia Johanson." Accessed September 15, 2016. http://patriciajohanson.com/.

Pelham, Abigail. *Contested Creations in the Book of Job: The-World-as-It-Ought-and-Ought-Not-to-Be.* Leiden: Brill, 2012.

Pels, P. J. "The Spirit of Matter: On Fetish, Rarity, Fact and Fancy." In *Border Fetishisms: Material Objects in Unstable Spaces,* edited by P. Spyer, 91–121. London: Routledge, 1998.

Petersen, David L. *Zechariah 9–14 and Malachi: A Commentary.* Louisville, KY: Westminster John Knox, 1995.

Pidcock-Lester, Karen. "'Earth Has No Sorrow That Earth Cannot Heal': Job 38–41." In *God Who Creates: Essays in Honor of W. Sibley Towner,* 125–32. Grand Rapids, MI: William B. Eerdmans, 2000.

Pollan, Michael. "The Intelligent Plant." *The New Yorker,* December 23, 2013. www.newyorker.com/magazine/2013/12/23/the-intelligent-plant.

Praet, Istvan. *Animism and the Question of Life.* New York: Routledge, 2014.

Pritchard, James B. *Ancient Near Eastern Texts Relating to the Old Testament.* Princeton, NJ: Princeton University Press, 1950.

——— ed. *The Ancient Near East: An Anthology of Texts and Pictures.* Princeton, NJ: Princeton University Press, 2011.

Rashkover, Randi. "Reasoning Through the Prophetic: A Reading of Isaiah 61, Leviticus 25 and Luke 4:16." *The Journal of Scriptural Reasoning* 6, no. 1 (2006). http://jsr.shanti.virginia.edu/back-issues/vol-6-no-1-may-2006-scripture-and-democracy/reasoning-through-the-prophetic-a-reading-of-isaiah-61-leviticus-25-and-luke-416/.

Reiner, Erica. *Šurpu: A Collection of Sumerian and Akkadian Incantations.* Graz: Im Selbstverlage des Herausgebers, 1958.

Reinert, Hugo. "About a Stone: Some Notes on Geologic Conviviality." *Environmental Humanities* 8, no. 1 (2016): 95–117.

Renard, Jules. *Histoires Naturelles.* Translated by Richard Stokes. Richmond, UK: Oneworld Clasics, 2010.

Revett, Jon. "The Fair Park Lagoon, and the Fate of Fair Park." Glasstire: Texas Visual Art. http://glasstire.com/2017/10/02/the-fair-park-lagoon-and-the-fate-of-fair-park/.

Richards, I. A. *The Philosophy of Rhetoric*. New York: Oxford University Press, 1936.

Ricœur, Paul. *The Rule of Metaphor: Multi-Disciplinary Studies of the Creation of Meaning in Language*. Toronto, ON: University of Toronto Press, 1981.

  The Symbolism of Evil. Boston, MA: Beacon, 1969.

Roberts, J. J. M. *Nahum, Habakkuk, and Zephaniah: A Commentary*. Louisville, KY: Westminster/John Knox, 1991.

Robertson Smith, William. *Religion of the Semites*. New Brunswick, NJ: Transaction, 2002.

Römer, Thomas. *The Invention of God*. Cambridge, MA: Harvard University Press, 2015.

Rooney, Caroline. *African Literature, Animism and Politics*. London: Routledge, 2000.

Russell, Brian D. *The Song of the Sea: The Date of Composition and Influence of Exodus 15:1–21*. New York: Peter Lang, 2007.

Sahlins, Marshall. *The Western Illusion of Human Nature: With Reflections on the Long History of Hierarchy, Equality and the Sublimation of Anarchy in the West, and Comparative Notes on Other Conceptions of the Human Condition*. Chicago, IL: Prickly Paradigm, 2008.

Santmire, H. Paul. *The Travail of Nature: The Ambiguous Ecological Promise of Christian Theology*. Philadelphia, PA: Fortress, 1985.

Sarna, Nahum M. *Exodus = [Shemot]: The Traditional Hebrew Text with the New JPS Translation*. Philadelphia, PA: Jewish Publication Society, 1991.

Savoy, Lauret. *Trace: Memory, History, Race, and the American Landscape*. Berkeley, CA: Counterpoint, 2015.

Schifferdecker, Kathryn. *Out of the Whirlwind: Creation Theology in the Book of Job*. Harvard Theological Studies 61. Cambridge, MA: Harvard University Press, 2008.

  "Of Stars and Sea Monsters: Creation Theology in the Whirlwind Speeches." *Word & World* 31, no. 4 (September 2011): 357–66.

Schmitz, Kenneth L. "World and Word in Theophany." *Faith and Philosophy* 1, no. 1 (January 1984): 50–70.

Schroer, Silvia. *Die Ikonographie Palästinas/Israels Und Der Alte Orient: Eine Religionsgeschichte in Bildern*. Vol. 3: Die Spätbronzezeit. Fribourg: Academic Press Fribourg, 2005.

Schüle, Andreas. *Die Urgeschichte (Gen 1–11)*. Zürich: Theologischer Verlag, 2009.

Seeger, Anthony, Roberto Da Matta, and Eduardo Viveiros de Castro. "A Construção Da Pessoa Nas Sociedades Indigenas Brasileiras." *Boletim Do Museu Nacional (Rio de Janeiro)* 32 (1979): 2–19.

Seow, C. L. *Job 1–21: Interpretation and Commentary*. Grand Rapids, MI: William B. Eerdmans, 2013.

Simkins, Ronald. *Creator & Creation: Nature in the Worldview of Ancient Israel*. Peabody, MA: Hendrickson, 1994.

Skinner, John. *The Book of the Prophet Isaiah, Chapters I–XXXIX: With Introduction and Notes*. The Cambridge Bible for Schools and Colleges. Cambridge: Cambridge University Press, 1985.

Smith, Mark S. *Poetic Heroes: Literary Commemorations of Warriors and Warrior Culture in the Early Biblical World*. Grand Rapids, MI: William B. Eerdmans, 2014.

———. *The Early History of God: Yahweh and the Other Deities in Ancient Israel*. Grand Rapids, MI: William B. Eerdmans, 2002.

———. *The Priestly Vision of Genesis 1*. Minneapolis, MN: Augsburg Fortress, 2009.

———. "'Seeing God' in the Psalms: The Background to the Beatific Vision in the Hebrew Bible." *Catholic Biblical Quarterly* 50 (1988): 171–83.

———. *The Ugaritic Baal Cycle*. Supplements to Vetus Testamentum 55. Leiden: E. J. Brill, 1994.

———. "Warfare Song as Warrior Ritual." In *Warfare, Ritual, and Symbol in Biblical and Modern Contexts*, edited by Brad E. Kelle, Frank Ritchel Ames, and Jacob L. Wright, 165–86. Atlanta, GA: Society of Biblical Literature, 2014.

Smith, Ralph L. *Micah-Malachi*. Word Biblical Commentary 32. Waco, TX: Word Books, 1984.

Smith, Theresa S. *The Island of the Anishnaabeg: Thunderers and Water Monsters in the Traditional Ojibwe Life-World*. Moscow, ID: University of Idaho Press, 1995.

Sommer, Benjamin D. "Nature, Revelation, and Grace in Psalm 19: Towards a Theological Reading of Scripture." *Harvard Theological Review* 108, no. 3 (July 2015): 376–401.

———. *The Bodies of God and the World of Ancient Israel*. Cambridge: Cambridge University Press, 2009.

Soskice, Janet Martin. *Metaphor and Religious Language*. Oxford: Clarendon Press, 1985.

Stevenson, Kalinda Rose. "If Earth Could Speak: The Case of the Mountains against YHWH in Ezekiel 6:3–5–36." In *The Earth Story in Psalms and Prophets*, edited by Norman C. Habel, 158–71. The Earth Bible 4. Sheffield: Sheffield Academic, 2001.

Strathern, Marilyn. *Partial Connections*. Updated ed. Walnut Creek, CA: AltaMira, 2004.

———. "Partners and Consumers: Making Relations Visible." In *Readings in Indigenous Religions*, edited by Graham Harvey, 50–71. London: Continuum, 2002.

Swenson, Kristin M. "Care and Keeping East of Eden: Gen 4:1–16 in Light of Gen 2–3." *Interpretation* 60, no. 4 (October 1, 2006): 373–84.

TallBear, Kim. "An Indigenous Reflection on Working Beyond the Human/Not Human." In "Theorizing Queer Inhumanisms." *GLQ: A Journal of Lesbian and Gay Studies* 21, no. 2–3 (2015): 209–48.

èTaylor, Glen. *Yahweh and the Sun: Biblical and Archaeological Evidence for Sun Worship in Ancient Israel.* Sheffield: JSOT, 1993.

Terrien, S. "Quelques Remarques Sur Les Affinités de Job Avec Le Deutéro-Esaïe." In *Volume Du Congrès, Genève, 1965*, International Organization for the Study of the Old Testament. Congress, 295–310. Supplements to Vetus Testamentum 15. Leiden: E. J. Brill, 1966.

Tigay, Jeffrey H. *Deuteronomy = [Devarim]: The Traditional Hebrew Text with the New JPS Translation.* 1st ed. Philadelphia, PA: Jewish Publication Society, 1996.

Tolkien, J. R. R. *The Letters of J. R. R. Tolkien.* Edited by Humphrey Carpenter. Boston, MA: Houghton Mifflin, 1981.

Tolstoy, Leo. *War and Peace.* Translated by Louise Maude and Aylmer Maude. Oxford: Oxford University Press, 2010.

Tönsing, Detlev. "The Use of Creation Language in Job 3, 9 and 38 and the Meaning of Suffering." *Scriptura* 59 (1996): 435–49.

Trudinger, Peter L. "Friend or Foe? Earth, Sea and Chaoskampf in the Psalms." In *Earth Story in the Psalms and the Prophets*, edited by Norman C. Habel, 4:29–41. The Earth Bible. Sheffield: Sheffield Academic, 2001.

Tsumura, David Toshio. *Creation and Destruction: A Reappraisal of the Chaoskampf Theory in the Old Testament.* Winona Lake, IN: Eisenbrauns, 2005.

Tull, Patricia K. "Persistent Vegetative States: People as Plants and Plants as People in Isaiah." In *The Desert Will Bloom: Poetic Visions in Isaiah*, 17–34. Leiden: Brill, 2009.

Tylor, Edward B. *Primitive Culture: Researches into the Development of Mythology, Philosophy, Religion, Language, Art, and Custom.* Vol. II. New York: Holt, 1889.

———. *Religion in Primitive Culture.* Vol. II. Gloucester, MA: Peter Smith, 1970.

Uehlinger, Christoph. "The Cry of the Earth: Biblical Perspectives on Ecology and Violence." In *Ecology and Poverty*, 41–57. Concilium. London: SCM, 1995.

Utzschneider, Helmut, and Wolfgang Oswald. *Exodus.* Translated by Philip Sumpter. Stuttgart: Verlag W. Kohlhammer, 2015.

Van Dooren, Thom, Eben Kirksey, and Ursula Münster. "Multispecies Studies: Cultivating Arts of Attentiveness." *Environmental Humanities* 8, no. 1 (May 2016): 1–23.

Viveiros de Castro, Eduardo. "1. Cosmologies: Perspectivism." *HAU: Masterclass Series* 1 (July 8, 2012). www.haujournal.org/index.php/masterclass/article/view/106.

———. *Cannibal Metaphysics: For a Post-Structural Anthropology.* Translated by Peter Skafish. Minneapolis, MN: Univocal, 2014.

———. *From the Enemy's Point of View: Humanity and Divinity in an Amazonian Society.* Chicago, IL: University of Chicago Press, 1992.

———. "The Transformation of Objects into Subjects in Amerindian Ontologies." Presented at the 98th Annual Meeting of the American Anthropology Association, Chicago, IL, November 17, 1999.

Vizenor, Gerald. *Everlasting Sky: Voices of the Anishinabe People*. St. Paul, MN: Minnesota Historical Society, 2000.
von Rad, Gerhard. *Genesis: A Commentary*. The Old Testament Library. Translated by John H. Marks. Philadelphia, PA: Westminster, 1972.
  Old Testament Theology. New York: Harper, 1962.
Wagner, Roy. "The Fractal Person." In *Big Men and Great Men: Personifications of Power in Melanesia*, edited by Maurice Godelier and Marilyn Strathern, 159–73. Cambridge: Cambridge University Press, 1991.
Wakeman, Mary K. "Biblical Earth Monster in the Cosmogonic Combat Myth." *Journal of Biblical Literature* 88, no. 3 (September 1969): 313–20.
Walsh, Brian J., Marianne B. Karsh, and Nik Ansell. "Trees, Forestry, and the Responsiveness of Creation." *Cross Currents* 44, no. 2 (June 1994): 149–62.
Waltke, Bruce K., and Michael Patrick O'Connor. *An Introduction to Biblical Hebrew Syntax*. Winona Lake, IN: Eisenbrauns, 1990.
Watson, Rebecca S. *Chaos Uncreated: A Reassessment of the Theme of "Chaos" in the Hebrew Bible*. Berlin: de Gruyter, 2005.
Watts, John D. W. *The Books of Joel, Obadiah, Jonah, Nahum, Habakkuk, and Zephaniah*. Cambridge: Cambridge University Press, 1975.
Weiser, Artur. *The Psalms: A Commentary*. Philadelphia: Westminster, 1962.
Welker, Michael. *Creation and Reality*. Minneapolis: Fortress, 1999.
Wellhausen, Julius. *Prolegomena to the History of Israel*. Atlanta, GA: Scholars, 1994.
Westermann, Claus. *Genesis 1–11: A Commentary*. Minneapolis, MN: Augsburg, 1984.
  Isaiah 40–66: A Commentary. Philadelphia, PA: Westminster, 1969.
Widmer, Michael. *Standing in the Breach: An Old Testament Theology and Spirituality of Intercessory Prayer*. Winona Lake, IN: Eisenbrauns, 2015.
Willerslev, Rane. *Soul Hunters: Hunting, Animism, and Personhood among the Siberian Yukaghirs*. Berkeley, CA: University of California Press, 2007.
  "The One-All': The Animist High God." In *The Handbook of Contemporary Animism*, edited by Graham Harvey, 275–83. Durham, UK: Acumen, 2013.
Williams, Rowan. *Dostoevsky: Language, Faith and Fiction*. Waco, TX: Baylor University Press, 2008.
Wolfers, David. *Deep Things Out of Darkness: The Book of Job, Essays and a New English Translation*. Grand Rapids, MI: William B. Eerdmans, 1995.
Wright, Christopher J. H. *God's People in God's Land: Family, Land, and Property in the Old Testament*. Grand Rapids, MI: William B. Eerdmans, 1990.
  Old Testament Ethics for the People of God. Leicester: Inter-Varsity, 2004.
  The Message of Ezekiel: A New Heart and a New Spirit. The Bible Speaks Today. Leicester: InterVarsity, 2001.
Wright, G. Ernest. *The Old Testament Against Its Environment*. London: SCM, 1950.

Wright, Jacob L. "Warfare and Wanton Destruction: A Reexamination of Deuteronomy 20:19–20 in Relation to Ancient Siegecraft." *Journal of Biblical Literature* 127, no. 3 (September 1, 2008): 423–58.

Wurst, Shirley. "Retrieving Earth's Voice in Jeremiah: An Annotated Voicing of Jeremiah 4." In *The Earth Story in Psalms and Prophets*, edited by Norman C. Habel, 172–84. The Earth Bible 4. Sheffield: Sheffield Academic, 2001.

Younger, K. Lawson. *Ancient Conquest Accounts: A Study in Ancient Near Eastern and Biblical History Writing*. Sheffield: JSOT, 1990.

General Index

Affect, 39, 115, 130, 132, 140–41, 154–55, 166, 170
  Anger, 117–20, 127, 136, 176
  Awe, 11, 111–12, 114–15, 170
  Fear, 82, 111–17, 129
  Grief, 8, 41–44, 108, 114–15, 129–31, 133, 139–45, 151, 199, 212
  Hostility, 121, 137–38, 175
  Joy, 39, 116, 145–54, 158, 170
Agency, 28, 31–33, 85–86, 149–50, 207
Agriculture, 23, 97, 191
Animism, 2, 7–8, 37–38, 54–55, 97, 120–22, 197–99, 204
  Art, 200
  Contemporary, 209
  New Animism, 15–16, 19–36, 45–46
  Perspectivism, 131–33, 141
  Racism, 15
Anthropocentrism, 4–5, 96, 155
Anthropology, 14–15, 19, 37
Architecture, 185, 199–201
Artefacts, 199–201
Assyria, 38–39, 179
Atonement, 93–94
Attention, 11–12, 46, 97, 144, 154–55, 170, 212, 215, 219–20

Baal, 70–72, 83–84, 112, 118–19, 141–42
Babylon, 55, 112, 118, 130–31, 147–48
Blessing, 59, 64, 97, 137, 152, 218
Blood, 14, 35, 58–61, 93–94, 174–75
  Blood Rites, 61–64
Buber, Martin, 6, 11, 41, 44, 47, 208

Categorization, 27–31, 43, 56–57, 132, 198, 202, 207, 209
Causation, 27, 33, 142
Chaoskampf, 82, 111–12, 119–20
Clouds, 88, 111, 149, 163
Comfort, 8, 12, 44, 138, 145–47, 151–52, 212
Command, 49, 51, 60, 63, 71, 77–78, 105, 133–35, 165–66
Conquest, 76, 101, 177, 179
Consciousness. *See* Interiority
Consolation. *See* Comfort
Cosmology
  Hebrew Bible, of, 24
  Western, 26–27
Covenant, 34, 48, 64–66, 72–73, 79, 87–93, 137–40, 218
Creation, 48, 65, 83–85, 149–50, 165, 216
  Days of, 55–58
  Interrelatedness of, 33–34
  Of Humans, 24, 55, 69, 174
  Of Vegetation, 48–50
Cult, Israelite, 33, 35–36, 48, 52–53, 77, 80, 137, 150, 169
Cult, Solar, 105
Curse, 58–60, 64, 97, 137

Death, 69, 71, 83–84, 104, 141–42, 173, 178, 193, 218
Deforestation. *See* Trees
Desert, 138, 145–46, 191
Diamond, Cora, 17–21, 28, 43, 94, 198, 201–10

Divinization, 51–55, 74–75
Drought, 97, 108, 129–30, 140–42, 150
Dualism, 30–31, 199, 209
    Cartesian Split, 31, 208

Earth, Actions of
    Creating, 48
    Devouring, 63, 79–83, 138
    Prostitution, 76–78
    Resting, 78, 95, 147
    Swallowing, 60–64, 70–72, 83–84, 173, 176–77
    Vomiting, 73–77, 80
    Witnessing, 54, 87–89, 172, 174
Earthquake, 11, 97, 112
Emotion. *See* Affect
Empiricism, 15, 109, 202
Enuma Elish, 55, 112
Environment, Contemporary, 98, 201, 210–12
    Climate Change, 96, 98, 156, 204, 208, 216–19
    Crisis, Environmental, 155–56
    Ecology, 8
    Ethics, Environmental, 3–5, 9–10
Ethics, 7, 97, 150, 201–2, 207
Ethnography, 15, 20–21, 45
Exile, 73–75, 78–80, 99, 137, 143, 175

Fertility, 57, 65, 94, 135, 138, 145–46
Forests, 18–19, 100, 103–4, 130–31, 164, 190, 214
Form-criticism, 111, 125

Gardens, 146, 185–89, 191–93, 199
Genre, 49–50, 87–89, 91, 111–12, 125–26, 159
    Prophetic Lawsuit, 87–89, 91

Heavens, the, 4–5, 54–55, 87–93, 125–26, 129, 132–34, 146, 148–51, 160–64, 168, 175–76
Historicizing, 119
Holiness Code, 74
Humanness, 23–24, 26, 184–85, 197–99, 203, 207

Icons, 40
Idioms, 81, 94–95
Idolatry, 77

Imperialism, 39, 130–31, 147–48
Interiority, 111, 113, 184, 198

Jezreel, 101, 134–35
Jordan, the, 166
Judge, Office of, 89–90, 172, 181

Land Tenure, 34–36, 180, 183–84
Laws, Dietary, 23, 34–36
Leviathan, 55, 118, 184, 216
Lightning, 108–9, 115, 164, 183
Literary Devices
    Apostrophe, 122–26
    Intertextuality, 178–79
    Merism, 126
    Metaphor, 16, 18, 38–42, 44–45, 95, 113, 142, 144, 149–51, 161, 186–88
    Metonym, 68, 77, 90, 95, 124, 127
    Parallelism, 126–27, 142
    Personification, 16, 31, 38, 142, 199
Luminaries
    Moon, 50–55, 65, 104–7, 109–10, 113–15, 169
    Stars, 22, 53, 101–2, 107, 114, 182–83
    Sun, 17, 50–55, 65, 104–7, 109–10, 113–15, 160, 168–69

Metaphor. *See* Literary Devices
Mind, Philosophy of, 31–32, 206–7
Modernism, 8, 26, 29–30, 33, 56, 109–10, 139, 150, 199, 204, 209
Monolatery, 53
Monotheism, 53–55, 107
Moon. *See* Luminaries
Mountains, 32, 88, 100, 108, 111, 113, 115, 122, 124, 127, 135–36, 138–39, 146–47, 166, 170–71, 181, 191
Myth, 70, 84, 118–20, 141, 149
    Demythologizing, 105–6
    Mythologizing, 81–82

Nature, Animate. *See* Nature, Inanimate
Nature, Inanimate, 2, 55–57, 72, 92
Near East, Ancient, 53, 61, 131, 148
    Iconography, 200–1
    Myths, 111–12
    Nature Worship, 74, 106–7
    Treaties, 54, 87–89
Negev, 100, 137

Obedience, 92, 106, 169–70, 183
Ontology, 20, 22, 25–27, 31, 131, 200

Pantheism, 54
People Groups
   Amazonian, 198
   Apache, 20–21
   Chewong, 31
   Maori, 199–200
   Mi'kmaq, 132
   Nayaka, 38
   Ojibwe, 26–29, 51–52, 108–9, 121
   Sami, 9
Personalistic Nature Texts
   Definition of, 3
Personhood
   Definition of, 15–16, 20
Philosophy, Moral, 17, 202
Plants
   Flower, 186, 189, 214
   Fruit, 49, 59–60, 140, 148–49, 151, 153, 187–90, 192, 218
   Grain, 68, 133–35, 151–52, 217
   Henna, 185, 187, 189
   Lily, 186, 188
   Mandrake, 190
   Myrrh, 187
   Pomegranate, 151, 187–89, 200
   Rose, 186
   Vine, 140, 151, 153, 187–88
Polemic, 52–55, 82, 105–7
Praise, 93, 158–61, 164–68, 170–71
Purity, 61–63, 76, 137

Relationality, 29–30, 38, 40–41, 45, 47, 103, 121, 137, 172, 199–200, 213
Righteousness, 148–53, 171–72, 174, 180, 183–84, 194

Sabbath, 8, 36, 74, 78–80, 137
Sacrifice, 9–10, 34, 169
Sea. *See* Water

Sex, 188, 190
Siege, 144
Source, Priestly, 82, 84, 136, 169
Spirits, 32–33, 132
Stars. *See* Luminaries
Suffering, 67–70, 130–31, 136, 143–45, 171, 173–74, 178–79, 184, 193
Sun. *See* Luminaries

Theophany, 11, 110–22, 133, 157, 164–65
Thing Theory, 200
Thunder, 22, 108–9, 121, 163–64
   Thunderbirds, 108–9, 121
Traditions, Canaanite, 61, 71, 75, 91, 105–6, 118–19
Traditions, Hittite, 61, 88
Translation, 59, 176, 180
Trees, 1–2, 6–8, 28, 31–32, 38–40, 103–4, 132, 147, 200, 203, 207, 214–15, 219–20
   Apple, 152, 186–87, 189
   Cedar, 32, 38, 130–31, 148, 164, 190
   Cypress, 32, 130–31, 147–48, 155, 190
   Deforestation, 130
   Fig, 151, 187
   Oak, 130, 164–65
   Palm, 152, 189, 199

Warfare, 99, 101–10
Water, 95, 98, 120, 149, 165
   Chaos, 71, 101, 107
   Dew, 108, 145, 153, 183
   Rain, 92, 98, 108, 112, 145, 149–52, 183, 218
   Rivers, 88, 101–2, 117
   Sea, the, 52, 55, 71–72, 88, 117–18, 133, 166, 182–83, 216–17
   Wells, 86
Witness, Office of, 54–55, 65–66, 87–89, 127–28, 175–76

Bible Index

Genesis, 24
 1, 48, 65, 80, 118, 146, 169, 182
 1.4, 55
 1.6-10, 56
 1.10, 55
 1.11, 149
 1.11-13, 57
 1.12, 48-58
 1.14-15, 169
 1.14-18, 51, 57
 1.14-19, 56
 1.16, 18
 1.18, 55
 1.20-25, 57
 1.21, 55
 1.22, 57
 1.25, 55
 1.28, 57
 1.31, 55
 1-3, 56
 2, 146
 2.5, 69
 2.7, 174
 2.22, 53
 2-3, 191
 2-4, 174
 3.17, 65
 3.18, 65, 175
 4, 14, 66, 84
 4.2, 58
 4.2-3, 59
 4.3, 58
 4.6, 58
 4.8, 58
 4.9-15, 58
 4.10, 175
 4.10-12, 58-65, 84
 4.12, 175
 9.4, 35
 9.13, 95
 9.20, 18
 12.1, 183
 21.23, 95
 22.1, 183
 22.11, 123
 31.42, 116
 31.48, 65-66
 31.52, 65-66
 37.34, 43
 41.36, 68
 42.9, 68
 47.13-26, 66-70
 47.19, 67, 80, 93
Exodus
 3.6, 116
 15, 83, 102, 118
 15.12, 63, 70-72, 84
 20.19, 116
 25-30, 199
 36-40, 199
Leviticus
 1.2, 34
 5.2, 35
 11.8, 35
 18, 73, 79
 18.24-28, 75-77

18.25, 72–73
18.28, 72
18–27, 72
19, 76–77
19.9, 213
19.19, 213
19.27, 213
19.28, 77
19.29, 73
19.30, 77
20, 73
20.22, 73, 77
25.2, 8, 73, 78
25.4, 73
25.4–5, 22, 78
25.5, 73
25.19, 8
25.23, 36, 69
25.25, 69
25.39, 69
25.42, 69
26, 73, 137
26.4, 8, 59
26.9, 139
26.16–20, 78
26.34, 73
26.34–35, 8, 22, 78
26.38, 73, 79
26.42, 9, 93, 146
26.42-43, 79–80
26.43, 73–74
Numbers
  13.32, 80–83
  16, 86, 177
  16.3, 83
  16.13, 83
  16.28–30, 83
  16.30-34, 63, 83–86
  21.17–18, 86–87
  26.10, 83
  33, 73
  35.33, 93
Deuteronomy
  4.26, 2, 5, 54, 66, 87–93, 176
  11.17, 8, 92
  11.6, 83
  18.9, 34
  19, 93
  19.10, 93
  19.13, 93
  21, 93

21.8, 93
26.1, 34
26.15, 93
27.25, 93
28.23, 92
30.19, 5, 54, 66, 87–93
30.19–20, 176
31.19, 87
31.28, 66, 87–93
32.1, 5, 54, 87–93
32.23–25, 94
32.43, 93–94
Joshua
  2.11, 115
  10.12, 5, 124
  10.12–13, 102, 104–7, 109–10
  24.23–27, 66
  24.27, 66
Judges
  5, 106
  5.20, 22
  5.20–21, 101–3
1 Samuel
  8.11–18, 68
2 Samuel
  1, 124
  1.21, 102, 108, 122
  1.24, 108
  8.14–15, 103
  18.8, 18, 102–4
  18.9, 103
1 Kings
  6, 199
  13.2, 129, 199
  13.4, 141
2 Kings
  2.21–22, 95
  3.19, 95
Job
  5.20, 173
  5.23, 173, 179–80
  7.1–2, 173
  7.7, 178
  7.9–10, 177–78
  7.10, 173
  8.18, 173, 176–78
  16.18, 60, 174
  16.18–19, 175
  20.9, 173, 177–78
  20.27, 174, 176
  20.28, 176

Job (cont.)
  21.33, 174
  28.22, 164
  29.6, 174
  31.5, 181
  31.7, 181
  31.9, 181
  31.13, 181
  31.16, 181
  31.24, 181
  31.35–37, 181
  31.38, 174
  31.38–40, 60, 174–75, 181
  38.1–38, 182
  38.4, 182
  38.7, 182
  38.8, 216
  38.8–11, 182
  38.12, 184
  38.12–13, 183
  38.13, 182
  38.19, 184
  38.28–29, 183
  38.31–33, 183
  38.34–35, 183
  38–41, 154, 182
  42.10, 180
Psalm
  19, 160–64, 167–70, 182
  19.2 [1], 163
  19.2–5 [1–4], 160
  19.3, 167
  19.5–7 [4–6], 160
  19.8 [7], 163, 168
  19.8–15 [7–14], 160
  19.14 [13], 170
  24.7, 199
  24.9, 199
  29, 120
  29.5–9, 164–65
  37, 177
  37.10, 177
  37.25, 178
  42.8 [7], 167
  50.1–6, 165
  50.4, 165
  50.6, 158, 165
  65.9 [8], 158, 167
  65.10 [9], 76
  65.13–14 [12–13], 158, 167
  68.17 [16], 166
  69.35 [34], 41, 166
  74.14, 55
  76.9 [8], 165
  77.18 [17], 163
  78.23, 165
  89.6 [5], 41
  89.13 [12], 167
  93.3, 158, 164, 167
  96.11–12, 41
  98.7, 167
  98.7–8, 164
  98.7–9, 22
  103.16, 177
  104.4, 165
  104.5–9, 165
  106.17, 83
  106.23, 100
  107.25, 165
  110.5, 176
  111.10, 115
  114.5–6, 166
  145.10, 167
  145.4, 167
  147.15–18, 165
  147.19, 165
  148, 5
  148.3–10, 22, 41
  148.8, 165
Proverbs
  17.22, 141
Song
  1.4, 185, 191
  1.6, 193
  1.14, 185
  1.15–17, 190
  2.1, 186
  2.2, 186
  2.3, 186, 188–89
  2.7, 193
  2.8–14, 186–87
  2.8–9, 186
  2.10, 186
  2.11–13, 187–88
  2.13, 186
  2.14, 186
  3.4, 193
  3.5, 193
  4.1–7, 185
  4.9–5.1, 192
  4.12, 187
  4.12–15, 187–88

Bible Index

4.13–14, 188
4.16, 188, 192
4.16–5.1, 188
5.1, 188
6.1, 188
6.2, 188
6.4–7, 185
6.9, 193
6.11, 188
7.2–7 [1–6], 185
7.9 [8], 189
7.12–13 [11–12], 189
7.14 [13], 190
8.1–2, 193
8.4, 193
8.5, 193
8.13, 191
8.14, 191
Isaiah
  1.2, 22, 126, 180
  3.26, 43, 199
  6.5, 116
  11.3, 115
  14.31, 130
  14.7–8, 148
  14.8, 131
  23.1, 130
  23.14, 130
  24.4, 8, 41, 139
  24.4–7, 140
  24.7, 43
  24.8, 142
  24.11, 140
  26.21, 175
  27.1, 55
  28.15, 218
  32.16, 151
  33.9, 8, 41, 139, 141
  34.1, 126
  34.3, 127
  34.4, 127
  35.1, 220
  35.1–2, 145–46
  35.3–4, 145
  40.1, 146
  41.17–20, 191
  44.23, 5
  44.24, 133–34
  44.27, 133–34
  44–45, 148
  45.8, 148–51
  49.13, 124, 146, 148
  50.2, 55, 117
  51.3, 44, 146
  55.12, 2, 32, 39, 124, 147, 219
  60.5, 116
Jeremiah
  2.12, 5, 125
  2.12–13, 129–30
  2.25, 192
  3.2, 77
  4.28, 8, 41, 139–40, 180
  6.10, 127
  6.11, 127
  6.17, 127
  6.18–19, 126–27
  6.19, 125
  12.4, 8, 41, 139, 141, 180
  12.10–11, 142–43
  12.11, 8, 41, 139, 180
  14.2, 199
  22.29–30, 128–29
  23.10, 8, 41, 139, 141, 180
  31.12, 191
  31.27, 147
  33.10–11, 147
  51.48, 148
Lamentations
  1, 199
  1.4, 199
  2.1, 176
  2.8, 43
  4.8, 141
Ezekiel
  1.28, 116
  6, 138
  6.1–7, 135
  6.2, 135
  6.3, 139
  6.4, 139
  6.5, 139
  7.2, 135
  7.3, 136
  16.15, 192
  21.2 [20.46], 135
  21.7 [21.2], 135
  22.30, 99
  24.7–8, 175
  31.3, 38
  34.26–27, 218
  35.2, 135
  36.1, 135

Ezekiel (cont.)
  36.6-15, 138
  36.8–11, 156, 191
  36.10–11, 139
  36.11, 212
  36.12, 139
  36.29, 134
  37.4, 141
  40–46, 199
Hosea
  2.23–25 [21–23], 134
  2.9 [7], 192
  4.1–3, 143
  4.3, 8, 41, 139, 212
  7.9, 175
  10.8, 124
Joel
  1.4, 151
  1.7, 151
  1.9, 151
  1.10, 8, 41, 43, 139, 141
  1.10–11, 151
  1.12, 151–52
  1.13, 151
  1.17–18, 152
  1.19–20, 152
  1.20, 152
  2.10, 114–15
  2.12, 152
  2.12–14, 217
  2.14, 152, 155
  2.18, 152
  2.18–19, 191
  2.19, 152
  2.21, 116
  2.21–23, 151–52
  2.27, 152
  4.15–16, 114–15

Amos
  1.2, 8, 41, 139, 141
  5.8, 133–34
  8.8, 43
  9.1–6, 135
  9.5–6, 133–34
Micah
  1.2, 127, 180
  1.3–4, 127
  1.4, 115
  1.5, 127
  6.1, 181
  6.1–2, 22
Nahum
  1.4, 55, 117
Habakkuk
  3, 115
  3.8, 117–18
  3.8–15, 55
  3.10, 32
  3.10–11, 113–14
  3.11, 109
  3.12, 117
  3.15, 117
  3.16, 116
Zechariah
  6.13, 153
  8.10, 153
  8.11, 153
  8.12, 152–54
  8.16, 153
  8.17, 153
  8.19, 153
  9–14, 131
  11.1–3, 130–32
  11.2, 32
  11.17, 141

Printed in Great Britain
by Amazon